Praise for *Inside Ocean Hill–Brownsville*

"*Inside Ocean Hill–Brownsville* makes a vital contribution to a much-needed reinterpretation of the epochal struggles over community control of the New York City public schools in the 1960s, and the divisive UFT fall 1968 strikes in opposition to that community-based movement. Writing from the firsthand perspective of a young Jewish math teacher at JHS 271, Isaacs brings this important story vividly to life with insight, candor, and humor. He evokes the attitudes and actions of a rich array of ordinary teachers, administrators, students, and parents who fought to defend the community-control experiment in the face of the lies and distortions perpetrated by UFT officials and the mainstream press. A must read for anyone interested in creating successful public schools, this book helps us remember what democratic public education might look like."

— Stephen Brier, The Graduate Center,
City University of New York

"Charles Isaacs's *Inside Ocean Hill–Brownsville* is a firsthand account of the dramatic events of New York City's greatest school crisis. Isaacs debunks many of the popular myths of black militants waging assaults on teachers. Instead, he demonstrates that the episode in Ocean Hill–Brownsville was a case of black and Latino parents, with the support of a number of teachers at JHS 271, struggling for the education of their children and for a more democratically run educational system. These parents faced one of the most powerful unions in the city and a bureaucratic board of education that wanted to protect the status quo. There have been many books written on the 1968 teachers' strike, but Isaacs's well-written, detailed account is by far the best."

— Clarence Taylor, author of *Knocking at Our Own Door: Milton A. Galamison and the Struggle to Integrate New York City Schools*

Inside Ocean Hill–Brownsville

Inside Ocean Hill–Brownsville

A Teacher's Education, 1968–69

Charles S. Isaacs

excelsior editions
State University of New York Press
Albany, New York

Cover Photo: Children pass through a police gauntlet to the doors of JHS 271 (Fall 1968)

Published by State University of New York Press, Albany

Printed in the United States of America

Excelsior Editions is an imprint of State University of New York Press

For information, contact State University of New York Press, Albany, NY
www.sunypress.edu

Production by Diane Ganeles
Marketing by Kate McDonnell

Library of Congress Cataloging-in-Publication Data

Isaacs, Charles S., 1945–
Inside Ocean Hill-Brownsville : a teacher's education, 1968–69 / Charles S. Isaacs.
pages cm. — (Excelsior editions)
Includes bibliographical references and index.
ISBN 978-1-4384-5296-8 (pbk. : alk. paper)
1. Strikes and lockouts—Teachers—New York (State)—New York. 2. Ocean Hill-Brownsville Demonstration School District (New York, N.Y.) 3. Discrimination in education—New York (State)—New York. 4. Isaacs, Charles S., 1945– 5. Teachers—New York (State)—New York—Biography. I. Title.

LB2844.47.U62N485 2014
331.88'113711—dc23 2013042569

10 9 8 7 6 5 4 3 2 1

This book is dedicated to the memory of

Bill Birenbaum
Thelma Hamilton
Major Owens
Annie Stein
Jitu Weusi
Preston Wilcox

Teachers . . . Warriors . . . Friends

This experiment does not concern just New York City, but the whole nation, wherever people tried to make democracy work.

—Rev. C. Herbert Oliver
The *New York Times* (November 1, 1969)

The 1968 battle over school decentralization in an obscure Brooklyn district called Ocean Hill–Brownsville ripped apart New York City as nothing has before or since.

—John Kifner
The *New York Times* (December 22, 1996)

Over forty years (later), Jews' and African-Americans' relationship remains deeply affected by the Ocean Hill–Brownsville strikes . . . This episode looms large in the American collective consciousness because it solidified the national splintering and collapse of generations of collaboration.

—Melissa Weiner
Power, Protest and the Public Schools (2010)

Contents

Illustrations

Acknowledgments

> I have never done anything but write, but I don't possess the vocation or talents of a narrator, have no knowledge at all of the laws of dramatic composition, and if I have embarked upon this enterprise it is because I trust in the light shed by how much I have read in my life.
>
> —Gabriel Garcia Marquez, *Memories of My Melancholy Whores*

This book was written without a publishing contract, or even a reasonable expectation that it would ever be published. Three experienced, sympathetic literary agents predicted that it would never see the light of day. I had no experience with book publishing, no agent, no interns or researchers, and no financial assistance, university post, or any other reliable source of income. What I did have, and what proved indispensable, was the ongoing support of good friends and old colleagues who believed that this was a story worth telling, and who kept my spirits up when clouds of pessimism gathered. My thanks to Lynne Slater, Fran Barrett, Mac Barrett, Alan Shulman, Carol London, Dorothy Williams, and Maurice Reid; to my sons, Marc and Steven Stern; and particularly to Wayne Barrett, Helen Birenbaum, Steve Bloomfield, Dr. Stephen Brier, Monifa Edwards, and Jitu Weusi, each of whom took the time to read drafts or excerpts and offered valuable, though sometimes conflicting, comments and suggestions. It's also about time that I thanked my JHS 271 colleague, Steve Mayer, who contributed many of his own experiences back in 1969.

I owe a huge debt of gratitude to Steve Brier, whose interest in the subject first triggered the idea for a book. Steve held my hand throughout the entire process. He digitized some of my old notes; he showed me the modern methods of referencing sources; he copyedited my first draft (without being asked); he opened doors at publishing houses; and he gave me thoughtful answers to an endless series of questions. Without his expertise and his patience, as well as his own commitment to this story, it would never have been told.

My wife, Carole, and I were brought together by the Ocean Hill–Brownsville struggles. She has put up with me for almost forty years now. Carole was the first to encourage me to take on this project, and her enthusiasm never flagged for a moment. She was always available for sounding out ideas, and for good advice based on her own deep community organizing experience. Never once did she suggest that my time would be better spent in a more remunerative activity.

The writing of memoir has a Rashomon-like quality to it. Since we experience the world solely through our own individual senses, and filter the input through our own mindsets, no two narratives can be exactly the same. I am grateful to each of my interview subjects for broadening my story by offering their own perspectives and viewpoints.

Filling out the context of the memoir required research. Once I exhausted my own library, Vassar College gave me complete access to its vast collection, including borrowing privileges. NYU's Tamiment Library opened its Robert F. Wagner Labor Archives to me. The staffs at both institutions were knowledgeable, helpful, and patient to a fault. I think librarians are the world's nicest people.

During the long year of submitting the manuscript to publishers, dozens of editors who didn't accept it nevertheless supported the work's value. Many suggested submissions to other publishers, and several recommended SUNY Press. Eventually, the manuscript reached Amanda Lanne and Rafael Chaiken there, who believed in this book and to whom I will be forever grateful. I am grateful as well to the historians who reviewed the manuscript for SUNY Press, and whose generous comments helped advance the project to the Editorial Board and to Diane Ganeles, who guided the project through a smooth, author-friendly production process. When all was said and done, I was glad that SUNY Press was the first publisher to accept the manuscript.

Finally, I have to thank my grandchildren: Emily, Malcolm, and Mason Stern. Many, many hours of spinning tales and reading books to them during their early years honed whatever skills I may now possess as a storyteller. When they read this book, they'll learn about what their Grandpa did way back in 1968, during the days of New York City's Great School War.

Preface

The confrontation over community control of schools that engulfed New York City during the 1968–69 school year changed that city in unexpected yet lasting ways. It sent shock waves reverberating across the nation, dramatically redefining the civil rights agenda and changing the national conversation about race relations. It transformed the way racial and ethnic groups thought of one another, and of themselves. It also thrust into sharp relief serious questions about the limits of liberal democracy in the United States.

Its setting was the city's public school system, the nation's largest, with a student enrollment larger than those of Chicago, Detroit, Boston, and Cleveland combined. United in struggle for radical changes to that system were the city's African-American and Puerto Rican communities, both of which were also the nation's largest. Arrayed in defense of the status quo was the nation's largest union local, the predominantly Jewish United Federation of Teachers, along with the nation's largest municipal bureaucracy, the New York City Board of Education. Drawn in, and pitted against the forces for change, were the city's overwhelmingly white trade unions and its Jewish community, which was then the world's largest. Among those caught in between were a mayor, a governor, the governments they led, and more than one million children.

The focal point of the conflict was a small neighborhood called Ocean Hill–Brownsville, a single square mile housing one quarter of one percent of the city's population in 100 city blocks. There, an experiment in community control briefly empowered black and Puerto Rican parents with an opportunity to rescue their children's futures from the abysmal, endemic failure of their racially segregated schools. In opposition to that experiment, the 92 percent white teachers' union launched the longest teacher strike in American history, closing nearly all of the city's schools for 36 of the school year's first 48 days, fully a fifth of that term. As those ten long weeks passed, and during the ensuing months, charges of white racism and black anti-Semitism triggered rising racial tensions that threatened to rend the city's rapidly fraying social fabric.

The eye of that storm was Junior High School 271, which quickly became the nation's most famous, or infamous, public school. This book tells the inside story, for the first time, of what happened in that school during that conflict. It also tells the story of its author, a young Jewish novice teacher in that time and place. It is a story about a momentous struggle over the education of children, through which this teacher was himself blessed to have gained an extraordinary education.

During the course of that year, political and educational issues long simmering under the surface burst into public attention: race and class; institutional and individual racism; parent and teacher empowerment; standardized testing, cultural bias and the "achievement gap"; teacher training and evaluation; school leadership; and the relationship between school and community. In succeeding decades, some of these issues have been addressed, not only in New York but in other cities as well. Most, however, remain unresolved, still the focus of controversy. The story of how teachers, parents, and community leaders dealt with them during Ocean Hill–Brownsville's experiment in community control offers fresh perspective on issues that still bedevil the schools, the cities, and the nation.

The genesis of this book's core, based on personal experience but written more than forty years after the fact, is a bit unusual. While in college during the mid-1960s, when I was active in many student organizations, I developed a habit of taking copious notes of what was going on and being said around me. In classes, clubs and political meetings, of which there were many, this habit, sometimes bordering on compulsion, served me well. When I started teaching in Ocean Hill–Brownsville in September 1968, it felt natural for me to continue jotting down notes at every opportunity, on whatever scraps of paper were close at hand. Shortly afterward, in the midst of the strikes and the controversies that made national and international news, I was asked to submit an article about my experiences at JHS 271 to the *New York Times Magazine*. My note-taking then became more disciplined. At night and on weekends, I put my scribbled notes into typed form, reconstructing my experiences while they were still fresh in my mind. After the article was published, I just kept the same routine. I also saved, and tossed into file drawers, nearly every document, leaflet, and related publication that came to my attention during that year.

I originally assembled all of this material into manuscript form during the summer of 1969. That manuscript didn't find its way into print, and I soon forgot about it, but I never disposed of it. Most of the source material also stayed with me as I moved from place to place during the next four decades.

During those intervening years, the Ocean Hill–Brownsville conflict has been studied by scholars of various disciplines. While some have produced thoughtful and nuanced analyses and histories, all have been handicapped by the absence of a contemporaneous eyewitness account from within the eye of

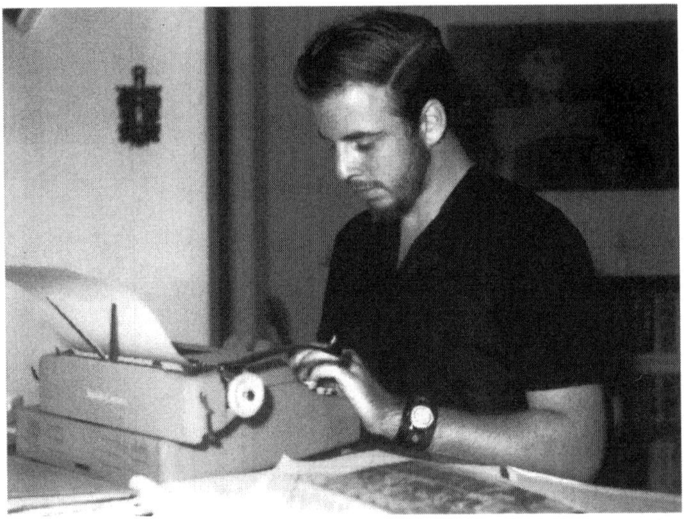

Figure 0.1 The author typing notes of school experiences (1969)

the storm. Since much of the primary source material was propaganda-driven, geared to associate the pro-community forces with violence and anti-Semitism, and since outright lies have gone without effective challenge for so long, truth-seekers have had much to overcome.

Some scholars have attempted to surmount that handicap, but the standard historical record of Ocean Hill–Brownsville is, I would argue, a distorted and biased one, a record that bears little resemblance to the actual events in which I participated, and to which I bore witness.

The fundamental inaccuracy of this historical record is of more than academic interest. It has informed educational policy and political behavior throughout the country during the succeeding decades, affecting the lives of many millions more children, and skewing the debate about all those still unresolved educational and political issues. It has poisoned the well of public discourse over matters that are critical to the nation's future.

In April 2011, I received a telephone call from Prof. Stephen Brier of the CUNY Graduate Center, asking if I was available to be interviewed for his doctoral seminar's oral history project. In preparation for that interview, I excavated my old notes of meetings and classroom experiences, and the unpublished draft that I wrote back in 1969. While reviewing that material, I was reminded anew of remarkable achievements that have been largely forgotten, and angered anew at the litany of lies and slanders that have adhered to the parents, teachers, and leaders of Ocean Hill–Brownsville, who accomplished what they did in the face of overwhelming odds. I was also struck by the continuing relevance of the issues brought to the forefront during that moment in history, and by how the standard historical record has distorted efforts to deal with them. I decided then that I would add my eyewitness account to the efforts of the few revisionist historians who had been chipping away at the established edifice.

Because of my compulsive note-taking during that eventful year, I have been able to tell this story now without having to rely solely on my memory of the events, of what people said and of what they did. In many cases, I have been able to relate the actual conversations, debates, and classroom interactions that transpired at the time. Since I could not have been everywhere, I have referenced the sources for my descriptions of events at which I was not present. All of the unreferenced dialogue that appears in this book took place in my presence.

Further, I have not employed any of the truth-fudging devices that have become accepted in historical memoirs. This narrative employs no compression of events, and introduces no composite characters. The story, which has undergone more than enough distortion by others, is presented here as it actually transpired. I have, however, made no attempt to present a "fair and balanced" narrative. Instead, I have told the story as I experienced it, and as I understand it. I make no attempt to hide my point of view. Others might offer a different interpretation, but the facts are the facts.

My original plan was to simply edit the 1969 memoir and attempt to get it published. I quickly found, though, to my astonishment, that it wasn't nearly as well-written on the page as it was in my memory, so I had to start over, using it only as a source. I also realized that most Americans alive today were born after these events, and that an introductory section was needed to put them into context. Another challenge arose when I shared drafts and excerpts with friends who are deeply involved with the schools today. Each of them commented that the issues the system faced back then are still the issues facing it today, though they did not agree on what the solutions should look like. This led me to add a concluding section bringing the evolution of those issues into the twenty-first century, and suggest a few of my own ideas based on the Ocean Hill–Brownsville experience.

In telling this story, decisions had to be made regarding a linguistic term that evolved like few others during the second half of the past century: Negro; black; Black; Afro-American; African; African-American. I have tried to choose the term that would have been generally accepted at the time in which particular events took place. Some readers may be offended by some of the choices I made, but I hope the difficulty I had in making those choices will be appreciated.

So, where to begin? The background to the narrative could start with the seventeenth-century arrival of Africans in the New World, or with the nineteenth-century origin of free public schools in the South during Black Reconstruction. Either of these, though, would require another book. The choice I made was to introduce the story with a brief summary of the events that took place in New York City between 1954, when black and Puerto Rican parents began to demand an end to school segregation in the wake of *Brown v. Board of Education*, and 1968, when 54,000 white teachers locked horns with those communities, opposing a new phase of the Civil Rights movement and generating a confrontation that brought the city to a historic standstill.

I

Prelude to Confrontation

Tales of Two Cities

By the middle of the twentieth century, the American labor force was characterized by two distinct, racially defined sectors. Workers of color were hired in certain industries, by certain companies and in certain job classifications. Other industries and occupations were reserved for white workers. "An accurate rule of thumb," wrote one economist, "is that the lower the pay, and the more disagreeable and dirty the job, the greater the chance of finding a high proportion of Negroes."[1]

This pattern pervaded the entire economy, including the civil service. New York City was no exception. Its low-paid black and Puerto Rican workers toiled as hospital orderlies, hotel and office cleaners, dishwashers, domestic servants, and unskilled factory workers, while also supplying the military with cannon fodder. A mayoral report concluded that, outside of Harlem, there were two categories of businesses: "those that employ Negroes in menial positions and those that employ no Negroes at all."[2] Their chronically high level of unemployment provided a reserve labor force for times of high demand, and served to suppress wage levels in general. White-collar office and managerial jobs, and skilled blue-collar jobs, were reserved for whites, whose unemployment rate was never more than half that of blacks, regardless of occupation, gender, age, or educational attainment[3] (a ratio that has persisted into the twenty-first century).[4]

The city's school system mirrored and replicated the dual labor market. There were, in fact, two school systems, segregated by color, each of which churned out workers prepared and programmed for the job classifications that awaited them. Both systems had a teaching staff that was almost entirely white.[5] Basic skills, such as reading, were required for the white-collar jobs reserved for white graduates, so white children were taught to read in the public schools. Academic skills were not required for the "colored" labor market, so the public schools produced huge numbers of illiterate graduates, dropouts, and pushouts.[6]

Paradoxically, the school system's abject failure to properly educate its black and Puerto Rican students contributed to its success in reproducing the city's economic, political, and social life.[7] Their segregated schools, wrote one journalist, "overcrowded, full of the violence and turmoil of the ghetto, were staffed by administrators and teachers from an alien culture who looked upon their work as combat duty. The result was that the schools were run as semi-reformatories, and learning was nil."[8] This was an overstatement, but it did capture the essence of ghetto schools, where both teachers and union officials conceded that custodial methods had taken the place of actual teaching.[9]

New York City's economy was changing during mid-century, though. Its industrial base peaked right after World War II, when there were more unskilled and semi-skilled manufacturing jobs in Manhattan than in any U.S. county except Chicago's Cook County.[10] Its industrial output, larger than those of Detroit and Pittsburgh combined, dwarfed that of every other city.[11] During the next twenty years, while it absorbed a wave of black and Puerto Rican migration, the city lost almost half of those jobs. Seventy thousand disappeared from the garment industry alone during the 1950s. The entry-level opportunities that sustained previous waves of immigrants, including the Italians and the Eastern European Jews who settled Ocean Hill and Brownsville earlier in the century, vaporized just as the new immigrants arrived. Expanding opportunities were increasingly limited to the construction trades, where discriminatory union practices denied employment to black workers,[12] and to the white-collar sector, which required a level of education that the city systematically denied to black and Puerto Rican children. By 1956, white-collar jobs outnumbered those involving manual labor, but federal studies during the 1960s showed a near total absence of black workers in the city's banking, insurance, communications, and advertising firms.[13] In 1961, the New York City Youth Board reported that "black youth coming out of both general and vocational high schools were untrained, unskilled and ill prepared for anything but menial work."[14]

It would have been expected that the city's new citizens would follow the economic path to the middle class journeyed by previous immigrant groups, employment in municipal services. The Lyons Law required municipal workers to live in the city. Whites were moving out; blacks and Puerto Ricans were streaming in. In 1962, though, the Lyons Law was repealed. The city's workforce, especially its police and fire departments, quickly became the province of white suburban commuters. The police force, and sometimes even the firefighters, became identified in the ghetto as an alien, occupying army.[15]

This whole arrangement, of a dual labor force fed by a dual school system, was challenged by a massive, grassroots movement of black and Puerto Rican parents. The movement began in 1954 with a call for desegregation, and culminated in the late 1960s with a demand for community control of the city's still segregated schools.

Triggering the movement was the U.S. Supreme Court's 1954 ruling in *Brown v. Board of Education* that racial segregation in public schools violated the Equal Protection clause of the Fourteenth Amendment to the Constitution. The Court reversed its 1896 *Plessy v. Ferguson* ruling that "separate but equal" accommodations satisfied the Constitution, and announced that, "Separate educational facilities are inherently unequal."[16] In a subsequent decision, it ordered integration of the nation's public schools, "with all deliberate speed."[17]

In case any New Yorkers hadn't noticed the landmark decision, it was quickly dropped on the city, with a loud thud, by Dr. Kenneth B. Clark, a prominent black psychologist and CCNY professor, whose own research findings had been extensively cited in the Supreme Court decision. In his 1954 keynote address to the Annual Meeting of the Urban League of Greater New York, Clark charged that the city's school system was racially segregated, and that its black and Puerto Rican students were receiving an education so inferior that they fell further behind the longer they stayed in school. He cited evidence that black children did worse in New York City's segregated schools than in those of the Jim Crow South. In a soft voice, he loudly challenged the Board of Education to immediately implement the Court's decision.[18]

Within a few weeks, the Board responded by passing a resolution praising the *Brown* decision, and boldly declaring that it would conduct a study of the problem. Noting, perhaps, that the promise of a study satisfied exactly no one, it took a stronger position before the year ended:

> It is now the clearly reiterated policy and program of the Board of Education of the City of New York to devise and put into operation a plan which will prevent the further development of such (segregated) schools, and integrate the existing ones as quickly as possible.[19]

At the time, New York City was experiencing substantial population shifts, which began in the 1940s when a massive migration from the American South and Puerto Rico to Northern cities was triggered by automation and other changes in agricultural economics. Between 1943 and 1960, fully a third of Puerto Rico's island population relocated to New York City, Chicago, and Philadelphia. During the same period, 60 percent of black-owned farms were lost, sending more than five million migrants to Northern cities and three million to the ten largest of these.[20]

The demographic shift accelerated after World War II, when a housing shortage for returning veterans was ameliorated by government programs that built highways, bridges, and tunnels, and provided low-interest financing for housing. These programs triggered a boom in suburban development, creating new communities that were largely restricted to whites.[21] The nation's largest government-aided all-veteran housing development, Long Island's Levittown with its 17,450 homes, sold houses only to whites and had deed restrictions that prohibited buyers from ever reselling or even renting to blacks. During the postwar period, all the Northern cities became less white, and more black and/or Puerto Rican. (Immigration to New York from Central and South America was minimal at the time.) By 1960, the once-rural, Southern non-white population was overwhelmingly urban, with half living north of the Mason-Dixon Line.[22]

New York City's black population grew by 250 percent between 1940 and 1960, reaching 1.1 million. During the 1950s, its Puerto Rican population doubled, from 245,900 to 612,600. State law didn't ban discrimination in multifamily housing until 1957, and enforcement after that was spotty at best. Landlords found it profitable to restrict the new migrants to certain neighborhoods, which were widely referred to as "ghettos." The Brooklyn Real Estate Board, whose membership included nearly all of the borough's banks and realtors, had made racial and ethnic segregation its official policy way back in 1927.[23] The nation's largest urban redevelopment housing project, Manhattan's Stuyvesant Town, was built exclusively for white veterans.[24] Brooklyn's Bedford-Stuyvesant surpassed Harlem as the city's black metropolis. East Harlem and "El Bronx" became Puerto Rico's mainland outposts.[25]

During these decades, the children and grandchildren of Eastern European Jewish immigrants were replacing the Irish teachers and supervisors who had long dominated the school system. These new teachers, mindful of past religious discrimination, lobbied hard for institutional changes that would protect them, including seniority rules, an examination system, guarantees against arbitrary dismissal and, eventually, a union contract.[26]

Meanwhile, 1.7 million white people moved out of the city, at an astonishing pace. People who lived in the "changing neighborhoods" at the time recall that all it might take to empty an apartment building of white families was for a single black family to move in. This phenomenon, which became known as "white flight," could generate 100 percent turnover in just a few months. Looking back, it seems like overnight. It provided the Temptations with the opening lyrics of their hit song, "Ball of Confusion."

People movin' out,
People movin' in,
All because of
The color of their skin.

Brownsville's turn-of-the-century tenements, which had historically been inhabited by working-class Jews who couldn't afford to live anywhere else, were rapidly overcrowded with poor and working-class black and Puerto Rican migrants, who spilled over into seven new, hastily and poorly constructed, public housing projects. While Brownsville reformers had once pleaded with city officials to replace its shacks and tenements with new public housing, these projects, according to one study, "rather than stemming the tide of decay, seemed to accelerate it."[27] Municipal services, particularly sanitation, declined when whites moved out, even as the increased population density multiplied residents' need for them.[28] Living conditions steadily deteriorated, to the point that Boston mayor Kevin White, following a tour of the area, remarked that it "may be the first tangible sign of the collapse of our civilization."[29] Similarly colorful language was employed by other visiting politicians after their obligatory tours of the area. Some compared Brownsville to European cities devastated by World War II bombing raids. Others even extended the analogy to Hiroshima.[30]

The schools that served ghetto neighborhoods were racially segregated and, by every measure, inferior. They had antiquated textbooks. They were physically neglected. They were staffed primarily by white teachers who were either inexperienced or had been transferred from white schools because of incompetence or character issues.[31]

School segregation, a violation of the state constitution since 1938, was justified as the inevitable consequence of residential segregation. Much was made at the time of the distinction between the "de jure" (by law) segregation of the South, and the "de facto" (by practice) segregation of the North. Northern racial segregation didn't "just happen," though. Federal, state, and local government programs and agencies were largely responsible for both establishing and exacerbating it. The federal Housing Act of 1949, for example, provided massive amounts of federal funds to private developers who, with city and state cooperation, cleared out mixed communities and replaced them with high-rise apartment blocks that did not rent to blacks or Puerto Ricans. Redlining, the policy that banks used to deny financing for the purchase or renovation of homes in black and Puerto Rican neighborhoods, was institutionalized by the federal Home Owners Loan Corporation, a product of the New Deal that probably did more to cement racial segregation than any other single program.[32] New York City's Board of Education zoned children into schools that were even more segregated than the residential patterns. In Brooklyn, for example, only 35 percent of black families lived in census tracts that were more than 80 percent black in the early 1950s, but nearly all of their children were zoned into segregated schools.[33]

Brooklyn's PS 11, on the edge of Bedford-Stuyvesant, provides a case study in the Board's segregationist policies. At the time of the *Brown* decision, the student body in this century-old wooden building with outdoor toilets was 100 percent black. Directly across the street, though, was a large all-white housing development. The zoning for PS 11 drew its northern line on its front sidewalk. White children who lived across the street travelled to all-white schools farther away. Ironically, the favorite slogan of whites who would organize to defend segregation was "Neighborhood Schools for Neighborhood Children."[34]

This slogan was stretched in a different way for PS 6, on Manhattan's Upper East Side, probably the city's best public elementary school. Its zoning followed a narrow north-south band for almost three miles, zigzagging from east to west in order to include only townhouses and apartment buildings populated by wealthy and upper-middle-class white Protestant and German Jewish families. PS 6 was popularly referred to as the free private school of the rich.[35]

When the PS 11 parents protested the poor conditions and the deliberately segregated zoning of their children's school, the District Superintendent promised to replace it with a new, integrated school. A group of black parents were told by a nearby principal, though, that integration was unrealistic. "How would it look," he rhetorically asked them, "to have the children of the madams attending the same school as the children of the maids?"[36] What the parents got instead was another segregated black school.

What the city soon got was its first grassroots civil rights movement.

The Fight for Integration

> If we ever expect to see the influence of prejudice decrease and ourselves respected, it must be by the blessings of an enlightened education.
>
> —*Resolution of the 1832 National Negro Convention*[37]

In 1955, another new school was completed, Junior High School 258 in Bedford-Stuyvesant. Parents, civil rights activists and teachers, black and white, had organized to pressure the Board to zone this new school for integration, which officials promised to do. When the school opened, though, it was zoned to enroll a student body that was 98 percent black.[38] Only eighteen of its seventy teachers held a regular license to teach in a junior high school.[39]

Annie Stein, president of the JHS 246 Parent-Teacher Association (PTA) in Brooklyn, was among the civil rights activists frustrated by the Board's duplicity. She approached Rev. Milton A. Galamison, the charismatic young pastor of Bedford-Stuyvesant's Siloam Presbyterian Church, to discuss what might be done about the ghetto schools. They began contacting PTAs around the city, inviting parents to meet at the church. Soon, the parents (nearly all were mothers or grandmothers) formed an organization. When a member raised a problem with a particular school, the group would travel with her to meet with the principal, thus providing local parents with organized citywide support in resolving their issues. They called this the Parents Workshop.[40]

The Parents Workshop's early successful campaigns included the creation of after-school and gifted programs, the opening of school libraries, getting a new roof for a school, even forcing one principal to have homework assigned for the first time. Word of these accomplishments spread, and its membership grew by the hundreds, including officers of 64 PTAs.[41] As the issues it addressed broadened to protesting racist practices by teachers and supervisors, and advocating for black history in the curriculum, the parents realized that they had common problems which could only be addressed on a system-wide basis. The overarching crisis was the inferior education that plagued the segregated black and Puerto Rican schools. The Workshop's parent leaders were convinced that segregation was the reason those schools were inferior, that the system would not assign properly trained teachers, or relieve overcrowding, in classrooms that had no white students. They were not mollified by the Board's claims that the schools could not be integrated if housing was segregated. Annie Stein had documented, in a case study, how JHS 258 was segregated deliberately, not as the inevitable result of housing patterns. They began to strategize a campaign for racial integration. The group now became the Parents Workshop for Equality in NYC Schools.[42]

Rev. Galamison was the group's charismatic leader, powered by a deep personal conviction that desegregation was the key to building a democratic society. Annie Stein was a brilliant researcher, statistician, and strategist with deep experience as a civil rights activist, and a former union organizer. During the prior decade, she had helped to organize black hotel maids, and lead the first lunch counter sit-ins, in a Southern town called Washington, DC.[43] Wrote one historian, "No white person was more intimately involved in the struggle to integrate New York's schools than Stein."[44] They were joined in 1960 by Thelma J. Hamilton, a 49-year-old, multi-talented mother of eight from Brownsville, who was already a well-known local parent and tenant organizer. She would travel the city, bringing audiences to their feet with both speech and song. Under their leadership, and the leadership of the many black and Puerto Rican mothers they trained, the Workshop grew within a few years to 4,000 members. It was, by far, New York's largest independent grassroots civil rights organization.

The Workshop's first campaign was a modest one. The influx of blacks and Puerto Ricans to segregated communities and the white exodus to the suburbs, combined with the Board of Education's racial gerrymandering, created, within short distances of one another, both underutilized white schools and severely overcrowded black and Puerto Rican schools. The Workshop proposed that the Board allow voluntary transfers by students in the overcrowded schools to those with empty seats. Its proposal was implemented, on a very limited basis, but the program met adamant opposition from white parents in the receiving schools. In Queens, black third-graders were met by angry white mobs, yelling "Blacks Go Home!" White opponents to any form of desegregation began to organize citywide, forming an organization they called "Parents and Taxpayers" (PAT).

Figure 1.1. Rev. Milton A. Galamison (undated, c. 1962).

By the end of the 1959–60 school year, the Board had done nothing, other than this half-hearted effort, to implement its lofty 1954 resolution to end segregation. The Workshop began organizing for a citywide boycott, demanding a plan and timetable for the desegregation of all city schools and voluntary transfers for any ghetto student to any school that had empty seats. Before summer ended, thousands of parents had signed up, pledging to keep their children home when schools reopened. The Board offered to negotiate, but offered nothing that the parents would accept. At the last minute, after the intervention of Mayor Robert F. Wagner, Jr., the movement won what appeared to be its first major victory. Through a new program called Open Enrollment, students in any segregated elementary and junior high schools would be permitted to transfer to white schools that had excess capacity.[45]

Now, opposition came from another quarter. As white parents flocked to PAT to keep their schools pure, the bureaucracy of the school system itself emerged to frustrate this new plan for limited integration.

The New York City Board of Education, as an organization, was a strange animal. The lay members of the Board itself, appointed by the mayor and often progressive in outlook, had no staff of their own. They were totally dependent, for information and for the implementation of policy, on the Superintendent of Schools. The Superintendent, in turn, had to rely on a sprawling bureaucracy, larger than those of entire European countries. The bureaucracy was comprised of dozens of bureaus, departments, and divisions, each of them operating as an independent fiefdom focused on little more than protecting its own prerogatives and sometimes nonsensical rules. Its Bureau of Supplies, to cite a ridiculous example, would refuse a request for requisition forms if the request was not made on a requisition form. Board headquarters, at 110 Livingston Street in downtown Brooklyn, was a maze of warrens, where it might take a visitor all day to find a particular office. One management expert described it as "a model of bureaucratic pathology."[46] Among the few things it did well was resist any kind of change.

Even when a new policy was strongly supported by the Board and its Superintendent, implementation was frustrated as it moved through the system. If the headquarters staff supported it, the field staff (principals and district superintendents) would sabotage it. If the field staff supported it, the headquarters bureaucrats would kill it. This inertia machine was more powerful than any Superintendent, a position that wore out every occupant after no more than a few years. Superintendents, who often came to NYC with sparkling records of accomplishment in other cities, were no match for what they found here. "In Pittsburgh, when I gave an order, it was carried out," Superintendent of Schools Calvin Gross once exclaimed in frustration, "Why doesn't that happen here?"[47] In 1965, Gross was replaced by Bernard E. Donovan, his top deputy and a 30-year insider at 110 Livingston Street, who would nevertheless soon characterize the bureaucracy as "monstrous."[48]

Open Enrollment was a case study in sabotage by every level of the Board bureaucracy.[49]

- Many parents of eligible children were never told they had this opportunity. Others were given transfer forms the day before they had to choose among several receiving schools, about which they were given little or no information. (The program was most successful in areas where the Parents Workshop itself prepared parents for it, including distribution of the information they would need.)

- Principals in the home schools warned parents of dangers that might await their children: an unfriendly new principal; unfriendly students; bad weather; a sudden illness far from home. One parent reported a principal asking, "What would happen if an atom bomb were dropped?"

- The bus schedules were poorly prepared, so the routes were longer and more time-consuming than they needed to be.
- Principals at the receiving schools did little or nothing to prepare their staffs or students. The incoming children were rarely welcomed, often ostracized, and typically assigned to segregated classrooms in their newly "integrated" schools.

By 1962, only 9,000 students had taken advantage of Open Enrollment, less than three percent of those eligible. Thousands of these returned to their ghetto schools after experiencing hostile, racist receptions at their new schools.[50] The other limited, pilot, and experimental integration programs offered by the Board met with even less success.

Another Parents Workshop strategy focused on school location. Between 1957 and 1965, the Wagner administration built no less than 300 new schools.[51] It did not go unnoticed that these schools were being built by construction workers belonging to segregated white craft unions, which had successfully fought off antidiscrimination protests since the 1920s. The apprenticeship programs that opened the doors to employment in the building trades were more than 99 percent white.[52] The Board of Education's approved list of contractors did not include a single black-owned firm.[53]

New York City's building boom of the 1950s and 1960s extended far beyond schools. Almost 90 million square feet of high-rise Manhattan office space was built in these two decades. Between 1970 and 1972, 49 million additional square feet were completed, as Manhattan reached its pinnacle as the headquarters of international capitalism.[54] White union labor had more work than it could handle. Rather than open its ranks to blacks and Puerto Ricans, though, it met the demand by importing white workers from other states.

The same pattern held true in large-scale residential and institutional construction, much of which involved government subsidies and loan guarantees. During the summer of 1963, a broad coalition of civil rights organizations participated in an intense series of demonstrations at three large publicly subsidized construction sites—a Harlem Hospital annex in Manhattan, Downstate Medical Center in Brooklyn, and Rochdale Village, a massive housing complex in Queens—demanding the implementation of federal laws prohibiting racial discrimination in such projects. At Downstate, 600 people were arrested in July, and the picket line swelled to 1,200. Nightly church rallies, recalling the spirit of the Southern Civil Rights movement, drew thousands. In each case, though, the craft unions cowed the politicians into submission, and nothing was accomplished.[55] As Herbert Hill, the NAACP's Labor

Director, characterized the building trades, "A form of caste psychology impels many workers to regard their own positions as 'white men's jobs,' to which no Negro should aspire."[56] Many of those whose first experience in direct-action protest, and whose first acquaintance with trade unions, took place that summer would soon become activists and leaders in the movement for community control of the schools.

The new schools that were planned to relieve overcrowding in the old ghetto schools were sited by the Board where they would be just as segregated as the ones they supplemented or replaced. Following the debacle of Open Enrollment, the Parents Workshop demanded that the new schools now be built in "fringe areas," near the borders between white areas and the ghettos, so they could draw students from each direction and still be neighborhood schools.

One of the most intense fights over this issue concerned the construction of JHS 275, which was originally planned for a site deep inside Brownsville.

Figure 1.2. Thelma Hamilton at Board of Education hearing (undated, mid-1960s).

This was Thelma Hamilton's home turf. She formed the Emergency Committee for Integration of JHS 275, which conducted a six-year struggle to have the site moved to the border between Brownsville and Canarsie, and to have it zoned "50-50," drawing students from both sides of Linden Boulevard, East Brooklyn's Mason-Dixon Line.[57] Canarsie was a white outpost developed for, and largely populated by, Italian and Jewish families fleeing the black and Puerto Rican influx into the surrounding communities of Brownsville, East New York, and East Flatbush during the 1950s and 1960s. Its surge in population, from 30,000 to 80,000 during those years, and corresponding boom in real estate values, were largely attributable to white flight.[58]

The Parents Workshop and its allies across the city joined Brownsville's parents in their effort to have the new school built where it could be an integrated neighborhood school. Some parent support was lined up even in white Canarsie. Hundreds were mobilized to picket a series of the Board's site selection meetings. It was hailed as a huge victory for integration when the Board moved the construction site to Linden Boulevard, precisely on the line that divided the two communities. Jubilation faded, though, when the school finally opened in 1963, zoned only for the Brownsville side of the boulevard. The students assigned to it when the doors opened were 90 percent black.[59] (In 1984, shortly after Thelma Hamilton's death, the local school board renamed JHS 275 in her honor.)

The Parents Workshop now turned to citywide direct action. A new coalition was built, joining it with the Harlem Parents Committee, several chapters of the Congress of Racial Equality (CORE), six chapters of the NAACP and other groups in a new organization, the New York Citywide Committee for Integrated Schools, which made Galamison its president and chief spokesman. The Committee demanded of the Board a specific plan and timetable for desegregating the city's schools. To enforce this demand, it called for the first citywide boycott of schools on February 3, 1964. While the massive organizing effort for the boycott proceeded, the Board called meetings, held negotiations, and made various promises. When nothing came of these, support continued to grow. Bayard Rustin, architect of the historic 1963 March on Washington, made the elaborate logistical planning for this boycott his next project. Churches and community organizations opened their doors for meetings and rallies, and for the 500 "freedom schools" that children could attend on the day of the boycott. Demonstrations and sit-ins, and the inevitable arrests, kept the movement in the news. The Urban League, the National Association for Puerto Rican Civil Rights, parent groups, and many teachers' organizations joined the coalition.[60]

The boycott was, as expected, opposed by all those who had resisted earlier attempts at desegregating the schools. It was also opposed by important liberal voices, including the American Jewish Committee, the Anti-Defamation League, the New York Civil Liberties Union, and the Liberal Party. The New York Times ran several editorials expressing its opposition as well.[61]

Where Are the Teachers?

> By the mid-sixties, it was not difficult to conclude that the reason for the union's success was that the teachers were primarily white and the community was increasingly black.
>
> —Marjorie Murphy[62]

Most notable in withholding support for the boycott was the teachers' collective bargaining agent, the United Federation of Teachers (UFT). Rev. Galamison appealed in person to its Executive Board for the union's support, or at least a recommendation that its members not cross picket lines, but to no avail.[63] The UFT's governing body, the Delegate Assembly, passed only a mealy-mouthed resolution of "support" for individual teachers who would refuse to cross the picket lines, and urged "negotiations between the civil rights groups and the Board of Education in order to achieve quality integrated education."[64] It vowed to support its own members, but not black and Puerto Rican children and parents. It called for "negotiations" as though the delegates were on another planet during the entire past decade, during which continual rounds of negotiations produced a net result of zero.

The UFT's position on this issue echoed those of most Northern, predominantly white trade unions, which opposed segregation in the South while supporting racist policies in their own backyards.[65] In New York City, one such policy concerned teacher assignments, which permitted experienced teachers to avoid serving in ghetto schools. The UFT took great pride in having kept the Board from improving the staffing of those schools through teacher transfers from other districts. It had successfully opposed such efforts since 1957, before it had even consolidated as an actual union.[66]

The UFT's failure to transcend its own parochial interests was a reflection of its brief history, and a forerunner of conflicts still to come. Before 1961, there were more than sixty different teacher organizations, none of which had collective bargaining rights. Chief among these were the Teachers Union (TU), which positioned itself as part of a larger social justice movement, and the smaller Teachers Guild, which had a more conventional craft union philosophy. Since 1935, the TU worked to forge bonds with parents in the city's black and Puerto Rican communities. It developed a complete curriculum in African-American history, exposed and fought to eliminate racist textbooks, and collaborated with parents and civil rights activists in the integration movement. It was a significant force, for example, in the effort to integrate JHS 258.[67]

The TU was one among dozens of Communist-led unions that once led the entire labor movement in the pursuit of racial justice. During the Cold War, though, they were targeted by red-baiting politicians. The omnibus anti-labor Taft-Hartley Act of 1947, for example, required union leaders to swear non-Communist oaths before any union could be certified as an elected collective bargaining agent.[68] In 1950, the Board of Education banned the TU from operating in the city's schools, after which it could no longer hold meetings or represent its members in grievance proceedings. The Board followed this by purging the TU's leaders, and hundreds of its members, from the school system. The TU survived, barely, as an advocate for civil rights, but it would no longer be a contender ten years later, when the Board agreed to hold a union representation election.[69]

In 1960, the Teachers Guild merged with some other professional associations and renamed itself the United Federation of Teachers. The national AFL-CIO cast its lot with the 7,500-member UFT, supplying organizers and campaign funds. In 1961, the UFT won recognition as the collective bargaining agent for the city's teachers.[70] By 1964, the TU and the other rival organizations existed only in memory. The UFT elected its second president that year, a 35-year-old former math teacher and Guild organizer named Albert Shanker.

While many teachers and some individual union chapters supported the 1964 integration boycott in various ways, the UFT leadership was missing in action. The union achieved rapid success in negotiating improvements in wages, benefits, working conditions, and job protections for its members. It never sought to recreate, however, the unity that the TU had developed with communities of color.[71] This was a portentous strategic decision. With its decision against supporting the boycott, wrote one union member, "The UFT started to slide down the road toward the Great Strike of 1968."[72]

During this period, the seeds were sown for a new rival to the UFT. In early January 1964, Galamison received a visit from two young black teachers, Albert Vann and Leslie R. Campbell, who asked how they could help. The minister asked them to do one thing: "Organize the black teachers." They did just that, assisted by their colleagues' negative reactions to the UFT position on the boycott. On April 12, fifty teachers gathered in a meeting room in Brooklyn's Bedford Avenue YMCA. They voted to establish the Negro Teachers Association (NTA), and to elect Vann as its president.[73] Before long, this group would become a significant force in the city school system, and a constant thorn in the side of another Albert, UFT president Shanker.

Boycotts and Dead Ends

According to Board of Education statistics, 464,361 students participated in the February 3, 1964 citywide boycott, nearly half the city's total school enrollment. Pickets marched outside 300 schools. Thousands marched to 110 Livingston Street for a noon rally. The city's black and Puerto Rican schools were deserted that day. Freedom Schools attracted almost 100,000 children. Organized by ordinary people at the grassroots level, the boycott was one of the nation's largest civil rights demonstrations, and the high point of the city's integration movement.[74]

From then on, though, it was all downhill. The Board, which had promised a plan and timetable for integration, but never delivered, stopped even promising anything. The Citywide Committee did not have a "Plan B." It had pinned all its hopes on the boycott, which was hugely successful in execution, but did not succeed in overcoming the Board's intransigence. When Galamison called for a second boycott, expanding the demands to include black principals and black history, the coalition splintered, leaving only its more militant members on board. While they were joined by such prominent figures as Adam Clayton Powell and Malcolm X, their Puerto Rican organizational support fell away. The city's Puerto Rican leadership lost interest in the movement after the first boycott, citing cultural and political differences with the black community and its leadership. Galamison found himself overextended in trying to organize another complex citywide action so quickly.[75]

Meanwhile, white opposition to integration was mounting. PAT, the segregationist group, held its own show of strength. Led by the Canarsie chapter, fifteen thousand white people marched against "bussing" on March 12, 1964.[76]

Considering its hasty mobilization and smaller base of organizational support, the second boycott, on March 16, was remarkably successful. Total absenteeism was about 26 percent, and closer to 90 percent in the majority black schools. Parents and activists manned picket lines at 150 schools. A militant, boisterous rally was held at 110 Livingston Street. The Board president, though, pronounced it a failure, and still refused to implement the Supreme Court's mandate.[77]

The reality had become undeniable. The NYC Board of Education had no intention of integrating its schools. If it was honest about this, it might have echoed the much reviled words uttered by Alabama Governor George C. Wallace a year earlier: "Segregation now! Segregation tomorrow! Segregation forever!"[78]

Its intransigence did not escape the notice of the State Commissioner of Education, James E. Allen. A study commission he appointed, almost a decade after the *Brown v. Board* decision, issued a damning indictment in May, 1964:

> Nothing undertaken by the NYC Board of Education since 1954, and nothing proposed since 1963, has contributed, or will contribute to any meaningful degree, to desegregating the public schools of the city. Each past effort, each current plan, and each projected proposal, is either not aimed at reducing segregation or is developed in too limited a fashion to stimulate even slight progress toward desegregation.[79]

Allen put forward his own desegregation plan, which was praised by many civil rights groups, but largely ignored by the Board of Education. Moderate groups entered a round of negotiations with the Board, but got nowhere. PAT went public with its opposition to any and all desegregation plans, and announced its own boycott for September. During 1964 and 1965, Galamison continued to lead actions aimed at forcing integration. Some attracted impressive participation, but none produced concrete results.

The poor and working-class communities of Ocean Hill and Brownsville at the time were completing a rapid transformation from predominantly Italian and Jewish, respectively, to almost completely black and Puerto Rican. These neighborhoods were changing not only in complexion, but in density. Tenement apartments formerly housing one or two people were now occupied by eight, nine, even ten. Sanitation and other city services, which were never good, worsened. The schools were so overcrowded that they had to function on split shifts. None of the children had a full day of school; they attended either from 8 a.m. to noon, or from noon to 4 p.m. Parents had to choose between working a full day or caring for their children. There were no parochial schools, which could have alleviated the overcrowded public school conditions. The parents took their complaints to Father John Powis, a 30-year-old white Catholic priest at Our Lady of Presentation Church, located at the intersection of the Ocean Hill and Brownsville neighborhoods. Father Powis organized a group to work on a solution. While some in the group were interested in integration, their primary objectives were to relieve the overcrowding and provide their children with a full school day.[80]

Fifteen minutes away, in the Glendale and Ridgewood sections of Queens, sat half-empty public schools, deserted by families who had enrolled their children in local parochial institutions. Father Powis's group petitioned Superintendent Donovan to bus some of their children to those schools, which would free up space for full-day programs in their own schools. In 1965, they were offered a compromise: Queens was out, but they could send children to underutilized schools in some white Brooklyn neighborhoods, including Bay Ridge, Canarsie, Borough Park, and Gravesend. These areas were about an hour away, but the parents were desperate. They signed up 1,700 children for the bussing program.[81]

It quickly proved to be a disaster for the children, exceeding even that of Open Enrollment. The busses were met by angry white mobs. The children were called "niggers," and pelted with eggs and tomatoes, by white parents. On the very first day, Father Powis, exiting the bus in Bay Ridge wearing his clerical vestments, was struck by eggs thrown by Italian Catholic women. The children were provided no police protection. Once they made it into the schools, they were crowded into separate segregated classrooms, sometimes on segregated floors, and ignored by the teachers. After just a few weeks, the parents had no choice but to bring them back to their inferior, overcrowded schools.[82]

The lingering trauma of this experience is reflected in these lines of verse, penned three decades later by an Ocean Hill survivor of bussing to a white neighborhood at the age of ten:

> where was my mother
> when i was bussed to Gravesend
> and rivers of people
> people
> people
> screaming
> screaming
> shaking the bus
> what was the meaning?
> we don't want them with us?
> people
> people
> white people?
> ***i am a nigger?***[83]

The final effort to relieve overcrowding and achieve integration in Brooklyn centered on a vacant 96-acre plot of city-owned land, located at the intersection of Brownsville, East New York, and Canarsie. Led by Thelma Hamilton, Father Powis, and other Brownsville leaders, a coalition was formed to pressure the city into building an "educational park" on the site, including junior high and high schools that would draw students from all three communities. Their vision encompassed a state-of-the-art campus, with facilities not feasible in individual schools, and 11,500 black, white, and Puerto Rican students. Thousands of parents in the three communities signed petitions supporting the proposal. Also signing on in support were the NAACP, the American Jewish Congress, the American Jewish Committee, the Urban League, and the Catholic Interracial Council. Meetings were held at City Hall and at the Board of Education, which agreed to study the plan.[84] When the young, reform-minded John V. Lindsay was elected mayor in November 1965, with the overwhelming support of the black and Puerto Rican electorate, many thought this plan could become a reality.

The outgoing Wagner administration, however, had a different idea for the site. It was planning an industrial park. This plan was supported by Canarsie's elected officials and local school board members, all of whom were white. Its main impetus, though, came from powerful real estate interests closely connected to the mayor through Brooklyn's Democratic Party political machine, which saw land values soaring when factories relocated out of the city's established commercial districts. On New Year's Eve, during his final hours in office, Wagner formally approved a long-term lease of the land to a politically connected developer with a shady reputation. During his first week as mayor, Lindsay tried to delay implementation of the lease, but Wagner's actions ensured that nothing could be done.[85]

The industrial park's July 1966 groundbreaking ceremony was disrupted by more than a thousand angry protesters, separated by police from the visiting dignitaries. Lindsay arrived at the peak of the demonstration. He stepped out of his car and walked, by himself, into the crowd, waving off police protection. After a few tense moments, a group of young black men lifted the mayor onto their shoulders and carried him to the podium, through the now cheering throng of demonstrators.[86] It was a unique moment in the city's political history. The Educational Park, though, quickly receded into bitter memory.

These experiences triggered a search for new solutions in Ocean Hill-Brownsville. They taught the activists and the parents that the only hope of improving their children's education was to improve their own neighborhood schools, leading them directly to the Community Control movement. Had the Board of Education ensured the success of the bussing program, while building new schools to relieve the overcrowded conditions, or built the integrated Educational Park, the history of this period could well have unfolded quite differently than it did.

By 1966, the 12-year struggle for integrated schools faded away in defeat, but new voices were being heard in the black community.

New Voices at a New School

> The issue of integration, in the ghettos at least, has paralyzed everyone and wasted energies in symbolic controversies that have done nothing to improve the schools. And each year, as the talk goes on, another crop of miseducated children is sown.
>
> —Joseph Featherstone[87]

> Suppose that now, bitter and disillusioned but clearer in our vision and wiser in our aims, we turn to another source of power, the only power sufficient for that fundamental change demanded by the times? Suppose we now *turn to ourselves* in answer to our needs!
>
> —Ossie Davis[88]

Rev. Galamison's vision of integrated schools as the key to building a truly democratic nation was consistent with that of Dr. Martin Luther King and the Southern Civil Rights movement. Black support for it, though, was never unanimous, particularly in the Northern cities. Standing at another ideological pole was Malcolm X, who was then electrifying audiences with messages of self-reliance and self-determination. Malcolm's endorsement of Galamison's second boycott was primarily a reflection of his effort to become more inclusive after his recent pilgrimage to Mecca, and to form alliances with militant forces in the Civil Rights movement, which he had previously shunned. He never thought for a moment that the proximity of white children would actually benefit black children.[89] In 1962, he explained that integration was one of many possible tactics, but that the goal of the struggle was "freedom, justice and equality."[90] By the time of the boycotts, he saw the only path to this end as "black control of the black community's economic and political institutions," and cited this as the essence of Black Nationalism.[91]

The Black Nationalist perspective was first brought into the educational arena three years before the boycotts, by Preston R. Wilcox, an East Harlem social worker, community organizer, and secular follower of Malcolm X. In 1961, he conducted a study of a program that relieved overcrowding in two segregated East Harlem schools by busing 84 black and Puerto Rican children to an underutilized school in Yorkville, a nearby white neighborhood. In his conclusions, Wilcox challenged the fundamental theory of the *Brown v. Board* decision, which equated segregation with inferiority. "If one can believe that a segregated white school can be a good school," he asserted, "then one must believe that a segregated . . . Negro and Puerto Rican school can *also* be a good school." He argued that one-way desegregation programs like Open Enrollment did nothing to improve education in the sending schools, and in fact stigmatized them, leaving those left behind with the belief that their own success would not be possible there. As a result, students would not work hard, parents would give up on the schools, and, most importantly, the teachers' already low expectations of their students would be reinforced.[92]

The issue of low teacher expectations was amplified by Dr. Kenneth Clark in *Dark Ghetto*, his comprehensive critique of social institutions in segregated black communities. He charged that white teachers subscribed to a "cult of cultural deprivation," which was a pseudo-scientific justification of their failure to teach.[93] This argument was validated by studies showing that low teacher expectations were a "self-fulfilling prophecy," that students would learn to the extent that their teachers believed they could learn, and that black students were being penalized by their teachers' racist preconceptions.[94] Wilcox and others who lived or worked in the ghetto did not need to wait for these studies. They were convinced that the Board of Education was putting teachers in their schools who, because of upbringing or training, were not capable of educating black and Puerto Rican children. There was no reason to think those children would do better if they were sitting next to white children.

In 1963, while teaching Community Organizing at the Columbia School of Social Work, Wilcox found a white ally in the person of Prof. Richard Cloward. Cloward and his partner, Frances Fox Piven, were prominent advocates of the theory that the best way to attack poverty was to empower the powerless communities of the poor. Self-reliance, self-respect, and community empowerment became the touchstones of a new movement.

Meanwhile a new school was being planned for East Harlem, Intermediate School 201. In response to well-organized local demands that the school be zoned for integration, Board officials insisted that IS 201's state-of-the-art quality, combined with convenient transportation to and from white neighborhoods (despite their location on the other side of the East River), would have white parents clamoring to send their children to school in Harlem. This clamoring, though, did not materialize. A 10,000-family direct-mail campaign attracted only ten inquiries and not a single white child. In early 1966, the Board announced its new integration plan for IS 201: It would have black students, and it would also have Puerto Rican students. Local activists were neither pleased nor amused by this redefinition of integration. A leading force in the controversy, the Ad Hoc Parents Council, insisted that the school's September opening be delayed until the Board satisfied the community that it would provide its black and Puerto Rican students with quality education.[95]

During that summer of 1966, James Meredith decided to take a walk through the State of Mississippi. In 1962, he had integrated the University of Mississippi Law School, with the help of a court order and twenty-five thousand U.S. Army troops. Now, unaccompanied by supporters or personal security, he wanted to prove that black people, anywhere in the United States, had the right to go about their business unmolested, in any public place, and to promote their taking full advantage of the 1965 Voting Rights Act. The experiment failed when he was shot and seriously wounded by a sniper. The Civil Rights movement quickly mobilized to complete Meredith's march through the hostile state, which would become no less dangerous. On June 16, at a rally in Greenwood, Stokely Carmichael, the newly elected 25-year-old head of the Student Non-Violent Coordinating Committee (SNCC), raised his right fist and issued a call that resounded throughout the nation's black colleges and communities. It was not a call for patience or for "turning the other cheek" to violent attack. It was a call for self-identity and self-determination that would join the teachings of Malcolm X with the long history of ethnic groups' struggles to establish a political and economic foothold in the United States. "We need," he proclaimed, "BLACK POWER!" The call hit a nerve. Carmichael himself later said he was amazed at the level of enthusiasm it unleashed at the rally.[96]

Wilcox, a member of IS 201's Ad Hoc Parents Council, was perhaps the first to translate the call for Black Power into institutional form. He audaciously proposed that the parents of the segregated school elect a "School-Community Council," and that the Board of Education cede to this body its powers over hiring, curriculum, and policy. With democratic governance, he argued, the com-

Figure 1.3. Preston Wilcox at a 1968 parent meeting.

munity could be brought into the school through a multitude of programs. The school could become a reflection of the black community's culture, interests, resources, and values, instead of an institution that rejected all of these.[97] This revolutionary proposal, soon adopted by the parent leadership, was rejected by the Board. The new movement for Community Control, though, was born.

Opposition to the Board's bungling of the IS 201 opening immediately galvanized from every corner of the Civil Rights movement. Negotiations, picketing, and boycotts delayed the school's opening, and continued thereafter. Among the national leaders marching with parents on the picket lines were Stokely Carmichael and H. Rap Brown of SNCC and Floyd McKissick of CORE. A white principal resigned under pressure, but was reinstated within a few days. Nothing was resolved. However, the demand for community control of that single school touched a nerve, drawing more national attention than did the 1964 citywide integration boycott which closed down hundreds of the city's schools. It spread like wildfire, not only through New York City, but also to Milwaukee, Detroit, Boston, Cincinnati, Philadelphia, Washington, DC, and other large cities.[98] It was the nation's first institutional assertion of the Black Power movement.[99] In New York, it would also develop into the nation's first contest for civic control between African-Americans and Jews.[100]

In *Black Power,* which might be considered the manifesto of that movement, Carmichael and Charles V. Hamilton echoed the argument that Preston Wilcox put forward in his 1961 critique of the East Harlem–Yorkville bussing program.

> "Integration" as a goal . . . , is based on complete acceptance of the fact that in order to have a decent house or education, black people must move into a white neighborhood or send their children to a white school. This reinforces, among both black and white, the idea that "white" is automatically superior and "black" is by definition inferior. For this reason, "integration" is a subterfuge for the maintenance of white supremacy.[101]

Harlem activist David Spencer put it more simply. "Nobody from outside is going to tell us," he said, "what kind of segregated school we're going to have."[102]

People Power in Brownsville

> At the nexus of race and labor, at the nexus of race and housing, and at the nexus of race and education, is power.
>
> —Craig Steven Wilder[103]

A few months after the opening of IS 201, on December 19, 1966, the Board of Education held a public hearing, one of its periodic, tightly choreographed, exercises in public relations. This particular hearing was well attended by parent and community groups, a public that intended to be heard. When Board President Lloyd Garrison ruled an Ocean Hill–Brownsville parent out of order because her name wasn't on the official speaker's list, the Board heard from that public, loud and clear. Shouts of, "Let her speak! Let her speak!" broke out, growing louder and cadenced. Rather than make an exception to the Board's traditional procedure, Garrison adjourned the proceeding and its members left the hall.

Their seats were quickly occupied by parent and community activists from every borough. They declared themselves the "People's Board of Education," and announced that the hearing would now resume. They also announced that they were not leaving. The group sent word to Rev. Galamison, who quickly arrived and was elected president of the People's Board.

The People's Board, and scores of supporters, would occupy the Board auditorium for three days before the police arrested its members and carried them out. When Garrison tried to reclaim his seat on the second day, Galamison ruled him "out of order." As word spread, parents came from all over the city to participate. Dozens testified about the unspeakable conditions in the ghetto schools. After the occupation ended, the People's Board held hearings throughout the city's black and Puerto Rican communities. In February 1967, it passed a resolution calling for community control of public education in the City of New York. "Community Control" became the battle cry of the city's black and Puerto Rican activists.

Rev. Galamison, the leader of the battle for desegregation, had made a difficult personal decision to abandon that campaign. He later wrote that the long effort "to educate children in a spiritual atmosphere of racial unity" had brought about only "integration in teaspoon proportions" which "the educational structure threw out with a shovel." Reflecting on the negative experience of Open Enrollment, he acknowledged that, "Black people who had not previously thought the matter through decided it might not be an advantage to have their children educated beside the children whose parents sanctioned bigotry and hatred."[104]

In historical terms this shift in demand, from integration to community control, happened overnight. While it had quietly been evolving for some time within the ghetto communities, it came as a surprise to outsiders, including white liberals who had committed themselves to supporting integration. One analyst observed that

> Negro demands for control of the schools their children attend have moved from relative obscurity to crippling confrontation with

> astonishing speed . . . No wonder, then, that white liberals are substantially bewildered . . . They find the most articulate of their presumed beneficiaries engaged in a very different war.[105]

Ocean Hill–Brownsville was well represented on the People's Board by Father Powis, Thelma Hamilton, and Dolores Torres, a Puerto Rican mother of four boys. Earlier in the year, they had brought together a group of young Ocean Hill activists, led by Paul Chandler, Brother Sun and Frank Negron, who formed an organization called "Project Method." Their initial focus was on alleviating the abominable housing conditions created by absentee landlords in the area, including lack of heat, frozen pipes, flooding, collapsed ceilings, entrances caked with ice, rats, and even two-foot-long lizards. They tracked down and applied grassroots pressure on the owners they could find, and pressured the city to help find other homes for tenants when these efforts were in vain. When the young Ocean Hill group worked together with Hamilton's Brownsville Tenants Association, this effort expanded and its reputation grew.[106]

Before long, these activists were besieged by local parents with complaints about the schools. Conventional channels were closed to them, since their local schools (though not any of their children) were then zoned into the white East Flatbush district where they had no representation on the local school board and were ignored by district officials. The next step was the formation of the "Independent School Board of District 17," which held open, well-attended public hearings on school conditions and gave community residents a voice for the first time. Parents testified about overcrowding, 15-year-old books, lack of supplies, broken boilers, teachers who didn't teach, and principals who didn't care. These independent efforts generated the leadership core and mass base that would bring those schools into the era of community control.

Powis, Torres, and Hamilton were also leaders in the local chapter of Christians and Jews United for Social Action (CUSA) and, through that group, the Brownsville Community Council (BCC). The BCC had been formed in 1964–65 as a neighborhood coalition of PTAs, churches, tenants associations, political groups, and block associations. From the beginning, it attracted every local issue and advocacy group, who joined together in the BCC and supported one another in addressing their many common problems. At the top of the list were some of the city's worst public schools. The BCC's leaders were supported by a small core of veteran Jewish activists, who had refused to join the white flight from Brownsville, and were able to contribute valuable experience gained from the days when the community was a hotbed of Jewish left-wing activity.

The BCC had an elected board, composed of members from all walks of life. It did not, however, include politicians. Samuel D. Wright, a black attorney and the area's State Assemblyman, had run a slate of candidates in 1965, but lost. The leaders of the BCC distrusted Brooklyn's white-dominated

Figure 1.4. Father John Powis (1969).

Democratic Party machine, and did not want their organization turned into a patronage mill. Wright, like most machine politicians, viewed this independent force as a competing power center. They would clash again and again, well into the next decade.[107]

Following that election, BCC board members realized they needed a comprehensive plan of development. They recruited their local librarian, Major R. Owens, a 29-year-old Morehouse graduate who was also chairman of Brooklyn CORE and a well-known tenant organizer, to lend some technical assistance. First as a consultant, then as Executive Director, Owens led the way for the BCC to become the city's most advanced community organization. He designed the blueprint for the first antipoverty program, which led to BCC's designation as the area agency for the new federally sponsored War on Poverty.[108]

Now known as the Brownsville Community Corporation, the BCC published a newspaper, operated a Head Start program, ran dozens of service

Figure 1.5. BCC Director Major R. Owens.

programs in every area of community life, and served as a hub for organized community action. In three short years, the BCC had grown from a few volunteers to more than 100 paid staff members with a $2 million annual budget. The federal War on Poverty was a short-lived effort, though. After Richard Nixon came into office in 1969, the trumpet call of retreat was sounded. The stream of federal funding would gradually dry up.

By 1967, however, the BCC, along with the Independent School Board and the tenant movement, had created a grassroots infrastructure of experienced organizers and activists ready to fight on for community empowerment, and committed to community control of the schools. When the opportunity arose to make this a reality, Ocean Hill–Brownsville was primed for action.

An Experiment Is Born

The New York City schools, once controlled locally by political ward bosses, were centralized under the aegis of the Board of Education at the turn of the twentieth century. Since then, even the members of local school boards, left surviving with only an advisory role, were appointed by the central Board. By the 1960s, the Board's bloated bureaucracy controlled every aspect of school operations, from assigning teachers and supervisors to supplying books, chalk, #2 pencils, and erasers. Between 1933 and 1965, citing many failures, six "white papers" called for decentralizing the system, but nothing was done.[109] Its signature failure, though, was that of the segregated black and Puerto Rican schools, which by the mid-1960s housed a majority of the city's students.

The opening for decentralizing the school system came in early 1967, when Mayor Lindsay petitioned the State Legislature to fund the system as though it were five separate borough-wide school districts. This could have generated as much as $100 million in additional state aid because of the way the state's arcane funding formula was structured. Legislative leaders indicated they would respond positively if the city system's decentralization to the borough level became an actual fact, not just a paper one. In a deal negotiated by Commissioner Allen, they agreed to $54 million in additional funding if Lindsay would submit an acceptable decentralization plan by the end of 1967.[110]

The mayor then moved forward with his own agenda, which was to decentralize not just to the borough level, but to the local communities. He appointed a task force, led by Ford Foundation President McGeorge Bundy, to develop a plan for the legislature, and pressured the Board of Education to begin experimenting with some pilot programs. In May, the Board created three small "demonstration districts," where such an experiment could be tested. One district, called "Two Bridges," was an ethnic polyglot in Lower Manhattan. The other two were in communities where local organizing was already well advanced, and where something needed to be done before dissatisfaction boiled over into civil disorder. One was in Harlem, centered on IS 201, 92 percent black and 8 percent Puerto Rican; the other was in Ocean Hill–Brownsville, 80 percent black and 20 percent Puerto Rican. The Ford Foundation provided planning grants to joint parent-teacher Planning Councils in each district.

The Board issued vague guidelines for these districts. It envisioned a lengthy planning and review process, after which elected local boards would assume some of the central bureaucracy's administrative responsibilities, and the principals and district superintendents would have expanded powers.[111] Parents and the community would be more "involved," but would not actually run anything. The UFT supported this vision, and campaigned, though unsuccessfully, for labor-intensive additional services through its "More Effective Schools" program, which would have created hundreds of new union jobs and lightened teaching loads.

Black and Puerto Rican community leaders had something else in mind. As IS 201's David Spencer put it, "The Board of Education will call it Decentralization. We like to carry it further. We call it Community Control."[112] Some decentralization supporters "were taken by surprise when they discovered that the changes they endorsed involved actual control of the schools by local communities," commented one analyst. "They had agreed to produce a play, but when the curtain went up on opening night, the characters were reading from a different script."[113]

"Community Control," like decentralization, meant different things to different people. At a national Black Power Conference, a workshop headed by Preston Wilcox reported out an ambitious definition of the powers envisioned for elected local boards:

- Expenditure of local, state and federal funds;
- Hiring, firing, training and reprogramming all staff;
- Site selection, design and naming of schools;
- Awarding and supervising construction contracts;
- Purchasing of books, supplies, equipment, food services, etc.;
- Educational policy, curricula and programs; and
- Merit pay for effective staff performance.[114]

Charles V. Hamilton, perhaps best known as co-author of *Black Power* with Stokely Carmichael, added another dimension. He proposed thinking of the school "as a locus for the entire family, year-round, day and evening," and as the community's primary service/activity center. In his vision, welfare, pre-school child care, sports, medical care, and even law enforcement, all under democratic community control, would come into the schools, through a "family-community-school comprehensive plan" that would bring parents in to work as respected members of the staff.[115]

These visions circulated primarily among black educators and activists. For street consumption, leaflets like this one broke it down to the basic concerns of parents:[116]

OUR CHILDREN WILL LEARN
As soon as we ourselves control our schools
TEACHERS WILL TEACH
As soon as we ourselves control our schools
OUR MEN WILL HAVE JOBS
CONSTRUCTING SCHOOLS FOR OUR CHILDREN
As soon as we ourselves control our schools
TEACHERS WILL NOT BE ABSENT (except for darn good reason)
As soon as we ourselves control our schools
WE WILL HIRE AND FIRE OUR TEACHERS AND PRINCIPALS
(just the way it's done right now in all those rich white suburbs)
As soon as we ourselves control our schools
Stop saying "Decentralization." Start Saying:
COMMUNITY CONTROL

While the new community control agenda was being defined and debated, there was no disagreement within the movement with the diagnosis put forward by Charles Wilson, Unit Administrator of the IS 201 demonstration district:

> Decentralization is not enough. Not enough, because the public educational system's deterioration is too widespread, its cancers and malpractices far too deep and too well protected by various special interest groups. Because the present order denies its diseases, it cannot be cured.[117]

Those "special interest groups," though, deemed a little administrative reshuffling quite sufficient. Over this fundamental disagreement, a decisive battle would be fought.

As it turned out, as noted by parents, observers, and participants, as well as in a study by Queens College's Institute for Community Studies, the primary distinction among the demonstration districts' teachers was simply their presumption that the children were educable.[118]

A Preemptive Summer

> In Ocean Hill–Brownsville, there are people groping in the dark. They are people who for a long time have felt themselves outside the mainstream of public concern. The city takes no notice of them. These people are obscure, unnoticed—as though they do not exist. They are not censured or reproached; they simply are not seen. They are the invisible residents of a demoralized, poverty-stricken inner city.
>
> —Rhody McCoy[119]

When the 1966–67 school year ended in June, the teacher representatives on the Ocean Hill–Brownsville Planning Council joined their colleagues, pursuing summer activities in more pleasant surroundings. The parent and community representatives, though, had no such places to go. Further, they had no intention of falling into the Board's time-tested trap of endless planning and review processes. They were determined to take this bull by the horns, and were in no mood to wait for their staff counterparts to return in the fall.

Their first order of business was to find experienced professional leadership, someone *in* the system, who *knew* the system, but was not *of* the system. Onto the scene came Rhody McCoy, a 44-year-old, blue-eyed, pipe-smoking, black man. An 18-year veteran of the city school system, McCoy was then the acting principal of a "600-school."

Established in 1946, the 600-schools were dumping grounds for thousands of children, nearly all black and Puerto Rican, who were categorized as emotionally disturbed or as troublemakers, but could not legally be tossed into the street until they reached the age of sixteen. As Annie Stein sarcastically wrote, "As soon as the child reaches sixteen years of age, the task of the teacher is immensely lightened."[120] Black men with strong personalities were appointed to head most of these schools, but all served as "acting" principals on teachers' salaries, barred from advancement by a civil service examination process that the courts would years later abolish due to blatant racial discrimination.[121] Black applicants who passed the written exam nearly always failed the face-to-face oral follow-up, coming away convinced that they had been barred from advancement by complexion and/or dialect. McCoy refused to even apply for a promotional exam, convinced that no blacks would ever be allowed through that portal.

McCoy had spent many hours discussing education with Malcolm X, coming away convinced that the most important thing was to free up the minds of black children. "You may have to clean floors," he would tell them, "but that ain't got nothing to do with *how you think*."[122]

Figure 1.6. Rhody A. McCoy, Ocean Hill–Brownsville Unit Administrator (1968).

As Father Powis remembered the impression McCoy made on the Planning Council:

> He just caught everybody's imagination immediately. He was talking the language that the parents were talking. He was talking about . . . parents had to be involved in education, that a whole new way of teaching had to be done. And somehow or other, it would have to involve parents in the community. I would say as soon as we heard from him for about 45 minutes, there was no doubt this man was going to be selected.[123]

The Council offered McCoy a provisional appointment as Unit Administrator (the equivalent of district superintendent). A final decision would have to be made by an elected Governing Board, which would supersede the ad hoc Planning Council.

The next crucial task was to hold that election, where parents would vote for that Governing Board. The Council went to the central Board for lists of parents eligible to vote from each school. Here the reliably obstructionist bureaucracy sprung into inaction. The Council was told it would have to hire two of the Board's secretaries to examine its files. When it agreed to cover the expense, it was told that those two secretaries were, unfortunately, on vacation.

The planning group was hard at work that summer, determined to have a new regime in place by the opening of the 1967–68 school year. It was not going to wait until teachers, secretaries or anyone else returned from their vacations. Council members, nuns, church volunteers, BCC workers, and parents conducted a door-to-door campaign, and registered more than 1,800 prospective voters. Nominating petitions were circulated, generating 61 qualified candidates. The election was held on August 3–4, with 1,049 parents electing eight parent representatives to the new Governing Board, one from each of the district's schools. The 22 percent turnout, despite all the obstacles, was higher than had been achieved in previous conventional elections of local officials. It was also higher than the average middle-class suburban school board turnout, and dwarfed the turnout of all future school board elections throughout New York City.

While the election was taking place, the Board's liaison to the community and Superintendent Donovan were both away on vacation. A few days after Donovan returned, anticipating a leisurely return to the planning process, McCoy informed him of the election results and introduced him to the winning candidates. According to McCoy, Donovan's response was, "My God, what have you done?"[124] Presented with a fait accompli, after an election determined to be fair, though unorthodox, by an independent panel, Donovan was more or less forced to accept the results. He agreed to deal with the new Governing Board, although he left its legal status ambiguous and never defined its powers.

As McCoy said in a 1969 speech, referring to Donovan and the central Board, "What they really didn't reckon with was that they were dealing with someone with a little savvy, who knew how to pull a few stoppers out of the sink too."[125]

The parent members of the Governing Board, in accordance with its planning document, then elected five at-large community representatives: Father Powis and Dolores Torres of CUSA and the BCC; Walter G. Lynch, director of community services at JHS 271; State Assemblyman Wright; and the Rev. C. Herbert Oliver, a recently arrived local pastor who brought with him a wealth of leadership experience from the Birmingham, Alabama Civil Rights movement. Representing academia was Dr. Stephen Lockwood, a Brooklyn College education professor. Two principals were added, and seats were reserved for a teacher representative from each school. Rev. Oliver, 42, was elected chairman over a challenge from Assemblyman Wright.

The teacher delegates to the Planning Council returned from vacation in late August. They were invited to sit on the Governing Board until faculty elections could be held, and to participate in two crucial votes. The first was to choose between Rhody McCoy and the teachers' nominee, JHS 271 Principal Jack Bloomfield, for permanent Unit Administrator. McCoy won easily. Bloomfield applied for a transfer out of the district, which would be granted a few months later, in the middle of the school year. The white teachers grumbled.

The Governing Board's next decision, on September 2, was to replace the five principals who deserted the district upon its creation. Its consideration of unconventional appointments (detailed later in Part II) further alienated the white teacher representatives, who refused even to vote. They walked out of that meeting, and never returned for another. The UFT joined the supervisors' union in filing a lawsuit against the appointments. As the opening of the 1967–68 school year approached, storm clouds gathered.

Polarization

Just as the Governing Board had all the pieces in place for the new school year, the UFT called a citywide strike. Strikes by public employees, including teachers, violated the state's recently enacted Taylor Law, but this inconvenient fact aroused little public discussion. Ostensibly, the union was striking over the usual contract issues, but it also demanded a provision authorizing any teacher to unilaterally expel any "disruptive child," from the classroom and even from the school.

Parents in communities of color, who had supported the UFT in its previous strikes, were horrified at the prospect of arming white teachers with such arbitrary power. "Nothing more destructive to the rights of the ghetto child can be imagined than the UFT demand for the right of direct suspension without review," wrote a prominent educational psychologist, summing up the parents' legitimate fears.[126]

Vocal in opposition to this strike were the black teachers. The Negro Teachers Association had conducted a major organizing campaign during the 1966–67 school year. Inspired by the example set by Major Owens in his leadership of Brooklyn CORE, it established borough chapters, sponsored a popular lecture series, and began publishing a highly political newsletter.[127] These efforts quickly paid off. By the summer of 1967, half of the city's 4,000 black teachers were involved with the NTA in some way, ranging from newsletter subscribers to active members. In August 1967, it changed its name to the African-American Teachers Association (ATA), and declared its opposition to the UFT's "disruptive child strike." A month later, at a conference attended by several hundred teachers, plus a hundred parents, it called for "self-determination, self-control and self-defense" in the black community, and community control of its schools.[128]

Vann and Campbell were steering the organization away from its "professional" affiliations with the UFT, and into solidarity with both the black community and the worldwide anti-colonial struggle. As Vann would soon write in its newsletter, "ATA does not view its efforts in education as being separate from the total struggle of all Black and oppressed people fighting for human rights. In that regard, we support all organizations and individuals trying to lift the yoke of oppression and racism."[129]

A new national affiliation would also develop. In 1968, 3,000 black education professionals met in Chicago to establish the National Association of Afro-American Educators. Preston Wilcox, who convened the groundbreaking convention and was elected its president, now had a broad platform for a new educational agenda. "The educational process," he wrote, "must become one in which (the student) learns to think for himself, and about how to develop his own (Black) nation." Teachers could become "resource persons and learner-enablers rather than repositories of knowledge." Most importantly, "Students are being urged to learn about how to solve their own communities' problems, rather than memorizing negative descriptions about them."[130]

In the wake of the "disruptive child" strike, most ATA members resigned from the UFT, and the organization became a leading voice of opposition to its policies. One source of the UFT's opposition to any significant decentralization was the fear that, in some districts, the ATA might replace it as the collective bargaining agent.[131]

On the other side, white teachers who had never previously been interested in unionism suddenly became enthusiastic UFT supporters.[132] In its 1960 strike demanding fundamental union rights, less than one in eight teachers manned the picket lines. Member support for its 1962 strike over conventional trade union issues barely surpassed a majority. Now, with the "disruptive child" issue thrown in, more than three-fourths of the teachers stayed out.[133] "Once it took a racist stand," concluded Annie Stein, "the union became more powerful than it had ever been before."[134]

Not all white teachers, though, sided with the union. Many opposed this strike, as they would the long strike of 1968. These teachers were mostly young, but among their ranks were experienced teachers as well, including veterans of the old Teachers Union whose decades-long efforts to build community ties were now being upended by the UFT.[135]

In the demonstration districts, the 1967 strike was seen as a show of the union's power, directed against them, their children, and their new experiment in community control. All the Ocean Hill–Brownsville schools were kept open during the strike, staffed by parent volunteers and non-striking, mostly black, teachers. Parents, ATA members, and some white teachers kept 35 other Brooklyn schools operating as well. After two weeks, the strike was settled, with the teachers gaining salary and benefit increases totaling more than 20 percent.[136] The UFT did not win its "disruptive child" provision but, in the black and Puerto Rican communities, the strike would be remembered for that demand. When the striking teachers returned to Ocean Hill–Brownsville, there was bad blood on both sides. All the white teacher delegates resigned from the Governing Board.

During November and December of 1967, competing proposals for decentralizing the city school system were submitted to the State Legislature. The first, sent over Mayor Lindsay's signature and supported by the entire Community Control movement, was based on the report prepared by the Bundy Commission. It recommended breaking the system up into 30 to 60 independent local districts, which would function much like all of the state's other school districts. They would have the power to hire and fire their own staffs, create their own curricula, and control their own budgets, all subject to centrally negotiated union contracts. Staff qualifications would be based solely on state certification, and the discredited competitive civil service lists would be eliminated.[137]

This was anathema to the UFT, which immediately attacked the Bundy report. Shanker saw it as an attack on union power, since its perennial threats of system-wide strikes would lose their impact if policy decisions were made by several dozen independent local boards.[138] The union quickly came up with its own plan for "decentralization." Its plan kept the Board bureaucracy in place, retaining central control of salaries, benefits, working conditions, hiring, and firing. On the local level, it proposed to create 15 districts with boards that would only have very limited "consultative" powers. Nothing but paper-shuffling would actually be decentralized. The union justified its stand with a broad attack on democratic governance, and on the inability of "laymen" to set educational policies. This latter argument was self-contradictory, since the union's proposal left the existing Board of Education, composed of laymen, atop the still centralized school system. The UFT vowed to spend "whatever is necessary" to thwart the Bundy Plan.[139]

Other vocal opponents of the Bundy Plan included the Jewish Teachers Association, the Council of Jewish Organizations in Civil Service, and the Board of Rabbis.[140]

The Legislature was expected to vote on school decentralization in April or May of 1968. Meanwhile, back in Ocean Hill–Brownsville, the chasm between McCoy, the ATA, and the Governing Board on one side, and the UFT and the central Board on the other, only widened. A fifth of the teachers transferred elsewhere by the middle of the school year, taking advantage of relaxed rules negotiated between the UFT and the central Board. Seventeen of the district's 21 assistant principals were granted transfers as well. In February, Jack Bloomfield left JHS 271, along with all six assistant principals, five secretaries, and a third of the faculty. Teachers who wanted to replace them were stalled at the central Board.[141] McCoy's request to recruit replacement supervisors from outside the all-white civil service list was denied. Even his need for office space was frustrated by the central Board, which made him wait seven weeks until it provided him with a tiny unheated storefront and got him a telephone.

None of this caused as much damage as the behavior of many white UFT teachers, which was increasingly being characterized as "sabotage." Some were in open mutiny, telling parents that they would not work under black supervisors. Lateness and absenteeism ran rampant. Dozens of teachers in a single school called in sick on the same day, causing class sizes to be doubled. One teacher was caught pouring paint on the classroom floor, a prank he would blame on his students. When IS 55 was completed, and McCoy sent five elementary school classes there, the teachers simply refused to go.[142] When a fire caused a school's evacuation, ten teachers went home, leaving their students standing in the street. Children panicked. Coats and books were lost or stolen.[143] At JHS 271 especially, little effort was made either to teach or to maintain order. Often, there were more students running around the halls than sitting in classrooms. Teachers would spend their time reading newspapers and racing forms, sometimes leaving their classes to place bets.[144]

The Governing Board, denied the power to take corrective action, once again demanded the right to recruit its own supervisors, which was again denied.

In April, the Parent Associations of JHS 271 and IS 55 called a two-day boycott to dramatize the crisis. Even without any pickets posted at the schools, the boycott was 100 percent effective. At the district's elementary schools, parents extended the boycott further, without any organizational mandate, keeping about half of their children home. Despite this clear demonstration of unity, the central Board held firm.[145] It was allowing the UFT to poison the embryonic experiment. Project Method declared itself ready for a war of independence. If the Governing Board didn't assert itself, community support would fade away, and along with it the promise of community control.

The Governing Board Strikes Back

> One of our most serious problems is our expectation that those whom we have not allowed to participate in American life should now participate, playing the game according to our rules of competition (law and order, due process, etc.) knowing that *our* past failures load the dice against *them* at the outset. People who, according to every social index, realize they are regarded as failures, are not especially eager to play a game in which another failure is preordained.
>
> —William M. Birenbaum[146]

On May 9, 1968, thirteen teachers and six supervisors received a letter, signed by McCoy and Rev. Oliver, informing them that the Governing Board "has voted to end your employment in the schools of this district." It offered a hearing for those who wanted to question their removal, but directed them to report to the central Board for reassignment.[147] Among this group were five teachers from JHS 271, including UFT Chapter Chairman Fred Nauman, the district's most politically powerful teacher. (He actually taught a drastically reduced schedule, to allow sufficient time for his union business.)

Shanker met with the dismissed teachers, and they resolved to fight the dismissals. He charged that the nineteen had been "fired" without due process of law. McCoy responded that the Governing Board couldn't fire anyone, since the teachers were employees of the Board of Education, and that they had simply been transferred back to the central Board for reassignment (as the letter stated). By offering a hearing, the Governing Board actually went beyond the requirements of the union contract.[148]

While the method might have been a little clumsy, transfers had long been the accepted way for administrators to relieve themselves of problem teachers. David Rogers, in *110 Livingston Street*, the classic study of the school system which was written shortly before this particular controversy erupted, described the transfer practice in matter-of-fact terms.

> Usually, an unsatisfactory teacher is transferred, frequently from one ghetto school to another, but he is not given an unsatisfactory rating . . . Many principals don't want the responsibility of defending an unsatisfactory rating for fear it may reflect negatively on them, because they don't want to be bothered, or because they are afraid of union harassment.[149]

Principals who wanted to remove incompetent teachers preferred the transfer procedure, since taking action to fire them involved an endless, expensive, and time-consuming process, during which the teacher would remain in the school. Teachers generally accepted these transfers, since their records remained clean. The losers in this system were the ghetto schools, since that was where incompetent teachers ended up.[150] Even in this case, all six administrators and two of the thirteen teachers readily accepted transfers to other districts. After the one black teacher in the group was accepted back by the Governing Board, there were ten white teachers left in limbo, half of them from JHS 271.

Superintendent Donovan refused to recognize the Governing Board's action, and ordered the nineteen to report back to their schools. "It appears," commented Rev. Oliver, "as though he would rather transfer the whole community than transfer nineteen people."[151] Rev. Oliver himself had actually voted against the motion to transfer the teachers. Minutes before that vote, though, there had been another one, prompted by Chandler and the Project Method activists in the room. The question was, "Do we have the power to do this?" and that vote was unanimous in the affirmative. Everyone present agreed that the Governing Board, democratically elected to run the schools, had by definition the power to decide who teaches in them. Otherwise, the entire enterprise was a sham.[152] Even though Rev. Oliver was in the minority on the transfer vote, he would support it to the end, as the democratically arrived at decision of a democratically elected body. Neither Donovan nor Shanker would agree with, or even respect, that logic.

On Monday, May 13, the five dismissed JHS 271 teachers were met at the school's entrance by a wall of parents, students, black teachers, and community citizens, determined to support their board and keep them out. While 200 police were waiting for orders to break the blockade, the size of the blockade grew. More police arrived on the scene. Fearing a violent explosion, officials at the central Board allowed the day to end in stalemate, closing the school for the day and announcing that negotiations would be held downtown. That evening, while 600 attended a community rally at the school, Shanker announced that no union teachers would report for work in Ocean Hill–Brownsville until the disputed nineteen were allowed back in.[153]

Late that night, following the rally, parents and activists occupied the school. Tuesday morning, all the entrances were barricaded from the inside.

Figure 1.7. Activists block the entrance to JHS 271 (May 13, 1968).

Students and teachers were allowed in, but not Nauman and his cohort. They were blocked on the steps by another contingent of activists. Elaine Rooke, the PTA president, made it simple for them. "You're not coming to this school," she said. "You've been dismissed by the Governing Board." Further, she announced that any teacher who stays out in their support "will never be able to come to this school." She was referring to the 85 teachers who, following Shanker's instructions, stood across the street, behind police lines. Again, Donovan refrained from calling on the police to charge the steps while negotiations continued. Tactically, the day was a victory for the Governing Board and its supporters.[154]

Before dawn the next morning, the school was occupied again, but this time by the police. When the sun rose, 300 policemen established control of the school entrance by cordoning off the building with wooden barricades. They deputized Fred Nauman to screen entrants to the school.[155] When the police escorted the five dismissed teachers and their 85 supporters inside, though, all the other teachers and all the students walked out. Stymied, Donovan ordered JHS 271 and two other district schools closed for two days "to help reduce tension in the area."[156] The Governing Board raised his bet, by announcing that all the district's schools would be closed "until further notice," while it made plans to reestablish control.[157]

While all nineteen dismissed by the Governing Board continued to receive their paychecks, and while nine of them were actually working in schools, the UFT continued to insist that they had been "fired." At one point, McCoy indicated to UFT Vice President John O'Neill his interest in finding a compromise and it appeared that a resolution to the crisis might be on the horizon. But when O'Neill called Shanker on the telephone to report the possibility of a negotiated breakthrough, the response he got was, "Fuck you. I want those teachers in the classroom now."[158] Compromise was not on his agenda.

The boycott lasted three days. As soon as it ended, Donovan ordered the dismissed teachers to Board headquarters for hearings on possible transfers. Shanker ordered them to report to their schools instead. Donovan said he expected his orders to be carried out, and that refusal would amount to insubordination.[159] But the next day, he caved in and withdrew his order. Shortly after the teachers entered JHS 271 that afternoon, all the students walked out. McCoy invited the teachers to a "fair hearing" with the Governing Board, but the UFT had determined not to recognize the Board's authority.[160]

When Ocean Hill–Brownsville students returned to school on May 22, 350 of the district's 556 teachers were on UFT picket lines instead of in their classrooms. Shanker told them to stay out, and then proclaimed that it was a management lockout, not a strike. Donovan ordered the principals to take them back, threatening their own dismissal. McCoy took the matter out of the principals' hands, and said he might take them back, but not with teaching assignments. The 350 continued their walkout for the remaining six weeks of the school year. Non-striking teachers, assisted by BCC, Project Method, ATA, and parent volunteers, kept the schools open but barely functioning.

On the same day that the UFT walkout began, the union held a large rally at City Hall opposing the compromise decentralization bill that Governor Rockefeller had announced was close to passage. The UFT had invested a half million dollars in a rarely seen lobbying effort, marked by baseless accusations and appeals to racial fears, to kill the bill. At another rally of his 500 teacher-lobbyists swarming the state capitol, Shanker threatened, "If the bill passes, I will follow every legislator around who voted for it, and kill them politically."[161] By the end of the day, the compromise bill was abandoned in favor of a weaker version that would postpone for a year the decentralization of the school system and, in the meantime, expand the Board of Education from nine to thirteen members and authorize it to delegate some of its powers, including the hiring and discharging of teachers, to local school boards. There was also an understanding among legislative leaders, the Board of Education, and the Governor that these and other powers would immediately be delegated to Ocean Hill–Brownsville and the other two demonstration districts. This compromise would have delayed full decentralization, while giving the experiment in community control an opportunity to prove itself,

Figure 1.8. Albert Shanker leads UFT rally against Ocean Hill-Brownsville (May, 1968).

and defuse the tense situation that was rippling out across the city from Ocean Hill–Brownsville.

But it was not to be. Shanker was still opposed. His threats against the city's representatives in Albany and his wild charges held off passage. The *Times* report on the day's political jousting used the term "refusing to budge" twice in four paragraphs to characterize Shanker's intransigence. He insisted that the delegation of any personnel powers, the heart of the bill, be removed from it. "If they're against this," complained one Senate official of the UFT, "then what kind of decentralization plan are they for?"[162]

The answer to that question lay in the law passed the next day, specifically tailored to receive Shanker's blessing. By appealing to white legislators' racial nightmares, Shanker had grabbed for himself veto power over the most critical issue of the Albany session. The agreement to empower the demonstration districts was abandoned, and the union was given assurances that no personnel powers would be delegated to local boards by the expanded Board of Education. The new law was denounced by Lindsay and the Board of Regents as meaningless, even as a harbinger of civil disorder. The *Times* editorial called it "the worst failure" of a "disastrous" legislative session," and warned of "day-to-day warfare between the school establishment, which now clearly consists of a coalition between the union and the Board of Education, and the community forces in search of an effective and legitimate role in running their schools."[163]

In June, McCoy officially ordered the 350 striking teachers to return to their schools. When none did, they were dismissed for excessive absences.[164] There was no sign of dissent in the community when the Governing Board announced that it would recruit replacements for every one of those teachers, and that none of those who abandoned their classes would ever again set foot in an Ocean Hill–Brownsville school. The district's schools limped to the term's end, facing an uncertain future.

The mayor made his four new appointments in mid-July. Lindsay took a bold step, appointing Milton Galamison, *bête noire* of the Board of Education, to sit on the Board. Annie Stein came along as his chief aide. Other appointments included a Puerto Rican activist, a corporate executive, and John Doar, formerly the U.S. Assistant Attorney-General who enforced Southern compliance with federal civil rights laws. Installed by Senator Robert F. Kennedy as head of the Bedford-Stuyvesant Restoration Corp., a huge community development effort, Doar had cultivated good connections with government, foundations, the private sector, and the black community. After the mayor filled a few vacancies triggered by resignations, his appointees comprised a majority

Figure 1.9. Teacher-lobbyists gathering for chartered train to Albany (May, 1968).

of the Board's members. Like their predecessors, though, they would soon learn that the school system was actually run by the UFT and the bureaucracy, not by the Board of Education or even the Superintendent of Schools.

During August 1968, the new Board of Education announced its interim decentralization plan, which it would formally submit to the State Board of Regents on September 4. This plan gave the local school boards the power to bypass the civil service lists in hiring teachers, although with restrictions, and additional powers over curriculum, textbooks, and budgets. It also codified the longstanding practice of involuntary transfers of unwanted teachers, as long as another district would accept them. Shanker predictably denounced the plan, and threatened a citywide strike for the first time during this conflict. It would not take a stretch of the imagination to conclude that this interim plan was the actual reason for the first citywide strike, not little Ocean Hill–Brownsville.[165] Defense of the sclerotic, dysfunctional status quo might have garnered little public support, though, and the district's troubles, instigated by the UFT since the Governing Board first took office, provided the union with a convenient whipping boy.

On August 26, the UFT's position was bolstered through a report issued by retired judge Francis E. Rivers. The Board of Education had asked Rivers to review the issue of the transfers and rule on their legality, though without authority to subpoena witnesses. Rivers held hearings and heard evidence presented by both sides. In effect, this process put the case into the realm of dismissals, which demanded a high level of evidence and a low bar for exoneration. The charge of incompetence, for example, required the district to prove, by a preponderance of the evidence, that the teacher "failed to perform in a manner equal to that of the average performance of a teacher under like circumstances," and that the district had given the teacher adequate opportunities to receive help. Since the "average performance" of teachers in ghetto schools was so poor, it was preordained that the transfers would be denied. Which they were.[166] The UFT publicized the ruling as proof of due process violations. The Governing Board brushed the hearing off as a rump proceeding.

The UFT and the Governing Board each lined up support and prepared for battle. Efforts at negotiation, mediation, arbitration and judicial review all failed. Positions hardened on both sides, although 140 of the 350 dismissed teachers dropped out of the dispute. By summer's end, with the BCC's assistance, the Governing Board hired 350 replacement teachers, attracted from all parts of the country to work in support of the community control project. Mostly young and inexperienced, they included graduates of Ivy League colleges, a large number with graduate degrees, former Peace Corps and VISTA volunteers, civil rights and antiwar activists, and some just looking for a job that would keep them out of the draft. Seventy percent were white, and half were Jewish.[167]

In a last-ditch effort to prevent a strike, Mayor Lindsay convened a marathon negotiation session. The Ocean Hill–Brownsville delegation was isolated and consulted only from time to time, while the actual negotiations were taking place among the teachers' and supervisors' unions, the Board of Education, and the mayor. On Sunday, September 8, the day before schools were to open, following four days and nights of frustration, the Governing Board issued a statement and left the building. The statement claimed that they had "been used" during the "so-called negotiations," and concluded with a resolution:

a) We will no longer act as a buffer between this community and the establishment.

b) This community will control its schools and who teaches in them.

c) We do not want the 210 teachers to return to this district. Since the legal machinery of this sick society are forcing these teachers on us under threat of closing our schools and dissolving this district, the Board of Education should return to our district any of the teachers who wish to return. Our original decision remains as before. We refuse to sell out. If the Board of Education and the Superintendent of Schools force them to return to a community who does not want them, so be it.

d) The parents of our community demand that all our 8 schools be open on Monday, September 9, citywide strike or no.[168]

To Lindsay, paragraph (c) indicated a grudging willingness to accept the teachers back, which he thought was good enough. It wasn't enough for Shanker. His members were already casting ballots in an all-day vote. By a margin of 12,021 to 1,716 that represented about 25 percent of the teaching staff, the strike was on.[169]

The UFT's demands, with their anticipated effects in my italics, were these:[170]

1. The Governing Board must reinstate 210 teachers, including the original 10 plus the 200 who were replaced after the May–June walkout but still wanted to return.

   This would put into the schools 210 teachers hostile to the district, who would have no incentive to make the educational program successful.

2. Future "union security" must be maintained through special protection for union leaders, and an "agency shop" which would require non-union teachers to pay UFT dues.

   Union leaders would have immunity for acts of sabotage, as well as for incompetence. An agency shop would force ATA members to pay dues to both organizations.

3. Local school districts must not override existing "understandings" between the UFT and the Board of Education.

   These vaguely defined "understandings" between teachers and bureaucrats would override not only the local boards, but also the written, negotiated union contracts.

4. Discharge of professionals must only be for cause, with outside impartial review.

   Incompetent teachers would be frozen in place, denying supervisors even the ability to affect transfers without a lengthy, expensive, quasi-judicial process.

5. Only "properly licensed personnel" will be employed in supervising children.

   The demonstration districts' programs bringing parents into the schools as classroom paraprofessionals would be squashed, snuffing out what many saw as the most promising school-community linkage.

The stage was now set for the confrontation that historian Jerald E. Podair would later characterize as *The Strike that Changed New York.* It would trigger, in the words of scholar Fred Siegel writing thirty years later, "a conflict so intense that it was described in apocalyptic terms at the time." "Even today," he continued, "if you ask middle-aged New Yorkers which side they were on, you will see that the embers of their anger still burn brightly."[171]

II

Ten Weeks, Three Strikes

Opening Day
September 9, 1968

Dozens of reporters,
        Crowding the sidewalk.
Hundreds of police,
        On side streets,
        In the schoolyard,
        Everywhere.
Children,
        Wandering about,
        Confused and bewildered.
Parents and teachers,
        No less confused,
        Eyebrows raised,
        Eyes squinting,
        Trying to tell friend from foe.
A perfect setting, perhaps,
        For a political convention,
        Or a football game.
Welcome to the first day of school.
        Junior High School 271
        Ocean Hill–Brownsville
        Brooklyn
        New York City
        The United States of America.

Outside the school doors, chaos reigned. The challenge inside was to create order. It wasn't easy. Sixty-two of our 109 teachers were in the district for the first time, and 43 of us would be facing a classroom for the first time. There were still 11 vacancies. The striking UFT teachers, who had walked out during the last six weeks of the previous term, took door keys and roll-books with them, and had confused or lost many of the children's records.

Administrators were able to assign the 1,735 children enrolled to their official (homeroom) classes, where the sixth and seventh grades would spend the morning. Regular class assignments were scheduled for the afternoon. The school year began, fitfully but hopefully.

The eighth grade started the day with an orientation session in the auditorium. Filing in, the students, nearly all black, encountered a tableau unprecedented in the city's schools. On both sides of the stage stood black teachers, many dressed in colorful African-inspired garments, flanking ATA president and acting assistant principal Albert Vann. Tall and lean with a closely trimmed beard, the 33-year-old Vann had been a Marine sergeant as well as a civil rights activist. With an unmistakable air of authority, he opened with a focus on motivation.

"We are engaged in a fight for survival," he began, "the survival of the black race, of *our* race, of *our* people. Do you know what survival means?" Hands shot up. A brief dialogue ensued. A working definition was arrived at. "Yes, we must live together, and make it *as a race*. We must *survive*. And we cannot survive in this country without some very necessary skills, all kinds of skills, so we can get good jobs to help serve our people. We need the skills we can learn right here in 271: Math; Science; Reading; Typing; Languages. To survive and to prosper as a race of people, we *need* all these skills."

Having won the rapt attention of his audience, Vann went on to discuss student-teacher relations, a touchy subject in any ghetto school. "Now, to get these skills for survival, you must respect and listen to your teachers—*all* your teachers, be they black or white."

"However," he quickly added, "if *they* don't respect *you*, if we find that they can't do the job, there'll be some changes made. Now remember: Give your teachers, and many of them are new in this building, give them a chance. If you do find yourself in a dispute with a teacher, and you're right, we will defend you. You can depend on that."

Ending on a note of high spirit, Vann asked how many students listened to WWRL, the city's leading Afro-American radio station. As most hands went up, he gave them a full-throated cue from the popular James Brown recording: *"Then Say it Loud!"*

"I'm Black and I'm Proud!" thundered the unanimous response. Vann had indeed set a new tone for a new type of school for black boys and girls.

In his speech to the students, Vann had referred to the 43 teachers who were to face their first experiences leading a class. Many came to Ocean Hill–Brownsville with a fast-track teaching license, and possessed neither experience nor formal training to prepare them for the job. Among them was one Charles S. Isaacs, 22 years old and just a year out of college.

Back to Brooklyn

A few short months earlier, I was nearing the end of a reasonably successful first year at the University of Chicago Law School, which had generously provided me with a full-tuition scholarship. I was thankful for my good fortune. It gave me the opportunity to be in a place where, in my view, everyone was smarter than me. I liked that. The law school, though, was a disappointment. Both politically and intellectually, it was a very conservative place. Too many courses were geared to produce skilled corporate servants, I thought. Constitutional law, civil rights law, and criminal law were underemphasized.

This was, of course, a shortsighted view. During the succeeding decades, I have worked with dozens of civil rights and constitutional lawyers, and even corporate attorneys, who were able either to use or overcome their formal training to make major contributions to the causes, organizations, and people I cared about.

But this was 1968. During the past decade, the great European colonial empires had crumbled in the face of revolutionary nationalist movements. Only a few African nations had not yet won their struggles for independence. The people were in the streets, forging new societies in France, in Germany, in Hungary, in Czechoslovakia. Here, our antiwar protests forced a President from office. Columbia University was being turned upside down by its students. Riots, disorders, and rebellions had hit more than a hundred cities in the aftermath of the King assassination. Social upheaval was in the air, throughout the country and most of the world. I enjoyed my quiet hours in the law library, but I was young, restless, and hungry for action. I wanted to make a difference. Right now. Sooner if possible.

Additional pressure was coming from the Selective Service System, which was breathing down my neck. Draft deferments for graduate students had been discontinued that year, and my draft board seemed obsessed with the prospect of plucking me out of Chicago and dropping me into Vietnam. I was never going to participate in the genocidal wars in Southeast Asia, and was willing to go to prison if necessary to avoid it. Actual graduation from law school didn't seem to be in the cards. I was closer to needing a lawyer than to becoming one.

Meanwhile, New York City was trying to fill a critical shortage of teachers. As one observer put it, "The New York school system is so desperately in need of teachers that it is ready to accept almost anyone who has taken the required education courses without fatal consequences."[1] In some subjects, chief among them mathematics, the desperation was extreme. The Board of

Education sent recruiters touring the country, looking for prospects. When one arrived in Chicago, we had a talk.

The recruiter looked at my transcript from Long Island University's Brooklyn Center, and lit up when he realized he was talking to a math major. To my surprise, he told me that I could qualify for a license to teach junior high school math, if I would just take any two-credit education course during the summer and pass a few tests at the Board. I would have a wide range of schools to choose from, and would probably qualify for a draft deferment if I chose an inner-city assignment. My only question was, "Where do I sign?" The recruiter filled out all the paperwork for the application.

(The draft deferment for working in "critical occupations" turned out to be discretionary on the part of the local draft boards, but was usually granted automatically. It brought thousands of young men from the country's best universities into ghetto schools. My local board, though, would use its discretion to deny me that deferment. This triggered an interesting three-year relationship between us which is, however, another story.)

So, after final exams, I told the registrar I was dropping out. She told me I couldn't do that because, "*Nobody* drops out of the University of Chicago Law School!" My bafflement eased when she offered to put me on an indefinite "Leave of Absence." (I've been on that leave for almost a half century now. Maybe I'll go back and finish one day.)

Back in Brooklyn during the summer, I took a two-week night course in Philosophy of Education, breezed through written and oral tests at the Board, and soon found myself a certified "permanent substitute" junior high school math teacher. I spent the rest of the summer as a volunteer tutor and draft counselor at an antipoverty program in Fort Greene, a black neighborhood adjacent to the LIU–Brooklyn campus, and interviewing at schools in and around Bedford-Stuyvesant.

The recruiter was right; it seemed I had my pick of schools in Black Brooklyn. Everyone whose judgment I trusted, though, had the same advice: "Go to Ocean Hill–Brownsville!" One of those advisors was a former LIU classmate, Steve Bloomfield. In 1966, he and I ran against each another for the presidency of the Student Government. He was the "left-wing hippie" candidate; I was the conservative, fraternity-backed candidate, and a heavy favorite to win. After three recounts, I won the election, but in a sign of the changing times, by a mere 1.4 percent of a heavy turnout. The contest behind us, we became close friends and our politics soon converged.

Bloomfield had taught in a Brooklyn elementary school during the year I was in Chicago, and was frustrated by what he described as a list of school priorities in which the children came last. He was looking for a more promising environment. I had been closely following the Ocean Hill–Brownsville story in the news during the previous year, and the advice I was getting made sense to me. By now, it was almost universally acknowledged that the city's schools would never be desegregated, and that they would continue to fail black and Puerto Rican children unless some radical change was introduced.

We agreed that community control could be a historic leap toward both democracy and teacher accountability, promising a new day in quality education for the communities of color. There were also plenty of openings in Ocean Hill–Brownsville, since the Governing Board had resolved to replace all of the 350 teachers who had walked out on them during the previous spring. We decided that we would both apply for a job there, and that we would try to be assigned to the same school.

District assignments were made at the central Board of Education. I went to the Bureau of Personnel in downtown Brooklyn, and asked for assignment to Ocean Hill–Brownsville. The clerk looked at me like I was mad. "Why on earth would you want to go there?" I had a feeling that I shouldn't waste time explaining my decision, so I again asked for the assignment. With a sigh, he stamped and handed over the appropriate forms. His expression said, "You'll be sorry!"

There was one more hurdle to clear. Even though the central board had the legal authority to make assignments, the Ocean Hill–Brownsville Governing Board insisted on screening all new recruits. The screenings were conducted in a school cafeteria, where parents and board members sat at tables to which applicants were randomly assigned for interviews. I had no idea what to expect. I really had no reason to think any white teachers would be accepted in this experimental district spawned by the Black Power movement. (I had no way of knowing then that 70 percent of the teachers approved by the Governing Board would be white.)

I found myself sitting across the table from Rev. C. Herbert Oliver, the Governing Board chairman. After passing him my credentials, we talked for about ten minutes. In that brief time, we sized each other up. The soft-spoken Rev. Oliver conveyed an air of dignity, resolve, and intelligence that I instantly found attractive. He made me feel like a welcome guest in his home. I must have passed muster with him too; he shook my hand and sent me on a tour of the district's schools. Bloomfield and I met with some of the principals and district staff, and both of us asked for assignment to JHS 271.

The school, built in 1962, was named for John M. Coleman, the first black member of the Board of Education, appointed in the mid-1940s as the black migration began to change the city's demographics. Originally, it was a junior high school, with grades 7 through 9. During the mid-1960s, partly in response to the 1964 Allen Report, "intermediate" schools, comprising grades 5 through 8, came into vogue. Beginning with the 1968–69 school year, "271" was technically neither, since its grades were now 6, 7, and 8. Both terms were used to describe the school during that year, from press reports to the school stationery. Among the staff and students, and in the vast majority of outside reporting, it continued to be referred to as a junior high school. Its student body was approximately 90 percent black and 10 percent Puerto Rican.

Later, I thought about the formulation that popped into my head when I met Rev. Oliver: *Welcome Guest*. I decided I was comfortable in this role. I would not be a Missionary in Ocean Hill–Brownsville, or a Savior delivering enlightenment, and certainly not a Colonial Emissary. Nor would I be a Visitor, just passing through like a tourist. The act of accepting an invitation to be a *guest* implies certain obligations to the *host* that extended the *welcome*. In civilized society, these include a duty to behave with a certain measure of respect toward that host. In this case, the host was the community of Ocean Hill–Brownsville and, by extension, the larger black and Puerto Rican community of which it was a part and, in the eyes of many, its vanguard of the moment. I would consider myself a guest, behave accordingly, and stay as long as I was welcome.

Of course, I have no idea whether this was really what was in Rev. Oliver's mind that day, only that it felt right to me. Even if I was guilty of over-thinking this issue, I'm quite sure that no inkling of these thoughts ever crossed the minds of the UFT teachers who had sabotaged the community control experiment, and whose union now held the entire city hostage in its crusade to destroy that effort.

First Time at Bat

So, here I was a few weeks later, my first day as a teacher, and my first day at JHS 271. I was impressed by Vann's presentation to the students, and even more so by their response. I was hopeful that this new atmosphere, with its emphasis on respect, pride, and self-esteem, could open new opportunities for them. My own self-esteem, though, was beginning to waver. After all, I had been made to feel welcome based on the premise that I could actually teach math to junior high school students.

"Whatever made me think I'd be good at this?" I wondered. I had done a considerable amount of public speaking during the previous five years, but none of it in a classroom full of restless adolescents. I had been successful as a tutor in the housing projects during the two previous summers, but that was one-to-one, not one-to-thirty. I had read plenty of books about the schools, but hadn't been in a junior high school since my own (which, by the way, I hated). "Suppose what I have to teach really doesn't interest the kids," I thought. "Maybe math really is boring to everyone except me and a few other strange people. What will I do if I get hit in the face?" A river of self-doubt was roaring.

Not assigned to an official class yet, my first assignment was to cover a sixth-grade homeroom for a teacher who was late to arrive. I was told to help the students fill out index cards with such data as names, addresses, and emergency contact information. This sounded simple enough, until I discovered that almost none of these 11 and 12 year-olds could write their own names! Obviously, they were also unable to read the textbooks they were carrying around. Somehow, all their teachers during their five or six years of previous schooling had apparently managed to keep them illiterate. I could only imagine the depth of their alienation from the institution of school. My reading about ghetto schools should have prepared me for this, but I found myself overcome with emotion. I was relieved to see their official teacher come through the door.

My next assignment was to cover an eighth-grade class for another teacher who had sent a message asking to be relieved. Showtime was approaching now, and whatever confidence I thought I had was giving way to premonitions of disaster. I climbed the stairs, walked down what seemed a very long corridor, and opened the classroom door. I had no idea what was awaiting me inside, and barely an outline of a hastily improvised plan.

Instantly, my doubts and fears vanished in a surge of anger-fueled adrenaline. The students were playing tic-tac-toe, talking, passing and throwing notes, and otherwise keeping themselves busy with one another. The teacher was shouting over the din, insisting that they address him as "Dr. Fruitbine" because he had a law degree (*Juris Doctor*). This was what he was up to after two hours with the class? The kids were totally turned off, and I could see why. Fortunately, the good "doctor" was happy to turn the class over right away, so he could hurry downstairs to the cafeteria.

The class quieted down for the transition, so I quickly took advantage of the opportunity. "Good morning," I said. Following a reasonably polite response, I told them my name and wrote it on the board. "People call me 'Charlie,' and you can too," I added, surprising everyone in the room, myself included.

Reactions to this were mixed. Some smiled. Others were intrigued. A few protested that they were supposed to address their teachers as "Mr." or "Mrs." I said that would be fine if it made them more comfortable.

This might have confused them a little, but it did get me their attention. Without missing a beat, I started right in. "How many people," I asked, "don't like math?" Practically the whole class raised their hands. "How many people think math is a hard subject?" Now every hand was up.

I smiled and clapped my hands. "All right," I stated with great apparent conviction, "Now I'm going to show you how easy and how much fun math really is!" The room buzzed with disbelief.

"This man is crazy," said one boy. "Out of his head," agreed another. But they were still curious, maybe even more so now, and willing to give me a chance.

"Somebody tell me what the speedometer on a car is."

"I knew it," came a voice from the rear. "This ain't math."

"How many miles," called out another.

"You mean if I travel ten miles, the speedometer will say '10,' and if I go 100 miles, it will say '100'?

"No, not that," another student impatiently explained. "It says how fast you be going."

"So, if the speedometer says '60,' what does that mean?"

"It means you going sixty milezanour."

"Does everyone agree?" As the class nodded assent, I wrote on the board: "60 m/h."

"Now, if I drive for one hour, how far have I gone?"

"Sixty miles, of course!" I could see that this one was running out of patience with my thick-headedness.

On the board now: "60 m."

"In two hours?"

A little delay, then a minor discovery: "If you go sixty miles in the first hour, then you go sixty more in the second: a hundred and twenty."

"Does everyone agree?" They did. "And in three hours?"

A shorter pause. "180!" Now we had a chart on the board.

60 MPH

Hours	Miles
1	60
2	120
3	180

"What do you notice about this chart?"

"Every time the number under 'hours' goes up 1, the number under 'miles' goes up 60."

"Right. Now, if I travelled for ten hours, how many sixties would I go?"

"Ten!"

"And what's a short way of adding ten of the same thing together?"

"Multiply times ten."

"So you could get the number of miles by multiplying ten times sixty?"

"Right."

"And suppose I drove at 40 MPH for five hours?"

"Five times forty."

"How do you know?"

"The number of hours times how many miles each hour."

Now on the board: "Hours × Speed = Miles." Success!

This was fun. Now we went on to miles per minute, feet per second, and so on, until the class discovered the general formula for these calculations, commonly committed to rote memory as "*Rate* times *Time* equals *Distance*."

I hoped this formula would have more meaning for the class than something simply committed to memory. They had discovered it themselves, with a little help from the Socratic Method, and they understood it, even if they didn't memorize the words. Of course, some children still protested that this "wasn't math." Why? Because it wasn't boring, and there was no mindless drilling.

This whole lesson took no more than twenty minutes. I had no idea how much more time I would have with them, but I knew we were on a roll. I used the same method to introduce short, discrete, abstract topics, so we wouldn't be interrupted in the middle of a big project. They worked their way through Zero, Infinity, and Negative Numbers. I didn't expect them to remember all this, but I was committed to changing their attitude about math.

After an hour and a half, their "Dr." Fruitbine returned, bursting with one critical query: "*Were they quiet?*" Thankfully, they were not.

I just thanked the class, said my good-byes, and left the room, too satisfied with this first class to bother responding to the question. I knew this had been a very bright group of students, and that not every class would be so easy to teach, but now I had gained some confidence in my abilities. Performance skills honed addressing LIU and University of Chicago protest rallies translated very well, it seemed, to the classroom.

In fact, I soon found that teaching came very easily to me, even without any formal training. I did find this a little surprising, given all the bellyaching I had heard from white teachers in inner-city schools. It was only much later that I developed a theory that explained it.

Down in the lunchroom, I was introduced to Steve Mayer, a veteran Social Studies teacher. Mayer had transferred into Ocean Hill–Brownsville from another district, where he represented his colleagues in the UFT Delegate Assembly for three years, and served as the union's Chapter Chairman during the previous year. In his view, he had not deviated from the principles that attracted him to union activism; it was the UFT that had turned away from its own progressive origins.

I later learned that Mayer had been active in Brooklyn CORE during its most militant period, when it mounted massive campaigns against discrimination in housing, employment, and education. He had married another CORE activist, a black woman, at a time when interracial marriage was not only unusual, but illegal in almost half of the United States. His liberal-leaning Jewish family, having failed to dissuade him, cut him off over this decision.

I also found that Mayer had an encyclopedic knowledge of history. He soon became a trusted advisor.

On this day, Mayer invited me to sit in on his next class. Still without an assignment of my own, I happily accepted.

The New . . .

It was an eighth-grade class, ranked as "average" by whoever made these judgments, which Mayer was meeting for the first time. Hoping to counteract the restlessness triggered by the turbulent times, as well as afternoon fatigue, he began quickly and confidently to get the class's attention.

After a brief introduction, he began with the display of a colorful picture cutout from *Life Magazine*. It showed slum housing inhabited by poor black people. "Where," he asked, "have you seen buildings like these before?"

A slight pause, even though the whole class could easily have answered the question. Murmurs of discomfort, then recognition. Suddenly, responses burst forth.

"Hull Street . . . Herkimer . . . along Atlantic Avenue."

"Yes, right here in our own neighborhood. In Social Studies, we'll be studying housing problems in New York City, along with other problems, like education and employment and discrimination."

"For example," Mayer continued, showing other pertinent pictures of city life, "We'll try to answer questions like, "What are the most important problems in housing?"

"The slums," interrupted an unsolicited answer.

"Yes, and who is responsible for the slums? How can housing be improved? We'll deal with other problems too. First, I'd like you to read a poem (slight groans from corners of the room) about a conflict between a landlord and a tenant. It was written by Langston Hughes."

As Mayer showed a picture of the great black poet, trepidation gave way to interest and approval. "A colored man!"

"A man?" Mayer asked, in good-natured disapproval. The youngster was quickly corrected by many of his classmates. "Black Man!" "Afro-American!" Mayer went on to distribute copies of Hughes' "Ballad of the Landlord," and had the students first read it to themselves. The poem begins . . .

Landlord, Landlord
My roof has sprung a leak.
Don't you 'member I told you about it
Way last week?

Landlord, landlord
These steps is broken down.

When you come up yourself,
It's a wonder you don't fall down.[2]

It goes on to tell a simple story that instantly resonated with the class. The tenant urges the landlord to make necessary, overdue repairs. The landlord responds by demanding the rent. When the tenant refuses to pay until repairs are made, the landlord threatens eviction. The tenant threatens a punch in the face. The landlord calls the police, who arrest the tenant for assault and sedition. After a quick trial and conviction, he is sentenced to 90 days in jail.

When everyone finished reading, Mayer continued, "Let's take it stanza by stanza to see what actually happened to the tenant, and then we'll have opinions about the poem." The class jumped right to opinions.

"That landlord should be shot!"

"I woulda done the same thing the tenant did!"

"He shouldn't have gone to jail."

"I saw the same thing happen on my block last year."

"One minute," Mayer interrupted, "We'll get to all of you. Let's speak one at a time."

He asked a student to read the first three stanzas aloud.

Then, "Who is the main character in the poem?"

"The tenant . . . a black tenant."

"How do you know he's black?"

"By the way he talks," a girl answered, sucking her lips at the teacher for asking such an easy question. "Besides, it says so at the end."

"Good. Why is he angry?"

"You would be too if you had a leak that wasn't fixed. And falling on broken steps."

"It's an old, dirty, nasty house!"

"Garbage all around, and he has to pay rent for it too."

"Continue reading. What does the landlord do?"

"He shuts off the heat because he didn't pay the rent."

"And he was gonna throw the tenant's furniture out in the street."

"He got an ev-(with some help), an eviction notice against the colored, I mean the black man."

"What's an eviction notice?" Mayer interjected, while writing the words on the board.

Pause. A boy in the back of the room volunteered, "It's when they . . ."

"Who is 'They'?"

"When some men from the city and some cops make you get out your house because you didn't pay the rent or somethin'. And they throw all your things in the street. Like when I saw this happen on my block. This lady, she had her bed and clothes in the street, and everybody was watchin', and she was cryin' and everything." He continued to describe this experience in vivid detail.

"Good answer. Did the landlord evict the tenant in the poem?"

"No, but he was gonna."

"What does the tenant do then?"

"He hits him."

"And the landlord calls the cops."

"The pigs!" someone interrupted from the back row.

Most of the class murmured approval of the correction. Some looked at the teacher, waiting for his reaction. Mayer answered, "We can discuss *that* later!" I had a feeling that they would.

"Let's continue. Was the tenant justified in hitting the landlord?"

"Sure. I woulda done the same thing."

"He shouldn't have shut off the heat. There's children in those houses, and old people."

"I don't know. He might have waited a while longer."

"Yeah, but he was gonna evict him. He was a slumlord and he deserves it."

The spirited discussion continued, sparked by challenging questions. "What eventually happened to the tenant, and did he deserve his fate?" "Would the same thing have happened to a white man?" "Does this poem remind you of anything happening in your own neighborhood?"

Finally, "What do the police do in the poem?" And, "How does what they're doing here in Ocean Hill–Brownsville compare with that?"

Mayer's plan was to use the poem as a springboard to further discussions of the wider problems of inner-city housing and, eventually, of other urban issues. It looked to me like he knew exactly how to go about doing this.

This wasn't the first time I had seen "Ballad of the Landlord." I knew that Jonathan Kozol, author of *Death at an Early Age*, had used the poem in a Boston ghetto school. After a supervisor charged that the poem "could be interpreted as advocating defiance of authority," he was fired.[3] There was no chance of Steve Mayer being fired for using that poem in Ocean Hill–Brownsville, where it was an accepted fact that survival depended on defiance of authority deemed illegitimate.

I later asked Mayer what he thought would have happened had he used the same lesson in any other NYC school district. In all likelihood, he said, he probably would not have been disciplined. He explained that the administrators of ghetto schools usually don't concern themselves with such mundane matters as the actual content of classroom lessons. Their primary concern is the main business of education as they view it: Discipline, the teacher's euphemism for "Law and Order" in the classroom. The administrators he had encountered were rarely concerned with what went on in any classroom, as long as it was done quietly. Any teacher able to contain children in quiet rooms was rated

"Satisfactory" and retained year after year, up to and including the awarding of tenure.

Mayer summarized the logic behind what he said passed for educational philosophy in the city schools: "Only when you shut 'em up, can you learn 'em some." "Shut 'em up," took precedence over "learn 'em some," though. The actual content of a particular lesson was just not very important. So, a simple tacit agreement between teacher and student was often reached: As long as relative silence is maintained, each party leaves the other one alone.

No, Steve Mayer would probably not have been fired from a NYC school. At worst, there might have been some upturned eyebrows, some official discomfort, or some irrational mumblings of extremism or troublemaking, if anyone noticed at all. But most supervisors, he explained, would probably concede that, "After all, the lesson was confined to his own room," or, "At least he can control his class."

. . . Meets the Old

At the end of the school day, it became pretty clear to me how the eighth-graders I met that morning had learned that math was boring and difficult. A Mathematics Department staff meeting was presided over by Claire Devine and Ira Brand, two assistant principals who had been in the school system for many years. It was attended by all of our math teachers, most of whom were actually licensed in unrelated subjects and were teaching math out-of-license, plus elementary school teachers who were put in this department just because it had vacancies.

After ascertaining these shortcomings in the staff, Brand told the untrained people not to worry. "After all," he explained, "You probably do know more than the kids." Later, Mrs. Devine explained her philosophy of teaching mathematics. "I don"t believe in any of this 'New Math' business," she emphatically declared. "The only way to make these kids learn math is drill, drill, drill, and more drill!"

"Why," I asked, "do we have to *force* the kids to learn math?"

"Because they won't learn it if you don't force them," she replied. "You have to pound it into their heads!" By that time, my own head was pounding.

It had taken until the end of the first day for me to encounter, up close and in person, the then prevailing philosophy of education in the City of New York's public schools. Ocean Hill–Brownsville held the promise of something new, a new spirit that I had witnessed during the course of that first day, but it was very clear that the old ways were not yet ready to concede the field.

Most of our assistant principals represented these old ways. When Jack Bloomfield, the former principal, resigned during the middle of the previous term, all but one of the assistant principals went with him, along with thirty teachers and five of the school's six secretaries. While the Board of Education had allowed the Governing Board wide latitude in hiring new principals and teachers, the existing rules and union contracts required that replacement assistant principals be chosen from the top of the existing civil service list. The tests that produced the lists of certified supervisors, administered by the semi-independent Board of Examiners, were widely viewed as irrelevant to the jobs for which they were being certified.[4] As one observer put it . . .

> Like the former Chinese gentry, New York school administrators are ranked in a rigid hierarchy of status, achieved through the passage of Confucian examinations which fail to measure either the intellectual or temperamental qualities needed for the job.[5]

The examination process, which included an oral exam, was also notorious for racial discrimination.[6] (In 1972, a federal court would order the end of these exams, since they had the "effect of discriminating significantly and substantially against qualified black and Puerto Rican applicants." It concluded that the examination process constituted a "merit system" in name only, and that it bore no relation to job performance.[7]) Out of the 1,500 assistant principals in the city school system in 1967, twelve were black.[8] There were few blacks or Puerto Ricans even on the lists, and any who did get onto them would have to wait years for an actual supervisory appointment, since only the top three individuals on the list could be considered to fill a vacancy. As a result, four of our five certified assistant principals had been imposed on the district.

Once I understood this, I also understood how Norman Rabinowitz, an assistant principal in our supposedly community-controlled school, could have instructed the teachers, during the pre-school faculty orientation, not to grade any child higher than "75" in any subject in any marking period. "Students in this school," he proclaimed to any teachers who might have had higher expectations of their students, "are not capable of higher scores." What I still did not understand was how our principal, William H. Harris, could have allowed this remark to stand. Maybe he just knew that none of the teachers would pay any attention to it. I certainly didn't intend to.

Harris, like McCoy, was formerly the acting principal of a 600-school. He had been appointed by the Governing Board as principal of an elementary school a year earlier, and transferred to JHS 271 when Jack Bloomfield left in January. Before his appointment, there were a total of four black principals in all of New York City's 865 schools, all of them assigned to elementary schools.[9] The Governing Board's other appointments were Luis Fuentes, the city's first Puerto Rican principal; Ralph Rogers (black, Jewish), and Irving Gerber (white, Jewish). David Lee, appointed to succeed Harris at PS 178, became the city's

Figure 2.1. William H. Harris, principal of JHS 271 (1968).

first Chinese principal. The sixth appointee, for IS 55 which was under construction, was Herman Ferguson, a respected, experienced administrator, who was also a well-known black nationalist who had recently been indicted for conspiring to murder "moderate" civil rights leaders. Although it was widely believed that these charges were trumped up, Donovan vetoed his appointment and suspended his employment. McCoy and the Governing Board continued to back Ferguson, but IS 55 would open without him.[10] Ferguson was retained as a consultant to the IS 201 district.

None of the Governing Board's appointees were among the eligible candidates on the civil service list. As an accommodation to the experiment in community control, the State Commissioner of Education had created a new category of "demonstration school principal," which required only state certification plus a connection to the community. This innovation was immediately challenged in a lawsuit filed by the Council of Supervisors & Administrators (CSA), which was joined by the UFT, thus uniting white labor with white management in the defense of an indefensible status quo. The principals' appointments were invalidated in a March court ruling. Pending the Board's appeal of that ruling, they remained in place.

Most of the staff stayed in school long after the dismissal bell that first day, as we would most days during the school year. There was plenty of information to process, and planning to do for the days ahead. That was when I met John Mandracchia, the only certified assistant principal in the school who supported community control.

White, balding, and 40 years old, Mandracchia had voluntarily transferred from another district a year earlier. Teachers who worked with him told me that he quickly gained the respect of staff, students, and parents. He had been able to bridge the multitude of gaps that separated his background from those of the young black and Puerto Rican students. He had a deep understanding of the urban crisis, even though his home was far out on Long Island. His connection between thought and action necessitated starting the day at 4:30 each morning and, on occasion, spending the night in school because there just wasn't time for his four-hour round-trip commute. He was exceptional in more ways than one.

When I asked Mandracchia what our school's most important innovation was, he quickly replied, "For the first time, black kids have an opportunity to identify with black leadership in their school."

It had been quite an education for this math teacher, on my first day at JHS 271.

Strike One

Only 10 percent of the city's schools actually opened on September 9, most of them in black and Puerto Rican neighborhoods where opposition to the illegal strike was passionate. This was the most effective of the UFT's four citywide strikes during the past eight years, with 93 percent of the 57,000 teachers staying home or joining picket lines. Only 48,946 out of 1.13 million students were able to attend classes.[11]

The CSA held a rally at Manhattan Center during the school day, attended by 3,300 of the system's 4,000 school supervisors. Following an open "debate" during which not a single dissenting voice was heard, they voted, in violation of a court order upholding the Taylor Law, to not only support, but to join the UFT strike. Walter Degnan, president of the group, called Ocean Hill–Brownsville a "malignancy" that could spread, and proclaimed that the district's Governing Board "believes in anarchy."[12] This nearly all-white management organization, which had never fought for improved education and had consistently opposed the UFT, now emphatically joined forces with the union against black and Puerto Rican Ocean Hill–Brownsville, and would hold the entire city hostage to their demands. The principals vowed to keep their schools closed, both to children and to the non-striking teachers who wanted to do their jobs. Since the official policy of the Board of Education was that the schools were open, this was a case of massive, unprosecuted insubordination.

"Their course," editorialized the *New York Times* "on the part of unions and supervisors alike, can only spell disaster for the essential revitalization of the schools and the reconciliation of the community."[13]

In Ocean Hill–Brownsville, all eight schools were open and operating with enough staff to carry on fairly normal activity, considering that so many of the teachers were newly hired. The majority of the registered students came to school. At JHS 271, this entailed passing through a massive police presence and a boisterous UFT picket line just to reach the front door. I understood why the pickets were there, but could not fathom at the time why there were so many police on the scene.

Regular classes were assigned on the second day, September 10. I was to teach four eighth-grade classes in a second-floor classroom overlooking the street. I was pleased with the room location since the rear rooms overlooked the schoolyard, which had been commandeered as the staging area for the thousand-strong police occupation. This would have been an unnecessary distraction.

For the first lesson, I thought the most important objective was to engage the students in a "math can be fun" activity. I began by asking if they'd like to see a magic trick, which of course they did. I asked them to write down two secret numbers, the first between 1 and 9, the second between 10 and 99. The trick was that I would "read their minds" and tell them what those secret numbers were, but first they would have to play along with me for a little while. Intrigued by the challenge, the students responded, on paper, to instructions like the following:

1. Multiply your first number by two.
2. Add six to the result
3. Multiply your new answer by five.
4. Now multiply by ten (by tacking on a zero).
5. Add your second secret number.
6. Finally, subtract 271.

Once each student announced the final result, I could figure out the two original numbers by simply subtracting 29, then separating the difference into two numbers by drawing an imaginary line to the left of the tens digit. If, for example, the student's answer was 619, I would subtract 29 to get 590; the original numbers, then, would have been 5 and 90.

One by one, as the results were announced, I performed what appeared to be magic. As long as there were no mistakes in calculation, my little trick had to work. (Some classes required simpler instructions, but the principles remained the same.) At first, the students were mystified at the feat, but this soon gave way to intense curiosity, and they demanded an explanation of "how you got it." While there was no complicated theory behind the trick, the explanation did involve some understanding of place values in addition to the basic arithmetic. The general theory, which came next, introduced some basic rules of algebra. Through all this, very few of the students had trouble keeping up. By the time they realized they were actually doing math, it was too late to tune out.

Late that afternoon, the UFT, the CSA, and the Board of Education, over Galamison's objections, signed a contract that ended the strike. All the 210 UFT teachers who still wanted to go back to Ocean Hill–Brownsville would be sent there, with police protection, the next morning. Any dismissals by local boards would now be subject to the lengthy, expensive process of arbitration. Union officials, such as chapter chairmen, would have "super-seniority" that would protect them from involuntary transfer. All local boards would be forever bound by "present agreements" between the union and the Board. The City would not only pay the salaries of all the teachers for their two days of participation in the illegal strike, but they would also pay the 350 teachers who illegally walked out on Ocean Hill–Brownsville for the last six weeks of the previous term. The Board of Education had not only condoned, but rewarded, a double violation of the Taylor Law. "We have won on every basic issue," announced Shanker.[14]

The Governing Board, left out of the negotiations, had promised not to block the return of the teachers themselves, but made no promises of cooperation, and no guarantees regarding the actions of their constituents. The UFT ignored this statement, taking the position that the Governing Board must simply comply with the agreement. On September 11, the teachers were to return.

A Rocky Return

It was no surprise to anyone when the UFT group met a blockade on the steps of JHS 271 that morning, least of all the police force, which outnumbered the forces on every side of the dispute. The stalemate broke for the moment without incident, though, when the front door opened from the inside. Leonard Buder of the *Times* reported on what happened next, with a curious twist on the racial context.

> Lloyd Sealy, assistant chief inspector of police, emerged with three Negro policemen and William Harris, the school's principal. Chief Sealy, a Negro, asked Mr. Harris whether Mr. Nauman and his colleagues should be admitted to the school and the Negro principal said they should. There appeared to be no resistance, and the teachers went into the building.[15]

Buder documented for the record that no less than five "Negroes" paved the way for the UFT cohort to enter the school, as though the perimeter was not occupied by hundreds of white cops.

They were not in the school for long. Summoned to an "orientation session" with McCoy, they headed back out. Then, the day began much like the first two at JHS 271. Once the students and teachers waded through the police and press, once the classroom doors were shut, we were able to close out the disruptions, to teach and to learn.

What happened at the meeting with McCoy, held in the IS 55 auditorium, is a matter of some dispute. Buder noted that it was closed to the press. He relied solely on the UFT's Fred Nauman to report the story. According to Nauman, the one hundred teachers in the auditorium were joined by about forty parents, along with some militants who "carried crash helmets." "At 11:20," wrote Buder, "the teachers came out of the building, charging that the meeting had been totally disrupted by parents and community representatives."[16] McCoy ended it by telling them to take a lunch break, and then go back to their schools. The teachers griped about enduring verbal abuse going down the school steps, but none were assaulted.

In the histories of the conflict, this report has been embellished with varying degrees of hysteria, but never with named sources. The authors attribute their information either to each other, to anonymous teachers, or to no-one at all. In *The Strike that Changed New York*, for example, Jerald Podair states that the teachers were surrounded by men "brandishing sticks and bandoliers of bullets" who cursed them, threw the bullets at them, and threatened to carry them out in pine boxes. His source is Martin Mayer's *The Teachers Strike: New York, 1968*, which presents this story without referencing any source at all.[17] (As we will see, this freelance journalist's distortions of reality would play an important role in shaping the outcome of the community control experiment.) A similar account, in *Time Magazine*, quoted a single unnamed teacher.[18]

Perhaps the most florid account, in Barbara Carter's *Pickets, Parents and Power*, also offered no sourcing:

> "Why do you come back where you're not wanted?" the teachers were asked. "We don't want you," someone cried. Flick. A .30 caliber cartridge sailed through the air and fell among them. Flick. Another came. Someone switched the lights on and off. . . .[19]

And so on. In Shanker's 2007 biography, *Tough Liberal*, Richard Kahlenberg again has the militants "armed with sticks," and the teachers are warned that they're "going out of here in pine boxes," but he offers only the same old circular self-referencing sources, none of them primary.[20] The only named primary source is Nauman's quote in the *Times* account, which says nothing about sticks, bullets, flickering lights, or pine boxes.

Notably absent among the primary sources for these stories are the several Governing Board members who were present, even though Rev. Oliver was on record about it in a 1969 interview, published the following year. In that interview, he claims that most of the community people were women, that no lives were threatened, that the teachers expressed a sneering, condescending attitude, that they insulted Governing Board members, and that it was all on tape.[21] That interview has, to my knowledge, never been quoted by any historian. After more than forty years, no one has ever asked Rev. Oliver for that tape recording.[22]

In order to get a report from the "militants" who were in the room, I had to ask them myself, since no one else ever did. According to Project Method's Paul Chandler and Brother Sun, there were no cartridges thrown, and the teachers were never in any danger because the rear wall of the auditorium was lined with police. The mayor's Urban Task Force was also represented. There was lots of shouting, though, on both sides. When I asked about the flickering lights, which could certainly have been terrifying, Chandler (who later worked at IS 55 and knew the building well) told me something that has never before been reported: The auditorium lights were not operated by switches, but by turning a key in a lock. No one but the principal and the custodian would have such a key. There *could not have been* any flickering of the lights.[23] Anyone reporting on this story could have known this, had they only asked.

At about one o'clock, JHS 271's UFT contingent came down the block. The police presence now, surrounding just our one school, included 3,000 helmeted officers; 35 mounted police; 150 plainclothes detectives; three communications units; a mobile command center; helicopters hovering overhead; and sharpshooters stationed on the roofs of surrounding houses. This was the force considered necessary to escort the nine unwanted teachers who showed up that day.[24]

By then, about a hundred parents and community activists were back on the steps, blocking the front door. The UFT teachers headed toward the entrance, surrounded by a wedge of police in riot gear. Paddy wagons pulled up to the curb.

I began to watch from my second floor window when the noise of all this prompted some of my students to look out the window, tuning out their algebra lesson. My hopes for a classroom free of distractions were quickly dashed. A commotion began out on the sidewalk. One student shouted, "Hey! That's my mother!" and the entire class joined him at the window. Parents, including one very pregnant woman, were being dragged into the wagon. Others, trying to interfere, were beaten back. Meanwhile, facing empty seats, I had to decide whether or not to try forcing the class to sit back down and listen (if, indeed, I possessed the powers of persuasion to pull this off). I decided that nothing would have been worse. Those children needed to know what was taking place outside. It was an important moment in their education, and in mine as well.

It was a short, bloody skirmish, with many casualties. Dolores Torres later described the end of it this way . . .

> What I saw outside of the school, 271, was a reporter that had been beaten and was laying on the sidewalk bloody. When I turned to go back into the second door of the school to get a washcloth and come out to help him, before I could get out the second door, I saw through the window of the door Mrs. (Thelma) Hamilton being struck in the stomach with a policeman's club. Before I could open that door, across the street a line of the Black Panthers had shown up and were standing there with folded arms. And as a result of that no one else got hit that day by the policemen. They didn't do anything. They just stood there. But no one else was struck by a policeman.[25]

That afternoon, one of those Panthers, 18-year-old Joudon Ford, who was the group's East Coast captain, was arrested as he led a demonstration at the police precinct protesting the morning's arrests.[26]

When the returning teachers were finally herded inside, the absurdity of the situation could not be avoided. They were given no class assignments, and there was nothing for them to do. People had been beaten and arrested so that these teachers could sit in a locked room with a police guard for the remainder of the school day.

Jerald Podair claims that the UFT teachers were menaced, threatened, even terrorized, by the students of JHS 271. Again, his source is Martin Mayer's book, which first made this claim, but offered no source for it.[27] I saw no evidence of any such harassment or terrorism that day, nor, apparently did the police or anyone else in authority, since not one person in the school, child or adult, was detained or arrested. Further, it was simply not possible, since the teachers were guarded by police every minute they were inside, or even anywhere near, the building. It was true, though, that the UFT contingent was not welcomed back. Those teachers were not wanted by the community, by the parents, or by the teachers who had been keeping the school open and functioning without their assistance.

Scheduled for that afternoon was a walking tour of Brownsville, for fifty delegates of foreign countries who were in New York for a United Nations conference. The tour, arranged by the mayor's office months earlier, was to be hosted by the Brownsville Community Council. The delegates arrived at BCC headquarters just as Thelma Hamilton and other injured demonstrators were returning from the hospital. (Some were too badly injured to be released.) She described to the assembled delegates what had happened on the school steps. The tour was canceled for safety reasons, and because most of the BCC staff was at the stationhouse demonstrating against police brutality. It now threatened to become an embarrassing international incident, worthy of official cover-up and denial. The *Times* reported the next day that there was no police brutality, that the precinct received no complaints, and that the reactions of the foreign delegates were "varied."[28] Hamilton's recollection was that their reactions were not so varied, rather that they were "aghast" at what they were being told. She herself became the subject of an FBI investigation after that day.[29]

Strike Two

While the injured demonstrators were being treated at the hospital, and while several hundred community citizens were demonstrating against police brutality at the precinct, Shanker proclaimed that his teachers' lives had been threatened, and that the UFT would again close the city's schools. The second citywide UFT strike was called for Friday, September 13.[30]

On a morning TV talk show that weekend, Shanker speculated that "some element of anti-Semitism" was behind community opposition to bringing the UFT teacher contingent back to Ocean Hill–Brownsville.[31] This was news to me, and I never would have guessed that this charge would develop into the most inflammatory issue of the months to come.

As the second UFT strike began to paralyze the city's educational system, Ocean Hill–Brownsville, the only district with fully operating schools, was subjected to increasing external attack.

Some of these attacks, I thought, carried a touch of the unreal. The UFT and the CSA were striking, they said, because the Ocean Hill–Brownsville Governing Board had not complied with the September 10 agreement. The Governing Board, though, had not been a party to that agreement, had issued a principled statement clarifying its position on it, and had since not deviated from that position. Further, the strike was effective only in schools *outside* the jurisdiction of the Governing Board. Even if it was in the wrong, why was the UFT punishing the rest of the city? Yet it seemed that white parents of children being denied their right to an education blamed this on Ocean Hill–Brownsville, as though it was the Governing Board that had called the strike. Their schools were closed only because teachers chose not to enter them. It seemed reasonable to me that those parents should have directed their ire at those teachers and their union, which were the ones on strike, not at the Ocean Hill Board. But most whites were allying themselves with the nearly all-white UFT. Further, they were willing to sacrifice their own opportunity for greater local control as long as they could deny it to the communities of color. They were acting as whites first, and as parents second. "Whites flocked to the union's side," wrote Podair, "less because Fred Nauman was a union man than because his antagonists were primarily black."[32]

The crusade carried on by the UFT and its allies was no longer, if it ever had been, about teachers' rights. It was about race, and it was about power. As I believed then, as I believe now, it had always truly been.

Divisions Emerge

As charges and countercharges raged outside, JHS 271 went on functioning relatively smoothly. A meeting was called to form a faculty organization that could act to protect our interests as teachers, in the absence of the union, while supporting the Governing Board. It was quickly agreed to elect a Steering Committee that would initiate and coordinate organized action. This election was to bring to the surface contradictions among the faculty, and foreshadow internal troubles to come during the months ahead.

The initiator and chairman of the meeting was Marvand Holland, a black teacher who had been in the school since its opening in 1962, and had worked himself into a non-teaching position in the school's programming office. (These "out-of-classroom" positions were considered plum assignments in the city's schools.) Holland had been maneuvering to emerge as a leader of the faculty, and this meeting was designed to grant him the legitimacy he wished for. It appeared likely that many of the teachers who were new in the school would vote him on the Steering Committee merely because he had called and presided over the meeting.

Holland moved directly into calling for nominations. Before any could be offered, though, another black teacher threw a monkey wrench into his plans. She announced that there must be two elections, not one. The black teachers should form their own caucus, and from that group elect half the members of the Steering Committee; the white teachers (who were in almost a 2 to 1 majority) should do the same. I hadn't thought of this. A voice in my head told me to just shut up and listen (a new experience for me in meetings and debates).

Holland immediately opposed this proposal from the chair, and unsuccessfully tried to dismiss it. He knew that the two-caucus proposal would work against his personal interests, since whatever voting base he had was among the inexperienced white teachers, not from the more disciplined and experienced black contingent. The nominations were postponed, however, and issue was joined over whether or not to have two separate caucuses. As the debate went forward, factions began to emerge. The at-large plan was supported mostly by white teachers, but it had some black support as well. This was, after all, more consistent with the formal definition of democratic procedure that we were used to.

The two-caucus plan was initiated and pushed forward by a group of young black teachers, most of them ATA members. This bloc was led in debate by Les Campbell, who described himself as a "revolutionary black nationalist." (In 1969, Campbell changed his name to Jitu Weusi. He has been known as such ever since.)

Campbell, 28, had grown up in Bedford-Stuyvesant. He was one of a handful of black youngsters accepted into Brooklyn Tech, one of the city's three selective high schools. Isolated and unhappy in the school's nearly all-white atmosphere, he transferred to Franklin K. Lane, an inferior school zoned for Central Brooklyn's black communities. From there, he attended LIU–Brooklyn on a basketball scholarship. After graduating in 1962 with a major in history, he began teaching social studies at JHS 35 in Bedford-Stuyvesant, where he and Vann launched the NTA/ATA. In his classroom and in the community, Campbell challenged the prevailing view of history as a European phenomenon, and attracted a substantial following among black youth. In March 1968, after being charged with insubordination for taking a class on an unauthorized field trip to Harlem for a Malcolm X memorial service, he was transferred to JHS 271, a move that he welcomed. A score of colleagues from JHS 35 had joined him and Vann here this September.

As Campbell rose to speak for dual representation, all heads turned his way. Six feet eight inches tall, bearded, wearing wire-rimmed glasses and a colorful African dashiki, he cast an imposing presence. "Our fight for community control," he declared, "is a fight for the *self-determination* of black people, for our right to speak for ourselves and to be responsible for *our own* successes and failures. It is a war against domestic colonialism . . . Ocean Hill–Brownsville is one battle in that war, a major one. If the principle of self-determination is violated here, today, with black teachers being denied the right to choose our own representatives, then 271 will represent *a step backward*, not forward, in that struggle."

This argument impressed me. Campbell had set our little procedural vote in the context of international anti-colonialism. Who was I to decide who would represent the black teachers, especially in this time and this place? I continued to listen, struggling in my mind to reconcile the apparently competing concepts of democracy and self-determination.

The debate continued. Many of the new white teachers, myself included, found ourselves being swayed toward what had begun as a minority proposition. In order to bring it to a close, a teacher called for a vote between the two opposing proposals. The cloture motion gained widespread approval among the white teachers. By now, though, I could see that this would be an implicit concession to the single-caucus view. Steve Mayer explained why.

"If our white majority can vote on whether or not the black teachers can have independent representation," he asked rhetorically, "then what will we be? White folks deciding whether or not blacks should have self-determination! This would be nothing less than the colonial system with which we and this community are at war." No one rose in opposition to Mayer's argument. Suddenly, a vote no longer seemed necessary. The two-caucus plan was adopted by consensus.

Campbell and Holland represented two diametrically opposed forces among the black teacher corps, which would do battle again and again as the year went on. In terms that each side would use to describe the other, it was the "Revolutionary Black Militants" against the "Conservative Black Bourgeoisie." It was the new Black Nationalist outlook of the ATA against those of its more career-oriented predecessors, each of which would have adherents among the staff.

I was glad I had kept my mouth shut and my mind open. My education was continuing. It never would have occurred to me, on my own, that the substance of democracy could be best served by limiting the influence of a majority. Yet now, in this situation, it was becoming obvious.

It would soon prove to be necessary as well. Through the long debate, a basis of trust was forged between the black and white teachers, without which we might not have been able to work together. Its resolution turned out to be the most practical way, and probably the only way, to create a united faculty leadership with any hope of effectiveness.

The caucuses later met and elected their own representatives to the Steering Committee, which then elected its officers. Larry Bussey, a black Art teacher, was elected chairman. I was one of those elected to represent the unnamed caucus of "others."

One of the first actions agreed to by the Steering Committee was a division of labor, with each caucus concentrating on the tasks that its members could best accomplish. The Black Caucus assigned itself to canvass the community during the coming weekend in order to build cohesion and to encourage more parents to send their children to school, strike or no strike.

They would find that most of the parents keeping their children home had done so because of the massive police presence in front of the school. Well over a thousand men had been drawn from precincts across the city to patrol, and sometimes to barricade, the block. Since there had not yet been any major confrontations, and since the UFT teachers were out on strike, not trying to enter the school, it was unclear until this time why so many police were needed. There were far more than would have been required to protect the UFT pickets, who hadn't been physically attacked or seriously threatened. Now, many concluded that one function of the police presence, whether intended or not, was intimidation. It frightened many parents away from sending their children to school, and it provided a constant reminder to teachers and students that their every move was being watched.

As a Governing Board statement sadly noted, "We and our children and the city and nation are learning what 'democracy' really means for Black people."[33] When low attendance resulted from this intimidation, Shanker and his sympathizers publicly interpreted it as "proof" that the Governing Board did not have the support of the community.

The UFT Rallies Against Mob Rule

Meanwhile, our caucus met over the weekend with teachers from other Ocean Hill–Brownsville schools. We formed a district-wide Steering Committee, and agreed to intervene in the UFT's September 16 City Hall demonstration against community control, which it now equated with "mob rule." The plan was to counter-picket, talk to striking teachers and, hopefully, persuade some to switch sides and cross picket lines at their schools.

We prepared a statement to hand out at the rally:[34]

1) Our schools are open and functioning well with a fully integrated staff of licensed teachers, appointed by the Community.
2) We believe in quality education through community control and we support fully the position of the Ocean Hill-Brownsville Governing Board and Mr. Rhody McCoy.
3) The present bureaucratic system of education has proven itself unable to respond to the legitimate needs and aspirations of the Black and Puerto Rican community.
4) A dedicated staff of people supported by the elected community board offers the best form of job security for teachers.
5) We repudiate the many lies and fantastic stories carried by the communications media about our school district and the citizens of this community,

Armed with picket signs and printed copies of our five-point statement, and, we felt, the forces of right and reason, we sallied forth to the after-school rally. Our mission was to proselytize the UFT rank-and-file, naïvely hoping that our presence, our unity, and our statement might overcome all the misinformation that had been spread about our school.

Up to this point, we had been living a pretty insular existence, working around the clock with one another and with parents and community activists. This left many of us, even those who had been around the longest, unaware of the depth of emotion that prevailed among the UFT rank-and-file. The City Hall demonstration awakened us to this ugly reality within the space of a mere few hours.

Steve Mayer was in a small group of teachers chanting pro-community control slogans, holding up signs challenging the myths about Ocean Hill–Brownsville and imploring the UFT to end its racist policies. No sooner had they begun, though, than they were surrounded by a large group of jeering and shouting UFT demonstrators.

"Get a haircut!"

"Why don't ya shave?"

"Hey, draft dodgers, why don't ya join the army where ya belong?"

Mayer later told me that he found irony in this third remark. He knew that thousands of male UFT members were only teaching in ghetto schools (when they weren't striking) to obtain draft deferments. It was common knowledge that most of them would leave the profession when they aged out of the draft at 26, and that actually teaching children was not high on their list of priorities. (He himself was several years beyond draft age.) Our female teachers were, of course, not subject to the draft.

As time went on, the epithets increased in number and magnitude. Our counter-demonstrators were called scabs, idiots, and traitors, along with more vicious profanity. There were also threats of gruesome physical violence, which visibly shocked and embarrassed some less vocal UFT demonstrators.

On the fringes of the confrontation, Mayer encountered a group of former colleagues. One greeted him warmly despite their present differences. They had once fought with common conviction in civil rights and peace movements within the UFT, and their meeting under other circumstances would have been a happy occasion. But now they were on opposite sides of a burning issue, and didn't even agree on what that issue was. The UFT supporter saw the strike as a battle for due process and job security, the official union line, though he was troubled by the racial polarization it had spawned. He was sympathetic to Mayer's position but could not support the "forced transfer of tenured teachers."

Mayer told me he was saddened by the irrationality of his former friend's position. "He really feels threatened," he said, "but he shouldn't be. He's a terrific teacher, who could work anywhere. He went as far as he could but, when the chips were down and he had to make a choice, he lined up with his white colleagues."

The man's wife, also a teacher, told Mayer he was being "deceived." "You wait," she insisted, "They'll get you next. When they don't need you anymore, they'll dump you too!" As her husband quieted her down, they moved on.

Later, Mayer met other former coworkers, many of whom refused to even speak to him. Another irony, he said, was that many of these striking teachers had for years refused to join the UFT, and had even broken previous UFT strikes over the customary union demands for higher wages and better working conditions. But this issue, with its racial overtones, had so inflamed their passions that it pulled them into the UFT, the union they had once found "unprofessional."

The UFT's fear campaign was accomplishing what had been previously unimaginable, the solid unification of New York's white middle-class teachers. The racism that had historically polluted the American craft unions was now manifesting itself among the educated membership of a professional union in "liberal" New York City. By driving his union to the right, Shanker consolidated his base among his white constituency as he had not been able to do with any bread-and-butter issue.

Before long, the UFT demonstrators became more violent, tearing the signs of counter-demonstrators and shoving some around. Things were getting a little tense. The UFT crowd was estimated by the press at over 15,000 and we were outnumbered by about 100 to 1.[35] When the police finally intervened, they ordered our pickets to the other side of Broadway. "For your own safety," they said.

My assignment was to hook up a sound system to my car and, along with Steve Bloomfield and an Ocean Hill teenager named Tim, read our five-point statement over the loudspeaker and further explain the virtues of community control. This, it was thought, might be an effective way to reach the picketing teachers who might be persuaded, once they heard the facts. This little bubble of naïveté would be quickly punctured.

As soon as the UFT pickets noticed the car, we were loudly jeered from all sides. We were unprepared for such an immediate reception, since we hadn't even begun to use the loudspeaker. No signs were on the car yet, and there didn't seem to be any obvious way for them to even tell which side we were on. I soon realized what had given away our allegiance. The UFT demonstration was comprised entirely of whites. Bayard Rustin, a former civil rights leader but a Shanker ally and a scheduled speaker, was the only black face to be seen at City Hall that day . . . except for Tim. The pickets knew where Bloomfield and I stood as soon as they spotted a black teenager in the car.

Our mobile mission was something short of a smashing success. Although loudspeakers were blaring from the UFT crowd, which now resembled more a threatening mob than a peaceful demonstration, the police refused to allow us to turn on our sound system. Apparently, we had neglected to obtain the proper permits. So, we just drove around the block holding signs out the window and making short announcements over the amplifier whenever we thought we could get away with it.

Unfortunately, traffic was moving slowly enough for the demonstrators to catch up with the car, scream epithets through the windows, and kick at the fenders. At one corner, a large group of teachers knocked over barricades and surged into the street after us, held back only at the last moment by mounted police. When objects started flying at the car, we retreated back to Brownsville, disheartened to be sure, but with a more realistic understanding of the depths of the hatred and racism that Shanker had succeeded in tapping to fuel his crusade.

This was the UFT's "Demonstration Against Mob Rule." It wasn't the last time I would be surprised by my own youthful naïveté. And it certainly wasn't the last time I would be struck by the irony of one of the UFT's favorite slogans: "Dignity for All Teachers!"

That night, as I reflected on the day's events, it struck me that the UFT demonstrators were, by and large, the same people I had been to grade school with in Brooklyn: middle- and lower-middle-class first- and second-generation Americans, mostly descended from Eastern European Jewish immigrants. In college at LIU–Brooklyn, they were my friends and fraternity brothers. They even comprised the bulk of my constituents there, who had elected me Student Government President and followed me into political battle. How, I wondered, had we ended up, so passionate in *this* battle, but now facing each other on opposite sides of the barricades?

Looking back from a long distance, I still have no definitive explanation of why I made that political choice, why I "defected." It might have been gut identification with the underdog, derived perhaps from an unhappy suburban adolescence, surrounded by families with greater financial means than my own. Maybe it was a fellow named Quinn, my first best friend at my first job, at 13 years old, who happened to be black. There was Miss Lynn, my favorite teacher in the high school I hated, the school's only black teacher and one of the very few who I felt understood me, A huge influence was Bill Birenbaum, LIU–Brooklyn's Provost and my first mentor, whose sensitivity to racial issues was critical to the shaping of my social consciousness, and whose 1967 firing triggered a two-week student strike.

Then there were the early impressions, the instinctive revulsion I felt as a child whenever hypocritical, offhand, racist remarks were made by adults in my ostensibly "liberal" family. "Of course, they should have a right to vote," pronounced a loving uncle to a chorus of approval, "but you sure wouldn't want them living next door!"

Whatever the reason, there could be no going back after 1968. I may have sprung from the same roots as the teachers demonstrating that day, but their world was no longer mine.

The Jewish Holidays

At the end of that week, all Ocean Hill–Brownsville students went home with a leaflet printed on Rhody McCoy's letterhead in both English and Spanish, announcing that schools would be closed on the following Monday and Tuesday, "out of respect for the first two days of the Jewish New Year. This holiday is called Rosh Hashanah. . . ." It went on to explain what the holiday was about and why it was important.[36]

The closing of the city's schools for the Jewish High Holidays had been official Board of Education policy for decades, since even before Jewish teachers had become predominant in the schools. By the 1960s, though, its necessity was obvious. If the Jewish teachers observed the holidays in *shul*, not in school, the system would not be able to operate.

During the 1968 holidays, of course, the system was not operating anyway, because of the strike. In Ocean Hill–Brownsville, where there were no Jewish students, some of the large numbers of Jewish teachers would have been happy to help their colleagues and the Governing Board keep the schools open had it chosen to do so. The decision was made, though, to honor the religious holidays and to issue a leaflet explaining their meaning to the black and Puerto Rican community.

This gesture of respect would soon be completely forgotten when the UFT unleashed its propaganda campaign against "Black Anti-Semitism."

An Experiment in Testing

My classes taught me an early lesson in the limitations of testing. Based on "inventory tests" an assistant principal told me to administer, it appeared that some of my eighth-grade students could not add whole numbers, that most could not multiply or subtract, and that almost none could do long division. Was it possible that no one had taught these skills to the children during the seven or eight years they had been coming to school? In high school next year, this level of mathematical ineptitude would certainly keep them out of academic programs. This could determine the course of their entire lives; they would be beaten before they began.

This conclusion grew more problematic, though, when I recalled my introductory lesson, the "trick" in which I had "read their minds" and guessed their secret numbers. The trick had worked practically every time, but it couldn't have worked if the students had made errors in simple addition, subtraction, or multiplication. Those skills had to have been there. It was only on the tests that difficulties emerged. Clearly, most were still well below grade level, in both math and reading, but this was third- and fourth-grade material. Students who had made no errors while they played the game displayed almost total ignorance of how to do far simpler problems on the inventory exams. "Maybe," I thought, "the problem is the exam."

In order to test this hypothesis, I made up a short quiz, consisting only of the calculations that had been required for the game, but presented separately and out of sequence.

1. 10 + 6 (16)
2. 890 – 271 (619)
3. 80 × 10 (800)
4. 16 × 5 (80)
5. 5 × 2 (10)
6. 800 + 90 (890)

Only in one of my four classes did most of the students get more than two correct answers. Clearly, their actual mathematical deficit, serious as it was, was being amplified by the test environment. During the game, they wanted to do the calculations and did them; on the test, they either couldn't or just wouldn't. I wondered how many children were being drilled over and over, year after year, until they could perform arithmetic operations that they always knew how to do, just because of tests they didn't relate to; and how many kids eventually lost interest in math, or in school, because of boredom.

What I really wanted to teach was mathematical concepts as a path to creative problem-solving. My priority was to help my students to think, not to perform on tests. I knew from personal experience, though, that test-taking was important. I was reminded of my eleventh-grade Regents exam in English, where I scored highest in the grade, even though I hadn't read any of the assigned material. Based on a single multiple-choice test at LIU that I couldn't have known how to prepare for, the college awarded me a full scholarship. My scholarship to law school was partly based on a 97th percentile ranking on the LSAT. I never knew how these things happened, but I did know my performance had nothing to do with knowledge, talent, or studying. Maybe my brain was wired for multiple-choice tests. Maybe it was because I chose to take on these tests as challenges, and was able to focus in some peculiar way.

What I did know was that they changed my life for the better. If my students could not perform on tests at least to the level of their real knowledge and aptitude, they would be in trouble.

I talked to several of the experienced black teachers about this, trying to figure out what was going on. Few were surprised by what I discovered with my little experiment, but no one had a scientific answer. Some theorized that black people, particularly families with recent Southern roots, simply had a less competitive, less individualistic, outlook on life, and didn't much care about such things as tests. I had seen these same kids after school competing pretty hard on the basketball court, but the ultimate urban sport was also the ultimate team game. Individual sports like golf and tennis were dominated by whites.

Another teacher offered an experience-based theory. Based on the life experiences of friends and family, he suggested, these students had learned that grades, promotions, and report cards meant very little, that these pieces of paper would not improve their lives, open new opportunities to them, or even get them into good high schools. Taking it a step further, he argued that, unlike middle-class children with different family experiences, education itself would have little relevance for them unless it was either intrinsically interesting or of clear practical significance.

In my own middle-class junior high school, teachers were often able to enforce discipline by simply opening their marking books and threatening to give unruly students a "zero," or to fail them and make them repeat the course. In the ghetto school, where such threats often had no effect on the children, many teachers simply raised the stakes to a higher level. Thousands of black and Puerto Rican children were left back in the same grade each year, until they dropped out on their own. Thousands of others, who didn't disappear on their own, were suspended each year for minor infractions of order.[37]

These cultural and experiential theories made some sense to me. They were amplified by observing a phenomenon I never could have predicted. Cliff Lee was a music teacher who took on the task of creating a student jazz orchestra. Early in the process, he invited me to visit a practice session in the music room. It was the noisiest cacophony I had ever heard. About 40 kids were making whatever sounds they could out of their instruments, but none seemed to know how to actually play them. Sitting calmly in the middle of the room was Cliff Lee, I covered my ears. He winked at me. I left, shaking my head at the impossibility of his project.

About two months later, at a school assembly, the curtains parted for the debut of JHS 271's new Jazz Orchestra. Somehow, not by lecturing, but by working with these kids as a group over just a short time, helping them to explore their instruments, Lee had made a silk purse out of a sow's ear. I was awestruck by the result, a real jazz concert with the student musicians riffing off one another and making real music. Since that day, I have always thought of Cliff Lee as a genius. And I wondered, and still do, what kind of standardized test could have measured or predicted his phenomenal achievement. (Cliff's brother, Bill, was a musician too; he had an 11-year-old son named Spike who grew up to be a filmmaker of some note!)

All I could do about this was to make my own math lessons as interesting and enjoyable as possible. I could try to develop team activities, and link the math concepts to everyday life. But that wouldn't touch whatever built-in, cultural testing gap there was between poor black children and middle-class whites. I never did figure out how to close that gap, and I don't think anyone else has either.

Testing turned out not to present a huge problem for me as the term progressed. The old assistant principals would be leaving the school, and with them the pressure for frequent testing, The new guard's emphasis was on teaching and learning, not on measuring.

Escalation, Capitulation, Resistance

As the second UFT strike consumed the month of September, Shanker's demands multiplied. It was no longer enough to restore the teachers dismissed by the Governing Board, even with police protection. Now, he wanted the Governing Board suspended until those teachers were given classroom assignments. He wanted UFT observers posted in each Ocean Hill–Brownsville school with absolute power to close those schools.[38] He wanted "extremist teachers" who were inciting violence by "bands of youths" to be fired. At every opportunity, he railed against "extremists" and "vigilantes." He resurrected an old Joe McCarthy tactic, alleging that City employees (presumably antipoverty workers) had been harassing his teachers in Ocean Hill, but he refused to name these employees, or levy actual specific charges.[39]

Negotiations at Gracie Mansion, the mayor's official residence, continued through the weekend of September 28–29. The Ocean Hill–Brownsville Governing Board was not invited to participate (because, as Superintendent Donovan later said, "the people on strike were not the local board, but the union").[40] By Sunday night, both Doar and Galamison had walked out, expressing open disgust with Shanker's ever-escalating demands. Late that night, a deal was struck: All the UFT teachers who wanted to return (reduced from the original 350 to 210 on opening day, and now to 83 by voluntary transfers) would be guaranteed classroom assignments, and paired with those who had been running the schools in their absence; both the central Board and the union would station observers in the schools, though without the power to arbitrarily close them down; and, again, an arrangement would be worked out to restore the lost pay of the teachers who had participated in yet another illegal strike.[41]

On Monday, the Ocean Hill–Brownsville Governing Board issued its response in the form of a resolution:

Whereas the Governing Board was not a party to the agreements worked out between the Board of Education, the United Federation of Teachers and the Mayor, and

Whereas the Agreements are an insult to this community and contrary to the goals of community control, and

Whereas the Agreements call for the return of unwanted personnel with a swarm of unwanted observers whose very presence is disruptive of the education of our children, and

Whereas the use of police force to impose inferior education on our children is adequate testimony of the utter bankruptcy of the Board of Education and the United Federation of Teachers, and

Whereas neither the Board of Education nor the United Federation of Teachers showed any concern for our children all last year, and the present Agreements demonstrate even less concern, and

Whereas unwanted personnel are being reintroduced into our schools by force of arms against the better judgment of duly elected community representatives and the community itself, thus demonstrating their contempt for the community, and their moral bankruptcy, and their determination to destroy the minds of our youth by returning to the "normal" chaos of last year, and

Whereas the Governing Board has been in constant consultation with the community, and

Whereas our schools are operating beautifully and we are providing education for our children, we have no intention of returning to the old days of educational genocide perpetrated by the Board of Education and the United Federation of Teachers, and

Whereas the Mayor has abandoned his responsibility to the children of our community by bowing to the unjust demands of the United Federation of Teachers,

THEREFORE we cannot comply with the agreements made between the Board of Education, the United Federation of Teachers and the Mayor. We will continue to provide quality education for our

> children. In the event that these teachers and observers should gain admission to the schools of our District, then the Governing Board reserves the right to send in its own duly authorized observers to insure that no harm will come to the children of our community.[42]

Since the settlement was reached late Sunday night, the teachers loyal to the Governing Board had no time to plan a strategy, and had not even organized a meeting. (By this time, we were referred to in the district as "the loyal teachers," in contrast to the returning UFTers, for whom there were a variety of unflattering descriptions.) When I arrived at school Monday morning, I was one of many wondering how we could save the school and support the Governing Board. Out on the sidewalk, there was talk of a boycott, but it went nowhere.

I entered the lobby to find a large knot of other loyal teachers being addressed by none other than Board of Education member John Doar, an advocate for serious decentralization if not outright community control. Doar was known for persuasiveness and a sense of fairness, qualities that made an impression on me in this little meeting. Although he was the one who had been peppered with hostile questions, Doar was, within minutes, able to take control of the gathering. He appealed to us that we should follow our programs,

Figure 2.2. John Doar, NYC Board of Education president (1968).

and promised that we could trust him to bring about justice within the terms of the settlement. Giving him the benefit of the doubt, the group disbanded, agreeing to make an effort to keep order in the school.

Installed in the district's eight schools that day were 850 policemen, most of them at JHS 271, plus 38 observers from the central Board's professional staff, 5 from the Board itself, 16 from the UFT, and 8 from the Governing Board.[43] In order to prevent another blockade on the school steps, the police set up barricades at both ends of the block, past which even parents were not permitted to accompany their children. This did not look like it would be a normal day.

Once the police escorted them into the building, the 17 returning UFT teachers, the cause of all the tension, didn't help matters. They spent the day being deliberately obnoxious, goading the loyal teachers into taking retaliatory actions, so the Board observers could charge us with harassment. One teacher showed up in class almost two hours after clocking in, claiming that he couldn't find a pencil. Fred Nauman, their chapter chairman, spent his day compiling a list of 65 "grievances" to file on behalf of his constituents.

They did their best to provoke us. In keeping with our promise to Doar, we did our best to avoid them. When our math teachers entered a department meeting and found three of them already sitting there, arms folded with self-satisfied smiles on their faces, we turned around, left and met elsewhere. Confrontation averted.

But they could not be avoided. During one of my classes, for example, the door flew open and one of them strutted to the middle of the room and began picking up papers from the floor. The eighth-graders, their lesson interrupted in the middle of the period, stared in amazement, as did I. After a few minutes, I calmed down enough to ask the intruder what he was doing in my room and why my class was being interrupted.

"I'm not interrupting your class," came the smug reply, "You are!" He continued walking around the room, hands authoritatively placed on his hips, inspecting the walls and the decorations. One of the larger boys started out of his seat, prepared to physically escort the uninvited visitor out of the room. Barely containing my own rage, I asked him to sit back in his seat, not quite sure at the time why. I knew he would have been charged with assault and probably jailed. On the other hand, I really wasn't thinking clearly enough to anticipate future consequences. Maybe I just wanted the pleasure of throwing the stranger out personally. The student sat down, and the class watched the two adults. They seemed willing to let me handle the situation.

I told the provocateur to get out of the room. Receiving no reply, still restraining an impulse to use physical force, I opened the door, and started counting backwards from ten. He slowly and calmly strode to the door, stopped to rummage in the wastebasket, belched loudly, gave me the middle finger, and finally stepped out.

When I slammed the door shut, many students applauded. Others called out encouragement. But a good math lesson had been ruined, and one bewildered student in a front row expressed the tragedy of the day. "Why did they have to come back?" he asked. "*Everything was going so good!*"

By dismissal time, it had become clear that this was no isolated incident. The returning UFT teachers were not in the building to teach or do anything to assist in the running of the school. Their job was to provoke an incident that the official "Observers" could use to get the school closed for good.

Our Steering Committee drafted a statement addressed to the UFT cohort, representing the school's loyal teachers. It read, in part, "We don't want the police who must escort you into the schools. We don't want the so-called impartial observers. We do not want the union, and we do not want you!" At a community rally that packed the auditorium that night, our statement and the fifty black and white teachers who attended were met with a rousing reception. The mood of the rally was angry and defiant. Speakers denounced the humiliation of the community by the imposition of the UFT teachers and the police occupation. Rev. Oliver announced that none of those teachers would be given classroom assignments in the morning, and asked if anyone disagreed with that decision. Not a single hand was raised.[44]

On Sutter Avenue in Brownsville that day, September 30, the Black Panther Party for Self-Defense opened a new headquarters.

Walkout

Our Steering Committee gathered early the next morning and voted unanimously to shut the school for the day ourselves, rather than continue under the intolerable conditions introduced by the strike settlement. We commandeered the public address system, and the microphone was handed to one of our members, Fran Aurello, to make a brief, agreed-upon, announcement.

Fran Aurello, a soft-spoken white English teacher about five feet tall and maybe a hundred pounds, appeared an unlikely candidate to proclaim a revolt. Upon graduating from Brooklyn College with an English major, she hadn't applied for a NYC teaching license for fear of being assigned to a ghetto school, like this one, and spent her first year teaching high school in an all-white distant suburb. There, to her admitted astonishment, she found far more satisfaction tutoring poor black students in a neighboring town. She became intensely interested in the Ocean Hill–Brownsville controversy. During the summer, she applied directly to JHS 271, a 90-minute commute from her home.[45] Most of her eighth-grade students towered over her physically, but her commitment came through, and she found a way to connect with them and with their parents. At the previous night's community rally, she was the only speaker to receive a standing ovation. She was among our most committed loyalists.

Miss Aurello took the microphone and announced the walkout, including our message to the unwanted UFT contingent: "The community doesn't want you and neither do we!" From the front lobby, we could hear students cheering the announcement in their classrooms, which emptied in a matter of minutes.

The united faculty, black and white, silently filed out of the school, first around the knots of confused police, then past the puzzled newsmen, clamoring with unanswered questions. Down the street, across the street, joined now by many of our older students, heading for IS 55, six blocks away, where we hoped to bring its teachers and students out into the streets with us. We were joined, as we marched through each residential block, by parents, mostly mothers and grandmothers, and by children. Spirits were high. The march at this point was truly "Black and White Together," reminding many of the Civil Rights movement's high points.

Past the drab decay of Hopkinson Avenue, pocked by lots strewn with rubble, gifts to the community from the city's terribly misguided "Urban Renewal" program. On to Atlantic Avenue, the polluted boulevard that cut the community in half with six lanes of deafening noise. Stopping traffic in the middle of the block, marching across. Drivers, in a hurry to complete their passage through a "bad area," leaning on their horns in impatient protest. Pedestrians looking on in wonder, some catching on and joining the still silent march. Reporters sweating bullets, still trying to catch up with their notebooks, cameras, and equipment, and calling out, "What the hell is going on?"

It occurred to some of us that something was wrong. The massive police presence had remained back at the school. Not one officer made any attempt to prevent our disruption of a major thoroughfare. But on we went.

IS 55, hulking and virtually windowless, was an exemplar of the new "Riot School" of American urban architecture. It was ugly enough as it was, without being surrounded by grey wooden barricades and its own contingent of menacing police. As the march, now numbering in the hundreds, approached the entrance, a double line of police quickly assembled to keep us away. A negotiating committee, spontaneously created by the leaders at the front of the march, spoke briefly with the police commander, who consulted with superiors on his radio. After a few minutes, he surprisingly conceded, reporting that the school's occupants would be released through another door.

Nagged by a feeling that this was far too easy, we went around the corner to the other door. We found it not just closed but padlocked. Back to the main entrance. By this time, the police were better prepared. Barricades had been quickly set up to keep us yards away from the doorway, with helmeted officers lined up five deep behind them.

Suddenly, with neither provocation nor warning, the barricades were pushed into the crowd of men, women, and children by an enthusiastic contingent of burly white officers. The startled marchers, sent scrambling into the street, shouted in protest. New sets of barricades were now being set up, defended, and again used to expand the police-occupied territory. Bloodshed was averted only by some veteran plainclothes cops who managed to steady some of their overeager uniformed comrades. The police charge stopped and held its ground. The marchers refused to back off. Stalemate.

During the brief standoff, it looked like the plainclothesmen thought they might defuse the situation with a divide-and-conquer strategy. One began a friendly conversation with a small group of white teachers. Nearby, another mumbled to his partners, "They're all right," motioning to the interracial, neatly dressed, contingent of teachers from JHS 271. "But it's that scum we gotta watch," pointing toward a large gathering of community residents that was now assembling across the street.

Then the shouting began. "Pig!" "Oink, oink!" "Let us in! Let us in!" Someone grabbed a barricade and threw it, just missing a cop's head. Some young people across the street started lobbing eggs at the police. Most of them missed, but I clearly saw one egg graze a cop's shoulder. He dropped to the ground, somewhat theatrically, and I watched, dumbfounded, as a police contingent picked him up and carried him into the building, as though he had been wounded by a bullet. "Who do they think they're kidding?" I wondered. (My question was answered by the evening *Daily News*, which reported that the cop had been struck by a large rock, not grazed by a small egg, and had suffered a severe fracture.)

The police refused to admit parents who wanted to take their own children out of the school. Those parents, some of whom had been roughly turned back, now took up positions on the front lines. As tensions mounted, another detail of police was moving up from behind the demonstrators with more barricades. Then the police directly behind the front barricades drew the long planks out of their sawhorse supports. As those directly behind them raised their nightsticks, they raised the planks in front of them, and began pushing us back.

The crowd at first did not resist. We moved back as best we could, until one of the women in front was knocked over by the force of the oncoming barricades. Now, no one was moving, but the police line continued to push forward. I found myself on the front line now, scared out my wits, flanked by mothers who had come to take their children home from school and who probably hadn't meant to be part of any demonstration at all when they left home.

The nightsticks in the second line soon started swinging, and the front line barricade-holders coolly accelerated their push. After a cop's sudden shove, a woman on my left fell to the ground. My fears instantly vaporized, replaced by rage and hatred at the still-advancing blue (and white) machine. Hands reached out from behind to pull the woman back into the ranks as I pushed on the barricades with all my might, secure now in the knowledge that a swinging nightstick would soon get me out of this bad dream. I pushed, and others pushed, and we managed to hold our position long enough for someone to pull the bewildered woman back to her feet and into the (relative) safety of the crowd. People did get clubbed, but I wasn't one of them. It looked to me like the cops wouldn't strike a white face so long as a black one was available. In fact, no white teachers were seriously injured at any point during the day.

The demonstrators were now being squeezed into the street intersection by a pincer movement of the force advancing from the front and the other from behind. As the pincer tightened, panic began to set in. People started running in any open direction. Most of the police seemed content to have successfully broken up the demonstration, but some couldn't control themselves. I never found out how many heads were cracked in the rush to escape.

Sometime after we left the scene, IS 55 was quietly closed for the day by its principal.

But this would only be the beginning. Somehow, we regrouped, and a new march began toward PS 144, four blocks away. Parents and students were firmly in the lead now; the teachers were marching in their support. Our silent march was now getting loud. As soon as people caught their collective breath, following the hasty retreat from IS 55, a chant was picked up. "We want our schools! We want our schools!" Down the middle of Pacific Street, past the squalid tenements, the march grew louder and still larger. Some windows opened, and people leaned out to see what was happening, but pulled back in when they saw the police snipers who were taking up positions on rooftops down the street.

The students came first, charging down Howard Avenue, throwing over barricades, shouting insults at the police, now exposed as an occupying army. We reached PS 144 before their reinforcements could arrive. Outnumbered, the contingent at the scene retreated inside and locked the doors, sending out word that no children would be released, even into their own parents' custody. The crowd milled around in the street, unsure of what to do next. Advance was blocked by steel gates and wooden barricades. Retreat made no sense either, since there was no place to go.

In the midst of the confusion and indecision, a police car came up the street, now blocked by over 500 angry community residents. Within seconds, the car was surrounded. As sticks and voices were raised, it slowed to a barely perceptible crawl. Peering through the car's locked windows, I saw the faces of two detectives draining from ruddy to ghostly.

It would have been a simple matter for the people to overturn the car, set it on fire, do as they wished with its passengers. The police on the scene, locked inside the school and still outnumbered, could not possibly have acted quickly enough to rescue those detectives. One large man with a booming voice, though, urged people to back away from the car. "We're ready to die for our children," he called out, "but not to kill." The car was allowed through with barely a scratch.

After we left PS 144, the school was quietly closed for the day by its principal.

Now, the lead was assumed by the young "militants" of the community. "On to 73," was the cry, as the crowd gathered itself together for a march to PS 73, at the other end of the district. I was walking with Les Campbell now, and we found we had independently made the same two observations: First, that the length of this section of the march, seventeen blocks, would give the police more time to plan strategy and gather forces than they had enjoyed in the earlier confrontations; second, that most of the white teachers had peeled off from the demonstration. Both of these signaled trouble ahead.

"Beep Beep! Bang Bang! Ungawa! Black Power!" The march was now joined by about a hundred younger kids who looked between eight and twelve years old. On it went, as both its size and its militancy seemed to grow on every block. Also growing for many of us was an ominous sense of danger. If a way out with dignity had been offered at that point, most of the teachers and parents who began the march would have been happy to call it a day. But no such way out was offered.

As the front lines reached PS 73, they confronted hundreds of barricades, surrounded by thousands of very angry helmeted cops. Rifle-wielding police forced their way into homes, pushed aside terrified tenants, and went straight for the rooftops. Those in the street lashed out with their nightsticks, attacking anyone within reach, but arresting few of those injured. As I got to the corner, Paul Chandler was running back to send an alarm about what lay ahead. "It's war now!" he exclaimed.

By the time our contingent turned the corner to see what was happening, one group of police had turned their attention and their nightsticks to the younger boys and girls demonstrating across the street from the school. When one child fell, I ran to help him up and behind me heard a car door slam. Spinning around, I saw a huge red-faced cop waving his nightstick wildly, trying desperately to catch up to the scattering children. I couldn't run as fast as the kids, but I could outrun the cop, and I did. Not everyone was so lucky.

That was the end of the day's demonstrations. The marchers scattered in every direction. For the next hour or so, the cops spread out, threatening people for standing on street corners and chasing kids down the streets. Then PS 73 was quietly closed for the day by its principal.

The front-page story of the *New York Times* reported that, "Nine persons were arrested and ten police officers were reported injured in melees that threatened to explode into a major confrontation between the predominantly Negro and Puerto Rican community and the police."[46] It did not mention any of the numerous injuries sustained by demonstrators. Even though the march was initiated by our united JHS 271 Steering Committee, the *Times* reported that it was led only by Al Vann. By this time, with or without corroboration, he and Campbell were automatically blamed for every breach of established order.

Buried inside the paper, though, was another article, bylined by Earl Caldwell, one of the few black reporters employed by the *Times* (or any other daily paper).[47] He chronicled the police attacks on not only the demonstrators, but on other reporters and even small children. He reported that Sandra Nystrom, a white JHS 271 teacher, was "repeatedly struck in the stomach" by police; that a police officer grabbed the notes of another black *Times* reporter and threw them to the ground; that a *NY Post* reporter was clubbed in the ribs; and that a contingent of police chased a 7-year-old boy down the streets until he outran them. In an unprecedented breach of polite society, he also reported the shield numbers of the offending officers. This would be his last report from Ocean Hill–Brownsville. The *Times* dispatched Caldwell to California for the next few years.

Figure 2.3. Marching through Ocean Hill–Brownsville (October 1, 1968).

The events of the day reminded me of an antiwar march I had participated in after the King assassination, back in Chicago. I recalled National Guard troops, bayonets fixed, charging our group of children, parents, and college students; the brutal Chicago cops blocking the demonstrators' only path of retreat; the panic; the flow of blood. I could find many similarities in the two experiences but, because of one glaring difference, I knew there was no real equivalence. After that Chicago march, those participants who hadn't been injured could go home, relax, and talk about what had happened over a glass of wine, secure in the knowledge that it would not recur unless they in some way invited it. For the folks in Ocean Hill–Brownsville, this had happened in their home. They had no place else to go.

Union teachers did have a place to go. A dozen white teachers from IS 55 travelled to UFT headquarters to file a complaint because their black principal advised them to leave "for their own safety" that day. Advised that the police had beaten up a young black child, one teacher commented, "If they roughed up a few more of those kids, all this wouldn't have happened."[48]

A Brief Case Study in Manufactured History

Wednesday, October 2, 1968

The most important driver of this narrative, written almost 45 years after the events it describes, was a compulsion to correct what I considered a distorted historical record. Rather than contest that record, point by point, generating a rather tedious process for even the most motivated reader, I have chosen simply to tell the story as I lived it, set as necessary in a documented context. As a case study, though, I here offer a single instance, drawn from the historical record of the day following the above-described events of October 1, 1968. Trivial in actual consequence, this incident reflects in microcosm the way "facts" of all kinds were distorted by journalists, and then repeated over and over by historians years later.

In his 2002 history of the 1968 teachers strike that has become the standard reference, Jerald Podair writes that, "Donovan shut JHS 271 on Wednesday (October 2) after community residents, including local board members, invaded the school and engaged in altercations with observers and teachers."[49] (The school was, of course, actually empty on Tuesday, since we were out on the march through the community, but that's not my major point here.) Podair references the reigning authoritative history of the city school system, Diane Ravitch's 1974 *The Great School Wars*, which states without citation, "On Wednesday, October 2, the day after the disorders around JHS 271, Superintendent Donovan closed the school for a one-day cooling-off period."[50]

Both statements were patently untrue. Either of these distinguished historians could have avoided making them by simply consulting the front page of that day's *New York Times*, which stated quite clearly that "*All* public schools will be closed today *because of the Jewish holy day of Yom Kippur* (my italics)."[51] (A calendar might also have been useful.) There was, in fact, no need for Donovan to single out JHS 271 for closure. So where did they get this misinformation?

In his mischievous little piece of pro-UFT propaganda, published in the midst of the legislative debate over school decentralization in early 1969—devoid of footnotes, endnotes, bibliography or sources—freelance journalist Martin Mayer wrote, "Donovan ordered J-271 closed for the one day Wednesday, October 2, to allow some time for contemplation."[52] This sentence, trivial in itself, echoed without challenge through the years, illustrates the willingness of more serious scholars to accept without question the often times ridiculous assertions that appear in the manufactured anti-history of Ocean Hill–Brownsville.

For now, though, we return to the real story.

The "Settlement" Unravels

On Thursday and Friday, the unwanted teachers were back, but they were assigned rather irregular classroom duties. They were given programs and classes, but with phantom registrations. Most of the students on the rolls for these classes had been absent since the beginning of school. Many had moved or transferred; some were simply chronic truants. This arrangement, proposed by McCoy, was reluctantly accepted by the faculty since we saw no way of keeping the UFT contingent completely out of the school. We hoped that this gimmick might prevent further disruption of our educational program.

Neither the UFT nor the Board of Education, though, saw the wisdom of McCoy's compromise. Shanker was threatening another strike, and had called a meeting of the UFT's Delegate Assembly. On Sunday, October 6, Donovan suspended the Governing Board for its refusal to assign the returning teachers to real classes. He ordered McCoy to expedite those assignments. On Monday morning, McCoy responded that he took his orders only from the Governing Board, which Donovan had suspended. Seven of the eight principals said they took their orders only from McCoy. (The eighth had requested a transfer.) On Tuesday, fifteen minutes before the scheduled UFT Delegate Assembly meeting, Donovan suspended McCoy and all seven principals, and reassigned them to central headquarters. In Donovan's press statement, he said, "I regret having to take this action, but I have done so in order that the orderly operation of the schools may proceed." It didn't quite work out that way. McCoy's response to his reassignment was quick and direct: "He will have to carry me out of here!"[53]

That night, the auditorium of JHS 271 was packed, as more than 700 parents and supporters rallied to back the stance that the district's leaders had taken. McCoy's defiant speech was greeted by a standing ovation that lasted almost five minutes.

At 7:30 a.m. on Wednesday, October 9, about 200 parents and teachers marched from McCoy's office to JHS 271. Reaching the school, they were met by a scene reminiscent of PS 73 a week earlier. The entire block was cordoned off by several hundred police. They manned positions behind the barricades, on the corners, and on the rooftops. Overhead, a police helicopter buzzed about. Only students and teachers would be permitted past the barricades. No parents. Not even Governing Board members. No journalists. Exceptions were made only for UFT observers and for members of the mayor's crisis team.

"What is this?" Rev. Oliver asked rhetorically. "Czechoslovakia?"[54]

This is how one student, Karima Jordon, later remembered going to school that day:

Figure 2.4. Police bracing for trouble (October 9, 1968).

> We had to go through barricades to get to the school and we'd look up on the rooftops, across the street from school, the cops were with their helmet gear and their riot helmets and their night sticks and helicopters and, and the playground was converted into a precinct and walking up to the school you have just mass confusion. You have the community people out there. You have the UFT. You have the black teachers on the inside. It was, you were just amazed. You couldn't believe this, this was happening.[55]

The police had made one tactical change to improve their image, but it backfired badly. At the previous week's demonstration, only white cops were in sight. Today, the most visible police, directly behind the barricades, were all black. New York City did not employ very many black police officers in 1968; they may have all been called to duty at JHS 271 that day.

But this only heightened the level of anger. Shouts of "Uncle Tom" and "Dirty Worker" were met with silence and blank stares. As it became clear that neither side was going to budge, the parents began to lecture and harangue the black officers, arguing that they were being used to betray their own people. Despised though they were, the presence of those black policemen, some speculated, was the only thing keeping the white cops' weapons holstered that day.

Figure 2.5. Patrolling the skies over JHS 271 (October 9, 1968).

Teachers were eventually allowed into the school once the guards were convinced that we actually were teachers. (This was a little arbitrary, since we had no official identification. Access seemed to rest more on dress and speech than anything else, but we all did get in.)

Students were being held in the auditorium for the time being. The teachers caucused, and agreed to recognize Vann's authority until the principal was returned to the school. Donovan had his own ideas. He appointed Evelyn Farrar, an assistant principal with 35 years in the system, to be acting principal. Ironically, she was one of Vann's teachers back when he was in elementary school.

Miss Farrar was one of the few black assistant principals to survive the Board of Examiners screening process. Like our other assistant principals assigned from the civil service list, though, she was antagonistic to community control, and appeared disinterested in any educational ideas developed since the Roosevelt Administration. In the school, she was best known for her admonition to new teachers to wear rubber-soled shoes, as she did, so they could "sneak up on the kids" in the hallways.

Official Acting Principal Farrar's first official act was to panic. Over the PA system, she announced that school was now closed; the children should pack up and leave immediately. All the children who had come through the barricades and the confusion outside in order to learn that day were to be expelled, without preparation or warning, back onto the street, back into the police lines, where chaos still prevailed.

This order did not hold. Vann quickly took control of the PA system and countermanded it. He announced that the school would indeed remain open, and that everyone would follow the regular class schedule. A teacher opened a side door, and students who had already gone outside rushed back into the building.

Perhaps realizing the impossibility of enforcing Farrar's hastily conceived order to close the school, Donovan gave Vann's reversal official cover, telling him over the telephone that the school could stay open "in the interests of safety," and that he himself would soon be there to "supervise the situation."

By the time Donovan arrived, the school was functioning as normally as it ever had been, with one glaring exception. There were police at all the entrances and exits, in the cafeteria, in the boiler room, in the teachers' lounges, in the hallways and the toilets, and everywhere they might be called upon to protect the unassigned and unwanted UFT teachers. But the students and the loyal teachers were in their classrooms, and tranquility prevailed. Donovan made a quick inspection and left the building.

The events of the preceding week had taken a toll on the patience of many of the school's teachers. We had all seen our efforts to teach the children smashed by the mere presence of these seventeen UFT functionaries, some of whom were now, as if to add insult to injury, passing the time playing blackjack in the teachers' lounge. All the legal and police power of the world's greatest city had been mobilized to crush the expressed will and aspirations of the community, so that the unwanted teachers could spend their day playing cards with each other at JHS 271.

At 1:20, during the seventh period of the day, about twenty of us entered the lounge. We had no plan in mind, but were intent on telling the card players, to their faces, what we thought of them. The UFT contingent quickly withdrew to one side of the room, gathering around Fred Nauman, their chapter chairman. We gathered on the opposite side. Police lined the wall in between.

Dorothy Hopkins and Lillie Curtis, two black teachers, immediately launched into an angry, emotional harangue. They verbally berated the UFT teachers for sabotaging the school, for abandoning the children, for forcing their way back in where they were not wanted, all of which culminated in accusations of racism. The UFTers squirmed uncomfortably in their seats. It looked to me like they were terrified of being told off by a black woman.

At one point, Vann entered the room. He looked around, took stock of the situation and left. He wasn't going to interfere with these proceedings, but he knew that he couldn't get involved either. Nevertheless, he would later be identified as its chief instigator.

The only near physical confrontation of the session occurred when an eighth-grader came in and verbally assaulted one of his old teachers, who had walked out on his seventh-grade class the previous spring. The boy had to be restrained by some of the black teachers until he calmed down and left the room.

Nauman, who could have strolled out of the room at any time (with police protection right there if he felt he needed it), insisted on sending a message to Miss Farrar. The intermediary was Norman Rabinowitz, the middle-aged, Board-certified assistant principal who had instructed teachers that none of our students would ever be capable of a grade higher than "75." Earlier in the week, Rabinowitz had told me that, "I've been through a war and seen men get battle fatigue, but even that was nothing like this. I really don't think I can take it much longer." He didn't.

A half hour after the confrontation began, Rabinowitz returned with a message inviting Nauman's contingent to meet with Miss Farrar, who was hunkered down in the principal's office. Our group followed close behind. Simultaneously and coincidentally, a group of parents also arrived in the office and harangued both Miss Farrar and the UFT group. They were calmed only when Vann came in and gave them his personal assurance that the school would keep on running.

The confrontation came to an end, but the unwanted teachers decided to call it a day. They left the building in an obviously morose frame of mind, resentful perhaps of the fact that they were not welcomed back more graciously. This was apparently also too much for Miss Farrar, as we would soon find out.

To those of us who were caught up in the spirit of the moment, this seemed a great victory. Even with the police right there in the room, we, along with the parents who arrived later, had established the fact that those teachers would never be able to return to JHS 271 again. Or so we thought.

"Your Papers, Please!"

At dismissal time, we were informed that Murray Hart, the Board of Education's Chief Observer in the school that day, had now placed *himself* in charge. He had decreed that no one except staff and students would be allowed in the school the next morning. We were handed slips of paper that would guarantee us safe entry. Signed by Hart, these passes indicated that the bearers were, indeed, teachers at JHS 271, and that Hart "would be responsible" for them. In order to report for work the next day, we would be required to display these passports to the police guarding the entrances.

Exceptions were made for observers sanctioned by the UFT, the CSA, and the Board of Education, but not for those appointed by the Governing Board, and certainly not for parents or other community citizens.

This scenario just didn't sit right with me. It brought to mind Nazi Germany and the apartheid South Africa regime, adding identity cards to the existing quasi-military occupation, and enshrining the second-class citizenship of community residents. I came up with a plan of non-cooperation. If the entire faculty left their passes at home, I thought, Hart would have to abandon his plan and let us in anyway. If he kept us out, he would only be demonstrating his own incompetence, his inability to maintain a stable atmosphere in the school. This, after all, was his only function in being there. I decided to sound out some other teachers on this. Since I wasn't particularly sure of myself, I went first to Campbell, Mayer, and a few others whose opinions I respected.

Then, with some encouragement from both black and white teachers, I began exploring less charted ground. More confident now of gaining wide support, I approached a less political white group and explained the proposal.

They listened in silence, then raised questions.

"But suppose they don't let us in. Will we still get paid?"

"Since Hart is in charge now, shouldn't we do as he says?"

"Why do we have to make things difficult?"

Three really stupid questions, I thought. Time to move on.

Another white teacher gave me an even more disheartening response. "Look, Charlie, I think these passes are a good idea," he explained. "How else could we be sure of getting into school and keeping those people out?"

"*Those people?*" I drew back in amazement, thinking, "Fool! This is their school, you idiot, not ours!" But I didn't say anything, except that maybe we should talk another time.

It was now dawning on me that our contingent of white replacement teachers was loaded with contradictions and uncertainties. I recalled the incident in the classroom the very first day, where the teacher insisted on being addressed as "Doctor"; the faculty meeting where some white teachers wanted to vote against black self-determination; the small group that had opposed the walkout a week before; the larger group that melted away from the march when the community took the lead; and the few teachers who told me that their only purpose in teaching here was to avoid the draft.

I started to wonder whether the Governing Board's teacher screening process had been too easy to get through. There was a substantial minority of teachers among us who were unreliable, who didn't belong in Ocean Hill–Brownsville at all, who were only going along for the ride, maybe even biding their time and waiting for an opportunity to institute or support a reaction. Before now, I had naïvely assumed that nearly the entire faculty had volunteered to teach in Ocean Hill for the same reasons I did. Now this assumption was shattered. More disturbing to me was the potential threat this group could pose to a pro-community united front. How long could they be expected to remain silent? When would the UFT realize that it had a potential fifth column in the school and begin to exploit it? Speculation aside, the configuration of forces was certainly becoming more complicated, and this was only the fifth week of school.

At any rate, the plan to leave the identity cards at home was never to be tested. Late that afternoon, it was announced over the radio that, because of the incidents in the teachers' lounge and in Miss Farrar's office, Donovan had ordered JHS 271 closed the next day. Teachers were ordered to report downtown, where the Superintendent would extract a pledge from us that we would work in harmony with the 17 unwanted teachers. Only then would the school be reopened.

Beginning with a new non-cooperation agreement among the Steering Committee, a chain phone call reached most of the loyal teachers, instructing them that they had not heard that news report, and that we would all report to school as usual in the morning. We were not going to leave our students alone with the police.

An Accidental Arrest

I arrived at school earlier than usual that Thursday morning. A few teachers had already preceded me there. They, along with a few confused children, were standing outside the police barricades. We decided to try going through the barricades if we could, walking around one end as though it were any other day.

Surprisingly, none of the police tried to block our way until we reached a second set of barricades closer to the school entrance. At that point, we were stopped and told we couldn't go any further. "Why not?" asked Judy Russell, one of our strongest pro-community white teachers.

"School's closed," answered one cop. "Why?" asked another teacher.

"Dunno. Orders is orders. Can't let anyone through."

Stymied, we all walked over to the benches that were between the two sets of barricades. We wondered why we'd been allowed through one row of police, but were stopped at the next. As the children sat down on the benches, a lieutenant approached and told them to get up. Russell, standing next to me, told the kids to stay where they were. She instructed the officer that the benches were public property, and that the kids had every right to sit on them.

"Now look," began the lieutenant, placing his hand on her elbow.

"Get your hands off of me," she interrupted angrily. She had a quick temper, and did not like police. It looked to me like she was getting ready to take a swing at him.

The officer looked my way, apparently expecting that he would find me more understanding. "What's she getting all excited about?"

"You didn't have to touch her," I explained, hoping to defuse the situation, or at least distract him.

"Now listen," said the cop, growing impatient. "I'm in charge of this area, and I have to make sure there's no trouble here."

I nodded in sympathy, and then repeated myself. "You didn't have to touch her." He was getting angry now, and grabbed my shoulder.

I was getting impatient too. "If you're not going to arrest me," I said, "let go." He did, but firmly instructed us before walking away that we were allowed in the area, but not on the benches. Temperatures were rising.

We walked back to the outer barricades, where a number of children had been stopped on their way to school. Armand, a skinny seventh-grader, was leaning on the wall of the building, staring at the cop nearest him. I knew he was trying to make the cop feel uncomfortable, a little game he had sometimes played on his teachers. The cop stared back, and then lost his temper, precisely the reaction that Armand was hoping for. "Get off that wall!" he ordered.

"No!" replied Armand defiantly, "I don't have to." The cop was beginning to turn red. "What's your name and address?" he demanded, pulling out a pad and pencil.

Armand stood his ground. "None o' your business!" Though small in stature, he was known around the school for his big mouth.

The cop must have realized by now that he'd put himself in a difficult position. Backing off would be an admission that a 12-year-old boy had faced him down. He could try to grab Armand, but probably knew he could never catch him. Now, more children were arriving at the corner, calling encouragement to Armand. We invited Armand and the other children to cross the barricade and join us. They had a right to go to school!

Faced with this mass of 11- and 12-year-old terrors and with teachers on the side of the kids, the fifty cops manning the barricades were becoming visibly uneasy. Finally, a captain took command of the situation and ordered everyone back behind the outer barricades.

Simultaneously, a cop standing near me grabbed my arm. I told him to let go, and took a step away. Perhaps frustrated by the events of the morning, he lost his temper and grabbed the lapels of my jacket. "Listen you," he began to shout. I pulled away, frightened by this outburst, and quickly walked to the place where the captain told us to go.

There, another cop grabbed my arm. More confident now that I was definitely on the "legal" side of the barricades, I again pulled away. Again, "Let go unless you're going to arrest me." He let go.

Five minutes later, I saw the captain approach the cop who had grabbed me, watched them speak for a few minutes, then looked on as the cop walked up to me and announced that they were taking my advice. "You're under arrest. Come along with me."

I was startled by this, since some time had passed between any incident and the arrest. I asked what the charge was. "Harassment. Hands behind your back." Handcuffs were applied.

The act was now complete.

Scene I: School closed because unwanted UFT teachers hadn't been welcomed.
Scene II: Cops unsure which barricades are passable and which are not.
Scene III: Twelve-year-old kid needles cops.
Scene IV: Cops push people around.
Scene V: Teacher arrested for harassing the cops.

It reminded me of that Langston Hughes poem, "Ballad of the Landlord."

I good-naturedly went along with the arrest, and even the handcuffs, convinced that the whole incident could easily be explained in court. Some of the cops even became kind of friendly once we had left the scene of the confrontation.

"Are you a teacher here?" one asked.

"Right."

"God help us." He closed the rear door of the paddy wagon, and away we went.

At the precinct station, I was put in a room with the arresting officer, whose name was Amadeo. He told me another wagon would soon arrive to take us downtown.

Meanwhile, papers had to be filled out: Name, address, occupation, etc. I was told that I wasn't in any real trouble, but would have to go through the formalities of a bail hearing anyway. If I brought a lawyer into the picture, I might have to stay in jail overnight. No phone call. My family read about the arrest in the afternoon tabloids.

The wait at the stationhouse dragged on for two hours, and after a while the two of us began to talk. Amadeo complained that he'd been pulled out of his normal Coney Island beat in order to come to Ocean Hill, and had been on duty for fourteen straight days. He felt he was being pushed around. I asked why the PBA, the police union, didn't protect the men from such conditions. "Look," he answered, "That's just the way it is, I guess. But if you think unions are so good, why are you against the UFT?"

I said wasn't against a union of teachers, that I was just against the policies Shanker was pursuing, which wouldn't be good for the children or their teachers in the long run. "Yeah," he agreed. "I think the PBA sells us out most of the time too. I think I know how you feel." I hoped maybe he did, but didn't really think so.

After a long while, I was led to another paddy wagon, and the added company of two plainclothes detectives. Sitting in the rear with me were two middle-aged, rough looking black men who were also on their way to the criminal court. Amadeo separated me from the other two arrestees; all three of us were handcuffed to the benches we were sitting on. I assumed that the two men were under arrest for some serious, maybe violent crime, and felt a little safer out of reach. Sitting behind the "cockpit," I was treated to a fascinating discussion among Amadeo, the driver, and the two detectives about what sounded like their favorite topics: sex and retirement, both of which couldn't happen soon enough for them.

Arriving at the courthouse jail, only blocks from Board of Education headquarters, I was led through a series of gargantuan barred gates, opened for passage by guards using what looked like foot-long skeleton keys. Up to now, I had considered this arrest little more than a freak accident, a mistake made in the heat of the moment. I was sure I would be released after sitting through some formalities to cover the police overreaction. The sight of the prison gates and the strict security conditions, though, now had me thinking different thoughts.

At one passageway, a guard noticed the "Community Control" inscription on my lapel button and muttered, "Let's take care of this guy," but my "buddy" Amadeo restrained him. "Nah, he's all right."

In another room, I was booked and fingerprinted. Another request to make a phone call for bail money was met with assurances that there would be no need for it. Then they asked if I wanted a Legal Aid lawyer. "I'd rather use my own," I replied. "If I can make a call, I can probably get one down here." I said "probably" because I really wasn't sure. Actually, I just wanted to call McCoy's office to tell them where I was. I had never felt more alone and powerless.

What I didn't know was that a lawyer was already in the building, vainly searching for me. It wasn't unusual for the police to hide the whereabouts of an arrestee, especially in political cases. After being given a full-scale runaround, he left to find more experienced help.

"Now look," explained the officer helpfully, "Why not use the Legal Aid for the bail hearing, and get your own lawyer for the trial?"

"Why would I want to do that?"

"Because Legal Aid will get you out of here right away. If you wait for someone else, it will take longer, maybe until tomorrow."

I was suspicious of these alternatives, but they had me over a barrel. If this was the only way to avoid an overnight jail stay, still totally out of touch with anyone who could help, I had to take it. I signed the paper he handed me, handed over my watch and wallet, and headed for the detention cells.

There were two cells, separated by a narrow walkway. One seemed particularly frightening; it was packed with men, mostly Puerto Rican, all of whom looked malnourished and desperate, as though subjects in a lab experiment. The other cell was thinly populated, with perhaps ten men in it. I was relieved to be put in that one. Another prisoner later explained the criteria of separation. "They're the junkies."

Glancing around the dimly lit cell, I noticed the two men whose paddy wagon I had shared on the trip downtown. We nodded recognition, and one of them asked for a match. I walked over, lit the man's cigarette, and asked what he had been arrested for. "Sneaking into the subway," came the unexpected reply. "I was going to work from the Franklin Avenue station and got caught."

"And your friend?"

"Same thing. We work in the same place and we were late. So we tried to save the time of buying a token. We had the twenty cents, but there was a line at the token booth."

I was furious with myself. I remembered my snap assumption that these men had been arrested for a violent crime, merely because two detectives had been assigned to take them in. Or were they ordinary plainclothesmen, and not even detectives at all? And had my assumption betrayed some pocket of *my own* racism? Would I have jumped to the same conclusion had the men been white, or dressed for business? I was more than angry with myself; I was ashamed. Something to think about. A lot to think about. I promised myself that I would never, ever, make the same mistake again.

A few minutes later, a turnkey called my name. I was led out of the cell, down a hallway, and into a cordoned-off area in a court room. There again was my new friend, Officer Amadeo, assuring me that the judge would set a trial date and let me go in no time flat.

And there we sat. Twenty minutes went by. A half hour. An hour. The two fare-beaters were brought before the judge. The charge was, indeed, sneaking into the subway. While they stood there, the harried Legal Aid lawyer engaged in a whispered conversation with his clients, the prosecutor and the judge. Finally, the judge asked, "How plead you?"

"Guilty, your honor," replied the lawyer.

"Have you anything to say before sentencing?"

"Your honor, this man has a steady job and a family. In his hurry to report for work this morning, he neglected to buy a subway token. He promises not to do this again, and he feels quite ashamed of himself." The defendant stood impassively, staring blankly as though uninvolved in the proceedings.

"Ten dollars or two days," proclaimed the judge. After another whispered conversation, the man was led back to the cell. He would have to call home for someone to come down to pay his fine. The process was repeated for the other man.

Brooklyn Justice had been done. For a twenty-cent fare, the men had lost a full day's pay and a ten-dollar fine, which might have been another day's pay. I wondered how many white people were so routinely convicted of that charge. Then, looking around the courtroom, I realized that I was the only white person in the place, except for police, lawyers, and court personnel.

Soon, the court was recessed for lunch, and I was led back to the detention cell. I was getting depressed and even lonelier. I hadn't seen anyone I recognized in the courtroom, and was beginning to envision spending the night in jail, alone and forgotten.

What had happened to the high-sounding rhetoric of my law school training? How absolutely irrelevant was all that in this courtroom? I had watched pathetic souls in alcoholic stupors sentenced to weeks in jail, and heard guilty pleas negotiated as though humanity had been reduced to a pile of fish or old clothes.

In the midst of all this, I was overtaken by a sense of overwhelming impotence. The novelty had worn off. When was I getting out of here?

Back in the holding cell, I got into a conversation with a couple of young black men. One was in for selling drugs, and calmly contemplating a lengthy prison term. The other was in for assault. They asked me what I was in for.

"Harassment," I answered, a little embarrassed at any comparison between my troubles and theirs. "I was going to school, and a cop got in the way."

"Going to school? What school?"

"I teach in Ocean Hill: 271. Know where that is?"

"Know where it is?" exclaimed one of the young men. "Man, you better get out of here fast, and take care of some more business back there!"

Eventually, lunch was served from a wagon. Jelly sandwiches on hard bread and watery lukewarm tea. Yeccch.

At: 2:30, after what had seemed like days of waiting, the court resumed its session, and I was brought back to wait for my case to finally come up. While in detention, I had gotten an idea, and suggested it to Amadeo.

"This is a waste of both our time," I argued. "Why don't you just drop the charges? After all, you know I'm no dangerous criminal."

"Are you kidding?" he exclaimed. "I would have done that hours ago if I could've, but they won't let me."

Terrific.

For the fiftieth time, I anxiously looked back into the crowded courtroom. As if in answer to a prayer, four community activists were standing in the rear, looking for me. Clenched-fist salutes were exchanged. All at once, I felt relaxed, for the first time all day.

They had brought an attorney from the National Lawyers Guild. Within minutes, my new lawyer and I were before the bench. After explaining the circumstances surrounding the arrest, the lawyer moved to dismiss the charges. Amadeo nodded his agreement. Maybe this would all be over.

But the prosecutor objected. "Only," he said, "Because this is a bail hearing, not a trial."

The judge sided with that argument, set a trial date, and released me without bail.

Free at last! Riding back to Ocean Hill–Brownsville, I felt as though I had been in jail for seven years, not seven hours.

My rescuers explained the runaround the police gave the lawyer that they had sent in the morning. They were only able to locate me after McCoy enlisted the assistance of William Booth, the city's Commissioner of Human Rights. They showed me a copy of an afternoon newspaper, which told the police version of the arrest. The article also provided readers with my home address, a common practice of the day, which I found a little disturbing.

No, this didn't have much to do with the theories of jurisprudence and the appellate brief-writing I studied in law school. This was like another country.

The high point of my day was arriving back at the district office, where I was surprised by a group of parents, teachers, and staff waiting to welcome me "back home." After our little celebration, I told the story of my day (minus the inner turmoil), and heard about the teachers' adventures that I missed.

"Now Play Nice Together"

Soon after my arrest, I was told, most of the loyal teachers reported for work as we had planned. They, too, were met by a cordon of police who stubbornly refused to allow entry to the building. Some teachers pleaded with the guards to allow them through, just to pick up personal belongings, even with police escorts, but all requests were met with a simple but final, "I'm only followin' orders, Mac." The teachers, without instructions from McCoy's office, simply milled about in front of the entrance.

At about ten o'clock, a messenger arrived with a directive for the entire staff to report to the Board's Bureau of Personnel, downtown at 65 Court Street (only a few blocks from where I was cooling my heels all day). Car pools were quickly arranged, and the teachers set out "to meet the man."

Sixty-Five Court Street was a modern office building, where the Board of Education had leased several floors in order to ease overcrowding at its old, archaic 110 Livingston Street headquarters, two blocks away. Outside, filling the wide sidewalk, were reporters, photographers, and television cameras. Inside, all normal activity ground to a halt as the white clerks and secretaries gawked at "the troublemakers from 271," whispering to one another about "extremist tendencies" and "known terrorists." Little gray-haired ladies scurried about the hallways, straining to catch a glimpse of the more well-known personalities.

The teachers slowly filed into a large meeting room with enough seats for both them and their UFT antagonists. As the two groups settled down in different parts of the room, they were greeted by Theodore H. Lang, Deputy Superintendent of Personnel, who was accompanied by an extensive entourage of assistants.

Lang began in a low-keyed monotone, seeming unsure of himself and intimidated by his audience. After a while, he got around to the orders of the day: The two groups were to be subdivided into small units, combining teachers from both factions, for meetings under the guidance of one of Lang's aides. These small group sessions, he explained with diminishing confidence as he glanced about the room, could "diagnose the grievances" that had been keeping the two factions from working together in harmony.

My colleagues looked at one another in amazement. Steve Mayer stood and objected, calling this plan a "scheme to divide and conquer" and to isolate the "troublemakers." Many called out in agreement. Lang was forced on the defensive, unable to persuade them to cooperate. After some back-and-forth, they insisted on time for a closed meeting amongst themselves. Lang, his aides, and the UFT contingent were asked to leave the room. Having clearly lost control of the meeting and needing further instructions from Donovan, Lang acceded to the request. The Board staff went to a second conference room, the UFT contingent to a third, and our teachers were left alone to decide on their next step.

Unanimously unimpressed with Lang, they were overwhelmingly opposed to his "sensitivity groups." Many expressed anger at having been forced to travel downtown at all. "If Lang wanted to know what the problem was," said one, "we could have written him a letter." "If he doesn't know what the problems are by this time," said another, "he shouldn't even be here." A proposal was floated that they all walk out of the building, but it was voted down since this would only give Donovan more of an excuse to keep the school closed. Ideas were called out, quickly debated and shot down for one reason or another. Finally, a consensus was reached to reject Lang's proposal and insist on speaking directly with Superintendent Donovan, the man in charge.

Apprised of the group's decision, Lang seemed more relieved than angry. After a break for lunch, he informed them that Donovan was busy that day, but would meet with them the next day in the same place. The school would remain closed.

On their way out, one of Lang's aides announced that Evelyn Farrar, Ira Brand, Norman Rabinowitz, and Claire Devine, all the "old school" assistant principals forced on the district because of their standing on the civil service list, had requested, and been granted, transfers out of the district. The general feeling was relief at this news but, although we kept the two supervisors we wanted, Vann and Mandracchia, two were not enough for a school the size of JHS 271.

I joined my colleagues the next morning at 65 Court Street, where we were told that Donovan would not arrive until after lunch. Our Steering Committee used the time to draw up a list of grievances and demands. By the time he arrived, at two o'clock, we had been waiting for more than four hours. He apologized for his lateness, but didn't mention that he had been attending a hastily called, and totally unproductive, Board meeting, aimed at dealing with the crisis.

Donovan announced that, since this was to be a meeting with "only the faculty of 271," he would ask his assistants to leave the room. This pleased everyone, including Lang and his aides, who made a beeline for the door. Once he was alone with the teachers, he expressed his disapproval of the recent events at the school and asked that the meeting concern itself only with reaching a *modus vivendi* between the two teacher groups, so they would be able to work together in the future. "Not as personal friends, necessarily," he added, "but as professionals doing a job."

We had other things on our minds. Hands went up. After being recognized by Donovan, a Steering Committee spokesman stood and presented our issues. Our primary demands were: (1) that the school be immediately reopened with Harris reinstated as principal; (2) that the large police presence be elimi-

Figure 2.6. Bernard E. Donovan, NYC Superintendent of Schools (1968).

nated or drastically reduced; (3) that JHS 271 again be open to the parents and the community; and (4) that the Board expedite orders for supplies and materials for which we had been starved since the beginning.

Nauman, speaking for the UFT group, said they were willing to return to the school, but expressed fear for their personal safety. Judy Russell objected, arguing that these fears were unfounded since not one of them had actually been physically assaulted inside, or outside, the school. Even the verbal abuse they endured paled in comparison to that dished out by the UFT pickets stationed outside schools across the city. There was no direct response to this, but the UFT group was not letting go of this issue, false or not. One demanded that the police be retained until the "extremists" were removed from the school. Donovan must have been in a good mood, although I couldn't imagine why. He parried this remark by asking who "the extremists" were. "Do you mean Albert Shanker?" The laughter broke the ice a bit.

I had been in a room with Donovan only once before, when he came to LIU for a few sessions with my senior seminar. I had found him pretty dull back then, and remembered only his lengthy lecture about why it was impossible to integrate the city's schools. Because of demographic shifts by that time, he was probably correct in that conclusion, but I found him singularly unimaginative in trying to craft solutions. Having been in the system since 1930, he was the ultimate insider. His appointment in 1965 ended a string of unsuccessful outsiders in the job, but he was not known for anything except his own string of administrative posts. To Annie Stein, he was "an old New York City hack with no serious educational qualifications or standing."[56]

In this place on this day, however, he was masterful. Somewhere along the line, he had certainly picked up some skills on how to "work a room." As the discussion continued, Donovan got the two groups talking to each other for the first time. Each remained suspicious of the other, but common ground was discovered regarding a few intra-school issues. We were never going to agree to anything until our larger issues were addressed, but it had become clear that these would have to be dealt with in another forum.

I was sitting quietly in a front corner of the room, just watching and listening. I felt like a latecomer, since (having been incarcerated) I hadn't been involved in the previous day's proceedings, and the discussion hadn't really grabbed my interest. In order to see the speakers, I had to turn and direct my attention toward the rows behind me. Facing the back of the room, my gaze was diverted when a rear door opened. A tall, familiar figure slipped in and leaned against the wall. I waited for someone to realize that Albert Shanker had joined the assembly, but no one seemed to notice. After a few minutes, I stood up and called out.

"Dr. Donovan, didn't you say that this meeting was exclusively for the faculty of 271?"

"Yes, I did."

"Then what's *he* doing here?" I turned and pointed to Shanker. Now all heads turned to the rear of the room. Friendly, though surprised, nods of the UFT teachers contrasted with the amazed stares of our contingent. Donovan was unruffled.

"Mr. Shanker, this meeting is for me and the JHS 271 teachers, only. I will have to ask you to leave."

Shanker calmly replied. "As the President of the UFT, Dr. Donovan, I have as much right to be in this meeting as you have. My job is to represent these people."

Donovan countered with the observations that the UFT teachers had been well represented by their chapter chairman all day, and that no harm had come to them. "If you refuse to leave," he added, "I will be forced to cancel this meeting."

Shanker insisted. "Whenever teachers meet with the Superintendent, they have a right to be represented by the president of their union."

Campbell suggested that Donovan use the police, dozens of whom were lining the outside hallway, to eject Shanker. Donovan angrily retorted that he "does not use such tactics." Many of us just smiled at that.

Finally, Donovan announced that he would not conduct the meeting with Shanker present. Quickly, he gathered up his papers and left the room by the front door. Shanker then stepped out the rear door. The teachers, left alone in the room, sat in stunned silence. The meeting had been brought to an abrupt end by Shanker's intrusion, and any possibility, however slight, of reaching a working agreement had been shattered.

"Now we know who really runs the Board of Education," mused Campbell, "Al Shanker!"

Some speculated that the confrontation between Donovan and Shanker had been staged. This was plausible, since the verbal exchange between the two men was calm and direct enough that it could have been rehearsed. I thought differently. Shanker had been promoting imagined threats of violence against his JHS 271 cohort as ammunition in his crusade against Ocean Hill–Brownsville and the Community Control movement. If there was any hope at all of the two teacher groups working together harmoniously (which there probably wasn't, anyway), he needed to torpedo it. That, I thought, was why he burst into the meeting, knowing his presence would force Donovan to cancel the effort.

At any rate, Donovan's attempt at forging reconciliation was over. And so was a very long week.

Early in the weekend, though, Donovan had a long meeting with McCoy, who assured him that the UFT teachers could get real classroom assignments if the school was reopened and all the suspensions were lifted. Then, after meeting with members of the central Board (who were reportedly furious with Shanker's disruption of the teacher meeting), he announced that he was reopening JHS 271 on Monday, and immediately reinstating McCoy and all of the principals (though not the Governing Board). It appeared then that two of our demands had been won.

Shanker was furious. He threatened another strike, a long one, unless JHS 271, which was being run by "gangsters," remained closed. Donovan caved in, reversing himself and recommending to the Board that the school's staff and students be dispersed to other districts. The Board, though, turned him down, calling what members thought was Shanker's bluff. It defied common sense that he would close more than 900 schools over what was happening in a single one.[57]

It was no bluff. Before that weekend ended, on October 13, Shanker announced that the UFT was closing all the city's schools once again, and that this strike wouldn't end until both McCoy and the Governing Board were removed, and the Ocean Hill–Brownsville demonstration district was *dissolved entirely*. Now, his primary demand was no longer the defense of his members' jobs, but an open attack not only on community control, but on the community itself.

The *New York Post* editorial page characterized the UFT's policy now as "rule-or-ruin . . . framed in a spirit of total war, requiring unconditional surrender not only by the local Ocean Hill-Brownsville board but by the central Board of Education as well."

Thus began the third, and most abrasive, citywide teacher strike of the young school year. Shanker had again escalated his demands, and there seemed little hope of an early settlement.

Strike Three, Week One

> It was a strike that went completely beserk, beyond reason, or logic, or hope, and nobody . . . could do a thing about it.
>
> —Barbara Carter[58]

> . . . the worst disaster my native city has experienced in my lifetime.
>
> —Martin Mayer[59]

> I don't represent children. I represent the teachers.
>
> —Albert Shanker[60]

The third strike was the longest and the ugliest. Throughout, JHS 271 was under siege. As soon as the strike began, a front-page headline in the normally staid *New York Times* screamed, "Death Threat Cited at Brooklyn School." The source for the story was a confidential report submitted to Donovan by his three observers, which was leaked to the *Times*. The report alleged that death threats had been made during the October 9 confrontation in the teachers' lounge, and that an observer had been physically shoved out the door of the principal's office by a "companion" of Rev. Oliver.[61] This was a legitimate news story, even several days after the fact, and the reporter had clearly gone to some lengths to obtain the observers' report. However, he apparently did not think it was worth his time to interview any of the loyal teachers who were there. Had he asked me, for example, he might have had a more interesting, though perhaps less sensational, story. He also could have interviewed a parent who was with us in the lounge, identified in the report as an "intruder." (Parents, of course, were more than welcome in the school. We recognized as "intruders" the observers, the police, and the UFTers.) This was typical of the news coverage JHS 271 received during this period, which relied almost exclusively on UFT and Board of Education sources.

Vann, Campbell, Hopkins, and Curtis were called downtown a week later to answer allegations in that report of harassment and insubordination. A strategic decision had apparently been made to charge only black teachers, even though our October 9 "welcoming committee" had been interracial and the observers' report also identified "other teachers." That morning, the Ocean Hill–Brownsville Teachers Steering Committee held a press conference at JHS 271, making our own charge: that the four had been "singled out as scapegoats to appease the UFT."[62]

Meanwhile, throughout the city, parents and teachers opposed to the strike again fought to open their schools. Middle-class white parents were arrested for trespassing at schools which were, according to the Board of Education, "officially open." Some succeeded in getting the schools open for a time, but many were thwarted by the school custodians, who joined the UFT and CSA on strike beginning October 18. Before leaving, they turned off the heat and power and, in some cases, changed the locks on the entrances. At the schools where it was the management keeping the doors closed, it was simultaneously a lockout and a strike. During the UFT's three previous strikes, custodians had walked right through the teachers' picket lines, but now they were in full support. The custodians, who at that time functioned as independent contractors, running lucrative, often corrupt operations that generated higher income than the principals' salaries, were 99 percent white. They had good reason to believe that their monopoly would end if the city's black and Puerto Rican communities ever got control of their school buildings.

Those communities quickly consolidated their opposition to the UFT strike, as well as their support for the three demonstration districts. As *Time Magazine* reported, "It was the black neighborhoods, where parents have long been accused of apathy toward education, that struggled hardest to keep their schools going."[63] Critical support for these efforts came from the Council Against Poverty, which represented the city's 26 designated "poverty districts," and from antipoverty programs all over the city. The Community Development Agency, which administered these programs, was headed by Major R. Owens, the original architect of the Brownsville Community Council.

Other citywide supporters included the Public Education Association, the Citizens Committee for Children, United Bronx Parents, the NYCLU, the United Parents Association, and EQUAL, a white civil rights organization. Labor leaders in support of community control included Sam Meyers of the United Auto Workers, Leslie Roberts of District 65, and Henry Foner of the Fur and Leather Workers' Union. Even in the UFT executive suite, the union's few black officers broke with Shanker and came out publicly in support of community control.

The tumultuous events of the third strike's first week reflected the passions and the polarization that had gripped the city.

On Monday, October 14, a hastily organized rally brought thousands of community control supporters to City Hall. (Estimates by police, reporters, and organizers ranged all the way from 5,000 to 75,000.) Joining with our teachers and parents were their counterparts from other school districts who opposed the strike, high school and college students, and activists of all stripes from all over the city. Black organizations that never seemed to agree with one another on anything were all represented, from the NAACP and CORE to SNCC, the Negro American Labor Council, the Black Panthers, the Nation of Islam, the Republic of New Africa, and numerous community-based groups. The crowd was about half white, which seemed to astonish the reporters who covered it. A small delegation met with a deputy mayor inside City Hall, and presented demands that the Governing Board be reinstated, and that the police and the uninvited observers be removed from our schools.

At about 5:30, at the peak of rush hour, the rally turned into a spontaneous arm-in-arm march over the Brooklyn Bridge, heading for Board of

Figure 2.7. Crowds assemble for the October 14, 1968 rally.

Education headquarters in downtown Brooklyn. Taken by surprise and vastly outnumbered at this point, although heavily armed, the police made a feeble effort to block the march or divert it to the pedestrian pathway. A small group of prominent ministers, among them Rev. Wyatt Tee Walker and Rev. William A. Jones, stepped up and persuaded the officers in charge not to force a confrontation. The clergymen's arguments may have had the support of the mayor and/or the police commissioner. Only 43 months had passed since "Bloody Sunday," when the world watched Alabama police attack voting rights marchers on the Edmund Pettus Bridge. A repeat performance on New York's most famous bridge would have been devastating to the city's image.

In any case, the police blockade soon melted away. We had taken over the bridge, and the commuters would have to wait. I couldn't see the traffic jam this created, but I don't think we made too many new friends in Lower Manhattan that day.

On the Brooklyn side, the police were waiting for us, but they were not going to attack or arrest thousands of people; instead, they gave us an escort to 110 Livingston Street, where we held another impromptu rally. As darkness began to fall, about a thousand of us marched the four miles through Bedford-Stuyvesant to JHS 271, and held yet another rally. As Father Powis later recalled the jubilant spirit,

Figure 2.8. Marchers take the Brooklyn Bridge. McCoy and Rev. Oliver are flanked by Claude Oliver and Governing Board members Elaine Rooke and Agnes Hansen.

> We marched right through Bed-Stuy. People on every corner were cheering, shouting. People in their windows, shaking bells and all kinds of things. It was a real party night. And we came to 271. We had a beautiful demonstration there.[64]

The people's supply of energy seemed inexhaustible.

The following night, Mayor Lindsay appeared at a Jewish Center in Midwood, a white, middle-class area of Brooklyn, where many Jewish schoolteachers lived. He and the rabbi had thought this would be a good setting for a conciliatory talk. The teachers didn't think so. Two thousand picketed the temple for an hour before the mayor arrived. Inside, a crowd of 1,700 shouted the mayor down at his every attempt to present the other side of the story, and could not be quieted even by the rabbi. When protesters surged toward the stage, the police decided that was enough. Lindsay and his aides tried to leave by the back door, but were now met with five thousand hooting, jeering white protesters. Finally, a large police escort was assembled to spirit away to safety the Mayor of the City of New York, and his wife, in a decoy car.[65]

Even with police surrounding it, the car was chased by the crowd. Fenders were kicked; objects were thrown. No arrests were made. Press coverage was extensive, but no newspaper called it what it was, a middle-class riot. No columnist thought to compare it with Lindsay's famous walks through the angry streets of Harlem and Bedford-Stuyvesant after Dr. King's assassination, with only a single aide at his side and no need for a police escort.

The UFT was not the only organization that mobilized for this occasion. Shock troops were provided by the Jewish Defense League (JDL), a paramilitary organization formed during the previous summer with the slogan, "Every Jew a .22." Openly racist in its philosophy, the group's members included a large number of Jewish teachers.[66] Despite its name, the JDL never actually "defended" anyone. Most of its efforts went into hounding its enemies, such as the mayor, and distributing material aimed at terrifying residents of the city's Jewish communities. Before long, it would forge an alliance with the Colombo crime family and evolve into a genuine terrorist organization itself.[67] Maurice Eisendrath, the leading figure in Reform Judaism, described the JDL as "no different from whites carrying robes and hoods, standing in front of burning crosses."[68]

It was a busy night of a busy week. While Mayor Lindsay was making his escape from Midwood, the Board of Education met to elect new officers. John Doar and Milton Galamison were elected president and vice president. By now, Galamison identified community control as the last, best hope of the ghetto schools, as "the struggle to abort colonialism in urban education." "It is our hope," he wrote, "that we can resurrect from these academic graveyards the children who belong to America's future."[69]

The UFT and CSA, meanwhile, were mobilizing for their own City Hall rally. One of the leaflets they distributed alleged that UFT teachers were cursed, spat upon, and threatened with death at JHS 271; that Miss Farrar transferred out of the school because she was physically threatened; and that "McCoy's teachers are teaching the three 'R's of Racism, Rioting and Revolution," none of which were true. The leaflet implored that "We MUST stop it now in Ocean Hill–Brownsville to prevent it from spreading!"[70]

Thursday's UFT/CSA City Hall rally, supported by several other labor unions, the AFL-CIO, and the Central Labor Council, drew an estimated 40,000 people, virtually all of them white. Well represented were the construction trades, the city's whitest labor force, which had benefitted greatly from the hundreds of millions of dollars spent on new schools during the 1950s and 1960s, and were intent on maintaining their racial monopoly. "Rather than let the Black and Puerto Rican communities have a decisive voice in who will build, repair and maintain schools in these communities," wrote James Haughton of Harlem Fight Back, "the building trades would cease to build, repair and maintain schools . . . The officialdom is as desperate as Shanker . . . to hold on to the economic power that has become their vested interest."[71]

As at the UFT's earlier rally, this one was "integrated" by the former civil rights strategist, Bayard Rustin. In a much-discussed 1965 essay, Rustin had called for a shift from direct-action protests to community institution-building aimed at building political power.[72] The Community Control movement was doing just that, though it could not abandon nonviolent direct action as a tactic. Still, Rustin chose to align himself with Albert Shanker, who was not only an ideological soul mate but also a financial supporter. A similar contradiction characterized his association with the pro-war AFL-CIO, which led him to abandon his pacifist principles (also expressed in his 1965 essay) and support the war in Vietnam. These two decisions would render him irrelevant to the Civil Rights movement, and a captive of his trade union patrons.

Notwithstanding the nearly monochromatic character of the UFT rally, one speaker incongruously called it "the largest civil rights demonstration since the March on Washington." Shanker shouted that, "We are not about to let our school system be taken over by Nazi types and gangsters!" Hundreds of police were on hand. The only arrests were of two women pulled out from a tiny band of counter-demonstrators.[73]

Few reporters remarked on the obvious paradox of these protests. The pro-UFT rallies, with all their signs denouncing racism, were virtually all white. The community control demonstrations, featuring signs supporting self-determination for people of color, were multiracial and integrated. At least one analyst concluded that this and other such journalistic failures evidenced a racial blind spot in New York's nearly all-white press corps.[74] I thought this explained quite a bit.

WHY WEREN'T YOUR SCHOOLS OPEN TODAY?

1 *Some teachers were threatened with death if they remained at J.H.S. 271.*

2 *Union teachers and supervisors were cursed and spat upon.*

3 *Mrs. Evelyn Farrar, Acting Principal of J.H.S. 271, an experienced Black Supervisor has under pressure of physical harm, transferred out of Ocean Hill-Brownsville.*

4 *McCoy's teachers are teaching the three 'R's' of Racism, Rioting and Revolution.*

5 *The Mayor, the Board of Education, the Superintendent of Schools have violated continuously their written and published agreements.*

6 *The intimidation, physical violence, rioting, illegal appointments and transfers have been going on in many parts of the city for the past several years. We MUST stop it now in Ocean Hill-Brownsville to prevent it from spreading.*

7 *Dr. Donovan's official observer recommended the closing of 271 because of the violence and chaos in that school.*

You Can Help Re-Open All Our Schools . . .

1 *GO TO THE RALLY AT CITY HALL ON THURSDAY, OCTOBER 17th AT 4 P.M.*

2 *SUPPORT YOUR TEACHERS -- LET MAYOR LINDSAY KNOW THAT YOU SUPPORT US.*

LET'S SAVE OUR SCHOOL SYSTEM.

Supervisors and teachers of
District 18, C.S.A., U.F.T.

Figure 2.9. UFT flyer promoting its October 17, 1968, City Hall rally.

Figure 2.10. Bayard Rustin and Albert Shanker rushing to the UFT rally (October 17, 1968).

Another distinguishing feature of the pro-UFT rallies was the absence of the city's many leftist organizations, which ordinarily were reliably pro-union. Shanker's sole supporter on the political left was the tiny Socialist Party, of which he was a member. That party, since its founding in 1901, had never made anti-racist work a priority. Its position was that racism would fade away once a classless society was established, and that the labor unions would blaze the trail toward that utopia.[75] Not surprisingly, the party attracted few black members. (A. Philip Randolph and Bayard Rustin were the most prominent of these.)

In contrast, the Communist Party (CP), which was hated by the Socialists, had always made the fight against white supremacy central to its work in the United States. It believed that the working class could not be successful until it was no longer divided by racism. It took seriously Karl Marx's dictum that, "Labor cannot emancipate itself in the white skin while in the black it is branded."[76]

Since 1928, the CP program advocated self-determination for the world's colonized peoples, and it even supported for a time the idea of an independent black nation carved out of five southern "Black Belt" states. Members risked their lives to unionize Southern black sharecroppers and other workers neglected by the mainstream labor movement. They fought for equal education and fair housing in the cities, blocked evictions, and organized the unemployed. They fought against employment discrimination, police brutality, and lynching. They could also be expelled for expressions of racism. These programs and policies attracted many blacks to the party, including W. E. B. DuBois, Richard Wright, City Councilman Benjamin Davis, Jr., and Les Campbell's father. They also drew the support of black luminaries, like Paul Robeson, Langston Hughes, and Adam Clayton Powell, Jr.

In 1938, the Communist Party had 7,000 black members. It also had a large Jewish membership. The high point of black-Jewish collaboration in pursuit of social justice was probably not in the later Civil Rights era, as the conventional wisdom would have it, but in the Communist orbit of the 1930s and 1940s. In New York, a case in point was the Teachers Union, which was predominantly Jewish and which championed the black freedom struggle since it elected Communist leadership in 1935. During this time, and continuing through that of the Civil Rights movement, the toxic ingredients of racism, anti-Semitism, and anti-communism all simmered in the same stew.[77]

Extending its doctrine of self-determination to what was commonly seen as the internal black colony of the U.S., the Communist Party was an active supporter of the Community Control movement. By then, the party had long since passed its peak, having been decimated during the 1950s by government repression, by Khrushchev's exposure of Stalinism's underside, and by self-inflicted wounds. Still, its support of community control overshadowed the Socialist's opposition to it.

Also in support was most of the predominantly white New Left, which had sprouted on college campuses during the early 1960s in support of the Civil Rights movement and in opposition to the Vietnam War. This loosely-defined movement spread into teaching, law, medicine, social work, and other professions as members of college organizations like Students for a Democratic Society moved off the campuses. The self-described "anti-imperialist" wing of this movement took the position that the leadership of the struggles against racism and imperialism must arise from the ranks of those oppressed by these systems, not from their white allies, whose proper role was a supportive one. This view was well-represented on the faculty of JHS 271.

During the week of the competing rallies, the Board of Regents was considering the city board's interim decentralization plan, which would grant local school boards substantive new powers and codify their authority to transfer teachers between districts. It voted to approve the plan at 5:30 p.m. on October 17 just about when, coincidentally, the UFT's City Hall rally was at its peak.[78] The next day, the Ocean Hill–Brownsville Governing Board began taking steps to break the impasse by accepting the transferred teachers back into the district as soon as the city's interim plan went into effect. Shanker rejected this offer, as he rejected the interim plan. Now, there was no way to mollify the UFT without the total destruction of the experimental districts and a reversal of the city's path to any meaningful form of decentralization.[79]

Meanwhile, a report issued by the New York Civil Liberties Union (NYCLU) during the previous week began to circulate around the city.[80] It began with a quote from Edmund Burke, lecturing the House of Commons in 1774 on the British suppression of the colonists in America.

> Reflect how you are to govern a people who think they ought to be free, and think they are not. Your system. . . . yields nothing but discontent, disorder, disobedience. Such is the state of America. . . .

The report, entitled, The Burden of Blame, was unequivocal in its conclusions:

1) From the beginning, the central Board of Education attempted to scuttle the experiment in Ocean Hill-Brownsville by consistently refusing to define the authority of the local Governing Board;
2) The UFT has used "due process" as a smokescreen to obscure its real goal, which is to discredit decentralization and sabotage community control;
3) . . . To the degree that the Ocean Hill–Brownsville Board violated due process, it did so only by following normal standards and procedures of the Board of Education; and
4) The major burden of blame for the chaos . . . must fall on the central Board of Education and, lamentably, on the United Federation of Teachers.

It went on to narrate the history of the controversy, validating every argument that had been put forward by the Community Control movement. It ended by calling on the central Board to "make the adoption of a plan for effective community control its first priority."

The report dealt a body blow to the UFT's claim to be fighting for any kind of civil rights or even workers' rights. Shanker retaliated by sponsoring a campaign within the NYCLU to undermine the report, and publicly called for it to be withdrawn. He was now losing this argument, though, and needed a new issue to keep the pot boiling. Otherwise, the experiment in community control just might turn out to be successful.

In what turned out to be a brilliantly cynical strategic move, the UFT escalated its campaign of fear, now claiming for itself the last line of defense against a mounting threat of "Black Anti-Semitism," even "Nazism" for those who didn't make the immediate connection. In an October 20 speech to an all-white audience in Houston, Shanker claimed that New York City teachers were threatened with death if they didn't leave their jobs and that, throughout the nation, schools were in danger of being taken over by black militants. If "black separatists" were able to take over the NYC schools, he warned, "How long will it be before it happens in Philadelphia, in Chicago, Detroit, Washington, and Los Angeles?"[81]

Battle lines had been drawn. Voices were growing louder. Racial rhetoric continued to intensify. And this was only the first week of the young school year's third teacher strike.

Eye of the Storm

> Virtually everyone who observed the schools in Ocean Hill, who talked to the teachers and watched the excitement of the children in the classroom, who reported the exalted mood and the sense of command among the parents . . . they are all persuaded that this change in the locus of control has exerted a profound change on the process of education, and that the level of teaching and learning has jumped significantly.
>
> —Dr. William Ryan[82]

As the storm raged, week after week, exacerbating tensions and fraying nerves throughout New York City, as Ocean Hill–Brownsville found itself under an intensifying state of siege, an inverse phenomenon evolved inside of JHS 271, the focus of all the commotion.

Here, in the eye of the storm, the pressure-cooker atmosphere generated a sense of unity among the staff, now freed of saboteur teachers and old-school administrators, along with a fierce determination to succeed. Among the students, the shared experience of crossing picket lines with their teachers, of enduring with us the verbal abuse of the white union pickets, as well as occasional physical harassment by the police, helped create a sense of solidarity inside the walls of the school. The students' parents welcomed the spirit and dedication of the new teaching staff, and were more than willing to participate in making the project a success. JHS 271 became a haven, where parents, community volunteers, students, and teachers joined forces to work on the business at hand: education. Through its struggle to survive, it both embodied and surpassed what John Dewey identified as the essentially social nature of a progressive school, "a community held together by participation in common activities."[83]

Not all students, parents, and teachers shared in this new spirit, but those who did were numerous enough and enthusiastic enough to set the tone of the school.

In a later interview, Les Campbell recalled that spirit:

> We had shown that this downtrodden community, faced with a crisis, using its own resources, could overcome, and there was a feeling of jubilation. The parents and community were so much behind us, and so supportive of us, this made it feel that much more exhilarating to know that we had community support. I used to walk through the streets of Ocean Hill at that time, and it was so beautiful. Parents used to come up and tell me to come in their house and have some fish, or have some chicken, or have some coffee, or have a cold drink. These were parents who were pouring out their heart to people who they felt were doing something to educate their children.[84]

One student gave me a red, black, and green Black Liberation pin he had made in metal shop. Another gave me a poem she had written:

Police Go Away
by Kathy, Class 8-211[85]

When I go to sleep, I pray
Police, please go away
We don't need you,
You nor your blue.
You sway your sticks,
You play your tricks.
You're in our schools,
You're playing us for fools.
Stay away. Stay away.
You're only in the way.
For you are there night and day.
When will you go away?
Go away, police.
Let me sleep in peace.

During this time, the typical ghetto school dynamic, pitting students, teachers, and parents against each other in an adversarial triangle of blame, was absent. With police on the streets and the rooftops, with UFT pickets marching and shouting in front of the school, with press reports distorting our own lived experience, the dynamic now was "all of us together" against what seemed like the entire outside world.

We also had a good time together. One Saturday, after someone (I didn't know who) arranged for free busses, dozens of teachers volunteered to take 600 of our students on a day trip to Bear Mountain State Park. Out in the country air, the children enjoyed ball games, hiking, exploring, and the park's zoo. There wasn't a single disciplinary problem all day. Everyone arrived home safe, sound, happy, and tired.

The doors of our school were once again open to all. Parents visited regularly, and were invited into the classrooms by their children's teachers. The young activists of Project Method seemed to be everywhere. Rhody McCoy, years later, remembered this corps of volunteers, and the atmosphere of the time . . .

> They'd pick up all of the young people who were late coming to school, or trying to play the hook, and kept the drugs out, and came into the schools and talked to the youngsters about staying in school, the value of education, and set some role models for them, and brought role models in—like Eubie Blake and others. Everybody in that community began to play a role in the schools. The school became the focal point of the community.[86]

Mass media accounts, which emphasized shouting, violence, finger-pointing, and accusations of black racism and anti-Semitism in our schools, bore no relation to the reality. It seemed to me, in fact, that the general opinion in the Ocean Hill–Brownsville community was becoming more, not less, tolerant of white teachers in its schools. Parents recognized the work that the new teachers were doing, along with our acceptance of accountability to the black and Puerto Rican governing body they had elected. Any journalist who took the trouble to notice, although few did, would have seen at that time a model of inter-racial cooperation on a principled, mutually respectful basis. This was, however, not widely known. Positive reports occasionally appeared, but they were in thinly circulated journals and newsletters, or buried on the inside pages of the *Times*; the tabloids, the TV news, the front pages only reported conflict, threats, violence. A few months later, in fact, I was asked to coordinate a panel discussion at a staff development center in Westchester, which had been titled, "White Teachers DO Succeed in Ocean Hill–Brownsville!" ("What a revelation," I thought.)

Our classes were visited not only by parents and other community citizens, but by journalists, professors, activists, students of education, and just about anyone interested in seeing for themselves what this experiment was really all about. This was in stark contrast to the policy in other ghetto schools, where security guards stopped, and sometimes frisked, everyone who came through the front door, including parents. At JHS 271, no one was even assigned an escort unless one was requested. Visitors were free to roam the school at will, even to sit in on classes if they wished to. Father Powis, a frequent visitor, recalled the atmosphere in an interview years later . . .

> During the strike, whenever I went into the schools, especially JHS 271 and IS 55, I saw something that I thought was so spectacular that I still thought we were going to win this thing. I knew the odds were against us, but . . . something was happening in those schools. Here you had mostly new teachers . . . but you had schools that were completely orderly, where classes were going on. People were coming in . . . and they were seeing this and saying,"*Who's so stupid to destroy this?*"[87]

Media interest was so high that some reporters and photographers rented rooms in houses across the street so they could monitor any clashes that might develop in front of the school.[88] Inside, press access was usually permitted without restriction, but there were some days that reporters were kept out. A few of these press-free days followed evenings of television or tabloid coverage that triggered anger because of pro-UFT bias and lazy reporting. At other times, the numbers of reporters and cameramen were large enough to create their own story, and to distract teachers and students from their own duties. The policy was inconsistently applied, but the press usually had free run of the school. In our view, they could have taken better advantage of it.

One of the most visited classrooms was that of Les Campbell, who had by now become the UFT's poster child for anti-white racism, black anti-Semitism, incitement to riot, and a slew of other charges. I had heard these accusations during the previous summer, and didn't know what to expect when I introduced myself to him after a faculty orientation session. That first encounter put the lie to all those charges. We chatted about our common alma mater, LIU–Brooklyn, and about a few people we both knew. (It was a Jewish LIU professor, in fact, who Campbell credited with inspiring his passion for history.) He had no problem with my ethnicity, religious heritage, or even teaching inexperience. As long as I was there to teach the children and support the community, I was okay with him. It was the beginning of a lifelong friendship.

Campbell's lessons were always open to observation by members of the faculty, independent observers, and media representatives. On some days, there might be as many observers in the rear of the room as there were students at their desks. The question on the minds of many outside observers was not Campbell's undisputed teaching ability, but the content of his lessons. Was he teaching “hate” and “black racism,” or was he simply attempting to teach some history, to instill pride and a positive self-image in his students?

His classroom was among the best decorated in the school, featuring posters and pictures of African-American heroes, the most prominent being Malcolm X. One bulletin board, entitled “Our Ancestral Homeland,” was filled with photographs of African life. Hanging in the front was not the stars and stripes, but the red, black, and green-striped banner of African liberation. As any of his students could have explained, its colors were “Red, for our blood; Black, for our skin; Green, for the vegetation of the land.” First popularized in America by Marcus Garvey during the 1920s, it was said to date back to a 15,000-year-old African empire.

I personally observed several of Campbell’s lessons. He invited me to more, and I wished I could have made the time to accept all those invitations. I was learning along with his students. His course traced the African people from ancient times through the European invasion, forced emigration to the New World, slavery and slave revolts, to the present day. According to him, it was designed to answer the questions: “Who am I? Where have I been? Who and where am I today?”

I walked into one lesson a few minutes after it began. Campbell was showing a series of slides on the origins of African civilization. They portrayed the anthropological discoveries locating the human species’ origin in eastern Africa’s Olduvai Gorge and depicted the builders of ancient Egyptian culture, highlighting their African facial features. This led into the next class, a discussion of social institutions in other early, highly developed African civilizations: Kush, Mali, Ghana, Songhay.

Student participation in Campbell’s lessons was not only high, but enthusiastic. In one that was typical, he began with a list of some prominent national groups in a column on the chalkboard: Italian, Irish, Japanese, Chinese, Polish, and German. Campbell explained to the class, “These are nationalities of people from foreign countries. When they got to this country, they were called ‘Americans,’ but they did not forget their original homeland, their ‘ancestral homeland’ where they or their parents or grandparents were born.” “What is the ancestral homeland of an Italian?” he asked.

“Italy,” responded a student quickly, as the teacher pointed to that country on the world map.

“What is he called when he comes to America?” After a slight hesitation, the student answered, “An Italian-American.” Campbell wrote the answer on the board and asked another student, “What is the ancestral homeland of the Irish?”

“Ireland.”

“Right,” pointing to the map, “And what is he called when he comes to America?”

Figure 2.11. Les Campbell at the blackboard (October 23, 1968).

"Irish-American."

The process was continued until the column on the board also listed "German-American," "Japanese-American," "ChineseAmerican," and "Polish-American."

At that point, Campbell introduced the term, "Negro." "Where," he asked, "is the Negro-American's ancestral homeland? Where does he come from?" The class hesitated, some students giggling in anticipation.

Campbell turned to the world map. "Can anyone find *NegroLand* on this map?" he asked sarcastically, to howls of laughter from his students.

Turning back to the class, "Seriously," he asked, "Where are we from?"

Almost the entire class burst out, "Africa!" and one boy located that continent on the map.

"Yes," continued Campbell, "Africa is our ancestral homeland. Then what should we be called?"

"African-American!"

"That's right, or Afro-American." These new terms were added to the list.

"Why then," he asked, "do we get the name 'Negro' if there is no NegroLand? Since we're from Africa, shouldn't we have always been called African-Americans?"

This led into a discussion of the term, "Negro," as Campbell impressed upon them the slave derivation of the word and its negative connotations.

"You see," he explained, "The white man wanted us to forget all about our ancestral homeland in Africa, where we once lived in freedom. So he didn't call us by our proper name, African-American, but gave us a new name instead."

"Negro," supplied the class.

"But what should we be called?"

"AFRICAN-AMERICAN!"

Campbell built on this motivation to discuss the component concepts of nationality shared by other ethnic groups, besides an ancestral homeland, such as common history and culture, and a shared language. He then compared different nationalist tendencies around the world with the Black Nationalism which was now becoming a force in their community. As the bell rang, he gave a homework assignment and the enthusiastic class went on to their next subject. I felt I had observed a master teacher at work.

Campbell wasn't the only one teaching about African heritage. McFadden specialized in this area as well, as did Floyd Sparrow and Alan Kellock. Kellock, one of the few genuine scholars teaching in the city's public schools, had studied at the Universities of Ghana and Cairo, and was now finishing his doctorate in African history at the University of Wisconsin. He had taken

Figure 2.12. A JHS 271 bulletin board.

a detour from his planned path to a professorship to do a stint at our junior high school, and now said he was inclined to stay. Extremely popular with his students, it mattered not at all that Kellock was white.

Many outsiders would have also been surprised to know that one of the standard textbooks used in these classes was *Eyewitness: The Negro in American History*, the author of which was William Loren Katz, who happened to be white and Jewish.

The lessons I had observed resonated when I spoke with other black teachers, and with parents, about their own schooling. They had been taught, not only in school but in popular culture as well, to be ashamed of Africa, which was populated, they once thought, only by primitive pygmies and cannibals, and was devoid of history. In 1950, when they and I were New York City public school students, the Harlem Committee of the progressive Teachers Union published an expose of racist bias in the school system's textbooks. Children were being instructed that slaves were happy and well cared for, that emancipation was responsible for all kinds of civic disorder, and that "niggers" were drunks, thieves, and liars.[89] Ocean Hill–Brownsville students were learning something different, that they had a place in the world and that they were connected to a proud historical narrative.

In 1968, teaching (accurate) African-American history had still not occurred to the Board of Education's curriculum planners. The idea of Black and Latino Studies was not only new, but highly controversial. Considering the experiences of previous waves of migrants to northern cities and towns, it need not have been. Back before the onset of the First World War, Scandinavian languages were being taught in Minnesota public schools, and German was the predominant foreign language taught in Wisconsin. Irish history was in the curriculum of the Boston high schools. New York City's Jews had successfully fought for Hebrew to be equal to French and German in high school offerings and Regents exams.[90] Yet it took the experiment in community control to expose the latest wave of migrants, blacks and Puerto Ricans, to their own history, and to create the city's first bilingual elementary school. To many observers, the failure of the Board of Education to do so was an indication of its unwillingness to prepare these children to succeed in the world, fueling the argument that it was perpetrating educational genocide.

At the time, even most universities' history and social science departments still seemed to define "World History" as European History. I was enrolled that semester in a course in Nationalism at the New School for Social Research. The professor asked all the students to choose a form of nationalism for the subject of a term paper. When I chose Black Nationalism, she insisted that there was "no such thing." I protested, to no avail, and finally took the path of least resistance. I wrote my paper on Jewish Nationalism (Zionism), which she found perfectly acceptable.

Our students' knowledge of American history got an unexpected boost when the comedian and history buff Dick Gregory arrived to address a student assembly. He was then running as the Peace & Freedom Party's candidate for President of the United States. His presentation, fusing humor with information, wouldn't soon be forgotten, but there was another surprise. The Gregory operation, being run on a shoestring budget, couldn't afford much in the way of campaign materials. His staffers did, however, bestow on his audience hundreds of "play money" dollar bills, with his picture in the center along with several catchy slogans. The surprise came when someone inserted one of these bills in a vending machine, which recognized it as an actual dollar bill. This quickly became a very poorly kept secret. All those campaign materials probably ended up in the hands of the beverage and candy companies.

African-American Studies was just one of the innovations introduced at JHS 271, and at the other district schools. We encouraged one another to experiment with new techniques, introduce new materials, or simply "tell it like it is," and were finding more success than anyone expected. Some experiments work, others don't; that's why they're called experiments. I believe that our successes stemmed more from the enthusiasm of the teachers, and the respect we showed our students, than from the mechanics of any new methods or techniques.

The siege situation also created an atmosphere of openness and flexibility in the classroom. In my own classes, I thought it was important to break down some of the barriers that were commonplace between students and teachers, particularly where the former were black and the latter white. I sometimes sat on my desk during a class, but never, ever behind it. On the very first day of school, following the encounter with the pompous "Dr. Fruitbine," I violated more conventions than I was aware of by impulsively telling the students they could address me simply as "Charlie." Some had a little trouble with that at first, and compromised by calling me, "*Mister* Charlie." I could only roll my eyes at that, and wonder what James Baldwin would think.

I also showed an interest in their families and home lives, and tried to meet as many of their parents as I could. So, it wasn't out of place for me to be asked whether I was married, what my wife's name was, where I lived, and other personal questions. I shared with them, and they shared with me.

At the beginning of one class, a boy asked me what my salary was. Instead of deflecting the question, I jumped on an opportunity to turn his curiosity into a practical math lesson. Shelving the work I had planned, I asked whether he meant "gross pay" or "take-home pay." The class seemed intrigued.

"What's the difference?"

"When you have a steady job," I explained, "you don't bring home all the money that you earn. Some of it is taken out for taxes and other things."

They expressed some suspicion about this practice, and wanted to know how much this "takeout" was, and how the whole thing worked.

"Let's suppose I make $100 a week. Okay?" They didn't know it, but this was more than the median household income in Ocean Hill–Brownsville.[91] As a starting teacher, I made a little more than that ($130).

"Okay," came the response. I wrote "$100" on the board.

"Now, before I get that money, ten per cent is taken out of it for state income tax." In another column, I wrote "10%."

"How much is that?" asked one student. Just the question I was hoping for!

"Percent means 'out of every hundred.' So '10 percent' means '10 out of every hundred.'" They were catching on that they were being tricked into a math lesson, but good-naturedly going along with it.

"How many hundreds did I say I started with?"

"One."

"So how many tens are taken out if the tax is ten percent?"

"Ten," a boy called out.

"No, stupid!" interrupted a classmate. "One ten. Ten dollars."

"Good. So the state tax is ten dollars." This information went into the appropriate column.

"After that, five percent is taken out for Social Security."

"That's not right," a boy objected. "Social Security is money you get, like my uncle, not money you pay."

"It's both. People who work and make money pay a few dollars every week, and all that money is collected and divided up among the old or disabled people who really need it. When you get old enough yourself, you can stop paying and start to collect."

"Not bad." Most nodded in general approval at the operation of Social Security. If they took this lesson home, though, many would find out that not everyone was covered by this program.

Back to percents. "All right. Now, five percent is how many out of every hundred?"

"Five."

"So, if five percent is taken out of $100 for Social Security, how many dollars is that?"

"Five." On the board went the purpose of the deduction, the percentage, and the amount.

"Another *deduction*," I slipped in a new term, "is federal income tax. This is the biggest: fifteen percent. How much is fifteen percent of one hundred?"

"Fifteen." answered a student quickly. Now this information went on the board.

"The deductions we figured out amount to how much all together?"

A little figuring (this was supposedly the slowest class in the grade), then someone called out, "Thirty dollars."

"Agreed?" Most heads nodded.

"So, if my gross pay is $100, and $30 is deducted, how much can I take home with me?"

"Seventy dollars," blurted a student in the front row, who had figured the answer before the question was asked.

"Does everyone agree?" They did. "And my take-home pay is what?"

"Seventy dollars," answered the class nearly in unison, sounding satisfied with themselves for having finished the problem.

But I wasn't finished with them yet. The lesson wouldn't be complete until we had worked with gross pay other than an even hundred dollars, so I quieted the class and announced, "But there's just one problem." (And a few groans.)

"You see, I don't get paid every week. I get paid by the month."

I continued quickly, hoping to sweep them along before any protests arose. Erasing the previous calculations, I asked, "How much do I make in a month if I get $100 per week? Let's say there are four weeks in a month."

"Four hundred dollars."

"OK. How much is the state tax now?"

"Forty per cent," called out a girl not yet heard from. A misunderstanding discovered.

I addressed her directly. "If that's true, then how much would it be if I made $800?"

"Eighty per cent . . . I think." She began to show misgivings.

"And if I made eleven hundred dollars?"

"Eleven . . . I think I got it wrong." Now I had to explain why her figuring didn't work.

"That was an easy mistake to make. Try it this way: If 'percent' means 'out of every hundred,' and I'm making more hundreds, then 'ten percent' just means one ten taken out of more hundreds. In other words, more tens."

"Ten percent of one hundred is one ten; ten percent of two hundred is two tens; ten percent of eleven hundred is eleven tens. Got it?"

The girl now corrected herself. "So it's still ten percent, but it's more money."

"Go on. How much is ten percent of four hundred?"

"Four tens. Forty dollars!"

"Right."

There was still time left before the bell, so we went on to figure out all the payroll deductions on my hypothetical monthly pay, yearly pay, and daily pay. After a brief introduction to other applications of percentages, I assigned some homework. The next day, I could build on what the class had just learned.

All this was made possible because they felt free enough, at the start of the class, to ask about my salary, and because I was not constrained by lockstep curricular requirements and lesson plans. I was free to make an unscheduled math lesson grow out of the curiosity they had about their teacher, and an enjoyable personal relationship.

But that wasn't the end of their curiosity. Just before the bell, some of the students returned to asking personal questions. I felt good about the lesson, and was happy to spend the last few minutes this way. Pasqual, a Puerto Rican boy from a big family, asked how long I had been married.

"About a year and a half."

"How many kids you got?"

"None. At least not yet."

The student was incredulous. "And you been married more than a year?"

"That's right," I answered, not quite sure what was strange about that.

"Wow!" shouted the boy, as he and many others rolled in laughter, "Charlie doesn't do it!"

The bell rang. Maybe later for a lesson on birth control. Maybe not.

Our teachers were very aware that doing the things which were working so well in this school would be discouraged, even penalized, elsewhere. Many had come to Ocean Hill–Brownsville specifically to find sanctuary from persecution they had endured in other New York City schools. Now identifying their opportunity for an inspiring and exciting teaching career with the survival of the community control experiment, they had both personal and professional reasons to fight for the survival of the demonstration district.

Steve Bloomfield, for example, had received a disciplinary transfer from his previous school for encouraging a cooperative spirit among his fourth-graders. Some colleagues had accused him of "teaching socialism" by not stoking individual cutthroat competition, and the principal agreed. Ellen Shumsky, our librarian, had deliberately kept herself on a lower status level (with a lower salary) than she was entitled to because this lower status gave her the freedom to voluntarily transfer out of a school whenever she encountered political harassment. Ron McFadden and other strong black teachers had undergone, for many years, the special treatment reserved for their "type" by racist administrators. Many new teachers, myself included, had learned from the experiences of others, and were pretty sure that our chances to flourish in any other district were limited. In effect, JHS 271 was a haven for political and professional refugees. Many could be relied upon to fight for this adopted community, with all the determination that characterized other types of refugees throughout history.

The excitement of this shared adventure had even captured some of the old guard. Marvand Holland, who distanced himself from Black Nationalism and all the other political ideologies debated daily in the teachers' lunchroom, had nevertheless become a passionate supporter of the educational program. In a *New York Times* interview, he compared being a teacher before and after the advent of Community Control: "The greatest joy (before) was the security of the job, the greatest sin was to rock the boat—to do something different. Now there is a new hope that we can really reach the children and do what we're here to do: Educate . . . If they succeed in killing this experiment, they will have killed a lot of hope." Several other teachers interviewed for that article, black and white, including me, echoed similar themes. Sylvia Vaughn, one of our experienced black teachers, described the staff this way:

> Here we have a new breed of teacher—both white and black—who has taken an interest in developing a better self-image within the children. We are instilling in them the desire to excel and the understanding that they can.[92]

She had resigned from the UFT and transferred to Ocean Hill–Brownsville because of the respective policies of each.

The atmosphere was contagious. The legendary independent journalist I. F. Stone reported on it after a late-October visit to JHS 271 and IS 55, where he observed classes and interviewed teachers:

> To visit the black-controlled schools . . . is like waking from a nightmare. The atmosphere was incredibly different from what I had been led to expect. I found black and white teachers, Jewish and gentile, working together not just peacefully but with zest and comradeship . . . The classes were orderly. There was none of that screaming, by teacher against pupil, and among the children, which is common in most NYC schools . . . I felt it would be a tragedy if this experiment in community control were shut down.[93]

Hanging over the heads of the loyal teachers was the much-discussed threat of being transferred to other schools, en masse, in the event the school was closed or the district dissolved. Having JHS 271 on a resume would be a kiss of death in many city schools. Shanker had demanded the wholesale removal of our staff, the closing of our school, and/or the dissolution of the district in many negotiation sessions. Superintendent Donovan had raised these ideas as well. Our teachers had good reason to fear being sacrificed by the Board of Education in order to appease the UFT. Still, we did not want to put the residents of the community in the position of having to fight for its teachers. These people were struggling for their own survival; we didn't want to become a distraction from that struggle.

The prospect of successful demonstration districts was an unspoken driver of the UFT's determination to destroy community control. The union had, from its birth, fought to protect mediocre and incompetent teachers who were retained, year after year, and even promoted based on nothing more than seniority and examination scores. Thanks to union contracts, only twelve teachers out of 54,235 had been fired for incompetence during the five previous years. Only 252, during that time, had even earned an "unsatisfactory" rating.[94] This in a school system widely regarded as a massive failure in educating its black and Puerto Rican students.

That the schools system was failing to properly educate black and Puerto Rican children was not in dispute. There was debate about the causes of the failure, ranging from underfunding to overcrowding to racist teachers to a "culture of poverty" that resisted education, but little debate about the end result. Even in the arguments and propaganda against radical change, almost none of it actually *defended* the status quo. Many individual teachers were understandably defensive about their own performance, which some had a right to be, but the case against community control could not be won on the grounds that things were really not all that bad. The closest argument to this was a remarkable statement from the lips of Albert Shanker himself:

> Sure, 80 to 85 percent are coming out of the slum schools after ten years as illiterate as when they started. But the 15 percent who are making it are not a negligible number. At least it's something.[95]

Since this was hardly a winning battle cry, it should have come as no surprise that the UFT and its allies worked so hard to shift the grounds of debate to such peripheral, invented issues as "due process" and "black anti-Semitism."

In Ocean Hill–Brownsville, we were teaching, and relating to children and parents, as though the change had already come. The forces of inertia and reaction were outside, not inside, our schools. Many of us were, in our most selfish, private thoughts, not really anxious for the strike to end, even though we were opposing it with everything we had. We knew we would have absolutely no influence over any potential settlement, and that the Governing Board, which represented only the community, not labor or management, would have little part to play in it either. We certainly hoped that our little experiment with community-controlled progressive education would survive the ultimate strike settlement, but we had good reason to worry that it might not. At the time, we had no idea how prescient these concerns would turn out to be.

Crossing the Lines

> (In) the first teachers' strike in 1960, those most concerned about job security were the ones that crossed the picket lines. Today . . . the success of the union . . . has made it the instrument of job security, and now the

> conservative and mediocre have become the union's majority. Now it is the radicals who break the picket lines. It is the conservatives, afraid of the black community, panicked about their jobs, who shout "scab" at those who oppose the strike.
>
> —Sol Stern (1968)[96]

Our educational sanctuary existed only within the four walls of JHS 271. Before penetrating those walls, both staff and students first had to get past raucous UFT picket lines and their massive police protection. I was never comfortable doing this.

I did not come from a union family, but I believed strongly in the trade union movement. Working since I was 13 years old in non-union shops, and in "part-time jobs" with full-time hours and no opportunity to join a union, I always looked forward to someday getting my first union card. My heroes included Joe Hill, Eugene Debs, John L. Lewis, Walter and Victor Reuther, and the thousands of workers who struck, picketed, sat down, slowed down, and laid down their lives for the right to organize.

Two years earlier, as president of LIU–Brooklyn's student government, I orchestrated the Student Council's first resolution concerning external events, a declaration of support for the striking teachers at St. John's University. A few months later, I found myself leading a two-week student strike, largely supported by our teachers, which led directly to the unionization of the LIU faculty.

For me, labor unions and strikes against management had always been presumed worthy of support. Picket lines were sacrosanct. But not this strike, not these picket lines, not this union.

Even for someone with no sense of labor history, crossing the picket lines had to be an unpleasant experience. When a teacher was spotted coming down the street on the way to school, the pickets would all turn in that direction, wave their signs around, and release a steady stream of invective.

"Scab!"

"Commie bastard!"

"Traitor!"

Surprisingly to me, the worst of this was not directed at the black teachers who had been accused of teaching "racism and revolution," but at the white teachers, like me. They considered us traitors not only to the teaching profession, but to the white race.

I tried walking past at a brisk pace, but didn't want to seem afraid of them. I tried staring back at them, but found this an unpleasant way to start the morning. Once, I tried shouting back, but felt stupid doing it.

On October 16, the third day of the third UFT strike, in a measure of desperation, I walked directly to one of the barricades that separated us from our tormentors, turned my back on them, folded my arms and simply stood there, smoking my pipe. It felt like calling out the schoolyard bully.

At first, the UFT pickets embraced this opportunity with enthusiasm, abandoning their circular march and gathering behind me at the barricade.

"Hey, Isaacs, where's your bodyguard? You'll need one!" I was a little startled that they knew my name, but probably shouldn't have been.

"Where are your lesson plans? Or don't you need any to teach hate?"

"Why don't you crawl back where you came from, you back-stabbing creep!"

And the inevitable, "Nigger-loving sonofabitch!"

I just stood there silently. A cop told me to move on for my own safety, but I wasn't moving until I was ready. A small, curious crowd gathered to watch. This attracted the press. Television cameras began whirring and flashbulbs popping. Failing to get a rise out of me, the UFT pickets became increasingly hysterical.

"You'll get yours, you miserable scab!"

"The Black Nazis will get *you* next!"

Finally, as the spectacle of their "professionalism" being captured on camera may have begun to dawn on the pickets, or just because they had exhausted their supply of invective, they lowered their voices and began to march back in their circle. The confrontation was over.

I quietly went on my way. Minor and insignificant though the incident had been, I felt pretty good about it.

The next morning, a parent ran over to me, the *Daily News* in hand. She opened it to the centerfold, where a photo featured a tall, sloppily dressed UFT picket, his mouth agape in a derisive sneer, shouting at me with my back turned. He had that ubiquitous sign hung around his neck, inscribed with large capital letters: "DIGNITY FOR ALL TEACHERS!"

The pickets harassed me much less after that incident, but when I found an alternate route to the school entrance, I often took advantage of that opportunity to avoid them.

I felt I had dealt reasonably well with the picket lines, but now I had to deal with notes that I found in my home mailbox, which must have been slipped in by neighbors who recognized my picture in the paper. For example,

> Dear Scab,
>
> Saw your picture in the paper.
> Hope you can live with yourself.
> Have you been intimidated yet?

My fan mail was also piling up. One anonymous letter called me a "commie bastard" and a "nigger-lover lout." It was handwritten in red pencil, in the neat cursive script of a schoolteacher.[97]

Neither side of any conflict ever thinks the press is treating them fairly. I had learned, though, that if you want your story to be told, you have to tell it. Even if only a fraction gets through, that's better than ceding the entire narrative to the other side. Some of the reporters covering Ocean Hill–Brownsville had also covered the LIU student strike, and knew I was approachable. So, by mid-October, my name had appeared in the news numerous times. I had also accepted an invitation from the editor of the *New York Times Magazine* to submit an article about JHS 271. (The deadline was November 15, my 23rd birthday.) Nearly every time I was mentioned in the press, there was a flurry of mail, most of it negative, some of it threatening. What spooked me most, though, were the anonymous little notes slipped into my home mailbox or under the door to my apartment.

The Leaflet Controversy

Shortly after the picket line incident, the postman delivered an envelope, without a return address, enclosing a single legal-size sheet. Handwritten at the top, it said, "Please circulate to your Jewish colleagues. Thank you, Rose Cohen." Underneath were reprints of two undated leaflets.

The first was introduced as the "VERBATIM TEXT of a leaflet distributed by the Parents Community Council of JHS 271." It called for the replacement of all white teachers with black and Puerto Rican teachers as soon as they become available for the jobs, and for community control of police, construction, contracting, repairs, and curriculum. Its overall tone was strongly pro-black and, it could be argued, anti-white. The contact shown was Ralph Poynter. The obvious reason for reprinting the leaflet was to portray Poynter as a "Black Racist" and connect him to Ocean Hill–Brownsville.

Certainly, there were individuals who would have agreed with the sentiments expressed in that leaflet, but it was almost certainly bogus. It was claimed to be a transcript of an "original leaflet" distributed in the community that had been "phoned in to a UFT representative." To my knowledge, no copy of that "original leaflet" has ever been produced. Further, there never was any organization called the "Parents Community Council of JHS 271." There was, at most, just one man with access to a mimeograph machine, who passed out a few flyers with that masthead near the school during the previous spring.

The alleged contact, Ralph Poynter, was a well-known black teacher who lived and worked in Manhattan. The contact phone number was listed in Manhattan, and was by then disconnected. At the close of the previous school year, his firing from a Harlem school for excessive absences provoked picketing, clashes with police, and arrests. I had met Poynter during the summer, and never considered him a racist. That was just my own impression of him. The more important point is that he had absolutely no connection to JHS 271 or to Ocean Hill–Brownsville. Why would an alleged Ocean Hill community organization be headed by someone not even from Brooklyn?

The "Poynter Leaflet," as it came to be known in the burgeoning controversy over alleged black anti-Semitism, said not one word about Jews.

The bottom half of the page was an alleged reprint of a flyer that it claimed had been "placed in teachers' mailboxes at JHS 271 and PS 144," but did not say when this had occurred or who had done it. That flyer was never in my mailbox, and I never met anyone who actually received it in theirs. McCoy said he did not see it until it after it became a public issue.[98] If any teachers actually did find these flyers in their mailboxes, they could have been put there by UFT teachers or functionaries, just to create an issue.

This second flyer was more inflammatory. It was crudely written. Every word began with a capital letter. Among its rantings were some of a decidedly anti-Zionist and possibly anti-Semitic nature. It was unsigned. Again, no original has ever been produced.

At the bottom of the page, printed in large capital letters was,

**IS THIS WHAT YOU WANT FOR YOUR CHILDREN?
THE UFT SAYS NO![99]**

My conclusion at the time was that someone at the UFT fabricated both of these alleged leaflets. I wasn't the only one who smelled fraud. Keith Baird, our district director of African-American and Latino Studies, was a trained sociolinguist. From his textual criticism of the leaflets, he concluded that "The locutions were not African-American, but in fact they were what a white European-American person would think an African-American person would say."[100]

Further doubt was cast by Jason Epstein, one of the nation's leading literary figures, who had taken a particular interest in the community control controversy. He investigated the "Parents Community Council" and reached the same conclusion I did, that it was nonexistent. "Either Mr. Poynter attempted to aggrandize himself by associating his views with an imaginary organization within Ocean Hill, in which case the UFT has perpetuated a fraud," he wrote in the *New York Review of Books*, "or the UFT is itself the source of the fraud, which, given the present bitterness within the city and the extremity of its racial tensions, is unforgiveable."[101]

More than twenty years later, another theory emerged when journalist Robert I. Friedman obtained FBI documents detailing the agency's campaign to disrupt the black Civil Rights movement and turn the Jewish community against it. "The Bureau's arsenal of dirty tricks," reported Friedman, "included mailing racist letters purportedly written by black extremists to white schoolteachers and union officials."[102]

Whether the leaflets originated in the offices of the FBI or of the UFT, and whether or not Albert Shanker was personally involved, their widespread dissemination became central to the UFT strategy. The union reproduced and distributed more than a half million copies throughout the city.

All these copies disseminated by the UFT combined the two leaflets. This method of reproduction associated the second leaflet, and its anti-Semitic tone, with the "Poynter Leaflet," which had the fictitious masthead associating it with JHS 271. Hundreds called the NYCLU to complain, most of whom were convinced that Ralph Poynter was an anti-Semitic official of the Ocean Hill–Brownsville district.[103] Even Fred Hechinger, education editor of the *New York Times*, conflated the two, writing that "Ralph Poynter . . . warned the 'Middle East murderers of colored people' to get out of Negro schools."[104] Even if Poynter was responsible for the first leaflet, which has never been verified, he was not in any way associated with the quote Hechinger attributed to him, which came from the second. The distribution of the document combining both alleged leaflets was an incredibly clever propaganda tactic.

The leaflet was reproduced and disseminated not only by the UFT and its members, but by a network of Jewish organizations and by Jewish merchants, who stacked copies on store counters. Jewish cab drivers handed them to passengers. They were distributed to commuters at subway entrances and to shoppers at store entrances. *Jewish Currents* magazine reported that it had received six different reproductions, from a variety of sources including Jewish War Veterans, the "Erasmus Hall Ad Hoc Committee," and others, and that it was reproduced in full in another Jewish publication's editorial. It warned that giving mass circulation to this leaflet "is to incite the Jewish community to a white backlash from which Jews too will suffer."[105]

The strategy, which would escalate during the coming months, was enormously successful. It consolidated Shanker's support within his own organization, and in the Jewish community as a whole. For many Jews, who were previously divided over the issue of community control, it changed the issue to "black anti-Semitism," overriding those divisions. For survivors of the European Holocaust, it resonated with terrifying memories.

Large sectors of New York City's Jewish community now felt themselves under siege. The fact that this widespread fear was based on misrepresentation and fraud made no difference. The fact that the Governing Board released a formal statement, printed in a *New York Times* advertisement, that disclaimed any connection to the leaflets and condemned "anti-Semitism in any form," made no difference.[106] The facts that half of the new teachers hired in Ocean Hill–Brownsville were Jewish, that not one of us expressed a single complaint about anti-Semitic attacks, and that 379 of the district's 541 teachers signed a statement denouncing the UFT fear campaign in a *New York Times* paid advertisement,[107] made no difference either.

The Anti-Defamation League investigated the leaflets. It concluded on October 23 that they were insignificant, and not the product of any organized effort (except that of the UFT). The NYCLU studied all the hate literature disseminated by the UFT (there were other leaflets as well), and concluded that the union's leadership had committed "multiple fraud." Furthermore, it said that the charges of "extremism and anti-Semitism" leveled at both McCoy and the Governing Board were based on "half-truths, innuendoes, and outright lies." Neither of these reports was widely reported in the press.[108] Neither made any difference at all.

Rabbi Marc Tannenbaum, a national official of the American Jewish Committee, charged that Shanker and the UFT were "using the Jewish community."[109] *New York Post* columnist Jimmy Breslin accused the UFT of "distributing the most unspeakable flood of racist literature since the days of Joe McCarthy." He began his column by stating, "Albert Shanker now stands as the worst public person I have seen in my time in the City of New York."[110] These made no difference.

Jewish Teachers for Community Control, an organization with 500 members, including myself as well as many UFT members, some of whom who were even supporting the strike, issued a statement at a news conference. It condemned anti-Semitism, but stated for the record that, "The struggle for community control of schools is NOT an anti-Semitic plot." It pointed out that half of the new teachers hired in Ocean Hill–Brownsville were Jewish, and that the Governing Board had issued two and only two statements concerning Jews: one explaining the observance of the religious high holidays; the other condemning anti-Semitism. It called on the UFT to negotiate with community-controlled school districts instead of trying to destroy them. Finally, it identified the interests of teachers with those of parents in the improvement of education.[111] This was reported in the press[112] and then forgotten, as was another plea issued by the nascent Council of Jews for Social Justice. Neither made any difference in the poisoned public atmosphere.

At least the teachers' statement got some press mention. In its coverage of indigenous community activists, the absence of anti-Semitism would have undermined the media plot-line. The young Ocean Hill activists of Project Method, for example, attended elementary school before the white exodus had even begun. "We would tell every reporter who raised the subject," Paul Chandler told me, "that we grew up with Jewish neighbors, that we had Jewish friends from school, that we celebrated Chanukah and other holidays with them." "But it never got into print," recalled Brother Sun, "and *that* was why we stopped talking to reporters."[113]

John O'Neill, an elected UFT vice-president and a union staff member, accused Shanker of "the most vicious racial demagogy ever practiced in this city," and said the UFT campaign had turned "a brush fire into a conflagration, sweeping across the city."[114] In his view, Shanker's exploitation of this issue, which was in its infancy at this time, was simply cynical. "He couldn't have held his side together without it," he said.[115] O'Neill's salaried staff position became a memory within a few weeks

Years later, the UFT's field representative in the district, Sandra Feldman, expressed her own second thoughts. "I believe it was a mistake to do that," she said. "I mean, to this day I don't think anybody knows exactly where that leaflet came from, or who put it in the boxes in that one school. And that did add to what was already a very difficult and divisive situation."[116] UFT chapter chairman Fred Nauman would also distance himself from that strategy.[117] In a 1996 interview, Ira Glasser of the New York Civil Liberties Union blamed the UFT for "whipping up" fears of anti-Semitism based on "manufactured" evidence, calling it "unforgiveable."[118] Shanker's authorized biographer, Richard D. Kahlenberg, wrote in 2007 that while the anti-Semitism gambit was tactically brilliant in changing the terms of the debate, "Even Shanker's defenders acknowledge that he overreached."[119]

Kahlenberg did some overreaching himself. In describing the May 13, 1968, blockade at JHS 271, aimed at preventing the dismissed UFT teachers from returning, he wrote that, "Extremists painted swastikas on the building."[120] His source for this could have been Shanker, who used it and other unsubstantiated charges in a furious late-May effort to kill the pending decentralization bill in Albany.[121] The source he cited, though, was Philip Taft's chapter on Ocean Hill–Brownsville in his adoring 1974 history of the UFT, which summarized a May 24, 1968, *Times* article where Shanker defended his references to Nazism.[122] (Taft's manuscript had been submitted to the UFT prior to publication.)[123] In the last two paragraphs of the referenced article, reported by Leonard Buder, McCoy accuses Shanker of "trying to turn the Jewish community against the ghetto community with emotionalism and talk of Nazism," and Shanker responds that, "Our references to Nazism are appropriate, in view of the fact that a school principal was removed from his school after extremists painted swastikas throughout the building."[124] He did not tell Buder that there were swastikas at JHS 271; Buder was on the scene that day, and would have known it wasn't true.

Buder apparently didn't ask Shanker where he alleged that the incident with the principal happened. In fact, it never happened. What did take place, a month earlier, was a four-day occupation of a principal's office in an ultimately successful protest against the appointment of a new principal. During a redecoration of the office, one of the occupiers pinned to the wall a picture of a swastika, with the words, "Stop Genocide of our Children."[125] The protesters were identifying Nazi-like genocide with the school system, not with themselves. (The principal was not "removed." He withdrew before taking office.) Nothing was "painted throughout the building." The school was located in the South Bronx.

This incident, which had nothing to do with Ocean Hill–Brownsville, was misrepresented by Shanker in his *Times* response, which was quoted without fact-checking in an article about Ocean Hill, then repeated in Taft's history, again without any apparent investigation. The greatest stretch, though, was where Kahlenberg used this chain of distortion to back up his claim that *swastikas had been painted on JHS 271*. It would be generous to charge him with "overreaching" in making this statement. It would not be unreasonable to conclude that he simply made it up in order to retroactively justify Shanker's campaign of fear. There were never any swastikas painted on the inside or the outside of JHS 271, and besides that claim, none of the other hostile press reports, articles, or books on the conflict, ever made this incendiary charge.

During the school wars, the UFT and its allies would repeatedly stoke these fires, raising the temperature in the climate of fear it had created. They would poison the well of reasoned discourse, and make reconciliation between the two sides impossible. The ties between the African-American and Jewish communities, forged through decades of common struggle against racism and discrimination, were quickly fraying. The consequences would be tragic.

As the strike dragged on through October and into November, cracks began to appear in the UFT juggernaut. Parents and teachers were able to open more schools around the city. Custodians, charged as defendants in numerous lawsuits, reevaluated the wisdom of their actions, and stopped trying to keep students and teachers out. Unions with large black and Puerto Rican memberships were breaking away from the Central Labor Council's united front of UFT support. Even within the UFT, a newly formed Black Caucus, including nearly all of the union's black leadership, announced "unequivocal support" for the Ocean Hill–Brownsville Governing Board.[126] On October 25, 100 black and Puerto Rican labor leaders, including UFT Assistant Treasurer Richard Parrish, announced their support as well.[127] On November 13, black officers of more than a dozen unions held an all-day sit-in at Council headquarters, and threatened an internal revolt.[128]

It was beginning to look like all that was holding Shanker's coalition together was its propaganda campaign against "gangsters, extremists, Nazis and anti-Semites." However, *Time Magazine* reported that, "Many New Yorkers were outraged by Shanker's own extremist rhetoric and by his arrogance in tying up the entire 1.1 million-pupil system over a dispute at one school."[129]

Meanwhile, negotiating sessions proliferated, virtually around the clock. Involved were not only Lindsay, Donovan, Shanker, and the central Board, but also State Commissioner Allen, labor mediator Theodore Kheel, Whitney Young of the National Urban League, Dr. Kenneth Clark, representing the

State Board of Regents, and many others. The Governing Board and McCoy were consulted on an arbitrary, inconsistent basis. Shanker's intransigence turned every creative proposal into a dead end. In the words of the *New York Times* editorial board:

> The union's refusal to accept an almost endless list of guarantees and commitments from city, state and district officials, even when backed by specific enforcement machinery, has taken the dispute out of any relation to even the most exaggerated definition of job security.[130]

Tensions continued to mount. The strike went on. In Ocean Hill–Brownsville, life, and teaching, went on as well.

The Wright Stuff

During this time, there were many evening community meetings and rallies. I don't think I missed a single one. When a meeting of the JHS 271 Parent-Teacher Association was announced, I made sure to attend. I had heard about the unprecedented levels of participation in the PTA's of the district's schools, so I was curious why this PTA waited until November to have the first meeting of such an eventful school year. My curiosity was soon satisfied.

After all the parent and community meetings I had been to, where the typical turnout was in the hundreds, I was amazed to find no more than a dozen parents attending a PTA meeting at the school on which the eyes of the city were focused. About half of those present were members of the executive board. The agenda consisted entirely of formalities, entirely lacking in content, and ended after about an hour. It seemed to me like sleepwalking through the apocalypse. I wondered whether I had made a wrong turn into some other school district.

Later that week, Clara Marshall explained it to me. She and I had spoken many times, but only about her daughter's progress in my math class. Mrs. Marshall was vice chairman of the Governing Board and a long-time community activist, so she seemed the right person to ask what was going on with the PTA.

As she explained it, the PTA was very active when Elaine Rooke was its president. When Mrs. Rooke became the school's parent representative on the Governing Board, it created a leadership vacuum at the PTA. This opportunity was quickly exploited by Josephine Wright, who "hijacked" the organization's leadership, and used her position as president to render the organization ineffective. Once she and her associates took control, the parents of JHS 271 lost their independent voice. A vehicle that would naturally have amplified the united voice of the parents and teachers of JHS 271 was rendered silent. But why?

It didn't take long for the rest of the story to be filled in. Mrs. Wright was married to Samuel D. Wright, the State Assemblyman and Democratic Party leader for the district that included Ocean Hill–Brownsville, and a dissident member of the Governing Board.

Sam Wright, 43, was a slim, good-looking man of average height with less than commanding oratorical skills. Still, he could attract attention from a block away. Always impeccably attired in perfectly fitting, expensive suits with bright, colorful accents, he was a small-time manifestation of what Major Owens recently labeled the "Peacock" species of African-American politicians.[131] Wright was a flamboyant, small-minded political ward boss, whose interest in empowerment extended only to the power that accrued to him.

Wright had been trying to depose the Governing Board for several months by that time, hoping to trigger a new election that his political club could control. He had a strong vested interest in preventing any voices being raised in support of the Board, especially from JHS 271. His close ties to Brooklyn's white-dominated Democratic Party machine were no secret. Neither was his long-term goal to put himself in charge of the school district, which he could use as a patronage mill to broaden his own power base. Community activists had little doubt that he would, quite willingly, cut deals with the UFT or anyone else that could help him accomplish those goals.

Assemblyman Wright, with his wife's help, had neutralized the latent power of the JHS 271 PTA. They had not, however, silenced either the parents or the teachers. He tried, but failed, to mobilize active, visible community-based opposition to the Governing Board. During September, he announced a public reconciliation, stating at a community rally that he "supports the Governing Board one thousand percent."[132] Up in Albany, though, he would spend the next several months laying the groundwork for a coup imposed from above.

Teaching Future Teachers

One evening, I was having dinner with Elaine Waldman, a friend who taught in LIU's Department of Education. A maverick in her profession, she gave me her view of teacher education in New York City.

"Education majors," she said, "have to sit through courses that are totally irrelevant to making them competent teachers. Too many of these courses are taught by people who wouldn't know how to make a course relevant if they had the chance. Middle-class white professors are assigned to teach middle-class white college students how to relate to poor black and Puerto Rican youngsters.

Instead, they propagate concepts of 'cultural deprivation,' 'non-verbality,' and other excuses for failure, instead of helping them become successful teachers. How can white teachers ever relate to black kids if their own racist beliefs are reinforced, instead of being challenged? Even the student teaching experience, which might provide them with their only experience in non-white communities, focuses on little besides enforcing discipline." "It's no wonder," she summed it up, "that so many teachers never survive their first year in a real live classroom."

Then came the idea that lay behind her dinner invitation. She proposed that I bring some of my students to her LIU classroom. The objective of the visit would be dialogue. Students would have an opportunity to confront future teachers, and vice versa, in an informal setting outside of their traditional roles and relationships. Perhaps, she hoped, the sensitivities of both groups could be sharpened. This sounded to me like it was worth a try.

Back at school the next day, I asked my sharpest eighth-grade class if they would be interested in this excursion. I wasn't prepared for the response. Some of the boys indicated, for example, that colleges, to them, were just sponsors of black basketball players. They had never personally known anyone who had gone to college except to play basketball. The idea of higher education was foreign to their experience.

A pretty sophisticated objection, for a 13-year-old, was raised by one of the class leaders. Brenda Martin had presented me with challenges since the beginning of the term. She was obviously very bright, and certainly capable of grasping the math concepts I presented, but she refused to do homework, paid little attention, and maintained a distant, suspicious attitude toward all of her teachers. The few occasions when I had broken through her shield were among my most satisfying moments, but she remained more a source of frustration most of the time.

"I ain't gonna be no guinea pig!" Brenda exclaimed vehemently.

"What do you mean?"

"People always be studyin' us. They say, 'Look at those animals. Let's put 'em under the microscope.' I ain't no animal, and I ain't gonna be studied."

Brenda had a point. There had been no shortage of social scientists, researchers, and various forms of voyeurs studying the denizens of the ghetto. Brownsville, because of its multitude of problems, was a favored subject. After testing, questioning, sampling, and analyzing, they had collected their grant money, written books, and pronounced themselves "experts." At the end of all the studies, and the expenditure of millions of dollars, nothing changed for the better in the lives of black and Puerto Rican people. Brenda was right. They had been subjected to the humiliating treatment of caged animals. All it had done was reinforce the impression among white people that the ghetto was, indeed, a zoo. She refused to be any part of it.

This wasn't what I had in mind, though, and I knew that the interaction, if it occurred, would have to be structured so that it wouldn't fit into this pattern. I had some explaining to do.

"Look at it this way," I said, "They won't be studying you. You'll be studying them! When they ask you questions, you can ask questions back. You won't have to defend yourselves about anything. *You'll be teaching the teachers.*"

The idea of role reversal intrigued many of the students, and they voted to give it a try. Brenda reluctantly agreed to come along, as well as to be on the panel that would represent the class, along with four classmates. It was also agreed that the rest of the class, sitting in the "audience," would be free to speak up at any time.

Some of the students' anxiety had been transferred to their teacher, though. I was wondering now whether this was really a good idea. The students would be on their own once the panel was convened, and my intervention under pressure would smack of paternalism. I had confidence in the class, but just hoped that it was justified.

It turned out to be more than justified. Five black students on the panel faced an audience of seventy-five white college students. The format was question-and-answer, with allowance for dialogue and debate. Hostile questions were met with the most honest answers. Ignorant innuendo was responded to with disarming frankness.

Generally, the college students, most of them probable future members of the UFT, reflected badly uninformed public opinion. One of the most startling moments, for all involved, came when the panel was asked, "Isn't there really a lot of bad feeling between blacks and whites in 271?"

Brenda jumped in with an answer. "No. The black people in the school get along fine with most of the whites. The only people who we don't get along with are *the Negroes*!"

Brenda's reply triggered a wave of condescending snickering among some in the audience. She was challenged to explain precisely what the difference was between a black man and a Negro. Once again, she came through.

"Let me put it like this," she explained. "Suppose the white massa drops paper on the floor and says to pick it up. Some ol' Uncle Tom Negro would just say, 'Yassuh,' and hurry on over to pick up that paper, jus' like he was told. Now, a black person, *or an Afro-American*, would stand up tall and tell whitey to pick up his own goddamn garbage. He'd say, 'We been workin' for you too long already. It's time you started cleanin' up your own house!' "

Brenda wasn't finished. "You see, I consider myself an Afro-American, and we gonna take care of business with the Uncle Toms just as soon as we done with the UFT." End of that question.

The session continued, the questions asked with diminishing smugness, and answered by all five members of the panel.

"What will you do if the UFT teachers come back? Suppose you're in one of their classes."

"Well, I just wouldn't do what they say. If the teacher says to copy something on the board, for instance, I just wouldn't do it."

"But he would still be your teacher. Shouldn't you do as he says?"

"He wouldn't be *my* teacher; I just might have to sit in his classroom for a while. After walking out on us like they did, we're not gonna let them strut back in and start ordering us around again, like nothing happened in between."

"Don't you think the UFT teachers have a reason to be on strike? Have you ever asked them about the cause they're fighting for? Have you ever tried to find out something about the other side?"

Another backfire. "I don't know why they think they walked out. I ask the UFT pickets all the time why they're walking around in circles in the rain and in the cold, and they never answer me. As far as I'm concerned, they're on strike because they're against me, because I'm a kid and because I'm black."

Not all the college students were hostile, and many seemed genuinely interested in finding out about the innovations and changes in Ocean Hill–Brownsville. One asked what was taught in the new Afro-American History course. He was given a few examples and referred to Malcolm X's lectures, which had been distributed to all eighth-grade students.

Another said she had read reports that children were running wild in the school and terrorizing the staff. She asked how school discipline compared with that of earlier years.

"Before, the kids used to act bad," explained one of the boys, "because they didn't respect the teachers. Nothing was being taught and the kids didn't see any reason to sit still and be bored."

"Right. Now things are different," added another. "We have mostly good teachers, so we do what we're supposed to do. Sure, we kid around with Charlie sometimes, but when he says we should do math, we do it. We're more relaxed, but we learn more too."

At a student's mention of a teacher's *first* name, mouths dropped open. Whispers of disapproval buzzed around the room. "*Charlie?* Who do those kids think they are?"

After the initial shock, one person asked, "Do you call all your teachers by their first names?"

"No, just him."

The collective sigh of relief was deafening. At least their whole world wasn't crumbling. There was apparently only one teacher who threatened the time-honored pedagogical perquisite of titled address. They asked me why I allowed students to take such liberties.

I explained, as well as I could, about transcending age, race, and class barriers. Some showed some interest in what I was saying. They asked how the kids reacted to the idea, and why more teachers didn't do the same thing.

"This 'name thing' is an experiment," I said. "Actually, it was totally unplanned, but the results so far seem to be good. At first, some of the students giggled and reacted immaturely, but it took hold within a couple of days. Those who felt more comfortable calling me 'Mr. Isaacs' kept on doing it, and those who were comfortable with the informality went ahead and called me by my first name. Now, there are many reasons why other teachers haven't tried this, like habit or fear, or legitimate disagreement on educational grounds. The black teachers have the strongest basis for projecting authority, because the children need this from them. This is why the black teachers have taken primary responsibility for maintaining discipline in the school."

The discussion continued, at a livelier pace than it had begun. I realized that I had unwittingly become a part of the panel, but also that my apprehensions about paternalism were baseless. The children had no need for any help, and I was only answering questions directed specifically at me.

Meaningful dialogue was actually being achieved, a rare accomplishment in any setting during those turbulent months. After an hour and a half, the session broke up, with the college students enthusiastically applauding their eighth-grade instructors. I happily joined in the applause.

I could not have been prouder of my students. I felt drawn even closer to them than I had been before. This was one of the high points of the year for me. Once again, I learned more than I taught.

The class spent that afternoon visiting the LIU Computer Laboratory, and being shown how to use some of the equipment. Leo Barnett, the lab's director, who was opposed to the UFT strike and was fighting to keep schools open in his own neighborhood, gave the students a warm welcome. While they learned about computers, which none of them had ever seen before, and about new careers in the field, they also learned that they had allies in white neighborhoods. But the visit to the computer lab, the "official" purpose of the field trip cleared by the administration, was anti-climactic after the morning session, for both the children and their teacher.

When I asked the class whether they thought they had taught their audience anything, Brenda was quick to answer. "Nah. They'll never learn." Others were less cynical, though, and I thought I even detected a slight gleam of satisfaction in Brenda's eyes.

It came as no surprise to me, a couple of years later, when I heard that Elaine Waldman had been fired.

Teacher Evaluations

At one point during the morning's discussion at LIU, the students brought up some shortcomings they perceived in a few of their teachers. One teacher, they felt, wrote too much on the chalkboard; another "talked too much"; another was too strict and authoritarian. I knew these teachers, I felt that most of them were trying to do a good job and might be unaware of their students' gripes.

During the subway ride back home, I asked the students why they didn't just present their complaints to those teachers. If they had complaints about me, I certainly would want to know about them. The children, so outgoing and articulate off school limits and in my classes, were too inhibited to confront other teachers with their grievances. I felt like I was on a roll with this class, and resolved to help them find a way to get their message across.

Two days later, following a brief discussion, the class chose a committee to prepare an evaluation form that they would use to rate their teachers. The committee drafted 15 questions, according to criteria they themselves selected, and brought them to the class for a vote. Following debates and amendments (a little lesson in democratic procedure), the questionnaire was finalized. In order to encourage honesty, it was agreed that they would be completed anonymously.

My job was to provide technical assistance. At first, all I did was edit the questions, strictly for grammar, and then type up and reproduce the questionnaire, so each student could fill one out about each of his or her teachers.

The following is the text of what was, to my knowledge, the first teacher evaluation form developed entirely by students in any New York City school.

Experimental Teacher Evaluation Project

Teacher's Name ____
Subject ____

1. Do you feel that you are learning?
   a (no)   b   c   d   e   f (a lot)

2. Does the teacher keep you interested?
   Yes   No   Sometimes

3. Does the teacher talk too much?
   Yes   No   Sometimes

4. Is the teacher too strict?
   Yes   No   Sometimes

5. Does the teacher write too much on the board?
   Yes   No   Sometimes

6. Does the teacher let the students be active in the class discussions?
   Yes   No   Sometimes

7. Does the teacher give too much or too little homework?
   Too Much Too Little OK

8. Do you think this is a good teacher?
   Yes No Undecided

9. Does the teacher answer students' questions?
   Yes No Yes, but not enough

10. Is the teacher a dictator?
    Yes No Sometimes

11. How is the teacher's personality?
    Excellent Good Fair Unsatisfactory

12. Does the teacher get along with the class?
    Yes No Sometimes

13. Does the teacher seem interested in the subject?
    Yes No Sometimes

14. Does the teacher grade fairly?
    Yes No

15. Is the homework interesting to do?
    Yes No Sometimes

Do you think these were good questions?

Why?______________________________
Why not? ____________________________

Would you like to continue this project?

Why?______________________________
Why not? ____________________________

The questions about homework resulted from a pretty high level of debate. The result was a rating based not only on whether the teachers assigned *too much* homework, but also *too little*. Personally, I was not a big fan of homework, and had done very little of it in my own junior high and high school years. In conversations with black parents when I was tutoring in the housing projects, though, I learned that one of their biggest grievances was that their children came home from school without books or homework. This was a clear signal to them that nothing was going on in the classroom, a generally accurate one. The phrasing of this survey indicated that the eighth-graders themselves felt the same way. They wanted to go home with some homework. All they asked was that the assignments be interesting.

Once the survey results were in, I showed the class how to tabulate them (a stealth lesson in basic percentages and statistics). We prepared two copies of the statistical results for each teacher being evaluated: one for the teacher and one, the students insisted, for the principal.

The class hoped to refine their technique after this experimental trial run, and to extend the project to a larger group of students, perhaps to the whole grade or even the entire school.

When the totals were tabulated and distributed to the teachers, their reactions varied widely. Some were grateful to have this opportunity to find out what their students thought of them. Since traditional teacher ratings were based primarily on classroom control, they welcomed the more substantive and meaningful student evaluation. Many took further advantage of the students' initiative and discussed the "report card" with them in class.

Others, however, primarily those few with seriously negative ratings, were not so appreciative. Some browbeat the class, trying to find out who was responsible for this mutinous action, and threatened the class leaders with disciplinary action. The students stuck together, though, because they felt they had exercised their rights. They weren't taking back anything they had said about those teachers, except perhaps to make their evaluations a little more caustic.

It was no secret that I had helped the students with the project. One teacher threatened to have me fired for "instigating rebellion." ("Stirring up the natives," was my translation.) There was no feedback, positive or negative, from the principal. When I mentioned it to McCoy a few weeks later, he just smiled and nodded. If there had been a functioning UFT chapter in the school, though, grievances would likely have been filed.

Tempers cooled after a few days, and the only lasting results of the evaluation seemed to be positive, minor as they might have been. Most important to me, though, were not any changes it may have brought about in teacher behavior or attitude, but rather what it had done for the students.

The encounter at LIU and the ensuing teacher evaluation project, both of which were possible only in the atmosphere that prevailed in Ocean Hill–Brownsville, had helped these students find their voices. Now, they had a taste of personal and collective power. They had functioned as citizens of a community, with rights that demanded recognition, and with thoughts of their own that demanded consideration. This aspect of the experience could be as valuable to them as any facts they might have been taught in the classroom. A new dimension of empowerment was evolving in the school that had become the symbol of the Community Control movement.

None of this was planned. I could never have predicted the direction these two projects would take. This had been another wonderful educational opportunity, for my students and for me. The environment that nurtured it, though, would soon be gasping for oxygen, strangled by the terms of the impending strike settlement.

Too Little, Too Late

The article I wrote for the Sunday *New York Times Magazine* appeared on November 24, 1968, a week after the final strike settlement. "A JHS 271 Teacher Tells It Like He Sees It" was featured as the magazine's cover story. (My suggested title had been, "A JHS 271 Teacher Tells It *Like It Is*.") It described our 70 percent white teaching staff, and the positive interactions evolving among black and white teachers. It told of some of the challenges we faced in the school, the innovative steps we were taking to overcome them, and the deliberate disruption of those efforts by the massive police presence and by the imposition of the returning UFT teachers. It testified to the positive qualities of the leadership provided by Vann and Campbell, and to my failure to discover the slightest evidence of anti-Semitism in either the school or the community. In so doing, it exploded many of the myths about conditions in the school that were circulating around the city.[133]

This article was the first, and ultimately the only, first-person insider's account to appear in a mass circulation publication, relating what was actually happening at JHS 271 during the teacher strikes. Nearly all of the extensive press coverage of the school until then had been about conflict. These reports hardly ever mentioned what was happening in the classrooms, and were nearly always biased in favor of the UFT. Typical was the lengthy, front-page *Times* report on the October 9 events, which quoted Fred Nauman and union observers in the school, but not a single one of the loyal teachers.[134] In a critique of his own profession, a veteran *New York Post* reporter wrote in *The Nation*, shortly before my article was published,

> I began to get an inkling of how poorly we were performing when I spoke to some of my colleagues in Manhattan. Most had gotten the impression that Ocean Hill was a wasteland, filled with angry warriors waiting for the signal to attack. Most believed that the schools were populated by angry children, defiant and ready to slit the throat of the nearest white man.[135]

The Sunday edition of the *New York Times* had a national readership of many millions in 1968, and the magazine was its most popular section. The editor, Harvey Shapiro, later told me that the paper received a record number of letters after the article appeared. The "Letters to the Editor," at least those that it published, were nearly all negative, the vast majority written by local teachers. One letter charged that we were "teaching hate," based on my account of Steve Mayer's "Ballad of the Landlord" lesson. Another attacked me for defending Vann and Campbell, charging that I must have been elsewhere, or not paying attention, when they were spewing hatred of whites and Jews. Others accused me of denigrating the history of teacher unionism, the city's entire teaching staff, and Western civilization's accumulated body of knowledge. The *Times* also came in for some hectoring for publishing the article at all.[136]

My own mailbox was bulging. The missives I received ranged from love letters to death threats. It was gratifying to receive "fan mail" from educational reformers like Jonathan Kozol and Nat Hentoff, and from local civil rights figures. But even more heartwarming were the letters of support written, some with obvious emotion, by ordinary people from all over the country, and some from other countries. A few even included little gifts. There were also many offers of speaking engagements, far more than I was able to accept. One lasting regret is that I couldn't possibly visit all of the high school and college classes that invited me.

Many publishers, authors, and college professors requested permission, which I readily granted, to reprint the article in anthologies and course materials. Even the U.S. Army War College made such a request. (In that one case, we were unable to agree on terms.)

In dozens of other letters, I was accused of being a fool, a naïve tool of dangerous extremists, an anti-Semite, and a nigger-lover. Many writers drew analogies to Weimar and Nazi Germany, and to anti-Zionist attitudes in the Middle East. Some were astounded that the *Times* would print an article written by such a young upstart, and a few questioned my ability, given my age, to even have actually written it.[137]

A ten-page, single-spaced "open letter" from an Alexander Kohanski argued, among other things, that calls to increase the number of black teachers in black schools are inherently anti-Semitic, because there would then be fewer jobs for Jewish teachers, and attacked me for collaborating with the enemy. In a way, this got to the heart of the matter, since any movement of the black poor into the middle class would inevitably bump into traffic posed by the Jewish teachers, social workers, and civil servants who then dominated these occupations. Kohanski's argument, which was achieving traction among Jewish intellectuals during the late 1960s, was that support for the black freedom struggle should be abandoned if its goals were not "good for the Jews." Rabbi Michael Lerner, my generation's voice of progressive Judaism, might have been responding directly to Dr. Kohanski when he pointed out that,

> The Torah tradition says that you have to be morally sensitive to the needs of others, even it's not in your self-interest. There's nothing in there that says, "Look, if it's in your interest, love your neighbors, but if it's not in your interest, screw 'em." It's just not what's in the Torah.[138]

So maybe Dr. Kohanski was the guilty party in this debate, not of being anti-Semitic, but of being anti-*Jewish*.

I was puzzled at the time why anyone would take the time to write me such a long letter. Six months later, when I went to Princeton University to address students at its Hillel Foundation, the mystery was cleared up. I was handed an issue of a Jewish bi-weekly, *Reconstructionist*, which was organized around its publication of that open letter. The journal's lead editorial somehow linked me to the Hellenist Jews who collaborated with Antiochus, the second-century Seleucid king whose forced assimilation policies included banning the study of Torah.[139] (I thought that was stretching the point a bit.) The students had been given copies in advance, and we had a lively, enjoyable conversation.

My hope was that my story's publication in the national "newspaper of record" might have some effect on public attitudes, and just maybe affect the course of events. If ever there had been a chance of that, however slight, events had already overtaken it. The strike would be settled, on the UFT's terms, a week before the article appeared. Based on the volume of positive mail, and on anecdotal reports, it may have changed a few minds, but it appeared at least two weeks too late to have an impact on events.

Mine was probably the most widely circulated positive report on Ocean Hill–Brownsville schools up until then, but it was far from the only one. *The New Yorker*, for example, reported that there was "much less disorder in the halls and in the classrooms than people have come to expect in slum district schools."[140]

Jason Epstein wrote that,

> The schools . . . lack the feeling, so common in New York City ghetto schools, of superheated aviaries, fetid, caged and shrill, but suggest a kind of purposeful gaiety, derived partly no doubt from knowing that they are parts of an embattled outpost on whose survival so much of the future depends.[141]

Dwight MacDonald, another noted New York intellectual, formerly a supporter of the UFT's position, was now one of its harshest critics. Critical to that conversion were his visits to four Ocean Hill–Brownsville schools, where he sat in on a dozen classes. His report:

> I was impressed . . . by the friendly, serious, relaxed atmosphere; by the easy way the young, mostly white teachers related to their pupils, talking to them without condescension; by the order, if not exactly quiet, in the halls . . . I don't remember hearing a teacher raise his or her voice the whole day . . . The teachers generally seemed to like their pupils and find them interesting and vice versa, so that a mild disorderly hum of cooperative effort was the usual classroom atmosphere. I'm told it used to be rather different. . . .[142]

There was also the testimony of Agee Ward, a social scientist on leave from his university post, who had been living in Brownsville for four months doing participant-observer research. In a journal published by a unit of the U.S. Department of Education, he summarized what his trained eye observed in Ocean Hill–Brownsville schools during this period:

> Repeated visits showed teachers and supervisors—white and black, Jewish and Gentile—enthusiastically working together with an obvious spirit of comradeship. Also present and ready to help . . . were parent volunteers . . . Inside the classrooms, orderly and attentive groups of children participate in lessons . . . Jewish teachers, who say they have encountered no anti-Semitism, relate happily that for the first time they are being allowed to use non-traditional teaching approaches, and speak enthusiastically about the positive results in student achievement . . . The observer roaming corridors, visiting lunchrooms, and watching playgrounds, sees plenty of youthful energy displayed, but fails to find any destructive rowdyism.
>
> It is being demonstrated now that a multi-ethnic but largely white teaching corps can function effectively in Ocean Hill, with loyalties to a largely non-white authority and in service to a program especially designed for black and Puerto Rican children. It would be hard to find in the United States today a more striking expression of the antithesis of racism in actual operation.[143]

All this was too little, too late. I had no idea at the time, though, of the magnitude of the threat that the strike settlement would pose to the atmosphere of learning and mutual, interracial cooperation that we had created in our school.

The Strike Is Settled

By mid-November, public pressure to bring an end to the strike became irresistible. Besides the educational damage it had caused by blowing a hole in a fifth of the school year, besides the racial tensions and antagonisms it had exacerbated, the economic costs to the city were staggering. The Transit Authority's loss of $5 million in revenue from student bus and subway fares would soon lead to a fare increase. School bus companies lost almost as much. Suppliers of food to school lunchrooms (where children missed tens of millions of hot meals) lost $3 million. The school system lost $25 million in daily-attendance state aid, while vandalism and thefts added to its costs. Untold numbers of hourly workers such as school bus drivers and lunchroom workers were laid off. Neighborhood candy stores, printers, five-and-dime stores, and other small businesses suffered collateral damage. With their children home, parents missed work or scrimped to pay babysitters. Winter vacations were canceled. The total economic cost was estimated at $7.8 billion, more than the annual budget of the entire New York State government.[144]

Early on Sunday, November 17, after Ocean Hill–Brownsville's representatives walked out of all-night negotiations in which they had been ignored, an agreement was reached among the UFT and CSA leadership, the Board of Regents, the Board of Education, Superintendent Donovan, Commissioner Allen, and Mayor Lindsay. Once it was ratified by the UFT Delegate Assembly that night, the third citywide strike would be over, after five long weeks. Their agreement contained the following main provisions:[145]

1. The Ocean Hill–Brownsville district was put under the direct control of the State Education Department. Dr. Herbert Johnson, an assistant to Commissioner Allen, was designated as its Trustee, with "total responsibility for the orderly operation of the schools."
2. Observers separately chosen by the Trustee, the UFT, and the Board of Education, would be assigned to each of the district's schools. The Trustee was empowered to remove any of our teachers upon reports of interference with the "rights" of any returning UFTers.
3. The suspension of the Ocean Hill Governing Board would continue until it was reinstated by Commissioner Allen or his Trustee, "in consultation with all the parties" and after he has been "assured . . . that it will comply with all orders and agreements, that orderly operation . . . has been restored, and that governance . . . may properly be returned to the community." Even after reinstatement, the Trusteeship would continue "until the orderly operation of the district has been assured."
4. Three principals—William Harris of JHS 271, Ralph Rogers of PS 144, and Luis Fuentes of PS 155—were removed from their schools and reassigned to central headquarters. The

invalidation of their appointments had been upheld by a 3–2 decision of the Appellate Division during the previous week, but the further appeal announced by the city would otherwise have kept them in their posts until the Court of Appeals issued a final ruling.[146]

5. Neither Rhody McCoy nor any of the district's other principals would be reinstated until they explicitly agreed to follow the orders of the Trustee.

6. Campbell, Vann, Curtis and Hopkins were reassigned to the district office, pending hearings by the Trustee on the charges filed after the October 9 incident (which not only violated the union contract, but contradicted the UFT's "due process" rationale for the first strike).

7. The 79 UFT teachers who still wanted to return to the Ocean Hill–Brownsville schools would receive "regular teaching assignments." They would get their programs in advance, including their room and class assignments, along with the names of their pupils.

8. Admission to the Ocean Hill–Brownsville schools would now be severely restricted, with registration procedures for those selected persons eligible to be admitted, including parents and those individuals specifically cleared in advance by the Trustee. (This provision was later interpreted to exclude even the members of the Governing Board.)

9. Both the pro-community teachers and the returning UFT teachers would now be prohibited from holding any meeting that excluded the other group.

10. A State Supervisory Committee (later known as the Israelson Commission) will be appointed, and staffed with investigators, to handle "teacher misconduct" throughout the city, with jurisdiction "concurrent with that of the Board of Education" and the unilateral right to suspend any teacher charged or under investigation.

11. Longer school days, and elimination of many of the remaining holidays, in all city schools were scheduled to allow the teachers returning from their illegal strike to recoup lost wages. They also received protection from any and all "reprisals."

12. The long-standing practice of involuntary transfers was ended, and would now be subject to the entire drawn-out UFT

> grievance procedure, including arbitration, as per the September 10 contract. With that stroke, the central Board's interim decentralization plan, which had gained State approval, was rendered moot. ("I just threw that in at the last minute," Shanker later admitted to an interviewer, "something you'd never do in ordinary, honorable negotiations.")[147]

This agreement represented a huge defeat for Ocean Hill–Brownsville and for the entire Community Control movement, neither of which had been represented in the negotiation. A foreign overseer was appointed to run the district's schools; McCoy and the Governing Board were stripped of their powers; the leadership of JHS 271 was removed from the school, and two other principals from theirs; the UFT teachers were not only returned but given preferential treatment; and the striking teachers would all be made financially whole for any inconvenience they might have endured during their illegal strike, notwithstanding the billions they had cost the city and its citizens. As word of the settlement spread that Sunday afternoon, each element of the Ocean Hill–Brownsville community mobilized to plan a response. Enforcement of the settlement was scheduled to begin the following morning.

Less than two hours after the deal was announced, the JHS 271 Steering Committee gathered in a teacher's apartment. If we were to have a collective response when school opened in the morning, there wasn't much time for planning.

After some discussion, a provisional plan of action was adopted by consensus:

1) We would urge our four suspended colleagues to return to the school as usual, not to accept their reassignments.
2) Since we couldn't verify the identity or authority of any outsiders, we would continue to accept and follow directives from Harris, McCoy and the Governing Board, either in person or by telephone.
3) We would follow our regular class programs.
4) Homeroom teachers would follow instructions from any parents to take responsibility for keeping their children away from returning UFT teachers.
5) All parents would be contacted, and we would urge the faculties of other district schools to adopt the same plan.

The thrust of our response was that the settlement was illegitimate and unworthy of recognition, since the Governing Board had not been party to it.

With this plan in hand, we adjourned to attend the evening strategy meeting that was called by the Governing Board.

Since the terms of the settlement weren't publicized until after Sunday church services, there was little time to publicize the meeting that had to take place that night. As a result, the hundred or so people who attended were among the Governing Board's most active supporters, including teachers, ministers, parents, and leaders of various community groups.

When our group arrived, two prominent Bedford-Stuyvesant ministers and civil rights activists, Rev. Calvin Marshall and Rev. William A. Jones, were beginning to address the gathering. I had heard both men preach, and was looking forward to an effective, if somewhat theatrical, presentation. My more experienced colleagues had more cynical expectations, which turned out to be correct.

Rev. Jones argued that the answer to the needs of the community lay in selective economic pressure. Pointing out that the Christmas shopping season was approaching, and claiming that the big department stores were overstocked with inventory, he unveiled his proposal of a "Christmas Whiteout," a "massive economic boycott" by black shoppers of every store in Manhattan, "from Central Park to 14th Street, and river to river." This would be, he said, "the greatest economic sanction in the history of the western world!" He forecast the threat of widespread bankruptcy among the largest chain and department stores, the owners of which would presumably pressure the Mayor and the State Legislature to finally grant the communities genuine control of their schools.

The ministers, though, were preaching to the wrong congregation. Most of the people present, tired and depressed at the prospect of defeat, were staring straight ahead with bored expressions on their faces. They had all heard enough utopian proposals during the preceding months to last them a lifetime, and the preachers' hyperbolic rhetoric was nothing new to them. The idea of pulling off such a boycott in a couple of weeks was patently ridiculous. Except for a few impressionable young white teachers, this proposal to "put capitalism up against the wall" excited no one.

Then, as Rev. Marshall was warming up for a second pitch, someone rushed in with unexpected news. The UFT Delegate Assembly, called together for pro forma approval of the settlement, had balked! Since the agreement did not include Shanker's most publicized demand, the total dissolution of the experimental districts, his deal was being labeled a "sellout" by his most rabid supporters. Many delegates were refusing to end the strike on these terms.

A television was brought into the room, just in time for the ten o'clock news. The report was accurate. The UFT Delegate Assembly was in disarray. Speakers on all sides were being shouted down by opposing factions. Shanker had clearly lost control of the situation, which he called "an atrocity" and "a disgrace." So angry and flustered was he that he utilized one of his own code words, which now had come full circle to boomerang right in his own union hall. "The constitution does not require me to conduct a mob," he exclaimed, "It requires me to conduct a meeting." With that, he adjourned the assembly and scheduled a membership referendum on the deal for the next day.[148]

In our gathering, this spectacle provided a welcome, totally unexpected, dose of comic relief. The room burst into laughter and applause. Shanker was sweating on television, rejected by his own union and left with a strike settlement he couldn't sell to either side. Some wondered what would happen if the UFT didn't ratify the agreement. "Maybe," someone mused aloud, "there's still a chance."

Whitney Young, Executive Director of the National Urban League, rose to address the meeting. During the settlement negotiations, Young had often urged the Governing Board to accept deals that it considered nothing less than humiliating. He now tried to convince the gathering that the strike settlement was actually good for Ocean Hill–Brownsville. He echoed some of the union delegates, who had argued that it was really a defeat for the UFT since the union hadn't won every single one of its demands. He pleaded with the people to accept the settlement, and to carry on business as usual, in order to "save the concept of decentralization." His audience was more interested in the realities of the situation to be faced in the morning than in "concepts," though. Young's organization did not have a base in the community, and some didn't even know who he was. His appeal was not favorably received.

Next to make a similar appeal was Dr. Kenneth Clark. Representing the State Board of Regents in the negotiations, he was a consistent advocate for the community, often the only one in the room. Here and now, though, Clark echoed Young in arguing for acceptance of the settlement. He presented this path as a strategic tactic in an ongoing campaign. "The fight has just begun," he said. Folks who had been fighting for real community control, attending meeting after meeting, rally after rally, breaking through police lines and being arrested, were getting the feeling, though, that the fight was just about over.

Clark went even further. He presented the apparent defeat as an actual victory, and appealed to the residents of the community "not to turn this victory into defeat." From time to time, impatient members of the audience interrupted Clark, but others insisted on allowing him to continue. People started drifting out of the room, though. It was now 11 p.m. Everyone was getting tired, but Clark was just getting started. He had just come from the weekend's round-the-clock negotiations, and still seemed to be bursting with energy. I couldn't agree with his argument, but I had to envy his stamina.

He spent the next half hour presenting a legal analysis of the strike settlement's terms, emphasizing again that a few of Shanker's demands, such as total abolition of the demonstration district, had not been granted. He argued that the agreement was "worded" in favor of the UFT so that the "substance" could favor the Governing Board.

At this point, even Rev. Oliver, whose patience usually seemed infinite, was showing signs of losing his temper. He interrupted to suggest that the community ignore the terms of the settlement, and simply "run our schools." Now, Rev. Marshall agreed. "We run the schools or they don't run! Suppose we believe what Dr. Clark says and it doesn't work out? At least we should plan for that!"

Clark went right on. He finally concluded by urging the community to go along with the settlement, and not cause any problems. That way, their "enemies" would not have "an excuse to close in."

Both Young and Clark did agree to withhold their public support for the settlement until the community reached a decision. The Governing Board decided not to take any position on the agreement since it had not been party to the negotiation. The UFT Delegate Assembly's inaction had postponed the projected confrontation for at least one more day.

The meeting was held in the IS 55 library, where Percy Jenkins, its principal, had taken advantage of the district's autonomy from Board of Education rules to fill shelves and tables with paperbacks relevant to his students' lives. These books were inexpensive, and could easily be replaced after they were stolen, which was one of Jenkins' objectives. "Do you know what it means when a kid steals a book?" he asked journalist Robert Campbell. "It means he's reading it. And when he's through with it, somebody else out there will be reading it. So what does that mean? It means reading's back in style." "I don't mind losing paperbacks," he added, "because I figure some cat's out there with that dog-eared book learning something . . . What the hell's a school for, anyway?"[149]

For the past ten weeks, parents and teachers had come up with some new answers to Jenkins' question, answers that put new kinds of books in a new kind of intermediate school library. We all left that library on that Sunday night, wondering whether any of this could survive the strike settlement. Now, it was time for everyone to go home. It was midnight, the end of a very long day. But would it also be the end of the new day in education that was the promise of community control?

III

The Vise Tightens

> Albert Shanker has participated in heaping as much degradation and humiliation on black people as is humanly possible. I think that some day there will come a reckoning, and God help him on that day.
>
> —Rhody McCoy[1]

Once the teacher strikes ended, the daily press largely lost interest in the schools of Ocean Hill–Brownsville. They woke up when trouble was reported at JHS 271, but none of that reporting was first-hand. Many press reports about the school were biased to the point that they could have originated in the UFT press relations office, which some no doubt did. What really went on inside the school was hardly ever reported, except in distorted, sensational accounts. Histories of the community control controversy, of which there have now been several, cover the strike period, but say little or nothing about our schools during the balance of the term. The UFT-driven media image of what happened, and what didn't happen, in and around JHS 271 was a major determinant, however, of decisions that would shape urban education for the next generation.

To my knowledge, the following pages include the only published eyewitness account of post-strike developments inside JHS 271.

Not Back to Normal

On Monday, November 18, as parents, community citizens, and outside supporters glumly milled about Governing Board headquarters, and as JHS 271 quietly experienced its last days without the unwanted UFT teachers, the union membership overwhelmingly ratified the strike settlement. That night, our auditorium was packed for what was billed as an "informational meeting." The evening's high point came when McCoy asked who supported the Governing Board, and was answered with a long, loud standing ovation. He and Rev. Oliver expressed a defiant attitude toward what they described as an illegitimate settlement to the strike, but they could not propose a program to prevent its implementation. They, the parents, the teachers, the community, were stymied.

The New York City schools reopened on Tuesday, November 19. In most parts of the city, this marked a return to what passed for normalcy. Not in Ocean Hill–Brownsville.

That night, parents and teachers mounted overnight sit-in protests at JHS 271, PS 155, and PS 144 to support the three principals whose removal was mandated by the strike settlement. Early the next morning, Dr. Herbert Johnson, the State Trustee now in charge of the district, met with the police commissioner to discuss using military power to clear out the buildings. Instead, he simply threatened to close the three schools if the protestors did not leave. They left in mid-morning, and the three principals reported to the district office.

At JHS 271, Wednesday's return of the 16 unwanted UFT teachers instantly triggered the near destruction of what had been a successful educational program. In order to give those returning teachers full schedules, as

Figure 3.1. Teachers voting to end the strike (November 18, 1968).

mandated by the settlement, loyal teachers had to be removed from their classes. They were now designated "above-quota," and could be assigned only to cover classes of absentees. Neither those loyal teachers nor the students they had been teaching appreciated these changes.

Administratively, the school was virtually leaderless. William Harris had been suspended as principal; Al Vann had been suspended as assistant principal; four other assistant principals had quit. Only John Mandracchia remained, one man to do the work of seven. In addition, Les Campbell, Lillie Curtis, and Dorothy Hopkins, three of the school's mainstays, were also under settlement-mandated suspension (which triggered not the faintest union protest against "due process" violations). Morale was low. In an effort to keep the school from exploding, and hoping to fill the gaps left by the suspensions and resignations, Mandracchia appointed Steve Mayer and ATA members Rudy Clarke and Edgar Morris to assume the responsibilities of assistant principals.

While we were desperately short of supervisors, there was no shortage of observers. There were State observers, UFT observers, Board observers, Mayoral observers, and an indeterminate number of plainclothes police. Since there were so many people involved in observing and reporting alleged infractions of the union contract, none of whom knew anything about the school, roles and identities were chronically mistaken. The situation sometimes approached the comic.

When infractions were reported, the observers were often confused about which "side" had committed them. Actions of loyal teachers were attributed to policemen. Those of State observers were charged to UFT teachers. Identifications were made by guesswork or awkward descriptions. A black teacher with an Afro was described by one observer as, "the tall one with the bushy hair." Once, when I was challenged by a State observer, I told him I wasn't a teacher at all, but a member of the mayor's staff.

Johnson brought in bureaucrats from the State Education Department to act as the chief observers. With one (temporary) exception, these men were all white. Culturally and professionally, they had much in common with the school's UFT contingent, and usually gravitated toward agreement with them.

All the observers, and all the police, though, could not protect the returning UFT teachers from their students. "It's been six months since the kids have seen these teachers," exclaimed one parent. "Since then, they've walked out on strike four times, and now they expect to be greeted with kisses? What nerve!"

If they really expected to be "greeted with kisses," they must have been pretty disappointed. They were greeted by hostile, aroused students, vocal in their objections to the UFT's return. These students confronted them in every part of the school with challenges and derogatory remarks. "Where you been all these months?" "Why weren't you here teaching us?" "Go on home. We don't want you here!" "Down with the UFT!"

Almost none of those teachers could function effectively in the classroom. One of them, an experienced social studies teacher who had taken over Mayer's schedule, lasted one day in class, then called in "sick" for a few days and soon transferred out of the district. Fred Nauman, their leader, was unable to control a seventh-grade science class on his very first day back in the school, and got into a physical altercation with Daryl, a child half his size.

Daryl, 4'9" tall and under a hundred pounds, said Nauman had grabbed him after he verbally blamed the teacher for the enforced absence of Harris, Vann, and the three suspended teachers. Nauman first said he was protecting himself after Daryl threw punches and chairs at him, then changed his story and said he "assumed" Daryl was getting ready to throw a punch. Undisputed was the fact that Nauman slammed the boy's hand into a desk and injured him. A teacher patrolling the hall came in when he saw the commotion. He took Daryl out and called his grandmother. The boy, bleeding profusely, was taken to the hospital.[2]

The following morning, parents, teachers, and community citizens gathered in front of the school entrance in time to block Nauman and his cohorts

Figure 3.2. Fred Nauman (undated).

from entering the building. After a four-hour negotiation, with police wagons standing by, Dr. Johnson reassigned Nauman to his field office at IS 55. Once Nauman was gone, the community blockade parted, allowing his colleagues into the school. Shanker called a press conference and threatened yet another citywide strike. He demanded the closing of JHS 271, and announced that, "Large numbers of children have been indoctrinated. They are full of hatred."[3]

The students didn't need any "indoctrination." They were acting from their own experience. They pulled out all their time-honored techniques of resistance. They forgot their pencils and notebooks; they drifted into class late; they refused to do anything once they got there. Some extended the anger to the loyal teachers, who they felt had "sold them out."

An eighth-grader, Gregory Jackson, wrote a poem protesting the teacher suspensions that his classmates later reprinted in the graduating class's yearbook:

The Fighting Four[4]

Miss Curtis, Miss Hopkins, Mr. Campbell, Mr. Vann
Miss Hopkins the lady, Mr. Campbell the man.
Each as we know has slightly different features,
But none of them want Mr. Shanker's teachers.
We want them back.
We want them bad.
So this is it,
I'll say no more.
We want them back,
The Fighting Four.

Acting entirely on its own, a class brought picket signs to school one morning and began marching in a circle near the front door. As more students arrived, they joined the picket line. When the late bell rang, the school was empty except for adults. The sidewalk was filled with hundreds of students, self-motivated and self-organized, marching to protest conditions in their school.

At ten o'clock, the picket line broke up, and the students streamed into the school. At the time, I was on patrol duty in the lobby. The student organizers asked me to store their signs in my classroom coat closet, and I agreed. From then on, I was constantly followed around by a State observer.

We could only look on helplessly as chaos reigned in the returning teachers' classrooms. Chairs flew out of open windows. Children ran in and out of doors. The yelling and shouting spilled into the halls. Fights broke out.

Steve Mayer was assigned to "coordinate the educational program" on the third floor. Most of his time was spent patrolling the area, and intervening when a UFT teacher lost any semblance of classroom control. This meant almost constant intervention. Conditions reached a point where UFT teachers were asking to be relieved of their classroom assignments, and Mayer asked loyal teachers to take over the classes. On some occasions, he took it upon himself to replace returning teachers even without their consent. State observers warned that this was impermissible, but none of the UFT teachers he replaced objected to it. Some couldn't hide the overwhelming relief on their faces upon leaving their classrooms. Mayer continued this practice on his own initiative to protect the health and welfare of the students and, on more than one occasion, the safety of UFT teachers.

Along with many other loyal teachers, I was spending all my free time patrolling the halls in a generally vain effort to at least contain the disruption, to keep it from spilling over into other classes. When children ran out of UFT-led classrooms into the hallways, I couldn't bring myself to force them back into the free-for-all taking place inside. Soon we designated unused classrooms for these "refugees," and loyal teachers volunteered their free periods to supervise them.

Hearing a great deal of noise emanating from one classroom, I looked inside. The teacher was calmly writing on the board, while the students were all over the room, tearing things up, fighting, and throwing books. As I stared at this spectacle, I noticed, out of the corner of my eye, a UFT observer on my right taking notes, probably so the disruption inside the room could be blamed on my watching from the outside. I was later ordered to stay at least three feet away from the door of any UFT-led classroom.

Throughout this whole experience, the two UFT observers, their presence dictated by the strike settlement for the protection of the returning teachers, were overly conscientious. They submitted a continual barrage of notes and memoranda to the State observers, complaining that the UFT teachers were being "harassed" by loyal teachers and community residents, and were being prevented from adequately fulfilling their teaching obligations. In addition, they constantly spied on classes conducted by loyal teachers, copying down words written on chalkboards to document charges that "sedition and extremism" were being taught. Our acting administrators had to answer these charges. They spent hours of precious time investigating dozens of unfounded accusations, which left them even less time to run the school. In our view, the true function of these UFT observers was to generate harassment, not to prevent it.

Despite exhaustive efforts by members of the loyal staff to maintain an educational atmosphere, the presence of the unwanted returning teachers proved too disruptive a force to cope with. They were not only unable to perform in the classroom, but usually couldn't, or wouldn't, help with less demanding administrative tasks such as supervising the cafeteria or patrolling the hallways. Within just days of their return, education at JHS 271 came to a standstill. What had begun in September on a promising note, with a new and dedicated staff and an enthusiastic student body, what had successfully survived months of attacks, lies, and slander, had been shattered.

The only good news was that four of the school's 16 unwanted teachers had voluntarily transferred to other districts. The bad news was that the remaining 12 seemed committed to provoking as much trouble as they could.

The school was paralyzed. We no longer had the luxury of operating in the calm eye of a raging storm. The storm was now raging inside the walls of JHS 271.

Nauman Returns, Sort Of

A week after the strike settlement, I reported under orders to the Midtown Manhattan offices of the State Education Department. Two other teachers and I were called as witnesses in Al Vann's hearing for "harassment" of UFT teachers, and of acting principal Farrar, on October 9. When we arrived at the hearing room, it was packed with community residents, including members of the Governing Board, who had come in Vann's support.

In one corner, protected by police, were the UFT complainants. Other than me, my two colleagues, and the State officials, they and the police were the only whites in the room. Miss Farrar was waiting in another office; she had refused to sit in the same room as the parents.

While Vann's lawyers negotiated with the State officials and the central Board's lawyer over procedural issues, the Ocean Hill–Brownsville contingent was growing impatient. Most felt that any hearing should have taken place back in the community, and resented the long subway commute to Manhattan. In addition, the room was too small for so many people. The crowded conditions irritated already frayed nerves. Some parents took out their frustrations in verbal assaults on the UFT teachers, whose discomfort was obvious.

"You gonna die!" shouted one.

"That's right," agreed another. "Everybody gonna die sometime!" Laughter filled the room as the community people enjoyed the UFT group's discomfort.

"It's nice to see them squirm a little," one parent whispered to me, "after the way they been treatin' us for so long."

Suddenly, a McCoy aide who had been summoned to answer a phone call from Mandracchia, rushed into the room, out of breath and angry. "Nauman's back!" he shouted.

Stares of disbelief greeted the announcement. After Nauman's physical incident with the seventh-grader, and the school-door protest that followed,

Johnson had agreed to keep him out of the school until a hearing on the matter could be held. Now, the Trustee had apparently gone back on his word. The messenger explained what happened at JHS 271 just a few moments earlier.

"Mandracchia wasn't told anything about it beforehand. About a half hour ago, fifty cops drove up and took Nauman back into the school. He's sitting in an office now with four detectives. Mandracchia's afraid he'll be ordered to assign him to classes. He wants the Governing Board to tell him what to do."

It didn't take long for the parents to decide what had to be done. They were sitting there all morning, waiting for a hearing on trumped-up charges against a black leader who had done nothing, but had been presumed guilty and preemptively suspended. Meanwhile, Nauman, a white man who injured a black child, had apparently been presumed innocent and sent back into the school. They quickly agreed to torpedo Vann's hearing as long as Nauman was in the school. They would return Vann to the school, collecting Harris and Campbell along the way, reinstate their suspended leaders, and get Nauman out by whatever means necessary. They informed the lawyers of their decision, waited courteously as the State officials postponed the doomed hearing, and headed back home.

My colleagues and I went along with the parents, as enthused about getting them back into the school as about getting Nauman out. We really needed parents to see what was happening to their school, and to help us restore the atmosphere community control had generated prior to the new regime.

After stopping at McCoy's office to pick up Campbell and Harris, the parents and teachers marched to JHS 271. As we came down the block, students on the top floors flocked to the windows, shouting excitedly. "Mr. Vann!" "Mr. Vann!" "Mr. Campbell!" "You comin' back for good?" "Hey! Look, everybody!"

Inside the school, the community contingent was met with the same scene that had prevailed over the past week. Dodging the flying debris, we entered the principal's office. Mandracchia was instructed to declare an early dismissal. One parent picked up the phone to call Johnson and told him, "Come over here, or we'll have to come and get you." Johnson agreed, but insisted that the school remain open. Otherwise, he said, he would close it permanently.

Johnson arrived in about ten minutes. On seeing the condition of the school, and perhaps wanting to avoid being caught in any crossfire, he agreed to the early dismissal.

The meeting was not an easy one for him. He had come into the district when the UFT teachers returned, tasked with enforcing the strictures of the oppressive strike settlement. The parents associated Johnson with the conditions the settlement had created in the school, and were in no mood to be mollified by meaningless gestures of conciliation. They demanded that the suspensions be lifted, and that both Nauman and his police protection be removed from the premises. There was no room for compromise. When the meeting finally broke up, no clear agreements had been reached. It seemed as though nothing had been resolved.

McCoy later asked Johnson to assign Nauman to the district office pending a hearing. Johnson refused. The Governing Board issued a statement of defiance. "Under these circumstances," it said, "our teachers are not to be tried by a State hearing officer. Returning Mr. Nauman to 271 is a deliberately provocative act. Our teachers and principals are to return to their respective schools to carry on the education of our children. We will not submit to this double standard of justice. We insist on the equal protection of the laws."[5]

That evening, after consulting with Commissioner Allen, Johnson partially relented and "temporarily" assigned Nauman to 110 Livingston Street.

Liberal educator and experienced conciliator that he may have been, Johnson's primary executive experience had been in Rockville Centre, a quiet suburban Long Island district with no racial conflict since everyone in town was white. He was over his head in this pressure-cooker, and his position was becoming untenable.

Trespass

The next morning, Al Vann and Rev. Oliver came to JHS 271 in hopes of easing the turmoil and restoring order. As soon as they arrived, a State observer called Johnson's office for instructions. The UFT representatives on site argued that both men were trespassing, since Vann had been suspended and Governing Board members were barred by the terms of the strike settlement. Johnson agreed with this reasoning and, in a supremely undiplomatic move, ordered them arrested for criminal trespass.

I was in the Governing Board office that afternoon, with some colleagues, when Rev. Oliver returned from court in time for an emergency board meeting. He asked us to sit in on the meeting so board members could hear the views of the staff.

Rev. Oliver began by relating his adventures of the morning. He said he was genuinely surprised to find out that he was barred from the school, since his copy of the strike settlement did not contain such a provision. He added, in fact, that Johnson himself could not produce a written clause to that effect, but expressed an opinion that the powers of the Trustee included the authority to keep anyone he wanted to out of the school.

One of the parent board members asked, "What are you going to do now?"

"What do you think?" Oliver answered, as though there were no need to do so. "I have to go back to 271 tomorrow!"

Several board members vehemently opposed this tactic, arguing that another arrest would not help the situation, and that they needed his leadership on the scene, not in a jail cell. Also, he might be held for high bail in a second arrest, not released on his own recognizance as he was today.

But Oliver was adamant. "We were elected by the community to run our schools. We cannot do this without being allowed inside them. Legal or not, Johnson's action in keeping me out is immoral, and I cannot condone it." This reflected Rev. Oliver's consistent position, that the Governing Board derived its legitimacy from its election by the people, not from any agency of the power structure, and that it could be held accountable only by and to the community. "If this board votes that I should *not* return to 271 tomorrow," he added, "I will simply have to resign as chairman and go there as a citizen of the community."

I could not help being impressed by Rev. Oliver's style, regardless of how effective his choice of strategy might or might not be. It was marked by uncompromising dedication to principle, unyielding yet suffused with the quiet dignity that characterized his every action. Before coming to Brooklyn, he was a civil rights leader in Birmingham, Alabama when that city was run by the Ku Klux Klan and its allies. He was there when Sheriff Bull Connor's men turned

Figure 3.3. Rev. C. Herbert Oliver, Governing Board chairman, after a long day (1968).

fire hoses and snarling dogs on child demonstrators, and when the KuKluxKlan bombed the 16th Street Baptist Church, killing three girls. He wasn't going to be intimidated by anything that he now faced in Brooklyn.

Some board members saw him as determined. Others saw him as stubborn. None questioned his leadership. Finally, the board gave in to Oliver's proposal. They could see that trying to change his mind would be an exercise in futility and they, too, respected his firm posture. He announced that he would enter the school the next morning, accompanied by other local ministers, and by white clergymen who had called to volunteer through the National Council of Churches.

The discussion then moved to conditions inside JHS 271. I described the effect that the imposition of UFT teachers and hostile observers had brought about in the school, and expressed my opinion that the staff could not last much longer at the pace we were all working. "Every day we go on like this," I said, "is a step backward for the students. It won't be long until they're right back where they were last year." Then I passed on a suggestion that other teachers had been talking about, something I disagreed with and desperately hoped would not be necessary. "If nothing can be done, maybe you should close the school. At least then we would be standing still instead of regressing." We would also be giving Shanker just what he wanted.

Ron McFadden, our faculty's representative on the Governing Board and one of the school's best teachers, elaborated on the decline in staff morale since the settlement. "Good teaching requires a great deal of planning," he explained. "Now, our teachers are so busy trying to keep order that they have no time to prepare for their own lessons. When they get home, they're too exhausted to even think about school, and too disgusted to want to. So, even the loyal teachers aren't as effective as they used to be."

The board members knew of the deterioration in the school's atmosphere, but not of its magnitude. Unfortunately, there was nothing they could do about it. Even the limited powers they once possessed had been taken away when the board was suspended, and they sadly came face-to-face with their impotence. The demoralization that gripped the faculty had now spread to the Governing Board.

Some members argued that the school should be closed until something could be done, but others countered that this would attract no community support, and could turn the parents against them. Another realization struck home. While the Governing Board had been fighting public relations battles during the past months, its level of everyday contact with constituents had eroded. Many board members had been spending all their waking hours composing drafts of statements, attending meetings, and answering unfounded charges. They feared losing touch with the community, and were now feeling insecure about their level of constituent support. The board appeared to be paralyzed by self-doubt. Some argued that only militant action could mobilize the community, but the only consensus that could be reached was to support Rev. Oliver in his promised return to JHS 271.

One Governing Board member who was not overtaken by malaise was Father John Powis, who had been in the leadership of the Ocean Hill–Brownsville school struggle since its very beginning. In a side conversation, he told me something would definitely have to be done to reverse the tide that was now sweeping away the vestiges of community control. He insisted, though, that the teachers would have to wait until community forces either bypassed the Governing Board or reawakened it. Until then, we would simply have to do the best we could. His position had consistently been, "Let the parents take the lead." It was the best advice possible under the circumstances.

At this point, as though on cue, we were all treated to a bit of comic relief when a young white teacher from IS 55 piped up. "If your problem is organizing the community," he said, "I can tell you how to do it!" Father Powis was struggling to hold back laughter. "I know how to do these things," he went on, oblivious to the hostile stares. "First we'll get some balloons of different colors, then . . ."

"Shut up!" He was interrupted by a black community worker. "Just don't say any more!" I considered sliding under the table in embarrassment. The board members were tired, but not tired enough to listen to this. Their self-styled savior was quickly hustled out of the room by a black teacher who could explain the facts of life to him.

The meeting was over, though. There was nothing more anyone could say or do. I went home, wishing that I had not been taken into the Board's confidence. Now I could only hope that parents would organize themselves, that everyone wouldn't give up.

In the morning, Rev. Oliver walked into JHS 271, accompanied by an entourage of 15 black and white priests and ministers. Johnson, instead of having them all arrested, opted to come and meet with them. While nothing was resolved in this meeting, or in a later one with community representatives, it was what passed for a relatively calm day. No one got arrested, and another early dismissal got us to a welcome four-day Thanksgiving recess.[6]

While the Friday after Thanksgiving was to be a "makeup day" for the schools, the Governing Board voted to close our schools as usual, since they had been open during the strikes and didn't need the UFT makeup days. Johnson, who needed a long weekend, also wanted them closed. This was a rare point of agreement. More than a third of the city's students boycotted classes that day. Black and white high school students, led by a coalition of student organizations that was headquartered at the ATA office, staged anti-UFT and "student power" demonstrations all over the city. Roving bands blocked subway lines and attacked school buildings. At one of the larger rallies, held at the

United Nations, Les Campbell delivered some inflammatory rhetoric, which was of great interest to the press corps.[7] He had become its favorite target.

The high school rebellion resumed on December 2, the first school day after the holiday, when the absentee rate was reported to be 28 percent. The students held a rally at Washington Square Park, then dispersed in every direction. Disorders and attacks were reported at twelve high schools that day. Subways cars were vandalized and entire lines were closed down. In the late afternoon, hundreds of students headed for JHS 271, where hundreds of armed, helmeted police were lying in wait. A pitched battle ensued, ending with a police offensive that scattered the students. They did not suffer the only casualties, though. Among those clubbed in the face by police were Governing Board member Elaine Rooke and a *Village Voice* reporter, who told the *Times* that "the cops started charging down the avenue, swinging clubs anywhere they could indiscriminately."[8]

The Synagogue Fires

During the Thanksgiving weekend, the *New York Times* reported that eleven synagogues in the five boroughs had experienced suspicious fires, of varying sizes, during the fall of 1968. The report was triggered by the arrest of four youths, who had been caught painting swastikas on the wall of another Jewish institution, and were being questioned in connection with several Bronx arson cases. "Police said one was Jewish, and the other three were Catholic," the paper reported. "All were white." Approximately 30 minutes after these arrests, Mayor Lindsay appeared on television. He announced the steps that were being taken to solve the outstanding cases and to prevent additional crimes, and emphasized that the eleven incidents "were not perpetrated by any single racial or religious group." After the broadcast, the mayor told reporters that he "did not believe the attacks on the synagogues were the result of Negro resentment against whites." Further, he disclosed that ten additional arrests had been made in connection with the desecrations, and "all the arrested persons were white."[9]

This was a sign of the times. First, the attacks on Jewish institutions in different parts of the city are pulled together in a single story, even though there is no evidence connecting them. Second, the mayor deems the arrests of a few teenagers worthy of a television appearance. Third, both the mayor and the *Times* emphasize, several times, that the attacks were not the result of racial animus, even though all of the suspects and all those arrested were white.

By that time, the UFT had distributed its half million copies of the bogus leaflets (which had been dismissed by the Anti-Defamation League as insignificant), hounded the mayor out of a Brooklyn synagogue, and conducted a widespread campaign against what it labeled "Black Anti-Semitism." UFT allies such as the Jewish Defense League were doing their best to spread fear in the Jewish community. The propaganda campaign, which first targeted certain individuals (some anonymous) and organizations (some fictitious), and then targeted Ocean Hill–Brownsville and the Community Control movement, was now indiscriminately branding the entire black community as anti-Semitic. If there were attacks on Jewish houses of worship, the expected public assumption was that they were carried out by "black militants." As one man put it at a community relations meeting convened by the mayor, "The first thing that happens when a synagogue is set on fire, you look for a black."[10] So tense was the city that the mayor, its police chief, and its newspaper of record clearly felt they had to act quickly to head off a racial conflagration that could threaten to consume the city.

During early January 1969, there were nine more fires. One temple in Queens was burned to the ground.[11] By the end of the month, the police had solved all the arsons. A total of 14 people were arrested, including 11 teenagers and a 10-year-old Jewish boy. All were white.[12]

In March, four more fires were set in two Manhattan synagogues. As if to cap off this strange series of events, the police quickly cleared these cases with the arrest of a single arsonist, the son of a Brooklyn rabbi.[13]

According to surveys taken after the arrests were announced, a quarter of the city's Jews still attributed the fires to a rising tide of black anti-Semitism. Only 12 percent identified the arsonists as white.[14]

Johnson's Welcome Wears Him Out

When JHS 271 reopened after Thanksgiving, it could barely function. Mayer, Clarke and Morris, the three teachers who had been assigned emergency leadership roles at JHS 271, visited Johnson in his office and presented him with an ultimatum.

As Mayer told me after the meeting, Morris presented their case. He characterized the school as "in chaos," and said this team could not control it without more support. "We need more assistant principals," he argued, "but most of all we need Al Vann returned and put in charge. Only he could possibly get the school back in order. If you can't meet these conditions, then, for the safety of the students, you might as well shut the place down." Clarke and Mayer added anecdotes to illustrate the urgency of this plea, and related the general feeling among the loyal teachers that the school could only function if its leadership was restored.

Johnson, reported Mayer, appeared shocked. In past days, he himself had threatened to shut the school down. Now, that bluff was being called. The loyal staff, unless conditions could be made bearable, refused to be held responsible for a deplorable state of affairs that we had no power to change. Flustered, Johnson replied that he would consider their suggestions, but that he did not have the power to implement them. "If you're the chief administrator and you don't have the power," asked Clarke, "who does?" No answer. End of conference.

A short time later, a group of about 25 parents did act. They marched through the police barricades, confronted Johnson in our principal's office, and angrily demanded immediate action. The door was closed, but loud voices could be heard in the outer office as the parents expressed their outrage over the turn of events. Many of these parents had not been active before, but now they were no longer content to leave matters to the Governing Board. Finally, Johnson promised that he would meet with Commissioner Allen and try to create more favorable conditions. He left the meeting quickly, visibly shaken by the vigor of the parents' harangues.

Reporters, who were barred from the school that day, were content to rely on the implanted observers as sources for their stories. When I read the *Times* account the next morning, I didn't recognize the school I had been in the day before. UFT observers claimed that mothers had entered the classrooms of male UFT teachers and physically attacked them, and a state observer claimed that Johnson had been "locked in a closet" and threatened with a knife by the parents. I wondered how these observers knew so much about what went on in rooms that they could not have observed, especially since Johnson himself was not making any such allegations. Even Leonard Buder, the *Times* reporter, had his doubts. "It was not clear," he wrote, "how this could happen with so many policemen, including Dr. Johnson's personal bodyguard, in the building."[15] He reported the following day that Johnson "flatly denied" either of these events had occurred, but did not conclude in the article that the observer's report to him was a lie.[16] A staffer at *The New Yorker* investigated the story and definitively concluded that the "closet and knife" story was a lie,[17] but the *Times* simply let the matter drop.

Later, Shanker held a press conference. Claiming that the strike settlement had been routinely violated at JHS 271, he threatened to call yet another citywide strike. He also singled out Campbell, who wasn't even at the school that day, implying nevertheless that he was personally responsible for the high school student demonstrations. "These aren't students organizing on their own," he said.[18]

That night, Commissioner Allen held a meeting at his Manhattan office with Johnson, Shanker, Kenneth Clark, and Harold Israelson, the Lindsay aide who headed the powerful State Supervisory Committee established by the strike settlement. When the meeting ended, Allen announced that JHS 271 would be closed "until further notice," and that Johnson, who was "pretty well worn out," would be replaced as Trustee by Dr. William D. Firman, one of his assistants.[19]

There was no official report of who said what in this meeting. One of McCoy's aides, though, told me that Allen, under pressure from Shanker, directed Johnson to close the school. When Johnson demurred, Allen replaced him with Firman. This seemed perfectly plausible. My guess was that the leak had to have come from Dr. Clark.

In any case, JHS 271 was closed indefinitely beginning December 3, and Firman, who had a much more authoritarian reputation than Johnson, took over as the district's Trustee.

Not long after this announcement, Rev. Oliver and about twenty parents and community activists entered the school. They announced their intention to stay overnight, and to open it in the morning for students and teachers. At 3 a.m., five dozen police arrived and escorted the group from the building.

Facing Down Firman

Firman's first official action after closing JHS 271 was to physically relocate the office of the Trustee from IS 55 in Ocean Hill–Brownsville to the Hotel Commodore in Midtown Manhattan. This set the tone that he would take in his relations with the community.

He announced that JHS 271 would remain closed, and McCoy would remain suspended, until McCoy presented him with a written plan of operation, specifying the supervisory personnel who would run the school and all procedures to be followed. If this plan met with his approval, he would reinstate McCoy and reopen the school. Many Ocean Hill–Brownsville supporters found this edict humiliating. The Unit Administrator, duly appointed by the elected Governing Board, who had successfully run the district's schools under the most difficult conditions, was now being forced to apply to an outside power in order to get his job back. Firman, who now held that power, had zero experience with inner-city schools. One response came the next morning, when 120 parents and students mounted a sit-in at Commissioner Allen's Manhattan office. It was eventually broken up by police.

When students and teachers arrived at school Tuesday morning, we found it closed and tightly guarded by police. Barred from meeting in any of the district schools, most of the teachers gathered in the community room of a local housing project to decide what to do. A substantial core was determined to fight along with the community until the bitter end, the shadow of which was now hovering overhead. Plausible concrete plans, though, were not immediately obvious.

Another blow came when we learned that John Mandracchia, our only remaining certified administrator, a white man who had earned the respect and affection of teachers, students, and parents, and who had been working around the clock for weeks, had been hospitalized after suffering a heart attack. He never told anyone that he had a weak ticker.

Partly out of respect, and partly out of desperation, the teachers agreed to ask McCoy to address the meeting and give us some guidance. McCoy had, on many previous occasions, displayed remarkable creativity in formulating tactics, and we were hoping for another of his brainstorms. He agreed and, without promising ideas of our own, we recessed until he could arrive.

First, he had to meet with a large group of parents, many of whom were clamoring for swift action to reopen the school, on their own terms, and to demand his reinstatement. McCoy told them that he expected to be able to resolve the situation favorably within a few days. He also cautioned that the police cordon around JHS 271 was now formidable enough to easily repel a community effort to reopen the school by force. The parents agreed to let McCoy try to settle things in his own way.

When McCoy arrived at the teachers' meeting, he opened with his observations of indecision and fragmentation among the members of the Governing Board, a few of whom had become ill under the accumulated tension of the past few months. He noted the danger of the school being closed permanently, but said he had hopes of personally bringing about a settlement. Finally, he said that the "community" did not want any demonstrations planned for the next few days, and that any mass action around JHS 271 could, in fact, alienate parents of children in the district's other schools.

He suggested that the teachers appoint two members of our Steering Committee to keep in close touch with him, and that we adjourn for the time being. Many were reluctant to simply let things ride, but we were not going to get out in front of the community. Larry Bussey and I were designated to act as liaison.

McCoy now had obtained uneasy votes of confidence from both the parents and the teachers of JHS 271. Thus armed, he called a press conference to respond to Firman's demand for a written plan of operation.

Anyone who first listened to McCoy's presentation to the teachers, and then his statements to the press over the next few days, could have been left with the impression that the "community" must be in a state of bipolar duality. After telling the teachers that the parents wanted them to "cool it," McCoy portrayed these same parents as "explosive" to the press. Where the "community was exhausted" in the private meeting, it was a "powder keg" for public consumption. McCoy said he would be betraying the parents' trust in him if he agreed to Firman's demands. Further, he accused Firman of injecting "Plantation Politics" into the situation. He said he could not and would not "submit to the directions of the overseer."

McCoy had exploited Firman's insensitivity to the history of African-Americans in order to highlight the colonial nature of the Trusteeship, and emerged as the sole individual who could resolve the impasse. The teachers were depending on him as their link to the community, while the parents were depending on him for contact with the loyal staff, and for resolving the issues with the State. In his public image, McCoy had become both the target of white oppression (because of his suspension) and the uncompromising spokesman for black liberation (by his refusal to accede). City and State authorities had to be sensitive to the unstated threat of civil disorder in and around Ocean Hill–Brownsville.

The suspended Unit Administrator, even with no legal authority, was quite clearly on top of the situation. Nothing could be done by any of the forces involved which would not enhance his position. If there was a disturbance in the community, he had warned of its inevitability; if things remained calm, he was temporarily holding the lid on. If he was further penalized by the authorities, he would become a martyr; if he was not, he would have stared them down. He held all the cards. Strategically, this was McCoy's finest hour.

Among our faculty, though, the seeds of factionalism, dormant for months, were beginning to blossom. While the school remained closed, we continued to meet. However, we had given McCoy a promise not to take any action, and the instability of our status prevented any serious teacher training or curriculum planning from even being discussed. So what was there to meet about?

Debates quickly turned to recrimination and buck-passing. Teachers began to blame one another for their accumulated frustrations and apparent impotence. Vital differences in purpose, philosophy, and political viewpoints, successfully submerged for so long, bubbled to the surface.

Much of the discussion centered on the chaos of the past two weeks. Rather than attribute that unrest to its root causes, the return of the unwanted teachers and the removal of the school's key personnel, some of the new white teachers chose to blame it on the children. One teacher called for more patrols, another for mass suspensions, and another for corporal punishment. "Blaming the Victim" was an old establishment game, but I never expected to see it played among this group.

Another teacher claimed that his hopes for a "return to normalcy" lay in "separating the politics from the education." This prompted a loud objection from Campbell, who himself was becoming frustrated. "Don't you see that you can't separate these two things? Don't you understand that the politics of who they are is the most relevant education for these kids right now? If we abandon politics and give up the fight, what hopes can we ever have for their education?"

An identifiable faction was beginning to coalesce, though, on the right wing of the faculty, mainly around the issue of "law and order." This faction was comprised primarily of older black teachers who thought the ATA was too militant, and white teachers who, it seemed to me, were overwhelmed by the charged environment in which they found themselves. The meetings were threatening to become as acrimonious as the confrontations that had taken place between advocates of community control and supporters of the UFT. Many of us in the pro-community faction were incensed by this development. Accusations and epithets were tossed around by both factions. Insignificant personal incidents were invoked, making some arguments too personal for reasoned debate. Castigation, accusation, and recrimination filled the room. Every meeting brought rising temperatures to the fore.

In an effort to keep the faculty from imploding before the school's reopening, whenever that might take place, the Steering Committee canceled future meetings and asked the teachers to just stay home until school opened. Otherwise, the faculty could well have torn itself apart. We might never have been able to function again as a unit. Still, much damage had already been done, and everyone knew this argument was destined to resurface. While McCoy was capturing the imagination of the nation, a key part of his home constituency was eroding from within.

McCoy continued to play out his hand. On December 11, after announcing he would reopen JHS 271 on his own authority, he walked up the steps to the school door. Firman had him arrested, removed him from his position as Unit Administrator, and sent police and state officials to occupy McCoy's office. These actions raised the stakes another notch. Firman's repressive tenure as Trustee was becoming increasingly costly to the public image of state authorities.

Kenneth Clark, who had tried to mediate between McCoy and Firman, blamed the State Trustee for frustrating his efforts. "Now I understand what McCoy was saying," Clark concluded. "He (Firman) does see himself as a plantation overseer and a white boss who has to contain the restless natives. Now I think this man has outlived his usefulness in Ocean Hill–Brownsville." Rev. Galamison and Whitney Young agreed, and called for Firman's removal.[20]

Blanche Pile, a parent member of the Governing Board, was even blunter. "He's treating us like slaves, not human beings."[21] Firman was becoming more of a liability than an asset to Commissioner Allen.

The next day, 80 percent of the teachers in Ocean Hill–Brownsville's open schools called in sick. Most of the parents kept their children home in a quickly organized boycott.

The following Monday, two weeks after he closed JHS 271, Firman was removed. He went back home to Albany, where he requested and received 24-hour State Police protection for several weeks.[22] Allen replaced him with one of his assistants, Dr. Wilbur Nordos, who was everything Firman was not. He came with a record of successful experience as a Bedford-Stuyvesant teacher and principal, where he encouraged parent involvement, and had a sophisticated understanding of race relations.[23] He knew that community support for the Governing Board was strong, and that McCoy's support was growing, based not only on his own observations, but on a private survey conducted for the state by Bert Swanson, a political sociology professor at Sarah Lawrence College. A Louis Harris poll found that McCoy was the single most popular person in Ocean Hill–Brownsville. Nordos was looking for resolution, not confrontation.[24]

On his first day as Trustee, Nordos reinstated McCoy as Unit Administrator and authorized him to reopen JHS 271 under his own direct supervision. He also rescinded Firman's long list of draconian ground rules for school operations, and tore up his tentative plan, unknown to us but one that we suspected existed, to replace both McCoy and the entire staff of JHS 271.

Asked about Firman in a symposium a few months later, Rev. Oliver commented that, "I think he might even have tried removing the whole district out into the ocean somewhere."[25] In the same symposium, discussing the failure of the two Trustees who preceded him (for whom he expressed personal respect), Nordos said,

> I think that many people had not accurately gauged the determination of the so-called little people, the ones who had been disenfranchised, the poor, those outside the mainstream who have not been given much status, or credit for enough ability to handle their own affairs. They have probably miscalculated the strength of this determination to play a determining role in the education of their children.[26]

McCoy had prevailed in his standoff with the State, and now had a Trustee he could work with until the Governing Board could be restored. Our faculty and students, though, as well as the community at large, had paid a heavy price for this victory. After two weeks of being closed, and with only a week left before the Christmas recess, JHS 271 had slid a long way from the atmosphere of unity that characterized it while the UFT teachers were out on strike.

Chaos to Camelot

During the two weeks that the school was closed, a panel headed by Dr. John Fischer, President of Columbia University Teachers College, conducted hearings on the charges against our suspended teachers. The panel had summarily dismissed the case against Dorothy Hopkins as having no merit. After a full proceeding, it also restored Lillie Curtis and Al Vann to their positions. Upon hearing the Board of Education's entire case against Vann, the panel concluded that he deserved *commendatory*, rather than punitive, action for the diplomatic steps he had taken to defuse a potentially dangerous situation on October 9.

The panel reserved its decision in Les Campbell's case, and he was temporarily assigned to the district office. Shortly afterward, he too would be reinstated. In the meantime, McCoy "moved" the district office into the school, so Campbell's reassignment kept him in the building. Nauman had refused to appear before the panel. His case was referred back to Donovan, so he wouldn't be back anytime soon. Things appeared to be looking up.

Although McCoy was officially put in charge of the school, he effectively delegated this authority to Vann when it reopened on December 17. Under his leadership, the staff forged a new unity, submerging for a time the differences that divided us. Black and white, we committed ourselves to do whatever it would take to reestablish the peaceful, positive educational atmosphere that prevailed before the UFT group was imposed on the school. Vann instituted a number of controversial innovations to restore the waning school spirit, many of which were so successful that teachers wondered why Harris hadn't thought of them months earlier.

Black Nationalism, a consistent undertone in the school's operation, was now out in the open. Teachers were given an option to replace or supplement the American flag in their classrooms with the red, black, and green flag of black liberation. Some also displayed the national flag of Puerto Rico. The ritual mumbling of the Pledge of Allegiance was replaced by the singing of *Lift Ev'ry Voice and Sing*. Composed by James Weldon Johnson 50 years earlier, it had come to be known as the "Negro National Anthem," and was now heard every morning at JHS 271, led with gusto over the school's PA system by the Queen of Soul, Aretha Franklin.

To start each day, the school vibrated with the rhythm of this anthem, as nearly every student stood and sang out . . .

Lift ev'ry voice and sing,
'Til earth and heaven ring,
Ring with the harmonies of liberty.

Let our rejoicing rise
High as the list'ning skies,
Let it resound as the rolling sea.

Sing a song,
Full of the faith that the dark past has taught us.
Sing a song,
Full of the hope that the present has brought us.

Facing the rising sun,
Of our new day begun.
Let us march on,
'Til victory is won!

Through classroom discussions and special programs, the students learned about the song's significance. These words of Paul Robeson, the great African-American "singer of the people," provided context:

> When Harriet Tubman went south in the dark days to lead the slaves, and perhaps my father, to freedom, thousands of human beings lifted their voices in song. And so it has been, wherever those of humankind have surged toward the light of liberation . . . men and women of every culture, color and clime.[27]

The students started each day in song, and the harmony of their voices helped to calm the lingering tensions. I found it remarkable how the students in the homeroom I had been covering, who used to mumble or ignore the words of the Pledge, now stood up straight as soon as the recording began, young men and women singing these verses of hope, loud and clear. In my role as "welcome guest," I was happy to sing along with them.

There were now eleven UFT teachers still in the school. Nauman had been reassigned downtown, and five others had voluntarily transferred out. These eleven, and their UFT observers, filed complaints about every pro-black innovation, each of which they interpreted as anti-white. Dr. Nordos, though, apparently did not agree, and was reluctant to intervene.

The Trustee's non-interference policy gave Vann the freedom to present a series of special assembly programs, aimed at enhancing student awareness of their history and culture:

- A group of students from Harlem's IS 201 presented a dramatized version of *The Autobiography of Malcolm X*, which many of ours had been reading in social studies classes.

- On another occasion, a film about the Black Panthers was shown. During the screening, the sound system broke down, and most of the film was shown silently. Even so, the students sat quietly throughout the program, watching attentively, and applauding enthusiastically when it ended. They followed it intently, even without the benefit of sound.

- As part of a Christmas program, the "Talking Drums" troupe was engaged to show, through song and dance, a side of African life and culture that few New York City students were aware of. It presented a series of colorful images, of strong and vital women, of beauty and of harmony. It was a portrait of life, not of death, of sunshine and light, not of some "dark continent." It added another dimension to our Afro-American History curriculum, recalling artistically the great African kingdoms that thrived while Europe was still in the Dark Ages. The students stayed in their seats that day until a half hour past normal dismissal time.

- On January 15, Martin Luther King's birthday (the first celebration since his assassination), the Muntu Players of New Haven's Lee High School put on a program of poetry reading, singing, and dancing, that continued along these lines. They read and acted out the poems of African-American poets Langston Hughes, Leroi Jones, Claude McKay, and others.

Les Campbell was the driving force in arranging for these programs. Any funds that needed to be raised were covered through voluntary faculty donations.

Vann also took strong measures to correct the breakdown in order that had developed after the unwanted teachers returned. New procedures were established to deal with lateness, truancy, and class cutting. We explained to the students that unprovoked confrontations with the UFT group could trigger another shutdown. A coherent disciplinary system was instituted for the first time, under the leadership of the new Deans, Rudy Clarke and Clarence Eastmond, and other strong black teachers. As this team met with parents, instilled new pride in students, and emerged not only as enforcers but as positive role models of self-discipline, the noise level in the school gradually decreased to manageable proportions. Many students went out of their way to assist and cooperate with their teachers. A student patrol force was formed, which became as effective as any teacher patrol had ever been.

One reason for the confidence the students placed in "Brother Clarke" and "Brother Eastmond" was their willingness to take the side of the students when a complaining teacher was partially or wholly at fault. Their investigations revealed classrooms where not enough was going on to engage the students' attention. The inexperience of many teachers and the shortage of training and adequate supervision were showing.

To address this problem, Vann instituted teacher training seminars during the 45 minutes before the opening bell twice a week. All teachers were required to attend. Led by respected, experienced teachers, the workshops concentrated on lesson planning, discipline, and techniques for teaching in specific subject areas. The program was flexible. Sometimes, any teacher who had an idea to present was given an opportunity to do so. Discussions ranged over such topics as team teaching, programmed learning, and field trips. Ironically, the teachers could be paid for the extra professional development time because of a controversial clause in the UFT strike settlement meant to help the striking teachers recoup the pay they had lost.

These innovations greatly improved the school's functioning, but, even as their effects were taking hold, other factors were dragging it back. Some white teachers, complaining that the Afrocentric programs compromised their own influence with the students, seized on them as an excuse for ineffectiveness. Others resented being required to attend training workshops. Some of the new teachers were learning that teaching was not the profession they had been cut out for.

In addition, we were still short of assistant principals and had no permanent department chairs. Supervisors who wanted to transfer in from other schools were prevented from doing so by the central Board's bureaucracy.

Finally, harassment and slacking off by the UFT teachers, unnoticed by the official observers, continued unabated. Many arrived late to their classes, and others claimed to have forgotten their class assignments entirely. Their sabotage, and their students' open hostility to them, rippled through the atmosphere.

Teacher vacancies and absentees sometimes reached 25 percent, burdening the remaining staff with covering multiple additional classes. One administrator had to spend nearly all his time figuring out and assigning class coverages.

Still, Vann had gained the confidence of most of the staff by assuming strong leadership in what had seemed an impossible situation. The faculty was publicly impatient for the principal's return, but the opposite sentiment was commonly expressed in private. Many teachers were hoping that Vann would remain as acting principal for the rest of the school year.

This was another occasion for irony. First, the UFT's three citywide strikes against Ocean Hill–Brownsville and against JHS 271 specifically, had helped bring about the cooperative school spirit that made our educational program so successful. Now, the removal of the principal from the school, meant to be punitive, actually allowed a new flowering of innovation and cooperation.

On December 19, just three days into this brief renaissance, a Brooklyn grand jury returned indictments on a series of misdemeanor charges against Vann, Campbell, and two other black teachers; Elaine Rooke and Hattie Bishop of the Governing Board; Esther Collins, a parent; and a colorful community activist known as Sweet Georgia Brown. The charges, obstructing governmental administration and attempted coercion, stemmed from allegations made by

UFT teachers and by the central Board's team of observers. As McCoy characterized the legal onslaught, "They're determined to get us one way or another."[28]

These indictments led to a May 1970, jury trial, which I attended in accordance with a subpoena. State Supreme Court Justice John R. Starkey ended the trial after eight days of testimony with a directed verdict of acquittal, and reprimanded the prosecution for bringing charges with no substantial evidence. The decision, though not the reprimand, received brief mention in the press.[29]

The January Offensive

> . . . And it is cowardly, and indeed a betrayal of whatever it means to be a Jew, to act as a white man, benefit as a white man, treat black people as white men do, and then accuse the victim, when the victim reacts, of anti-Semitism.
>
> —James Baldwin[30]

The dawn of 1969 brought with it a new session of the New York State Legislature. One of its most anticipated agenda items was a definitive decentralization law for the New York City school system. After almost two years of reports, modifications, and drafts, the original proposal of the Bundy Commission, which called for the system to be broken into about 60 community-controlled districts, had been considerably watered down. The surviving version, though, would still allow 20 to 30 local school boards to make their own personnel decisions, including the power to transfer teachers within their districts. The Board of Education and its infamous bureaucracy would be replaced by a small central agency to service these districts. Supervisors would have to pass an examination administered by this central agency, but the Board of Examiners' rankings and appointment lists would be eliminated. The local boards would have full control over their allocated lump-sum budgets to spend on supplies, construction, outside services, and other contracts. They would also be able to formulate their own curricula, as long as state standards were satisfied. This proposal, which would be finalized on March 3 by the Board of Regents, became known as "The Regents Bill."[31] In addition to the Board of Regents, it attracted support from the Board of Education, the Mayor, the Ford Foundation and, with varying levels of enthusiasm, most civil rights organizations. It was bitterly opposed by the UFT which, along with the CSA and its other allies, mounted a massive, sophisticated campaign to defeat it.

The political arsenal deployed by the UFT and its allies, in their campaign against any meaningful decentralization, included much more than an extensive lobbying operation. Their chief weapon was not debate or persuasion, but the exploitation of fear. Albert Shanker's public crusade over school governance was carried on as the defense of civilization against the specter of "Black Anti-Semitism."

A contemporary search for this term through the online *New York Times* archive (which, admittedly, is not an exact science) turns up 75 articles during the twelve months of 1968. A search for only the first two months of the legislative session, January and February of 1969, brings up 67 articles, more than one per day. After that, the frequency declines steeply, with only 46 articles surfacing during the remaining ten months of the year. In all of 1970, there were only 48, most of which had nothing to do with New York City.

"Overt Negro-Jewish tensions," wrote the authors of one book on the subject, "receded considerably by mid-1969," with no attempt at explanation.[32] What explanation could there be for this? Was the "rapidly spreading virus" of black anti-Semitism suddenly cured? Did the media just get bored with the story? Or was it all much ado about very little to begin with? What really changed after the spring of 1969 was that the UFT's campaign to defeat the Regents Bill had been completed. The circulation of the leaflets, the constant alarm-ringing, the demonization of black leadership, were by then no longer necessary to achieve its goals.

The year's campaign began in the pages of *Commentary*, then a respected intellectual journal sponsored by the American Jewish Committee. The theme for its January 1969 issue was "Conflict in the Cities." Featured were three major articles.

- "Is White Racism the Problem?" was written by Murray Friedman, one of the AJC's regional directors. He concluded that it was not.
- "The NYC School Crisis," a long article by Maurice J. Goldbloom, who usually wrote for the magazine on foreign policy issues, presented a history of the teacher strikes and the community control conflict. In every case where there was any controversy, where there was more than one side to the story, Goldbloom presented the UFT side as undisputed fact. Opposing points of view were dismissed out of hand or simply omitted from the story.

  Goldbloom introduced to the public discourse a preposterous conspiracy theory, in which the city's Protestant elite had joined forces with black militant extremists to crush the Jewish middle class, thereby distracting attention from the underfunding of the public schools. The absurdity of this theory did not prevent its reemergence, time and again, in the works of otherwise sane commentators.

This article was riddle with inaccuracies. In one that I found personally striking, Goldbloom wrote that Elaine Rooke, the JHS 271 parent representative on the Governing Board, had no children in the district's schools. Actually, her son Kevin was in one of my classes. This was only one small example of the gratuitous comments made in the article's attempt to discredit the Ocean Hill–Brownsville leadership.

- The most interesting article was "The Black Revolution and the Jewish Question," by Earl Raab, executive director of San Francisco's Jewish Community Relations Council. Its main thesis was that, "It is possible to be anti-Semitic without being an anti-Semite." This formulation reconciled the charges of anti-Semitism being leveled against the black community's quest for empowerment, with surveys and studies which found that black people were less anti-Semitic than any white Christian ethnic group. One major study, commissioned by the Anti-Defamation League in 1964, had additionally concluded that "militant blacks" were the least anti-Semitic of the black groups surveyed.[33]

These three articles laid out the historical and theoretical bases of the UFT's campaign against the alleged black anti-Semitism that supposedly permeated the community control movement. By the end of that month, Norman Podhoretz, *Commentary*'s editor, would call it "the most serious crisis confronting American Jews since the end of World War II."[34]

Vann and Campbell Meet the Press

After a shortened Christmas recess, teachers and students eagerly returned to our rapidly improving school. Among them was Les Campbell, who had been cleared of all charges by the Fischer Committee. A *New York Times* editorial blasted his reinstatement as "appeasement that undermines long-term peace" that would lead the city on the "road to guerilla warfare."[35] Shanker immediately vowed to file new charges against him with the Israelson Commission, the powerful quasi-judicial body established in the strike settlement.[36]

The campaign to discredit and destroy community control was largely carried out in the daily press and on television. In early January, a *New York Times* reporter discovered the November 1968 edition of the *African-American*

Teachers Forum, published by the ATA, and wrote a story identifying it as "the current issue."[37] The subject of the story was the *Forum*'s editorial entitled, "Needed: A Responsible Jewish Voice," the thesis of which was encapsulated in these paragraphs:

> Ever since the Hitler nightmare, American Jews have hidden behind the cloak of anti-Semitism as a broad shield against criticism . . . This would be bearable except for the great harm committed by those teachers and supervisors who have been incapable of instructing the youngsters committed to their care. The great pains we now suffer fill our eyes with tears which blind us to the European horrors of yesteryear. Don't tell us anymore about the six million slaughtered by Hitler. Tell us instead about the twelve million Blacks literally slaughtered in three hundred years of Black genocide. The Jews have recovered and now prosper. We Blacks, abused by slave traders and slave owners, hampered by vicious laws, beaten by sadistic police, exploited by employers, landlords and merchants, still exist in the stifling slums of our poverty-ridden ghettos. . . .
>
> It is time for a great responsible voice to speak up in the Jewish community. It is time to right these grave wrongs. It is time to declare that Albert Shanker and all those who support his racist diatribes do a disservice to the entire Jewish community. It is time to pour water on the growing fires of religious and racial hatreds in New York City. . . .[38]

The *Times* could have reported on this editorial in several ways. It could have focused, for example, on the cry of pain it expressed. It could have focused on the hand outstretched, reaching for Jewish allies and understanding. Instead, the headline was, "Negro Teacher Group's Editorial Assails Jews." For me, this brought to mind "Ballad of the Landlord," the Langston Hughes poem, yet again.

During the following week, almost immediately after the charges against Les Campbell were thrown out and he was reinstated at JHS 271, a new controversy arose.

On December 26, Campbell had been interviewed by Julius Lester, a popular folk singer, civil rights activist, and award-winning author, as the first guest of his new talk show on WBAI-FM, a small listener-supported radio station. Prior to the interview, Campbell showed Lester a number of poems written by students, including several by Sia Berhan, a 15-year-old high school girl. Lester picked out a few and asked him to read them on the air. "Les was uncertain" about reading one of them, he recalled in his memoir, "but I wanted him to, because it was indicative of the racial tensions engendered by the strike, and I wanted others to know how the strike was affecting black youth."[39] In an interview, he was more direct, quoting Campbell as saying, "You got to be crazy!"[40]

On the air, Lester summarized that exchange, and Campbell went ahead and read the poem. Entitled "Anti-Semitism (Dedicated to Albert Shanker)," it read, in part . . .

> Hey, Jew boy, with that
> Yarmulka on your head,
> You, pale-faced Jew boy,
> I wish you were dead . . .
> Hitler's reign lasted for
> Only fifteen years.
> For that period of time
> You shed crocodile tears.
> My suffering lasted for
> Four hundred years, jew boy
> And the man only lets me
> Play with his toys . . .
> Jew boy, you took my religion
> And adapted it for you.
> But you know Black people were
> The original Hebrews . . .
> Guess you know, Jew boy,
> There's only one reason you made it.
> You had a clean white face,
> Colorless and faded . . .
> I hate you, Jew boy,
> Cause your hang-up was the Torah,
> And my only-hang-up was
> My Goddamned Color!

In response to a flurry of angry callers, Lester again explained his motivation.

> An ugly poem, yes, but not one-hundredth as ugly as what happened in the school strikes, not one-hundredth as ugly as what some teachers said to some of those black children. I would hope that you would not have this automatic reaction, but raise a few questions inside yourself. I had it read over the air because I felt what she said was valid for a lot of black people, and I think it's time that people stop being afraid of it, and stop being hysterical about it.[41]

The interview, broadcast the morning after Christmas, probably had a listenership in the hundreds. Two weeks later, when Lester played the tape again, there were no calls to the station. The incident appeared to be over. It did not come to broad public attention until January 16, when the front page of the *New York Times* reported that the UFT had filed a complaint against WBAI with the Federal Communications Commission and called, once again, for Campbell to be fired. Shanker charged that his "proud reading of his student's anti-Semitic poem is an indication of his teaching approach" (even though he knew nothing of Campbell's teaching approach, but certainly did know that he was not teaching in any high school). The reporter threw in his own jab, indicating without any basis that the poem was *ostensibly* written by a high school student, thereby implying that Campbell was its actual author.[42]

Then the floodgates opened.

WBAI received thousands of hate letters. Lester's life was threatened in messages left on his home answering machine. The FBI told him they had uncovered a plot to kidnap him. Jewish organizations demanded that he be fired. The paramilitary Jewish Defense League sent several dozen club-wielding goons to raid the offices of WBAI. Twelve JDL members were arrested for trespassing and assault, some of whom were caught on the roof trying to loosen the elevator cable.[43]

(The JDL also staged an anti-Campbell demonstration in front of JHS 271, marching in a boisterous picket line within a set of barricades. Its substantial police protection proved unnecessary on that cold day. Teachers and students walked by the screaming pickets as though they weren't even there. I wondered if they felt as ridiculous as they looked.)

While the story was extensively covered by all of the New York media, and nationally by Jewish publications, Lester was asked for comment by only one newspaper and one television station.[44] Not a single one of those reporting the news bothered to ask Campbell what he himself thought of the poem.[45] Twenty years later, in an interview for the PBS *Eyes on the Prize* documentary series, this was his response:

> The child had very little knowledge of the whole, total picture of Jews and history of Jews. In fact, she had been taught most of her life by Jewish teachers who had taught her about the Holocaust, who had taught her about injustices to the Jewish people, and she was just finding it unusually strange that now some of these Jewish people were performing injustices to her people. That was what she was saying in the poem.[46]

Nor did any of them think to ask the young lady who wrote the poem what she was thinking, which was this:

> I had found out, doing reading and listening to some of those people who came to the school, that the original Semites were black. That the Falashas in Africa, East Africa, were the original Semites. I felt that instead of saying that we in the black community were anti-Semitic, I felt that the UFT, Albert Shanker, were anti-Semitic.
>
> The community wasn't anti-Jewish. It's true that a lot of the teachers were Jewish. But see, you shopped on Pitkin Avenue; you shopped on Belmont Avenue; you shopped on Delancey Street. You wasn't anti-Jewish.[47]

Based solely on the UFT-inspired press coverage, Mayor Lindsay asked the Board of Education to conduct an investigation, and "take appropriate action." This did not amuse Al Vann. "Are Jews beyond criticism?" he asked in a *Forum* editorial. "I don't think so. *Any* people who persecute black people will be criticized by blacks." He charged that the mayor had "played fast and loose" with Campbell's reputation, "in his hurry to appease the powerful Jewish financiers of the city."[48]

Whatever Vann had in mind, which may have been the financing of Lindsay's fledgling reelection campaign, writing these words was like pouring gasoline on an already raging fire. In New York at the time, almost any use of the word "Jew" in any but a positive sense was probable cause to be indicted, in the press and in the political realm, for anti-Semitism. A connection between Jews and anything in the financial realm would escalate that indictment to a summary conviction. These push-button responses, though, had not penetrated the black community. As Brandeis University historian Jacob Cohen observed, "Negroes have never learned that it is impolite to call a Jew a Jew in public, perhaps because they are called Negro so irrelevantly, so often."[49]

The mayor, speaking to an audience composed mostly of teachers in a Queens synagogue shortly afterward, escalated his own rhetoric. Now he prejudged the case, proclaiming that both Vann and Campbell "did not have any place teaching in the city's schools."[50] This was before any "investigation" had even started. At the Board of Education, though, a resolution directing Superintendent Donovan to bring charges against Campbell and Vann was defeated by the votes of Lindsay's own appointees. Instead, Donovan was directed to investigate further.

Simultaneously, the Jewish Defense League took the matter to court, and convinced a judge to issue an order directing the Board to "show cause" why the two should not be dismissed.

Shanker held a press conference, where he called on Commissioner Allen to remove the Trustee, Dr. Nordos, because he "failed to stop the harassment of union teachers by the suspended district Governing Board" and because he hadn't taken action against Campbell.[51]

Commented Julius Lester on the air, "It seems that white people believe in free speech only as long as they agree with what is being said."[52]

Campbell's initial reluctance to read the poem on the air was never reported until the *Columbia Journalism Review*'s Fall 1969 issue published an analytical article by Fred Ferretti, a former NBC television newsman.[53] He reported that WBAI's general manager told him that no one, before Ferretti, ever asked for a complete tape of the program, which meant that all the hysteria had been based on hearsay.

Lester, who equated Black Nationalism with Jewish Zionism, and respected both, was supported by WBAI's largely Jewish staff and management.[54] A few months later, he attempted to add some perspective. "I think one of the difficulties," he said in an interview, "is that people are equating the poem with the traditional anti-Semitism, which is rooted in God-knows-what, Christ-killers and what have you. That has no relationship to the black community."[55]

Accusations of anti-Semitism would stick to Campbell for decades after this incident, for reading a poem on the radio that he didn't write and was reluctant to read,[56] and to Lester as well, even after he converted to Judaism in 1982. (He ultimately became a professor of Judaic Studies and a lay leader of his congregation.)

In March 2011, State Senator Velmanette Montgomery introduced a resolution honoring Campbell (now Jitu Weusi), in recognition of his decades of leadership and community service. Like most bills of its type, it was rubber-stamped as a courtesy by the Senate. Almost two years later, and 44 years after the reading of the poem on WBAI, the *Daily News* apparently first became aware of the resolution. In an opinion piece, the paper blasted the Senate for making any positive mention of Weusi. It labeled him an anti-Semite and claimed, wrongly, that he was the actual author of the poem, "one of the most notorious anti-Semitic statements in New York history."[57] This gratuitous piece of slander appeared a few weeks after Weusi was diagnosed with the cancer that would soon take his life.

During 1969, though, Rhody McCoy held his ground, refusing to take action against any teacher based on any words spoken off school grounds. In a five-page February 1 letter to Donovan, responding to a vague request for recommendations regarding Vann and Campbell, he called on the city to "help us implement the Constitution's Fourteenth Amendment (guaranteeing equal protection to all), rather than lead an assault on the First (guaranteeing freedom of speech)." "I, for one," he continued "would take no part in the latter." He said the district would not tolerate anti-Semitism in its schools, but had received no reports of any such incidents, and reminded Donovan that he had no power to discipline any teacher for anything said outside the school system. He also reminded Donovan of the system's many shortcomings in multicultural education, and suggested a focus on these instead.[58] It appears that this letter put an end to Donovan's investigation; nothing was heard about it after that.

Donovan did circulate a memorandum throughout the school system on "Staff Responsibilities with Respect to Racial or Religious Bigotry," that included some curious statements.[59] "It has always been the pride of this system," he declared in one, "that teachers and supervisors treat all children and adults with equal consideration." (If that were true, there might never have been a need for the Community Control movement.) Then, "It has also been recognized (*by whom?*) that a teacher's public activities outside the classroom may reflect upon his ability to create an atmosphere of objectivity and justice within the classroom." (*Guess who?*) And, "The entire school system can be affected adversely if the public even believes that a staff member harbors ill will." Through all the years of complaints about white racist teachers and supervisors, neither Donovan nor his predecessors had expressed such a concern. (My italics added.)

After instructing school supervisors to initiate a "human relations" program, Donovan added that, "I am also assigning a small task force within my office to follow up on all complaints received . . . involving racism or other forms of bigotry and to bring to my attention those facts which may warrant disciplinary action." Since no action was taken against any white teachers, it must be presumed that no complaints of "racism or other forms of bigotry" were filed.

By this time, most of the city's teachers, approximately 30,000 of them, had signed up with the right-wing Jewish Teachers Association, which accused the Ford Foundation of anti-Semitism and uncritically allied itself with the terrorist Jewish Defense League.[60] For those unsure of this step, their leader made it an easy choice. "If community control as we see it in Ocean Hill–Brownsville wins," announced Shanker at a meeting, "there will be 'Jew Bastard' signs and swastikas in all the schools."[61] There were, of course, none of these actually in Ocean Hill–Brownsville.

Mr. Singer's Visit

In the midst of all this, life went on at JHS 271. Despite the vastly improved school operation, there was still tension in the air. The understaffing, and the nagging presence of the eleven remaining unwanted teachers along with all the official observers, generated plenty of stress and strain. Any opportunity for some comic relief was more than welcome. On January 14, 1969, one was provided by a visitor to JHS 271.

I was in the lobby at the end of the school day when I heard a PA announcement summoning me to the principal's office. This was completely unexpected. Steve Bloomfield told me he had seen someone he didn't recognize conferring with the State observers and then going into the office with two policemen. He and Steve Perry, another teacher, offered to come along with me, and they did. I proceeded to the office with some trepidation, wondering what I could possibly be wanted for. Bloomfield's observation made me a little nervous. "Well," I thought, "it's finally happened. They'll tell me I've done something that violates some obscure rule and revoke my teaching license."

I had imagined this happening many times before, whenever a telegram was delivered or I received an official-looking envelope in the mail. Jittery though I was, I also felt relief that the enemy was finally laying its cards on the table, whatever they were.

When we arrived in the office, Campbell, Vann, and Hopkins, who were under indictment, were already seated at the conference table. Relieved to have allies present, I began to relax. The other occupants were two police officers sitting in a corner, and a busy little white man at the head of the table, a mountain of papers piled in front of him.

Vann must have had advance notice of this conference. He was accompanied by Rita Murphy, a black attorney who, along with noted civil liberties lawyer Morton Stavis, had provided superb representation to the four teachers recently cleared by the Fischer panel. She was trying to ascertain what the session was to be about, but finding little success. The teachers were asked to be seated and the "proceedings" got underway.

The little man introduced himself as "Mr. Singer, an investigating officer for the Israelson Commission," and said he had called Campbell, Vann, Hopkins, and me together in order to explain the nature of charges that had been filed against us. The commission he represented had broad powers, not only to adjudicate charges but also to suspend those charged pending the outcome of a future hearing.

Mr. Singer's first order of the day was to write down the names of the other people in the room and their role in the meeting. "Just for the record," he said.

"Miss Murphy, I assume you are acting as consultant to Mr. Vann?"

"That is correct," she replied, "as well as to any of the other teachers who wish to be represented by me." That was music to my ears. All three of us quickly accepted her offer.

Turning to Bloomfield and Perry, he asked what their names were, one at a time. Steve Perry answered first.

"Is that spelled P-E-R-R-Y?" asked Singer, taking care to make his notes accurate.

"That's right, S-T-E-V-E-N P-E-R-R-Y."

"Very good," muttered Mr. Singer without glancing up from his paper. "And what is your business in this meeting?"

"No business," answered Perry. "I just came to watch. This isn't a closed meeting, is it?"

"Yes, this *is* a closed meeting," Mr. Singer abruptly declared, to the surprise of everyone present. "And I will have to ask you to leave."

Not if I could help it. "Wait a minute," I interrupted. "Mr. Perry misunderstood the question. He is here to act as my consultant." My newly appointed "consultant" stammered his agreement, as the eyes of the teachers around the table met in silent amusement.

"I see," mumbled the investigating officer, suspiciously copying down the information.

Turning to Bloomfield, "And what is your name and business here?" I broke in again.

"He's my assistant consultant." I had decided, without thinking about it, to have some fun on what might be my last day at the school.

"Mr. Isaacs," Mr. Singer impatiently retorted, "You are not permitted more than one consultant."

"Where is that written?" I asked, well aware by this time that the rules for such proceedings were usually made up on the fly. Mr. Singer, caught in his own procedural trap, was getting annoyed.

"Isn't Miss Murphy acting as your consultant?"

"Of course," I replied. "'She's my chief consultant. You see, in important matters, my consultants must consult with one another and . . ."

"Now stop this!" Poor Mr. Singer was losing his temper. "Mr. Isaacs, I must warn you that you are not treating this proceeding with the respect to which its authority entitles it."

Campbell, laughing so hard he could barely stay in his seat, made the obvious observation. "But that's just what he *is* doing!" This was becoming the best part of my day.

Mr. Singer, not wishing to provoke the group into walking out on him, and reluctant to appear to be violating anyone's "due process" rights, wrote down Bloomfield's name and title: "Assistant Consultant to Mr. Isaacs." Anyone reading the minutes of this meeting, with the list of my "consultants," might have thought I was either a Chief of State or a Mafia kingpin.

As Singer read aloud his list of names and titles, Vann winked to the group, walked to the telephone, and dialed a number. "Hello," he began, as everyone watched, wondering who he could be calling in the middle of the meeting. "Is this the Black Panther office?" Mr. Singer's pen began to shake as the teachers surveyed the ceiling tiles, struggling to look serious.

"It is?" Vann continued, "Listen, you better get some troops over to 271 right away." Pause. "That's right. We got some business to take care of." He hung up, stepped back to his seat, and gave Mr. Singer his most attentive pose.

The appointed representative of constituted authority was trying not to appear unnerved. He began to recite the charges that had been lodged against each of us. Those against Campbell, Vann, and Hopkins were identical to the ones they had just been cleared of by the Fischer panel. When the attorney pointed this out, Mr. Singer merely shrugged. His job, he explained, was not to bring the charges or to decide them, but only to inform the group of what they were. Further, he said, the Commission had not even decided yet whether or not it would formally pursue these charges.

This was harassment and double jeopardy. Shanker had struck out with the Fischer panel, and he had no reason to think Dr. Nordos would override it, so now he had filed the same charges with the Israelson Commission. What would be next?

The charges filed against me were new. According to unnamed observers, I was guilty of three violations of regulations: picketing during school hours; agitating students to harass UFT teachers; and harassing UFT teachers myself. Mr. Singer refused to divulge the identities of either the alleged victims or the complainants, or the dates on which the acts were alleged to have occurred.

After informing us of our right to remain silent, he asked whether any of the prospective defendants had any statements to make in response to the charges. None did, and the meeting ended. I had enjoyed it enormously.

Later, after entertaining a friend with an account of what had happened, she asked the simple question that I had been avoiding. "They can't do anything, can they?" I really wasn't sure how to answer. I knew that the charges, as presented, were trumped up; but I had little faith in this commission's ability, or even willingness, to sort out fact from fantasy. It was a politically appointed, UFT-approved panel, which I had no reason to believe would give me a fair trial. I knew that some support could have been mobilized in my defense, but did not want to become the center of that kind of controversy.

This scenario exemplified the power inequality between union and nonunion teachers. When complaints were made against us by UFT teachers or observers, they were carefully prepared, presented as formal charges, and litigated by the union's large staff of attorneys. Those lawyers were also on call to defend union members, like Fred Nauman, whenever necessary, against any charges filed against them. Without organizational support, we were on our own. Stavis and his colleagues at the Center for Constitutional Rights, including Rita Murphy, had been steadfast in various defenses of the Governing Board and the teachers brought before the Fischer panel. Would they defend me? I had no idea. Rather than worry about this until I really needed to, I just put it in my rapidly growing file of "things-not-to-think-about, yet."

Three weeks later, the Israelson Commission announced that a hearing would be scheduled only in the case of Campbell, regarding allegations of "harassment, intimidation and disruption" during November and December. I never heard from that panel again, although I would have welcomed another encounter with Mr. Singer.

The Principal Returns and Teachers Leave

On January 15, the State Court of Appeals, in a narrowly construed ruling, strongly implying that the Board of Examiners lists should never again be bypassed, reversed the decisions of the lower courts and reinstated principals Harris, Fuentes, and Rogers. The ruling allowed them to return to their schools the next day. However, the court upheld the suspension of the Governing Board.[62]

Harris had been enthusiastically supported in efforts to retain his position by our entire faculty, perhaps most vigorously by the ATA cadre, its most militant faction. This support, though, was more about upholding community control of hiring than about the specific person involved. Circumstances had made Harris larger than himself.

As Campbell mused, "Here's a black man, working for years in a white system, and being passed over for promotion, year after year, because of his race. Now that he's finally a principal, the first black junior high school principal in the city's history, will he take any risks that might endanger his job?" Some teachers foresaw new internal conflicts during the coming months.

Nevertheless, Harris was greeted with a warm reception. A sign over the main entrance proclaimed in large letters, "Welcome Back, Mr. Harris!" We put a small party together in his office. Some teachers brought homemade cakes for the occasion.

The ATA core faculty, which had been running the school, urged Harris to retain the practices that Vann instituted in his absence. At first, he was amenable to these overtures, sometimes even taking personal credit for some of Vann's ideas. As the spring semester approached, it appeared that the staff might still be able to overcome the challenges posed by personnel shortages and continued UFT harassment.

The staff shortages, though, were posing increasing problems every day. Many white teachers, realizing that Ocean Hill–Brownsville was not the place for them, were transferring to other districts or leaving the profession entirely. When I asked why, they offered a wide variety of reasons.

- One Jewish teacher confided that he didn't really want to leave, but that his "family was under too much pressure from neighbors."
- One was offered a good job in a progressive private school, and jumped at the opportunity to work in calmer surroundings.
- Some teachers, who had misinterpreted the promise of community control to mean all their anti-establishment notions would be indulged, were shocked when confronted with the

social conservatism of the black community. One decided on his own, for example, to teach sex education to sixth-graders, and was shaken when parents objected.

- One teacher, who had only been teaching to avoid the draft, actually enlisted in the army. I wondered if he thought he'd be safer there.
- Another Jewish teacher transferred, because, "According to my parents, there is anti-Semitism here," although he admitted that he had never experienced a single manifestation of this phenomenon.
- Another teacher simply disappeared for months without bothering to resign.

The remaining staff was not sorry to lose most of these people. Few of them had been particularly good teachers. The mounting class coverage assignments, though, were becoming more than even committed, effective teachers could handle. Sandra Nystrom was one of these. A Midwestern blonde of Scandinavian descent, she had bravely travelled to Sunflower County with a church group in 1964 to work with SNCC in organizing the Mississippi Freedom Democratic Party, so she was no stranger to controversy, even danger. In September, she had come to JHS 271 as one of the replacement teachers, and she was a good one. She had marched on the front lines in the October 1 walkout, and absorbed the blows of police batons. She had no problems establishing good rapport with her black and Puerto Rican students, and cultivated positive relationships with their parents. By February, though, the strain of covering extra classes, the internal conflicts, the presence of the UFT teachers and the outside observers, and the barrage of external UFT-inspired attacks, were more than she could bear. Her resignation hit me hard. Conditions had deteriorated to the point where we lost one of our best.

Since the beginning of the experimental district, the issue of teacher transfers had created difficulties. All the UFT-instigated turmoil of the spring and fall began when McCoy and the Governing Board tried to transfer uncooperative and incompetent teachers out of the district. Yet a special exemption from the union contract allowed any teachers in our district to transfer out *voluntarily* whenever they wished to do so, no questions asked. Meanwhile, roadblocks had been put in the way of teachers from other districts who wanted to voluntarily transfer *into* Ocean Hill–Brownsville.

The contract between the UFT and the central Board specified that teachers could not transfer out of any school without prior approval unless they had at least five years of experience. Further, no more than five percent of the teachers in any one school could transfer out in any one year. Without these restrictions, teachers could have jumped around from school to school, whenever life got a little difficult for them, instead of working through their problems; and the difficult ghetto schools would never be fully staffed. When the demonstration districts were established, though, the UFT demanded and won a waiver of these rules only for those three districts. Now, teachers could leave Ocean Hill–Brownsville whenever they wanted to, but they could not be replaced. This deal had injected a poison pill so that, under these circumstances, our teaching staff could only continue to shrink.

Even more ominous was the exhaustion of the community base. The Governing Board remained under suspension, and many parents were just worn out.

Still, there were reasons for hope. Ten new teachers were recruited, and finally cleared to fill some of the existing vacancies. While they were inexperienced, it was hoped that they would learn fast enough to be able to hold their own in a classroom. Two experienced black teachers, Allen Boyce and Milfred Fierce, were able to transfer in as acting assistant principals. Mandracchia had recovered from his heart attack, but the Governing Board asked him to accept a less stressful assignment as principal of PS 87, a feeder elementary school that had a vacancy. We would miss him.

In order to rationally integrate these changes, the entire school was reorganized. Children who had apparently been placed in the wrong classes were shifted. Teachers were given new programs so they could "begin fresh," which many welcomed the opportunity to do. The faculty seemed to get a second wind, and we resolved to do everything we could to overcome the still numerous obstacles ahead.

Our principal, though, was a competent administrator at best. Harris did not have Vann's leadership qualities. One of his very few innovations was a "Weekly Bulletin," a summary of instructions for teachers, and complaints about their performance. The introduction to one of these announcements provides a good example of his limited capacity to inspire:

> For better or worse our new semester is under way, and inasmuch as we are now in the water, we must sink or swim. Though sinking might seem easier at times, there seems to be an all-out attempt to swim the turbulent waters. There are many, many rough spots. In fact, it is difficult to find the calm areas; however, we must be persistent in searching for the silver lining.[63]

Fortunately, this missive was not distributed to the students, who were working to improve their English language arts. After six weeks, Harris discontinued the bulletins, because, as he correctly observed, "no one seems to be reading them."

Even though the principal was back in his office, Vann was still generally recognized as the school's top administrator, while Campbell became identified as its educational leader. At first, Harris seemed to accept this, often readily approving implementation of his nominal subordinates' ideas. On February 21, Malcolm X Memorial Day, he permitted Campbell to organize the entire eighth grade for a trip to a program at LIU. Harris only insisted that his own name be kept out of it. He similarly acceded to Campbell's recruitment of outside groups to present cultural programs, as long as any costs were covered through faculty donations. Harris, at this point, was trying to pacify all sides and avoid confrontations.

The ADL Report

January 16, the very day that the principals were reinstated by the court, was also the day that the controversy over Campbell's poetry reading broke. A week later, the Anti-Defamation League put its considerable weight behind Shanker's characterization of the Community Control movement as an anti-Semitic plot.

On January 23, the ADL published a major report, this one entitled, "Anti-Semitism in the New York City School Controversy." The report began,

> The use of anti-Semitism—raw, undisguised—has distorted the fundamental character of the controversy surrounding the public schools of NYC. The anti-Semitism has gone unchecked by public authorities for 2½ years, reaching a peak during the school strike . . . and in the post-strike period. It is still going on.

In the introduction to this report, the ADL repudiated through omission its own previous studies, which minimized anti-Semitic feeling in the black community. The author of one analysis of anti-Semitism that the ADL itself published in 1964 did not even think it worthy of mention.[64]

Now, the League took quite the opposite view, inflating minor provocations to major proportions in order to "prove" that the Jewish community was under siege. In addition, the introduction to the report, as quoted above, seemed to be self-critical since the ADL itself had not alerted the public to the existence of this menace during the two and a half years that it had allegedly been building up; it had, in fact, consistently done the opposite. In 1967, for example, the ADL's National Director, Benjamin R. Epstein, said, "The Jewish community would be well advised to focus its attention on the main sources of American anti-Semitism and to drop preoccupation with Negro anti-Semitism, which only serves to divert energy from the civil rights struggle."[65] Only a few months before this report was issued, Dore Schary, the League's Chairman, declared in his convention speech that the greater danger is not from black militants, but from "the radical right of the white extremists who stand for repression of the Negro *and* the Jews."[66]

Since this new report characterized and intensified the attacks from all quarters, and since it was widely accepted as proof of the "crisis situation," its methodology and content deserve particular attention. What follows is a summary of the ADL report, along with a running critique for which this author takes full responsibility.

The report began by presenting the "Philosophy of Mental Genocide" which, it said, is responsible for instigating anti-Semitic feelings in the black community. It presented an "early expression" of this philosophy in an article written by John Hatchett, then a teacher at PS 68, part of Harlem's IS 201 complex, in a late 1967 edition of the ATA's *Forum*. The article laid out the statistical facts of Jewish dominance in the teaching and supervisory positions of the city school system, and linked these overwhelming statistics to the miseducation that system has inflicted on black children. Further, he alluded to the self-fulfilling prophecy that those children could not succeed, which he attributed to the racist beliefs held by their (predominantly Jewish) teachers.[67]

There was no disputing the statistics, neither the overwhelming Jewish presence in the teaching staff, nor the system's abysmal failure to educate black students. The theory of the self-fulfilling prophecy had achieved widespread currency among social scientists by then, following several major studies, and had been in the public domain at least since the release of Kenneth Clark's *Dark Ghetto* in 1964.

The confusion of correlation and causation is a common statistical fallacy. The fact that two conditions exist at the same time does not mean that one necessarily causes the other. Hatchett did not make the case for causality, and could fairly be accused of statistical illiteracy. It could be argued that Hatchett's inference was justified by the massive data, but he did not adequately justify his conclusions from that data. A charge of anti-Semitism could not be logically sustained on this basis, though. Hatchett did not charge Jewish people with having anything in their religion or their nature that dictated hatred toward people of color. When he wrote, "I hate the misery, degradation, racism and cultural genocide daily practiced against my people by (those) whose entire history should have told them, 'No, this is morally and spiritually wrong,'" he indicted not the Jewish people, but only those Jewish schoolteachers who, he thought, should have known better.

Hatchett did not suggest that these schools would suddenly awaken to a renaissance if all the Jewish staff disappeared overnight. Rather, he implied that the education of black children would be of much higher quality if the

Jewish teachers would be true to the lessons their own history should have taught them. Jewish teachers, he argued, should know better.

Hatchett's condemnation of those who should have known better was not even limited to Jewish teachers. Most of the article was an attack on two specific teachers in his school who, he wrote, typified the "Anti-Black Jews and the Black Anglo-Saxons." These two groups, he argued, have joined forces to keep black children from achieving a meaningful education. The two teachers, one black and one Jewish, had been extensively quoted in the UFT's organ, *The United Teacher*, attacking community control and the IS 201 Planning Board. Commenting on their statements, Hatchett wrote that, "Their personal and political charges display an inordinate desire to crush those forces designed to free our Black children from the miserable education they have received, and are continuing to receive, from misfits, incompetents, and racists."

Hatchett, never a major figure in the Community Control movement, was fired because of unrelated charges a few months after the article's publication. The ADL's attack would later cost him his next job, as director of the Afro-American Center at New York University.

The next targets of this section were Les Campbell, whose reading of the high school student's "Anti-Semitism" poem on the radio was considered proof of his own anti-Semitism, and Al Vann, whose defense of Campbell was considered sufficient to paint him with the same brush. Rhody McCoy's support of both Campbell and Vann in other connections was noted in the report, suggesting that he, too, must be anti-Semitic.

Next was the above-referenced November editorial in the ATA's *Forum* that called for "a responsible Jewish voice." The ADL report cited it as "the most recent manifestation of a new twist in scapegoating."

In the second section of the report, "Pressures on School Personnel" was presented as further evidence of an anti-Semitic plot. It "documented" a total of four anonymous remarks allegedly heard at two demonstrations in 1966 and 1967, one anonymous leaflet discovered in 1967, and four reported verbal remarks, all in connection with "attempts to drive Jewish teachers and principals out of schools." Hardly a mountain of evidence.

As if to clinch the case against black leaders, the report quoted from a 1967 letter to Albert Shanker from Oliver Leeds, then chairman of Brooklyn CORE:

> If anti-Semitism is not to flourish and mislead the people, then the hypocrisy of being liberal has to end. We in CORE are demanding teacher responsibility. If they can't produce, go elsewhere. If they can't get these Black kids up to grade level, teach elsewhere. This to us will be the best proof against anti-Semitism.

Once again, the ADL deliberately misinterpreted an honest statement of a real problem.

The most slanderous section of the report was the one entitled, "An Ocean Hill Principal." This was an attack on PS 155's Luis Fuentes, the city's only Puerto Rican principal. The evidence here was the testimony of two unnamed assistant principals at the school, who transferred out of the district soon after Fuentes was appointed. The report lists nine statements allegedly made by Fuentes, out of context, and often in the heat of argument.

In my view, only two of these statements could conceivably be construed to be derogatory to Jews, one concerning the changing of obviously Jewish names, and the other alluding to "prominent (physical) characteristics." The other seven statements quoted in the report, although controversial, are either neutral or complimentary regarding Jews, or are about entirely unrelated subjects. The only conclusion I could draw from this was that these statements were included in order to "soften" the reader to the view that Fuentes was anti-Semitic. Whatever the nature of the quoted statements, the anonymity of the sources and the lack of any corroboration added up to a pretty weak case. (Four years later, when Fuentes was serving as superintendent of another district, the identical charges were brought in a quasi-judicial "chancellor's hearing," in which I testified. The hearing officer, Judge Vincent Broderick, dismissed those charges.)

This section of the ADL report then made an effort to discredit David Spencer, Chairman of the IS 201 Complex Governing Board. Here, the report should be quoted directly. "Spencer wrote,"

> What we see happening is that, with an ingenious display of verbal gymnastics, a large part of the Jewish Establishment (is) using the cry of "anti-Semitism" to imply that Black people are persecuting Jews. The only comparable situation that comes to mind is a rapist charging his victim with assault!

"Spencer then states that,"

> We *are* becoming more anti-Semitic—with very passing day that brings a new rash of news articles with new charges or resolutions by this or that Jewish organization . . .

"*After complimenting Jews who are 'working tirelessly behind the scenes for self-determination in Black and Puerto Rican communities'* (my italics), Spencer said,"

> Nevertheless, it is hard to keep from reacting against everyone Jewish when the full weight of the Jewish Establishment is not only

> beating our Black and Puerto Rican communities, but also accusing us of being the aggressor.

Spencer could have been referring to this very report. What reaction could the ADL have expected from blacks and Puerto Ricans after dealing with so many of their most popular leaders in this manner?

The next two sections of the report concerned the views of black officials of the city's antipoverty program. Together, they document four statements and two leaflets, some of which were anti-Semitic, some of which were alleged to be, and some of which were clearly not. Several of those quoted were officials, others allegedly were, and others were not. One statement was "alleged (to have been made) by the *New York Post*." Little of the material had been checked for accuracy. It appeared that these sections of the report were included to stimulate an investigation of the antipoverty program. The paucity of the evidence demonstrated, though, that such an investigation would invalidate its hypothesis.

The report's largest section was titled, "The Strike Incidents." These incidents consisted primarily of anonymous shouts made at demonstrations, and of threatening notes allegedly passed around during the UFT strikes. The UFT picket lines at ghetto schools were often scenes of verbal abuse, bordering on the violent on both sides of the barricades. To pick out remarks made at these emotional confrontations, and then to offer them as "evidence" of violence and anti-Semitism is hardly persuasive. As Rev. Oliver pleaded repeatedly at the time, "I wish people wouldn't interpret an exclamation of 'Drop Dead!' at a picket line as a threat on their lives."[68] Otherwise, I suppose the brickbats thrown by UFT members at non-striking teachers could have been enough to charge them with violence as well.

The report also discussed the questionably sourced leaflets that were reprinted in the hundreds of thousands by the UFT, which the ADL itself had dismissed as insignificant during the fall. Now it presented these same leaflets as evidence of widespread anti-Semitism in the Community Control movement.

Other "Strike Incidents" included a written attack on Shanker signed by Hal Koppersmith, an unaffiliated white gadfly on Manhattan's Lower East Side. Koppersmith charged that, "Shanker, in his mad search for power, has escalated a simple administrative transfer into a race war in order to preserve the white job monopoly based on racial discrimination, not [on] merit." Koppersmith also referred to "Adolph Shanker" as the "Jewish George Wallace of Education." I knew Koppersmith, and did not doubt these statements; he was a master of hyperbole. They were only anti-Semitic, though, if that term had become synonymous with "anti-Shanker."

The ADL report missed no angles, however obscure, in attempting to prove its point. For example, also listed as "strike incidents" were a letter to the mayor written by a pro-Arab lobbyist, totally unconnected to the school situation; and a leaflet distributed not by black militants, but by the Neo-Nazi National Renaissance Party, which was not only anti-Semitic but also anti-black.

The pattern continued in the section entitled, "Anti-Semitism Since the Strike—the Holiday Controversy." After quoting in full one anonymous leaflet that was distributed at a single school, it described various protests targeting a particular section of the strike settlement. This agreement had taken away parts of the Christmas and Easter holidays in order to allow teachers to make up back pay, while leaving all Jewish holidays intact. These "incidents and flyers," declared the report, "reveal anti-Semitism." Really?

The report's concluding section was entitled, "The Virus Spreads." It attacked the introduction to the published catalogue for a Metropolitan Museum of Art exhibit, which was entirely run by whites. It berated Human Rights Commissioner Booth, for "failure to take appropriate investigative action" on the anti-Semitism alleged to be in the show's catalogue. (Booth was removed from his position two weeks later.) It did not mention the fact that the exhibit itself was protested and picketed by black activists and artists.

The ADL report was designed to conclusively "expose the obvious bias against Jews posed by Negro extremists." Its failure to demonstrate the menace of black anti-Semitism only proved the very opposite to be true. Here was the city's black population, provoked daily by vicious lies and slanders, denigrated at every turn by a Jewish union chief, and attacked by the major Jewish organizations. Then consider the paltry findings of this report.

The report was the product of months of investigation, carried on by an experienced staff. At the end of that time, it could not cite even one anti-Semitic action, only a few defamatory remarks. Nowhere was it even alleged that blacks had kept Jews out of jobs, out of neighborhoods, or out of an educational system. Nowhere was it even suggested that blacks had lynched Jewish citizens, exploited Jewish consumers, attacked Jewish businesses, or destroyed the minds of Jewish children.

The report quoted a few threatening letters as though these were evidence of an anti-Semitic tsunami. Nowhere did it acknowledge the thousands of threatening letters sent by Jews to McCoy or to Rev. Oliver (or even to me). With the flimsiest of evidence, the ADL released this attack just at the time that negotiations for the reinstatement of Ocean Hill–Brownsville's Governing Board were going on, as were the State Legislature's deliberations over a new school decentralization law.

The *Times* published the ADL's "findings" on Thursday, January 23, the same day the report was issued. By the time I finished reading, I was incensed. In the long term, the report would inject fear into the legislative debate. In the short term, it would interfere with the educational programs we were trying to implement in Ocean Hill–Brownsville. It slandered colleagues who I knew not to be anti-Semitic. It strained my attachment to my own Jewish heritage.

Dissent and Rebuttal

Over that weekend, I drafted a statement of rebuttal. By Tuesday morning, it had nineteen signatories, about half of the Jewish teachers at JHS 271. Given more time, there would have been more signatures, but I didn't want to take any more time. No one I showed it to disagreed with its content and message. Just one teacher refused to sign, only because he said it didn't go far enough. The full statement read:

> We are members of the faculty at JHS 271, in Ocean Hill–Brownsville. We are colleagues of Leslie Campbell and Albert Vann,
>
> We are also Jewish.
>
> We have watched the white leadership of NYC work itself into a furor over the alleged anti-Semitism of Mr. Campbell and Mr. Vann. We can no longer remain quiet on this issue.
>
> Les Campbell is a master teacher, one of our best. Al Vann is an extremely effective administrator. Both these men have proved themselves indispensable to the smooth functioning of our school.
>
> Neither Campbell nor Vann is anti-Semitic.
>
> We acknowledge that there exist some anti-Semitic blacks. There are more anti-Semitic whites. These are difficult problems which will not disappear by simply being ignored. If, for example, a poem is written which expresses the roots of anti-Semitic feelings, it should be read and studied, not suppressed. And let us not be diverted from fighting what is still our society's most basic sickness: White Racism.
>
> It is a statistical fact that the educational bureaucracy in NYC is dominated by Jews. There is no question that years of miseducation, capped by the UFT strikes, have encouraged whatever anti-Semitic feeling there is among black youth.
>
> We are sorry that the legitimate aspiration of black people to get jobs which are now held by Jews is interpreted as anti-Semitism.
>
> We see this absurd attack on Les Campbell and Al Vann as one more strategy of the educational establishment to destroy the concept of Community Control, and to repress the self-determination of black and Puerto Rican people.
>
> This is nonsense, and we are tired of it.
>
> We demand that Mayor Lindsay, the Board of Education, and others who hold power in this city, end their harassment of

> Campbell and Vann, and that they deal with the issue of community control on its merits.[69]

During my lunch break, I walked over to Rhody McCoy's office, and showed it to him. McCoy and I were both pipe-smokers. Whenever we met in his small office, we would disappear in a haze of smoke after about ten minutes. This meeting didn't need ten minutes, though. He immediately instructed an aide to arrange a press conference for 4:00 that afternoon.

The press conference was well-attended. The story made the day's late tabloids,[70] and clips were shown on the evening TV news. Within a couple of days, the hate mail came pouring in, angrier and more vicious than almost anything I received after the *Times Magazine* article. In a typical letter,

> May I express the heartfelt wish that one of the first "Jew-boys" that are dead—if Campbell gets his wish—will be an object like you, who defends those who are murderers toward his people . . . you despicable flea![71]

There was another flood of mail after I appeared, with some of my students, on Alan Burke's TV talk show during the following week. On this platform, I again refuted the charges of anti-Semitism at JHS 271, and told of the positive working relationships that had been established between the white and black teachers, including those who were Jewish and those whose names were Vann and Campbell. I also tried to communicate the sense of closeness that had developed between teachers, students, and parents, mentioning as an illustration the day I took a few students to meet my own parents, who invited some of their friends. It was probably injudicious of me to relate that particular anecdote in more detail than was absolutely necessary. It prompted this, from an anonymous letter-writer . . .

> When you've shown yourself to be an ugly individual is when you told the story about bringing the negro (sic) children to your parents' home, and the sneers and faces the Jewish women made at you. Even if it were true, you should have kept your mouth shut. In short, you're a bigot and a rat.[72]

Rev. Oliver had the best line that night. In an obvious reference to the Anti-Defamation League report, he stated that, "No community has been more *defamed* in recent months than Ocean Hill–Brownsville!"

A common theme in the hate mail I received was the writers' insistence that black anti-Semitism was rampant in Ocean Hill–Brownsville, no matter what I reported from direct personal experience. After all, they read and heard about it in the media every day. Many references to Hitler's Germany

JANUARY 28, 1969

For the Defense

Post Photo by DeLucia

Charles S. Isaacs, a math teacher at JHS 271, defends Leslie Campbell and Asst. Principal Albert Vann against charges of black anti-Semitism. Isaacs, who is Jewish, presented a statement signed by 20 Jewish teachers at the school during conference that arose from a radio reading of a Campbell poem.

Figure 3.4. "Shame" scrawled on news coverage of author's press conference (January 28, 1969).

were made, but none to the Nazi's "Big Lie" propaganda technique, the very device that I argued was being employed by the UFT to spread the myth of black anti-Semitism. Often, at speaking engagements, people who never set foot in Ocean Hill–Brownsville would deny the veracity of my accounts of life at JHS 271, or just claim that I must have missed a lot. Once, I was invited into a Holocaust survivor's living-room to meet with his neighbors. The host was open to accepting my narrative, but most of his guests were more inclined to dismiss it.

Growing up Jewish during the 1940s and 1950s was to routinely hear references to European pogroms and concentration camps, sometimes from actual survivors. These stories were amplified for me through my own study of European history. I also had direct experience with anti-Semitism during my adolescence in a predominantly Italian and Irish Catholic neighborhood. I felt confident that I would recognize actual anti-Semitism when I saw it. (Ironically, Albert Shanker's children had their first personal experience with anti-Semitism when the family moved to a leafy white suburb in 1968.)[73]

Some of the letter-writers took the charge of denial to an even further extreme, arguing that I couldn't really be Jewish at all. Were they right? I needed to give this some thought.

Ten years earlier, when I was in junior high school myself, an unhappy Long Island transplant from Brooklyn, I was drawn to attend the religious services my father attended. Afflicted by numerous illnesses and addiction-related problems, often unemployed or hospitalized, he found solace in the familiar surroundings that recalled his Lower East Side upbringing. I was more than willing to be his companion there. I was also attracted to the communal atmosphere of the congregation assembled in its spare storefront synagogue, next door to an Italian deli. It was an escape from the sterility of suburban life. I memorized the major prayers and made my best efforts to sing the songs. I preferred Hebrew to English, experiencing this foreign language as a secret code known only the congregants. Even though I couldn't decipher much of that code, and was able only to read it, I found this more fulfilling than reading the English translations. I studied hard for my Bar Mitzvah Torah reading, hoping to make my father proud.

Shortly after that big day, construction was completed on the congregation's new synagogue, a soaring structure dripping with ostentation. The intimacy of the storefront *shul* was gone, along with the old rabbi I had studied under. I never had the old feeling of authenticity in that new place, but I still continued to go with my dad, who was investing his time and his identity there. The biggest event of the year was the Kol Nidre service on the eve of Yom Kippur, the solemn High Holy Day. Paradoxically, this was also the temple's biggest fund-raising night, since entrance required the purchase of an expensive ticket, and congregants were expected to promise a further contribution on "pledge cards" they were handed at the entrance. I was already a little turned off during this High Holiday season by the sight of women I had never seen before, milling about the entrance in their mink coats and big jewelry. These people, I supposed, fit in with the new building, but certainly not with the ascetic spirit of the holy day. Nor did they fit in with the weather, since the temperature was about 75 degrees. That, however, was just the beginning.

I sat by myself in a rear pew. Because of his hard work for the temple, Dad had been honored with one of the dozen seats on the altar, flanking the Torah scrolls. Pledge cards were collected before the service began. Within minutes, they were stacked in order of dollar amount and handed to the congregation's president, who took the podium. To my horror, he began from the top, reading the names and the pledged amounts. The first dozen pledges were for more money than my father earned, in that year or in any year. I could see him up there, in view of the entire congregation, shrinking into his chair. I could never go back there again. My teenage consciousness experienced this as a betrayal of the first magnitude.

By 1969, while I lived a secular life, I still identified as a Jew, although based in culture and history more than in religion. In my mind, I had abandoned neither my Yiddish-speaking grandparents who crossed the ocean to escape Eastern European pogroms, nor the victims of the Holocaust. I felt that I was honoring their memories, and fulfilling the spirit of Torah, that sense of meaning and purpose that once attracted me to *shul*, by joining with the freedom struggles of another Old Testament people. I took pride in the individual and institutional Jewish participation in the Southern Civil Rights movement, and welcomed the opportunity to support the new form that movement had taken in the northern cities. I experienced the established Jewish leadership's January Offensive against community control as a racist, deceitful attack not only on the black community, but on the progressive character of what I still considered to be my own tribe. This was another betrayal.

Now the Jewish communal leadership was casting all of us as *white*. My outrage at this appropriation was probably what made me feel responsible for responding to all the lies and fabrications, in any forum that would hear me. I refused to allow these people to speak for me, or for the many other Jews who still retained progressive values. In my fury, the rhetoric that ensued may have overshot the mark at times, but there were and will be no apologies for it.

I had taken my own personal stand, but stood not the slightest chance of actually stemming the tide. As Fred Ferretti reported in his *Columbia Journalism Review* (*CJR*) piece, "The ADL report was widely publicized, and since the ADL has long been the official delineator of what constitutes anti-Semitism, it was widely accepted." Ferretti also summarized two serious critiques, both written within two weeks of the report's release, neither of which had ever received public attention.[74]

The first was in a letter from Leonard J. Fein to Arnold Forster, the ADL's general counsel. Fein was associate director of the Harvard-MIT Joint Center for Urban Studies, and headed a commission on intergroup relations for the American Jewish Congress. He blasted the report.

- It was, he wrote, "a continuation of the vague, but panicked, rhetoric . . . which exacerbates an already volatile issue.
- It "neglects entirely the counter-provocations which, though they can never justify anti-Semitism, at least help to explain it."
- "It does not contribute to either understanding or corrective action; it merely inflames."

He further accused the ADL of "gratuitous slurs," and attacked the UFT for its circulation of "that scurrilous leaflet."

Fein analyzed the 43 instances of alleged anti-Semitism cited in the report. Of these, four surrounded the museum controversy, and had nothing to do with the schools. Four others reported the opposition of unnamed black students and parents to the holiday cancellations directed by the strike settlement. Three quoted white activists. Seven quoted remarks by unnamed pickets outside schools, and speakers at local meetings. Five were quotes from anonymously produced leaflets. That left twenty, he wrote, "including a number involving the same people, and a number not clearly anti-Semitic." Hardly a wave of anti-Semitism.

The other critique was from Henry Schwarzchild who had recently been an ADL national official, and was then a member of the Synagogue Council of America's Commission on Religion and Race. His study, which was limited to private circulation, was titled, "An Anti-Semitic Herring."

He began by reminding the ADL that, only a year earlier, its national director wrote, "The Jewish community would be well advised . . . to drop preoccupation with Negro anti-Semitism, which only serves to divert energies from the civil rights struggle."

He went on to ridicule the meager revelation of 43 allegedly anti-Semitic incidents after 2½ years of staff research. Had the staff focused instead on anti-black racist remarks "made by whites (or by Jews)," he hypothesized, "it could hardly be doubted that such a recital would comprise not 25 pages and 40 incidents, but literally thousands of statements and incidents. . . ." He continued,

> One needs only to remember the patently racist remarks of UFT President Albert Shanker . . . or teachers and supervisors screaming "nigger lover" at parents and children who crossed the UFT picket lines . . .
>
> . . . The ADL report should have comforted everyone who was concerned with an apparent rise in the noise level of Negro anti-Semitism. To find 40 incidents in 2½ years in a city of 1.2 million Negroes and almost 2 million Jews, beset with a multitude of social, racial and class problems that make for some inevitable

friction between ethnic groups, that is a surprising (record) of relative tranquility."

Though most Jewish organizations jumped on the ADL bandwagon, there were dissenters here as well. A notable such voice was the Central Conference of American Rabbis, the 1,000-member voice of Judaism's Reform wing which, it said,

> . . . must not be silenced by the summer soldiers and fair-weather patriots who were for racial justice when the going was easier, but now counsel abject silence or even outright opposition to the just demands of black Americans . . . We Jews should understand the overriding need of a powerless people . . . to gain dignity and pride along with a fair share of economic and political power. We, who for so long were 'the Jewish Problem' and were considered unworthy of being granted full civil rights, should better understand the black man and the 'Negro Problem.'[75]

These critiques received even less exposure than the statement issued by the Jewish JHS 271 teachers, probably not even enough to generate any hate mail. Ferretti's employer, the *Times*, never saw any of them as "fit to print." Instead, as he summarized the climate,

> Each day, the airwaves were filled with the catchphrases—"black militants," "extremists" and "outsiders" . . . Television dwelt only on confrontation . . . There was no real effort to present the black man's side of the conflict . . . The pattern demonstrates the frightening ease with which clever demagogues can manipulate a sensitive issue in a vast metropolis.[76]

This was the atmosphere, created by those demagogues, in which the public debate over a school decentralization law was taking place. This January Offensive, in a relentless campaign to discredit community control as an anti-Semitic plot, would continue through the passage of the new law. Meanwhile the suspended Ocean Hill–Brownsville Governing Board would fight for its reinstatement, and the teachers at JHS 271 would continue trying to teach the children.

Thoughts on the Black/Jewish Divide

> If Judaism cannot recognize the God within those who have previously been treated as "demeaned Other," it has no future.
>
> —Rabbi Michael Lerner[77]

Personally, I think Earl Raab had it backwards in his *Commentary* article. Even though I had not been subjected to, and did not witness, any expressions of anti-Semitism in Ocean Hill–Brownsville, I would never have argued that there were no black anti-Semites on the loose. African-Americans are, after all, Americans, and anti-Semitism had deep roots in American culture. Wrote Rabbi Arthur Hertzberg, a former president of the American Jewish Congress, "In the act of hating Jews, the Negro joins the majority."[78] African-Americans are also, by and large, Christian, a persuasion with anti-Semitism at its historical core.

As the poet/songwriter Tom Lehrer put it, in his 1964 song "National Brotherhood Week,"

> Oh, the white folks hate the black folks,
> And the black folks hate the white folks . . .
> The poor folks hate the rich folks,
> And the rich folks hate the poor folks . . .
> The Protestants hate the Catholics,
> And the Catholics hate the Protestants,
> And the Hindus hate the Muslims,
> *And everybody hates the Jews!*[79]

No one knew how deep anti-Semitism really was in the black community, although every study showed it to be a surface phenomenon. There were some open expressions of anti-Semitic animus at school meetings and in print, though none of these were connected to leaders of the Community Control movement. More important is that the record of anti-Semitic *acts* by African-Americans has been so meager that the smallest incidents had to be magnified into major events to even call it an issue. Every pogrom carried out against any Jewish community, anywhere in the world, has been committed by white people. Every one of the synagogue fires mentioned above was set by white people. While a few Jewish school principals may have been made uncomfortable by some black activists, the issue was never their religion. No black person or institution ever had anything to do with keeping Jews out of banking, insurance, architecture, college fraternities, or country clubs. Actions of a discriminatory nature required a degree of institutional power that African-Americans simply did not possess, whatever their individual opinions might have been.

If the schools in black communities ever came under real community control, would that create opportunities for real anti-Semitic discrimination? This is certainly possible, but even independent school districts operate under a myriad of state and federal laws and regulations, and they are all open to lawsuits. Local school boards (as well as central boards) are capable of doing stupid and small-minded things at times, and they do, but the apocalyptic fears generated in New York's Jewish community were far from realistic.

These fears were also inconsistent with my own experience. In Ocean Hill–Brownsville, where we had the city's closest approximation to true community control, the Jewish teachers who supported and respected the community were welcomed with open arms, even while the experiment was under attack by the predominantly Jewish teachers' and supervisors' unions. District teachers who didn't support the experiment were encouraged to leave, not because of their religion but because they were interfering with the political and educational program. In a 1988 interview, even Fred Nauman admitted,

> I had never felt . . . that our being Jewish had anything to do with our being fired. That was a coincidence caused partly by the fact that a good number of the whites in the district were Jewish. There was obviously a black-white confrontation, but the fact that many of the teachers who were fired were Jewish was, I think, incidental.[80]

It might have elevated the level of public discourse if he had expressed this feeling at the time, instead of twenty years after the fact. At the time, though, such a statement would have undercut his union's most inflammatory argument against black empowerment.

It might also have helped if more attention had been paid to I. F. Stone's call to conscience:

> The Jews, as the more favored and privileged group, owe the underprivileged a duty of patience, charity and compassion. It will not hurt us to swallow a few insults from overwrought blacks. It is no more wrong to invoke the better Jewish tradition against Jewish bigotry than to invoke the better American tradition against white racism.[81]

In a rare *New York Times* piece that presented both sides of the controversy, reporter John Kifner wrote that, "Older Jews cannot forget their history. Dogged by the memories of pogroms, persecutions, the Third Reich, and prejudice in America itself, they understandably react strongly to any criticism directed at them as a group."[82] I could understand that, but I, and I think many of my Jewish colleagues in Ocean Hill–Brownsville, felt that these attitudes belonged to another time and another continent. Power relations, then and there, were different.

Only a few days after Kifner's column appeared, Julius Lester said on WBAI,

> In German, the Jews were the minority surrounded by a majority which carried out heinous crimes against them. In America, it is we

> who are the Jews. It is we who are surrounded by a hostile majority. It is we who are constantly under attack. There is no need for black people to wear yellow Stars of David on their sleeves. That Star of David is all over us. And the greatest irony of all is that it is the Jews who are in the position of being Germans.[83]

As time went on, I agreed with him more and more.

In the racial pseudoscience that prevailed through most of American history, as well as in the old "colored folklore," the race of the Jewish people was somewhat of a mystery. At times, the Jews were considered "Oriental," as though they came from someplace in Asia. At others, they were considered mutated Africans. In the Negro folk culture, they were considered somewhere in between black and white, as in the jokes that began with, "There was a white man, a colored man, and a Jew. . . ."[84] By the late 1960s, though, American Jews were being called upon, both explicitly and implicitly, to identify one way or the other. This was a momentous decision.

Rabbi Hertzberg also remarked that, "If the Negroes can 'join' society through anti-Semitism, Jews can 'join' it as whites."[85] Racism has always opened the door for white minorities to escape being cast as a separate race, as the Jews had been as late as the 1940s. Nell Irvin Painter, in her modern classic, *The History of White People*, documents in great detail how the nineteenth-century Irish immigrants were denigrated and despised by white Americans as "Celts," an inferior race, and how, in description, in status, and in condition, they were lumped together with black people. This changed only after the 1863 New York City Draft Riots, when the oppressed Irish conducted terrorist pogroms against the city's black communities. By supporting the pro-slavery party, and by taking up arms against innocent blacks, the Irish-Americans "recognized how to use the American color line to elevate white, no matter how wretched, over black."[86]

By opposing the black community's aspirations to self-determination, New York's Jewish leadership took its constituency down this same road. It was now not enough for the Jews to be Americans. They were now to become *white* Americans. In this conflict, wrote historian Jerald Podair, ". . . they completed their journey to unambiguous white identity, the last group of Caucasians in America to do so."[87] The tragedy is that so many Jews in New York City were manipulated onto this path by demagogues interested only in power and in maintaining illegitimate prerogatives. In this environment, while anti-Semitic actions by African-Americans remained few and far between, anti-Semitic sentiment could only have grown.

In her 2010 historical study of the struggles of African-Americans and Jews with the New York City public schools, sociologist Melissa F. Weiner concluded,

> Over forty years (later), Jews' and African-Americans' relationship remains deeply affected by the Ocean Hill–Brownsville strikes. The very mention of these two groups in the same sentence often elicits comment about this historical breakpoint—and for good reason. This episode looms large in the American collective consciousness because it solidified the national splintering and collapse of generations of collaboration.[88]

Martin Mayer Spins a Tale

January's propaganda offensive against community control entered another dimension in February. Martin Mayer, a prolific freelance journalist, had written a short book about Ocean Hill–Brownsville and the 1968 teacher strikes.[89] While it was at the printer, a slightly condensed version was published in the February 2, 1969 edition of the *New York Times Magazine*. At 23,000 words, it was the longest article the magazine had ever printed. (The length of my article was more typical, at about 3,500 words.) Its 18-word title, also unusually long, put the imprimatur of the *Times* on a vicious, one-sided combination of political and personal attacks. Publication of "The Full and Sometimes Very Surprising Story of Ocean Hill, the Teachers' Union And the Teacher Strikes of 1968" was a heavy-handed, but effective, tactic to influence the legislative debate over the new decentralization law. It gave an obscure little book a mass readership, and drowned out alternative narratives of the events it covered.

Mayer built his account around a single thesis: The Ocean Hill–Brownsville Governing Board, in its quest for continual confrontation, had provoked all four UFT strikes, and prevented peaceful resolutions at every turn. In his narrative, the UFT, the CSA, and the central Board had simply reacted to these provocations in the only ways open to them. Donovan had no choice but to deny the May 1968 transfers. Shanker had no choice but to pull his teachers out of the district in the spring, and to strike the whole city three times in the fall. It was not the UFT, but the Governing Board's members and supporters in little Ocean Hill–Brownsville who had managed to turn New York City upside down (opposed only by the nation's largest local union, the Board of Education bureaucracy, the mass media, the police, the courts, the Mayor, the Governor, the Central Labor Council, and the AFL-CIO).

In order to "prove" his thesis, Mayer layered one-sided reporting, which included no voices from inside the community, with distortions and inventions of facts, and with slanders, slurs, and innuendos presented as facts themselves.

All of Mayer's reports on events that took place inside JHS 271 came from UFT and secondhand sources. Any of us who were actually there could have written the same review of the article that Aryeh Neier of the NYCLU did:

> When someone supplies as much detail as Mr. Mayer does, a reader is often led to believe that the reporting is accurate. At least with regard to those areas of the dispute over Ocean Hill with which I am familiar, such an impression would be unfortunate.[90]

Mayer made no effort to disguise his contempt not only for the Governing Board, but also for poor people, for social activism, even for the concept of local self-government. Note the tone of these few quotes, presented here with my italics of his words but without further comment . . .

- "The people's board was interested in 'community control'—*a slogan with no clear meaning, but implying a glorious freedom* which 'decentralization' somehow lacked."
- "The elected parent representatives *were all mothers, several on welfare* . . ."
- "(During the UFT's 1967 strike for "educational" goals), 'Teachers want what children need,' was their slogan. Most Ocean Hill parents thought that what children needed was an open school and *a shiny new governing board,* and that the strike was an abomination."
- "The Ocean Hill board *fell under the domination of people who had determined to use it to force what Father Powis liked to call a confrontation with a sick society.*"
- "It occurred to someone that the governing board *could make a big splash in the world by firing a bunch of teachers.*"
- ". . . the JHS 271 staff, which contained what everybody considered *some thoroughly disreputable elements in terms of politics or thuggery.*"

Mayer held nothing back in launching personal attacks. Reporting, for example, on a Governing Board motion to remove Campbell from the district, which was soundly defeated, Mayer felt obligated to add his own one-word judgment: "Pity." About Rev. Oliver, he wrote, without a single substantiating fact or even a quoted opinion from anyone who knew the man, that "his black separatist beliefs were not yet known" when he was elected chairman of the Governing Board.

Consistent with the editors' decision to turn the magazine over to Mayer, they even allowed him to write the captions under photos of the main players, which he happily used to slander the Ocean Hill leadership . . .

- "Rhody McCoy: . . . *Confusion followed wherever he went, as the fog follows the tide.*"
- "The Rev. C. Herbert Oliver: . . . *He used his position to promote a confrontation with the teachers' union and he worked against any settlement of the disastrous war which followed.*"
- "Father John Powis: . . . *His planned indiscretions heralded the confrontations which led to the teacher strikes.*"

And then,

- "Albert Shanker: . . . A *civil rights activist, he was goaded into extreme reaction by an arbitrary injustice to his members working in Ocean Hill.*"

There was no real need for anyone to read all 23,000 words. All they needed to do was look at the pictures.

Of the many rebuttals to Mayer's article, the one I found most interesting was a published Letter to the Editor by John O'Neill, the UFT vice-president who had broken with Shanker after the UFT's mass reproduction and distribution of the bogus anti-Semitic leaflets in the fall. O'Neill was fired from his staff job, but retained his elective position in the union.

O'Neill, who had an inside vantage point, wrote that it was the UFT forcing the confrontation,

> . . . to show them what power they did not have. They had to be taught that they could not act in the same manner as other boards and other administrators—make the same mistakes—commit the same excesses. The rules were different—one set for white boards and administrators and another set for black boards and administrators. The name of the game was color—as complex and yet as simple as that.

Further, he wrote . . .

> (Shanker) perceived that the way to solidify his power within the union, and to project himself into national prominence, was

> to become leader of a substantial backlash movement—symbol of the leadership needed to contain the black thrust for a share in power. Ocean Hill provided the opening, and Shanker seized it with both hands.[91]

During the previous spring, an article in the same magazine concluded with another rebuttal to Martin Mayer. The author of this article urged the Legislature to "suspend whatever sections of the Education Law may need suspending" in order to allow the Governing Board to carry out McCoy's ideas. That author gave this experiment in community control "an outside chance at rescuing" Ocean Hill–Brownsville's "9,000 unlucky children," but gave the "Board of Education, as presently owned and operated" no chance at all. That author was Martin Mayer himself who, less than a year later, was pursuing a very different agenda.[92]

Mayer's 1969 *Times Magazine* article was brought up in a State Senate debate a few days after its publication. His book came off the press about two weeks later. The book, like the article, was unsourced, though it was obvious to any close reader that Mayer's fount of information and misinformation was the UFT propaganda machine. In a lengthy, devastating *New York Review of Books* critique, Jason Epstein characterized it as the product of an "agitated imagination."[93] The UFT backed up its massive lobbying effort by sending a copy of Mayer's tract to every member of the State Legislature, one of the last places a reader of the *New York Review of Books* was likely to be found.

Notwithstanding its abundant errors of fact and flights of imagination, Mayer's account—because of its timing, its role in the legislative debate, and its endorsement by the newspaper of record—would in the future, without deeper investigation, become the basis for influential historical narratives. The travesty would be reinforced for decades to come, as those with no first-hand knowledge of the facts continued to repeat the slanders granted official credibility by Martin Mayer and the *Times Magazine*. Thus does reality give way to manufactured history.

Homeroom Math

Back at JHS 271, we were trying to make a success of the school's reorganization, which gave me my first official class. Earlier, I was content to avoid the tedious clerical responsibilities that came with this assignment, but now I welcomed it. I would have an opportunity to get closer with a small group of students, especially in view of the extended homeroom periods that appeared inevitable. Coincidentally, it was the sixth-grade class I had briefly met in September, the one where the students needed help to write their own names.

My first challenge was to get their attention. They had been failed by the school system for the six or seven years of their experience in it, and had only a tenuous attachment. Further, their previous official teacher never used the homeroom for anything except clerical duties and waiting for the bell to ring, so they were used to spending the time drawing, talking, fighting, or whatever else they felt like doing. I needed to pull them together.

I started off with a simple technique I had learned from watching the more experienced teachers. This involved sitting as little as possible, standing tall with the best posture I could muster, moving around, and speaking a little louder than I ordinarily would, often moving my hands as well. The substance of it was presenting the expectation that they could and would pay attention. The trick to it was making believe I was more confident than I actually was. This worked pretty well. It brought about an immediate improvement, but it never seemed to start working quickly enough. The first 10 or 15 minutes still remained a little chaotic.

After about a week, an idea came to me. I brought in a little phonograph and a single 33-rpm album: My Favorite Things, performed by John Coltrane and his quartet (which was one of my own favorite things). I set it up and turned it on before the students arrived, so it was playing when they came into the room. The calming effect was magical. I still don't know why this worked so well, but I think it may have provided some nonverbal structure to the classroom that set it off from the chaos of the morning hallway rush. We started each day this way, with the same music, for the entire semester.

Over the next few months, I developed a strong attachment to many of these students, as well as a deeper understanding of the complexities of the challenge at hand. The class was rated near the bottom in achievement level, although many of the children were exceedingly bright. It had gotten a reputation as a "bad" class, a disciplinary problem.

There was Jerry, who had been beaten by alcoholic parents until he was two years old, passed around from relatives to foster homes since then, and classified in his file as "disruptive," "emotionally disturbed," and "immature." Yet I noticed that Jerry would behave either well or badly in class, depending on which strategy would enable him to stay and help his teacher after school.

And there was Herman, who was once in a top class academically, but had stayed home whenever the weather turned cold because he didn't own a warm coat and wouldn't accept a gift.

And Henry, whose self-sufficient upbringing had made him a man before he could be a child. And Mario, the half-German, half-Puerto Rican boy who didn't like to "hang around with the colored kids." And all the others: each one a problem, a puzzle, a welcome challenge.

Even with the few additional staff that came on board, the extended homeroom periods quickly became necessary, so I began thinking about how to use that time for some educational adventures. They still had the old third-grade textbooks, and still hadn't learned the arithmetic in them. I decided to try teaching them mathematics instead.

Everhard Barrett, the district's math coordinator, gave me the building blocks of a solution, one that resembled actual building blocks. Cuisenaire Rods are multicolored rectangular wooden rods, each one centimeter thick, in varying lengths. The white rod is 1 cm long; the orange is 10 cm. In between, 2 cm through 9 cm in length, are red, light green, purple, yellow, dark green, black, brown, and blue. I could see right away that there were endless possibilities here, and I would discover new ones as time went on.

At the beginning of the next extended homeroom session, I told the class we were going to do something new and different. I found that novelty will always get the attention of sixth-graders, at least until they pass judgment on what it is. I gave each student a plastic box, labeled with his or her name, containing a set of Cuisenaire Rods, several of each color. I told them the box they had in front of them would be their property for the rest of the school year, and they would be responsible for taking care of it. Then I invited them to play around with the rods: build things; arrange things; whatever came to mind, but no throwing! They went right to it, as the music played on. No structure was needed now; they would see the patterns and relationships that could be used for teaching later on. But, as our time was drawing to a close, they did have to put the rods back in the box, put the cover on, and deposit the box in the case that it came from. No problem.

When our next opportunity arose, there was excitement in the air as soon as I opened the closet and took out the case labeled Cuisenaire Rods. The tactile aspect of manipulating the rods had grabbed their attention. It was play, and I wanted to keep it that way as we moved into math.

We started simply. I wrote W = 1 on the board, and asked the class to give me the length of all the others. As they came up with the answers, by comparing the rods to one another, I put the length of each one on the board, along with its alphabetical analog. (Five of these were the first letter of the color. The two greens were labeled L and D. For the three that began with B, we used the last letter. This may sound more confusing than it actually was.)

Then, to reinforce the relationships, we turned to addition and subtraction. Just by lining the rods up together, the students were able to see the relationships and call them out as fast as I could get them on the board. For example, L + Y = N became 3 + 5 = 8. At the same time, N – Y = L became 8 – 5 = 3. I didn't know it for a fact, but it sure looked like many of these kids were volunteering answers in class for the first time. After a little while, I had them take out their notebooks and write down their own equations. Everyone was engaged. As I walked around looking at their work, I saw surprisingly few errors.

The next time, now that they were comfortable associating the different rods with numbers and letter codes, we moved on to multiplication and division. Let's line up the purples with a brown. How many? Two. So $2 \times P = N$, and $2 \times 4 = 8$. Also, $8 \div 4 = 2$. How many of these equations can you find? Write them down.

Soon, we moved on to fractions, something they had never learned before. First, we had to turn our number ladder upside down. Orange, which had been ten, now became one. Let's see what are the others are. We started with the whites, which took ten to equal the orange, and labeled the white one out of ten, or 1/10, one tenth. Then we did the same with yellow, and saw that it was one out of two, or ½, one half. What about red? It took five reds to equal orange, so R (2) equals 1/5 of orange (10), and $2 = 1/5 \times 10$.

What about Light Green (3)? Uh oh, it doesn't go evenly. OK, let's compare it with white. Since 3 W's equal L, and $W = 1/10$, L must equal $3 \times 1/10$, or 3/10. Do the same thing with brown. Now we see $N = 8/10$. Compare it with red, and $N = 4 \times 1/5$, or 4/5. So 8/10 is the same as 4/5.

Now, let's put red together with light green, and see what they add up to. Yellow? Let's do the equations. $R + L = Y$, which means $1/5 + 3/10 = ½$. Then compare red with white, so $1/5 = 2/10$, and $2/10 + 3/10 = 5/10 = ½$. And so on.

As the weeks rolled by, we explored geometry, ratios, and proportions. Enthusiasm never waned. It never stopped being fun. I didn't teach them to do the arithmetic drill work in their useless textbooks. That wasn't my job. I was just their homeroom teacher, and now they were thinking mathematics.

After several sessions of this, I just asked the kids one day to play around with their rods, write down equations for whatever relationships they could create, and hand their papers in at the end of the session. They began writing furiously, manipulating the rods and filling sheet after sheet. Even after working with them on this for all this time, I was astounded when I reviewed their work after school. Some of the equations stretched across the page. One of the simpler examples was,

$$(2 \times R + Y - D) / 3 = W$$
$$(2/5 + 1/2 - 3/5) / 3 = 1/10$$
$$(4/10 + 5/10 - 6/10) / 3 = 1/10$$
$$(3/10) / 3 = 1/10$$
$$1/10 = 1/10 \text{ (!)}$$

"Quod Erat Demonstratum," I thought, recalling my only Latin phrase. "Not bad for a bunch of illiterate sixth-graders."

I wasn't the only one experimenting with the Cuisenaire Rods. Barrett had trained teachers to use them at PS 178, one of our feeder elementary schools.

Paraprofessionals, who were also trained in their use, made home visits with the rods, teaching parents how to help their children get the most out of them.

Getting the Right Answer

Not all of my classes were innumerate in arithmetic. The students in my advanced eighth-grade class were quite proficient in the basic techniques of adding, subtracting, multiplying, and dividing, at least as long as only whole numbers were involved. With this group, though, I was finding some difficulty in getting across some of the more abstract material, including concepts that less academically successful classes seemed to grasp more readily, sometimes with great enthusiasm. This class seemed to be so intent on mastering "ways to get right answers" that they often resisted solution paths that required more thought than procedure.

One day, I complemented them on their performance, and asked if they would help me understand how they did it. They readily agreed, and I put the following instructions on the board:

1. Do this problem: 260 divided by 5.
2. How did you get the answer? Explain each step.
3. Does this process make sense to you? Why? Why not?

The papers handed in by students I had been trying to teach, for months, to think for themselves, were startling. Among them were . . .

Tootie:

1. 52
2. I tried to get 5 into 26, it went 5 times. Which was 25. And 1 left over. 5 couldn't go into 1, so I brought down the 0 and then it was 10. 5 went into 10 2 times, so I put up the 2. And my answer was 52.
3. This makes sense because it is simplified and I do it this way because I can understand it.

John:

1. 52
2. By saying 5 go into 26 = 5 times and then carry one over in front of the zero and then going 5 into 10 = 2. Combine 52, which is your sum.

Curtis:

1. 412
2. I divided 5 into 26 and got 4 and 6 left over. I added 6 to 0 and divided.
3. It makes sense because it gets the answer.

Joyce:

1. 52
2. I got my answer by dividing five into the number twenty-six. After I divided I found that it went into 26 five times. Then I put down the twenty-five under the twenty-six, afterwards I put the five above the six. Then I found that it was one extra from the twenty-six. And then I brought down the zero and divided five into ten, and I came out with two. Afterwards, multiplied two times five and got ten.
3. Yes, because this is how I was taught.

Warren:

1. 52
2. I divided five into 260. Then I said five goes into 26 five times with remainder one. Then I take down the one. Then I'll say five goes into 10 two times. Then I will have my answer. The answer is 52.
3. No, it doesn't make any sense.

Tootie, Joyce, and Warren all performed the procedure exactly as they (and I) had once been taught, and parroted it quite well. Yet when I asked *what they meant* by "bringing down," by "putting up," and by "getting one number into another," they had no idea what I was talking about. They (as well as I) had once been taught to move the numbers around in a certain pattern in order to get the right answer, and did it almost on faith. The objective, after all, was to get the same result that the teacher did, not to understand the process. They (as well as I) could find satisfaction in this, as it provided an oasis of certainty in an uncertain world. This is a good thing. It just isn't mathematics.

Of these five, only Warren readily admitted that none of this made any sense to him. John had no comment, probably because he was afraid that "nonsense" was not the "right answer." Everyone agreed, though, that Curtis's method made just as much intrinsic sense as their own; it just wasn't the way that they were taught.

I explained the theory behind their manipulations, and showed the class what they were really doing when they moved the numbers around. I should have expected, though, that some of the students would find this explanation neither interesting nor relevant. They had always gotten reasonably good grades by blindly following the prescribed process, and, for the time being, that was pretty much all they wanted to do.

This was just the opposite of the experience I had with the "slow" classes, where I introduced abstract work, such as algebra and the Cuisenaire Rods, in place of the arithmetic drills that had turned them off in earlier grades. Their minds, less cluttered up with formulas and manipulative procedures, were eager to learn what the mystery of mathematics was actually about, once they were offered the opportunity. Even though most of its students still couldn't do long division, my near-bottom sixth-grade homeroom class seemed to be learning mathematics faster than the near-top eighth-grade class. They also seemed to be having more fun.

After teaching one of these classes, my enthusiasm got the better of me in a conversation with a black administrator who had begun his career as a math teacher. He didn't participate in any of the anti-community UFT strikes, but he also seemed totally uninterested in any of the political issues we were dealing with in Ocean Hill–Brownsville. He was just a hard worker, who always seemed to be in his office doing paperwork. I suggested, off the top of my head one day, that it might be worthwhile to include a lesson on "What is a Number?" in our math curriculum.

"After all," I said, "You can't see, hear, feel, or taste a number, but we talk about them and work with them all the time. This could be a terrific exploration in abstract thinking and symbolic reasoning!"

"Forget it," he advised. "It's too abstract. These kids will never understand it."

Nevertheless, I did present that lesson in a few of my classes, with a reasonable degree of success. The object wasn't to impart a definition, but to take an intellectual tour exploring something that really existed only in the realm of ideas. The adventure took a different path in each class, all of them ending with some students feeling pretty smart, others just shaking their heads, and still others displaying both reactions. All of us had a good time.

I never forgot, however, that administrator's reaction to the idea, his dismissal of the children's intellectual potential. It was even more disturbing to me that a black educator held this opinion of black children's abilities, an opinion that could be based on nothing but acquired racial prejudice.

(During the 1990s, scientists determined that rhesus monkeys were capable of abstract mathematical thought. In 2011, another study reached the same conclusion regarding the common pigeon.)[94]

The Splits Widen

Upon his return, Harris took over the compulsory preschool teacher training seminars, but did little to give them any value. After a while, they became a boring, annoying routine. Teachers, especially those having good classroom experiences, began to raise objections.

Many of us generally disliked being told what to do about anything, unless we could at least recognize a rationale in it. Our faculty was far from a randomly selected group, but questioning authority was rampant throughout the land. It was central to the *Zeitgeist*, the spirit of the times. Harris, though, had a way of requiring things without giving any reasons for them, a practice that tended to rouse our rebellious spirits. It might have worked in other schools, but here it was doomed to failure. Our staff had been formed in an atmosphere of rebellion, and it would not change its ways for the sake of Harris's more questionable programs. While it continued to follow his orders, a tide of resentment was growing, particularly among its more anti-authoritarian and militant members.

Sometimes, it was difficult even to take seriously some of Harris's instructions. After six months of school, during which formal controls had never been set up on the flow of textbooks, and two weeks after the second semester's start, when teachers had simply taken books from storage and distributed them to the students, Harris stated the following in one of his weekly bulletins:

> Most of the book rooms have been designated and books are being issued to pupils. It is very important that responsibility be established in this whole procedure. Pupils must know that books that are not returned, books that are lost, books that are stolen, books that are badly mutilated, will have to be paid for. A list will be issued shortly regarding the specific location of these rooms.

This horse had long been out of the barn. The memo read as though the principal didn't know what was going on in his own school.

A more significant conflict flared in March, when Harris announced that standardized reading examinations were to be administered. This directly contradicted a promise made by McCoy, back in September, that the children would not be forced to take any such tests, at least until our experimental district had a couple of years to generate positive results.

I had read about these reading tests. In 1964, they replaced Group Intelligence Quotient (IQ) tests, which were discredited during the previous two decades, largely because of cultural bias in favor of whites, as the basis for student placement in "bright" or "slow" classes and tracks. The result of this change, as with so many of the Board of Education's "changes," was no change at all. The reading tests were just as biased as the IQ tests, and black students were still disproportionately represented in the "slow" classes.[95] In fact, this made things worse, since these students now came to the plate with two strikes against them. First, they were penalized by the cultural bias of the tests. Second, their actual reading deficit, primarily the result of poor teaching, was now interpreted as lack of potential. Testing led to tracking, then to even lower teacher expectations, then to dropouts and pushouts, and finally to manual labor jobs if they existed. Street corners, the army or prison if they did not.

The material on the exam I was assigned to administer confirmed everything I had read about them. In order to do well on this test, the children had to not only be skilled in filling out computerized answer sheets, which they had never seen before, but also familiar with mallards, fossils, and sundew plants, which they had also never seen before. A question in the Word Knowledge section asked whether a "shrub is a (a) tree; (b) vine; (c) bush; (d) branch; or (e) shrug." This test might have measured reading ability in the suburbs, but not in the concrete inner city. My colleagues and I went along with the instructions, but I felt like I was collaborating in stacking the deck even higher against our students.

Being a city kid too, I didn't know much more than they did about shrubs. I did know, however, that if you plant one, you need to water it, maybe feed it, and otherwise leave it alone and see what happens. I was pretty sure that it wouldn't be helpful to pull it out of the ground every week to see how the roots were growing. Even if these tests were fair, forcing them on our experimental district, at this early date, was doing exactly that.

If the examination was a farce, some of my sixth-graders gave it its proper due. Jerry, who could barely read at all, guessed every answer without even trying to read the questions; he scored in the top half of his class. Herman, a good reader, got stuck on the second question, tore up the exam, and dropped off to sleep. Ricky, one of the more conscientious students, started to cry when time was called before he was finished with the first section, and refused to work on the second section. Pasqual was smart enough to just stay home that day.

As if to rub salt into the wound, the teachers were instructed to grade the tests after administering them. Steve Bloomfield told me that his former principal suggested that the teachers "correct a few wrong answers" on the exams where the child "did not perform up to his usual level." In this way the principal could claim that his administration "boosted reading scores."

Cheating was rampant in the city's schools. The exams were distributed to teachers weeks ahead of time. Drilling in vocabulary words was standard procedure, wasting class time on a project with no educational value. In some schools, the same reading test was administered multiple times until the scores were acceptably high. Results were often doctored before they were sent to headquarters. Teachers who challenged these practices were persecuted by their supervisors and colleagues.[96]

I graded the tests honestly, and found that, according to the tests, my sixth-graders were almost all reading on second- or third-grade level. I knew they were behind, but not that far behind. Now these test scores could be translated into future class placement, and the teachers of their "slow classes" could be depended on to expect little from them. With little expected of them, they would produce even less, and the cycle would continue until they either dropped out, or were pushed out, of school. I turned in the graded exams, went home, and took a long shower.

Ultimately, McCoy kept his word. He never reported the test results to the central Board or entered them in the children's records. However, the fact that none of us built a bonfire out of those test papers was indicative of a spreading mood of resignation. The Governing Board was still under suspension, we were exhausted from covering extra classes because of staff shortages and absences, and our leadership was under constant attack.

This mood was exploited by Josephine Wright, the Assemblyman's wife, who asked Harris to approve a PTA-sponsored field trip to Albany. The children would get to witness, in person, the big debate over the school decentralization bill. Many teachers were suspicious of her motives, and disappointed in Harris's ready agreement to promote the trip. These suspicions turned out to be well-founded, for the Albany excursion emerged as one of the year's greatest fiascos.

Hundreds of children had paid a small fee for the trip, and were enthusiastically waiting for the busses at 8 a.m., when they were scheduled to leave from the school entrance. But the busses had not yet arrived. By 9:30, the students were growing impatient and unruly. Teachers were beginning to ask Harris to cancel the event because of its obviously poor organization. He advised patience, and assured them that the journey would soon be underway. Finally, it was, but the last bus did not leave until almost eleven o'clock, three hours late, after many children had already walked home in disappointment.

Upon reaching Albany, after 2½ hours on the bus, the children were let out at the State Capitol for a brief meeting with Samuel D. Wright, their honorable Assemblyman, who had arranged for the occasion by having three photographers present. Once that encounter had been accomplished, and all the necessary pictures had been taken, the children were loaded right back onto the busses for another 2½-hour trip back home. They never even got inside the Capitol. Each student, though, had been given a button on the bus, which they unknowingly wore home as an ironic souvenir of their day travelling the New York State Thruway. The buttons, quite predictably, were inscribed, "Elect Sam Wright." For them, it was a frustrating waste of time. For Mrs. Wright, who had planned the trip to promote her husband, it was a political gold star.

Our somber mood broke when the Israelson Commission announced that Campbell's hearing was now scheduled for March 6. This roused a spirit of resistance. We resolved not to allow him to be "knocked off" so easily. Our Steering Committee proposed to Harris that the student body, en masse, be taken to the hearing on a "field trip." To the surprise of all, he agreed. Letters were distributed to the parents with an explanation for the trip, and with permission slips to be signed and returned. On the night of March 5, while a rally in support of Campbell was being held in the auditorium, the hearing was postponed indefinitely. No reasons were given. It was never rescheduled.

It seemed to me that our side had scored a rare victory, one that was sorely needed to boost morale. Steve Mayer, though, speculated that the announcement of the disciplinary hearing might have been no more than a "trial balloon" to measure Campbell's strength, and to see where it would come from. If so, the commission would have learned that he was supported actively by a large part of the faculty, the ATA, the ASA, and the coalition of community organizations that banded together to organize the rally and mobilize people to attend the hearing.

It might have been surprised to find that Ocean Hill–Brownsville's Governing Board was mute on the matter. On the surface, it appeared that the Governing Board's silence was the result of internal divisions and the demoralizing effect of its five-month suspension. But there was more going on behind the scenes.

On March 1, the State Department of Education awarded Ocean Hill–Brownsville a $2.2 million Urban Education Grant to open and operate a Community Education Center during the remainder of the school year. An additional $4.5 million was contemplated for the following year. The Center would operate sixteen programs for community residents, including adult education, English as a second language, peer counseling, African-American and Puerto Rican history, preschool training, after-school tutoring, career guidance, and media training. Hundreds of local jobs would be generated. Hiring would be controlled by an advisory board chosen by the Governing Board, when and if it was reinstated. Curriculum was mandated to be locally developed, though it would need the approval of the central Board bureaucracy. This grant promised not only a high level of community control, but also jobs for local people, economic development and an unprecedented integration of the schools with the broader community.

Perhaps it was coincidental that the Governing Board was silent on the current in-school controversies while it was awaiting the final outcome of the grant process, and that it was finally reinstated on the very day of Campbell's cancelled hearing. Perhaps not.

In mid-March, Fred Hechinger, the *Times*' education editor, revisited the schools of Ocean Hill–Brownsville. His report gave sparkling reviews to the district's elementary schools, where he found teachers, paraprofessionals and parents working together on both conventional and innovative approaches to teaching the children.[97] By that time, 327 community people had been trained to work with teachers in classroom instruction as paraprofessionals, something no other district had even attempted. Other successful innovations included the city's first bilingual school at PS 155, the non-graded classes at PS 144, and the preschool reading and math program at Rev. Oliver's church. The promise of community control was, in many ways, being fulfilled.

However, "The new harmony that has begun to take hold in the elementary schools," Hechinger then wrote, "is not paralleled in JHS 271, the focal point of much past conflict." He did not give many details, but painted a picture of a shrinking white teaching staff, many of whom were thinking of joining the white exodus that had already begun, feeling "unappreciated" by their black colleagues. He was struck by what he called "the segregated cafeteria," where black and white teachers sat at different tables.

He also noted the "hostility of some older pupils toward white teachers not generally their own (many of whom have achieved good personal rapport)." I read this sentence many times, but could make no sense of it.

The morale problem was real, but not because of a "lack of appreciation." We were all under enormous stress, which could no longer be blamed on the returning UFT teachers. Of the seventeen who had caused so much trouble to force their way back into the school, only four now remained. The other thirteen slots, though, were left vacant, contributing to an already severe staff shortage. All five of our assistant principals were operating in an "acting" capacity. Under such stressful conditions, it is inevitable that tempers will rise, that whatever internal contradictions exist will sharpen.

What I never could understand, though, was the segregation he reported in the teachers' lunchroom. It was not absolutely accurate, but his observation was largely correct. This late in the school year, many white teachers had still not developed any relationships with their black colleagues. Months before, I had taken a seat at the "ATA Table," because I thought that would be where I could learn the most, and I had been welcomed by the black teachers. Since then, that was where I went for lunch on most days. The African-American social scientist C. Eric Lincoln has written that, "The Jew is not *compelled* to be a stranger in the black community."[98] He could be, in the words that came to me when I first met Rev. Oliver, a "welcome guest."

While on the subject of lunch, one more thing needs to be mentioned. All our cafeteria food was prepared by local women, using their own "down-home" soul food recipes. We had the best tasting school food in the city, maybe in the country. I was lucky that my own education about cardiovascular health came later in life.

The Madison Project

Harris's hands-off policy was welcomed by those teachers who were reasonably self-sufficient in their teaching methods and programs. Since there were no supervisors looking over my shoulder, I was able to do whatever I wanted to in class, which was just how I liked it. The irony was that this privilege could only last as long as the door stayed closed, and that no noise, debris, or students made it outside that door during class. This recalled what I had heard and read about the city's ghetto schools, the salient difference being that some of us were using that freedom to experiment with new, hopefully more successful, ways of teaching.

When I was assigned to take over a low-performing eighth-grade class, I thought it would be a good opportunity to try out a program that Everhard Barrett told me about, called The Madison Project. This was a newly developed curriculum that presented abstract algebra, coordinate geometry, and matrices in relatively early grades, and Barrett had already introduced in some Ocean Hill–Brownsville elementary schools. Its central idea, as I understood it, was to create opportunities for students to discover for themselves the concepts that undergird abstract mathematical structures. It promised to be a program for learning, more than for teaching; for understanding, more than for remembering. For my debut performance with this class, I chose "Signed Numbers," to which I was sure the students had never before been exposed.

I began by explaining that they were now in the pet-shop business, and that their first customer is entering the store.

"Donald, you're the salesman. What does the customer buy?"

"A dog?"

"All right, a dog. And how much does he pay for it?"

"How do I know?" Donald was a bit suspicious, wary that he was being tricked into giving a wrong answer. I knew by now that I could expect to receive the benefit of the doubt on whatever new thing I was doing, but not for very long.

"Well, you're the salesman. How much do you want to charge?"

"Okay. Ten dollars." He had decided to take a chance on this.

"Ten dollars it is." I wrote $10 on the board.

"Valerie, do we now have more money than when we started or less?"

"More, of course!" Valerie was humoring me.

"How much more?"

"Ten dollars more."

I wrote "+10" on the board, and asked, "Mark, here comes our second customer. What does he buy?"

Mark's imagination had not yet been totally dulled by his schooling. "A dinosaur!" he shouted out, joining in his classmates' laughter

"Excellent. And how much does he pay for it, Mark?"

The boy held up an outstretched finger. "One dollar."

"Now, William, do we still have more than when we started?"

"Sure we do," he confidently answered. "Eleven dollars more."

As I wrote "+11" on the board, students with exotic animals to sell shouted out to be called on next. I had to quiet them down.

"Just a minute. Our next customer bought a horse from the store last week, just before we took over. But it wouldn't fit in his apartment, so he wants to return it. How much do we give him for the horse, Barbara?"

"We'll give him eight dollars for the horse," declared the girl with great assurance, as though she had looked it up on a price list. I wrote "–8".

"Okay, Barbara. Do we still have more money than when we started? Don't forget that you just had to give away eight dollars."

"Yeah, but we were ahead by eleven. So we're still ahead three dollars." Her classmates and I agreed, so I wrote "+3" in the appropriate space.

"Wilma, just before lunch, a lady comes into the store to return something else. What is it, and how much do we give her for it?"

"It's a rat!" squealed Wilma, "and we give her five dollars for catching it!" Many children protested at the high price for the too-common rodent.

"Are we still ahead?"

"No, we're losing money now."

"How much more did we give out than we took in?"

"Two dollars."

"That's right," I answered, and recorded the new symbol on the board: "–2".

After the next two transactions, the pet store was still losing money, and it took a big sale, that of a twenty-dollar alligator, to get it back in the profit column. By this time, our list of balances read:

+10
+11
+ 3
– 2
–12
+ 8

"How do we read these numbers?" I asked. The students, well aware that the signs were not for addition or subtraction, readily accepted that they were called "positive" and "negative" numbers. To reinforce the concept, I drew a number line, with zero in the middle, positive numbers to the right, and negative numbers to the left.

"Which would you rather have? Positive five or negative five?"

"Positive five," answered one student confidently, while another called out a more sophisticated reply. "Depends what it is. Could be roaches!"

"Good answers. Positive five is more, but more isn't always better, is it? But let's say we're talking about a good thing, like money. Would you rather have positive five or negative five?"

"Positive five!"

"Positive zero," I asked, "Or negative zero?"

Not such quick answers now. After a few guesses fell flat, one student confidently solved the riddle. "With one, you're ahead by nothin'. With the other, you're behind by nothin'. Either way, you're even, so it don't matter. And anyway, look at the number line: Zero isn't on the positive side or the negative side!" And on we went.

In this short, fun lesson, the students had discovered "positiveness" and "negativeness" of numbers for themselves. In subsequent days, they learned how to add and subtract signed numbers in much the same way, and the device of the number-line was extended to analytic geometry.

Periodically, some student would ask the question that always made me smile: "When are we going to start doing math?" I was often able to make my classes fun, but there were always doubts about whether this was really math. It was music to my ears.

This lesson typified the teaching style with which I was comfortable. I tried my best to maximize the fun of math and to encourage spontaneity. I didn't expect my young charges to sit still with their hands folded, silent until spoken to or called upon to speak. For me, a good lesson was one in which my teaching resembled Cliff Lee conducting his jazz orchestra, improvising and shaping new thoughts and interactions, surprising the students with their own discoveries.

I enjoyed it the most when interaction was at its highest level, when I worked the room with questions, eliciting shouted answers, and building on this dynamic toward new revelations. One day, a boy yelled out, "Preach!" and I realized that this method resonated with the call-and-response rhythm of the black church.

The students generally enjoyed this approach as well. Many parents, expecting a more traditional approach, found it a little curious. They were fine with it, though, as long as the children were learning. They could also accept a diametrically opposite style, responding well to strict teachers who demanded quiet, orderly classes at all times. Some even shared fond memories with me of the Deep South schools that they came from, where classroom order was often enforced with a hardwood paddle. There was no paradox here. The common denominator was that the teacher *cared about the children*. Teachers who cared tended to have classes that behaved and did the work, whatever the teaching method, and they enjoyed parent support.

Teachers who cared, though, were in short supply in most ghetto schools. Far too many behaved as though the schools existed for them, not for the children. It was unsurprising to hear, time after time, of teachers who spent class periods giving an assignment to keep the class quiet, then reading a newspaper or a racing form until the bell rang. Nor was it surprising to hear of students that did everything they could to make a misery of those teachers' lives. Breaking that cycle of failure was our job.

This was why our students reacted so negatively to the imposition of the returning UFT teachers. To them, these teachers' attitudes were succinctly articulated many times by their leader and chapter chairman, Fred Nauman, when he told his classes, "If you monkeys don't learn, I get paid anyway!"[99] Our young, inexperienced replacement teachers made plenty of mistakes, but statements like that were never among them.

Civil Liberties Revisited

Soon after Nauman was reassigned to 110 Livingston Street, following the seventh-grader's injury, he sued the Board of Education. His argument was that, since he was a tenured teacher, he could not legally be removed from his position until the resolution of formal charges, including hearings and appeals. On March 20, the judge ruled against him, concluding that Nauman had been "transferred," rather than "removed."[100] This was precisely the argument of the Governing Board since the previous May, when it reassigned the 19 teachers and supervisors. The UFT's "due process" argument, the rationale for four teacher strikes, had been defeated in court. The Governing Board and the NYCLU's *Burden of Blame* report had been vindicated by a judge. This story was relegated to four short paragraphs on an inside page of the *Times*. No-one connected the dots.

The UFT had never stopped pressuring the Civil Liberties Union to withdraw its report. Since its October release, approximately 300 members had resigned from the NYCLU. This was only about 1 percent of the state-wide membership, but hundreds of resignations over a single issue was a rare event for the organization. A small pressure group kept up a steady drumbeat, calling for a special membership meeting to debate the issue.[101] That meeting was scheduled for March 23, at New York University's Loeb Student Center.

Nancy Mamis, a member who was then working for Preston Wilcox in Harlem, invited me to join her at the meeting. The auditorium was packed, standing room only, and virtually all white. The format for the debate was an open one. There was a standing microphone in each of the two aisles. Anyone who wanted to speak could line up behind the mikes to wait their turn. The moderator tried his best to enforce a time limit on the speakers.

The speakers, and the spirited audience reactions, were polarized. It seemed to me that the audience supported *Burden of Blame* by about a 2 to 1 margin, but feelings were strong on both sides.

About two hours into the meeting, the floor was taken by James Peck, one of the early white heroes of the Civil Rights movement. Peck was on the first Freedom Rides in 1961, when he suffered two severe beatings at the hands of the Alabama Ku Klux Klan. Dozens of his bones were broken, and he needed over a hundred stitches. Following these attacks, the televised pictures of him, his black and white comrades, and the torched busses, shocked the conscience of the nation.

Peck spoke as a supporter of *Burden of Blame*, of community control, and of Ocean Hill–Brownsville. It seemed everyone knew who he was, and his opponents sat on their hands in respect, until he made a passing, admiring comment about my *Times Magazine* piece that had appeared five months earlier. At that mention, he was shouted down by a sizable section of the audience that suddenly turned into a hooting, jeering mob. "Where's *Charlie?*" shouted some. It became obvious to me then that the UFT had made an effort to pack the room. This was one of the few moments during the entire year when I felt physically unsafe. Nancy and I looked at each other, and knew we were thinking the same thought: "Let's get out of here before someone recognizes me."

The NYCLU board stood by its *Burden of Blame* report. Aryeh Neier, its executive director, continued his support of the Governing Board and his firm opposition to the UFT's campaign of fear.

A Downhill Slide

In early April, a conflict arose concerning the Easter vacation. The terms of the strike settlement had changed the dates of the traditional spring recess by eliminating four days, and moving it back one week. The four additional school days would help the UFT teachers recoup wages they had lost during their illegal strikes. This, like the rest of the agreement, was to apply uniformly to all schools, including those, like ours, which had been in session during the strikes.

Parents and community activists insisted that the old schedule be maintained, since many children had scheduled customary trips "down home" during the break, and because it was unfair to force the children to make up strike days they had never missed. Aggravating the situation was the fact that moving the recess back that one week retained the closing of schools for the Jewish holiday of Passover.

McCoy and the Governing Board, so soon after their reinstatement, had to decide once again whether to fight for their community's self-determination or conform to the dictates of the strike settlement. They chose not to fight this particular battle.

They didn't have to. Parents took matters into their own hands. During the newly scheduled vacation week, the school was required to be closed. On the previously scheduled vacation days, though, when the schools were now to be open, almost all of the students stayed away. Those who were going on vacation trips went ahead with them. Most of those who remained in the city joined a citywide high school student strike, which was then paralyzing those schools over the same issue. In this case, as in many others, it was the children who were taking the lead.

The students and their parents had empowered themselves. For those who did come to school, JHS 271 teachers looked forward to teaching very small classes for those few days. The principal, though, decided that this arrangement would be inefficient. After an extended homeroom period, Harris announced that classes were to be combined into groups of thirty, until the school's attendance figures were back to normal.

What might have been a rare educational experience had been aborted, for no apparent reason. Teachers and students who did not know each other were now shifted from room to room, generally wasting their time. This increased teachers' hostility to Harris. Many opposed his reliance on conventional methods and routines, while a little flexibility could have allowed us to take full advantage of the unusual circumstances. On the second day, attendance declined even further. It did not return to normal for the rest of the week.

By now, the educational program was on life support. The staff had been reduced from a full complement of 120, to 109 in September, and now to 85 in April. Only two of the ten new teachers hired in February remained, and it seemed that more were leaving each week. Applications were on file from enough qualified teachers to fill the vacancies several times, but the required Board of Education approvals never came through. This was only the latest case of personnel policies being used as weapons of sabotage. The Board's unwillingness to fill the vacancies, combined with the transfer policies that Shanker had successfully negotiated, would keep our staffing level below 70 percent during the remainder of the term. The school was being slowly starved to death.

The regulations did allow day-to-day hiring of per-diem substitute teachers, if they could be found. This apparent source of relief actually made the situation even worse, for we were now dependent on a revolving-door contingent of part-time staff. Each week, there would be a turnover of ten to fifteen per-diem teachers, none of whom ever stayed long enough to make any positive contributions or develop any relationships with their classes. Students, alienated from the school experience once again, acted out their frustrations.

The most ironic aspect of the personnel situation was the fact that the unwanted UFT teachers, who had fought so hard and long to return to the school, who had paralyzed the city in their fight to do so, who had cost the community so much in the battle, had, within a short time, nearly all retired or exercised their options to voluntarily transfer to other districts. Predictions that those teachers would never be able to function in JHS 271 were proven correct, but at great cost. Having won their point and done their damage, they wasted little time in abandoning their hard-won positions. The four who remained, which would soon become two, were totally ineffective. Of the UFT contingent, only the union "observer," who was still roaming around the school, presumably to protect these few people, did the job he was assigned to do. He aggravated the situation by sitting in on all faculty meetings, taking copious notes, provoking arguments, encouraging dissension, and being generally obnoxious. His constant refrain was, "We wouldn't have these conditions in a UFT school!"

The students reacted to these conditions predictably. Cutting classes became common, particularly where each day saw a different substitute teacher in the room. When caught, the students might ask, "Why should I go to that class? These new teachers are no good, we're always getting new ones, and we never learn nothing from them." It was a formidable argument, one which could only be countered with dogmatic authoritarianism. In order to avoid this dilemma as much as possible, some of us were spending our free periods with groups of students who were escaping from their custodial classes. At least that way, they stayed out of trouble, and had an opportunity to learn something, or to do some of the homework assigned in their remaining real classes.

Those students who did go to their classes could not long be expected to sit still while they were shuffled around, though, and they did not. Discipline was becoming a major problem. Invariably, disruptions in the classes of incompetent teachers spilled over into those of teachers who would otherwise be in control. Classroom doors had to be locked from the inside.

Comparisons began to be made to the chaotic periods of the previous spring's teacher walkout and of the November strike settlement's immediate aftermath, but there was one major difference: This time, the "enemy" was less visible.

All this had an inevitable effect on the relations among the teaching staff. Our teachers were drawn from a potpourri of different ethnicities, political persuasions, backgrounds, philosophies, and styles. During the many months when we were under open siege, fighting against huge odds for a new day in inner-city education, all these differences had somehow been submerged in the common effort. Under this new silent siege and the deteriorating conditions it generated, contradictions rose to the surface, testing friendships, dividing alliances, and creating an atmosphere of suspicion and hostility.

Our cafeteria, once a beehive of open debate and exploration of ideas, was becoming a caricature of Fred Hechinger's recent observations, which now seemed pathetically prophetic. We had black nationalists and their allies sitting in one corner, bourgeois black conservatives in another; white "moderate-liberals" dominating one group of tables, white reactionaries in another. There was one table of hickory-stick educators, another of Summerhillians. Communists, Trotskyists, Social Democrats, and Democratic Socialists spoke to each other only in argument. Even those affiliated with the Peace and Freedom Party avoided their counterparts in the Freedom & Peace Party. Prodded by the insecurity that resulted from frustration and disappointment, each group blamed one another for the school's intolerable conditions instead of the real architects of the rapidly developing disaster. There were exceptions, but these were few. Factionalism, distrust, and defensiveness abounded. On only one hope was there widespread agreement: "Let's just hold things together until June."

In an effort to keep the school functioning for the remainder of the term, Harris reorganized it a second time. Since staff shortage was the overriding problem, the number of class periods was reduced from eight to six, and the length of each period was increased from forty minutes to an hour. The first period of each day was designated a "remedial reading hour," to be conducted by homeroom teachers. All minor subjects were eliminated, so that the major ones could be staffed. Schedules were arranged to minimize room changes during the day, so the children would spend less time out in the hallways.

This presented me with a new challenge. I didn't mind having an hour every morning to teach reading, especially since my official class was so far below grade level. The only problem was that I knew absolutely nothing about how to teach reading. In search of something that might help, anything at all, I rooted around the school's storeroom. There I found unopened cartons of brand new sets of "programmed learning" materials for reading. I didn't know what that was, but I was desperate. I took a sample home with me, and spent a weekend trying to understand it.

The program must have taken much thought to develop, but it was incredibly simple to administer. Each child was given a kit with several little books, each book divided into very short chapters (a page or two), with a little quiz on each chapter. They worked individually, at their own pace, and moved on to a slightly more advanced chapter as they successfully completed each quiz.

I introduced it to the class with a great flourish, as though it was a new invention designed just for them. It was an instant success, equal to that of the Cuisenaire Rods. Every student worked on it intently, and the positive reinforcement offered by mastering the short quizzes powered their motivation. They all started at an elementary level. Some advanced slowly, others quickly, but, day-by-day, each moved forward. For me, this was much easier than teaching math. All I had to do was go along with the program, and facilitate their quite visible improvement. Anyone could have done it. I had been lucky to find this solution, but it made me wonder once again why some teachers found their chosen profession so difficult.

While this reorganization brought about some logistical benefits, it was far from a solution. The students, for example, did not appreciate losing their minor subjects, such as art, music, and especially Afro-American history. These were, for many, their favorite subjects. Furthermore, some math, science, and English courses were now being taught by art teachers and music teachers who, in most cases, didn't know much about these subjects. Rather than take advantage of the hour set aside for remedial reading, some teachers didn't even attempt to provide instruction. They used the time as a babysitting and paperwork period, even after I personally related my discovery of the joys of programmed learning. While an hour may have seemed a long time for these teachers, the students were often scheduled to remain in their seats for three of these hour-long periods without a break, a near-impossible feat for early adolescents.

The new reorganization was obsolete almost before it got underway. As a result of its failure, conditions deteriorated even further. The only solution Harris could come up with now was to dismiss the eighth grade two hours early and the seventh grade one hour early. The philosophy behind this move seemed to be that the school could function best without students in it.

School morale took another hit when a group of students stumbled on a male teacher in a compromising position with a female student. The teacher was immediately removed from the school, partly for his own safety, but no other official action was taken. This was not the first time such a matter had been swept under the rug. Two months earlier, a teacher had broken under the strain and nearly gone berserk; he had to be restrained by two colleagues who happened to be passing by the classroom. This teacher was removed from the school, but was allowed to simply transfer to another ghetto district. To the experienced teachers, this was reminiscent of the Board of Education's "teacher shuffle," which bounced around incompetent, and even dangerous, teachers from one ghetto school to another. This had been one of the very frauds that community control was meant to stop. As Steve Mayer expressed his frustration, "Now, this could be any ghetto school in New York City, except that the sabotage makes it a little worse."

This observation was reinforced by the attitudes of the children, who had reached that conclusion long before their teachers. The students of JHS 271, who had been at the epicenter of the preceding months' turmoil, and who had experienced a taste of real education during that time, could not be expected to endure the deteriorating conditions without protest. Harris, by undermining the Dean's office, had weakened a bridge to reconciliation between the angry students and the administration, but even Clarke and Eastmond would have had a tough time of it now.

The Season of Student Revolts

JHS 271 wasn't the only school populated by angry students. All over the city, student groups such as the High School Student Union and the African-American Students Association had been organizing, demonstrating, and striking for better conditions in their schools. Their demands included democratization of high school governance, elimination of racist material from textbooks, removal of police from the schools, designation of the birthdays of Martin Luther King and Malcolm X as official holidays, and expansion of community control. During a three-week "Spring Offensive," the Board of Education recorded "eighty riots, fires or disruptive demonstrations" at high schools and junior high schools, "all of which concerned pupil demands or racial and ideological conflicts." Student rebellions caused early dismissals or full-day closings at 60 of the city's 90 high schools.[102] Nearly everywhere, it was a season of discontent and revolt.

Ellen Lurie, a prominent white civil rights activist and former People's Board member, drew a direct connection between the teachers' strike and the high school uprising.

> During the teachers' strike of 1968, the students witnessed the adults fighting over the school system; law and order was brushed aside by principals and teachers who participated in the strike. When the strike was over, the students proved that they were not slow learners. They began to organize, protest, picket, march, demonstrate—and even strike.[103]

Black and Puerto Rican students at the City University of New York (CUNY), supported by white allies in Students for a Democratic Society and other groups, were also agitating for change. During the spring of 1969, there were major protests at every unit of the university in a new movement that was organically linked to the community control struggle. The CCNY students, for example, quickly attracted widespread community support in Harlem, including a working relationship with the parents and activists of the IS 201 district. The Brooklyn College students were led by Orlando Pile, who had cut his organizing teeth as one of the young Ocean Hill activists working out of

new york
HIGH SCHOOL FREE PRESS

ISSUE 1

OCTOBER 9-22, 1968

Five Cents Cheap

"Of, by, and for liberated High School Students"

H.S. Free Press is born...

Figure 3.5. First issue of the revolutionary *High School Free Press*.

Father Powis's church. His mother, Blanche Pile, was a parent representative on the Governing Board.

The college students' demands were closely linked as well. Just as the demonstration districts pioneered in the teaching of African-American history, the CUNY movement demanded new campus institutes in Black and Puerto Rican Studies. Further, they insisted that those institutes be controlled by black and Puerto Rican students, not by the virtually all-white faculty and administration. They also fought to add African-American and Puerto Rican history and culture courses to the degree requirements for all education majors.

Another demand was that the public, tuition-free, tax-supported university open its doors to the entire taxpaying population of the city, end its policy of basing admissions solely on test scores and grade-point averages, and provide remediation for high school graduates who hadn't been academically prepared for college work. Brooklyn's high school population was then 43 percent black and Puerto Rican, yet the Brooklyn College student body was 96 percent white. CCNY, in the heart of Harlem, was 91 percent white.

These campaigns dominated CUNY's spring semester. There were demonstrations, rallies, building takeovers and, at CCNY, a two-week shutdown that led to the president's resignation. At Brooklyn College, there was also arson and vandalism but, despite predawn police raids and the arrests of 17 student leaders, no link of the student movement to these incidents was ever found.

The students' demands echoed calls for change that were already being made within the CUNY administration. Most outspoken was Dr. William M. Birenbaum, then serving as president of Staten Island Community College, whose prescriptions for reform were even more radical than those of the students.[104] The Board of Higher Education actually had major changes to admissions policies on its agenda, but was not planning any implementation until at least 1975.[105] The 1969 campus upheavals moved this issue to the very front burners.

Considering the massive institutional resistance that was encountered by the desegregation and Community Control movements, the college students were remarkably successful. The various CUNY units fairly rapidly established courses, departments, or institutes in Black and Puerto Rican Studies, a development that was soon adopted by virtually all of the nation's universities. Only a year after the revolts, the Board of Higher Education established a policy of Open Admissions, guaranteeing a place at CUNY, plus remedial help and financial aid when needed, to every graduate of a New York City high school. As a result, the 1970 freshman class was 75 percent larger than that of 1969, and a quarter of the new students were black or Puerto Rican. By 1975, there were five times as many of these students attending the senior colleges as there had been during 1969. These dramatic gains would be rolled back, beginning with the city's 1976 financial implosion, but they continued to play a major role in the development of a black and Puerto Rican middle class. Thousands of civil servants, lawyers, doctors, and social workers, as well as new public school teachers, got their start through Open Admissions.[106]

Signs of a Feud

At JHS 271, Harris had to react to the rising student revolt with shrinking resources. Increasingly, his solution was the same administrative repression that was taking place in the high schools. Our students, the victims of the deteriorating situation, were blamed for their own plight. Harris reproduced and distributed a Board of Education bulletin which warned, among other things, that:

> Firm action shall be taken against students who commit disruptive acts. Charges, prosecutions, and suspensions, where appropriate, shall be pursued. Encouragement by teachers of disruptive activity by students shall be considered "conduct unbecoming a teacher" and shall be the basis for disciplinary action.[107]

The principal backed up this warning with a wave of student suspensions, which soon became his first resort rather than his last. It was ironic that the system's sanctions, those used by administrators to control unruly students and those promulgated by the central Board to suppress supporters of Ocean Hill–Brownsville, were now being used within the district as "law and order" devices.

To many teachers, this constituted conclusive evidence that Harris had "gone over to the other side." He and Campbell, once supporters of each other, now became symbols of opposing viewpoints. A bitter rivalry was developing.

Campbell told me he had looked forward to working with Harris when he was transferred to JHS 271 the previous spring. That term was marked by the UFT strike against Ocean Hill–Brownsville, the prelude to the succession of citywide walkouts that occurred in the fall. Harris and Campbell tried to work closely to hold the school together during the remainder of that school year, along with parent volunteers and the small number of teachers who did not strike. They disagreed frequently, though, over how this should be done.

One point of disagreement concerned the school's assistant principals, whose union was not then on strike, but who were in sympathy with the picketing teachers. Campbell was incensed to see these administrators chatting amicably with pickets outside the school while, on the inside, "all hell was breaking loose." He recommended that Harris remove these people since their presence hurt matters more than it helped. He viewed them more as infiltrators than as colleagues. The principal demurred.

Before that semester ended, they disagreed again over the same issue. On one occasion, while Campbell was breaking up one of the many fights taking place among students in the grossly understaffed school, he noticed one of the assistant principals watching the fracas, then calmly turning and going down the stairwell. As he put it, the administrator was just "letting the little niggers kill one another." Incensed, Campbell demanded that Harris at least remove that one person. Again, Harris refused, and Campbell began to feel that the principal's caution would stand in the way of the school's success.[108]

This conviction deepened in September when, even supported by a militant and politically conscious loyal faculty, Harris failed to control his subordinate supervisors. On this issue, Campbell turned out to be correct. Those assistant principals proved a constant irritant to the loyal faculty during the few weeks they lasted until voluntarily transferring out of the district.

He grew more critical of Harris as the year progressed, particularly of his unwillingness to create meaningful innovation in the educational program. Our program was being developed by the faculty, more in spite of Harris than through his leadership. At times, the two agreed in the abstract on the need for radical changes, but Harris's extreme caution always stood in the way of implementation.

Campbell argued that Harris should have prepared for the contingency of the school being closed in December by securing locations in the community where classes could meet and, even more important, by doing more to communicate with parents in such emergency situations. He felt that the principal was not exerting strong enough leadership within the school even to ensure that his moderate policies were being adhered to, and pleaded with him to take bolder, more decisive action to make sure that his authority was maintained.

After the conflicts over the reading exams, the Easter recess, and the preschool training workshops, each of which had seen the two men on opposite sides, the feud worked its way into the open. Forces among the faculty began to align themselves around the two opposing figures. In mid-May, their rivalry was to come to a head, not only rupturing their relationship, but climaxing the evolving tragedy that was the history of JHS 271.

Decentralization Debacle

> There is nothing new about the idea of community control—as public school boards around the country well know—or the idea of participatory democracy—as old as the dreams of Jefferson . . . Nothing new, that is, but the participants: the poor, the powerless, the black.
>
> —Barbara Carter[109]

> All America will be the loser if we can not find the wit, the patience, and the courage to give this experiment a chance.
>
> —Dr. Ewald Nyquist,
> Deputy Commissioner of Education[110]

While we were trying to hold the school together (and using what little free time we had for our factional infighting), the State Legislature was debating the new decentralization law. The UFT flooded Albany with an army of lobbyists that far outnumbered the legislators. It issued veiled and not-so-veiled threats against those who were leaning toward the Regents Bill.

At the end of April, after five weeks of torturous negotiations and a final, unproductive, ten-day marathon, the Republican majority proposed a bill on a take-it-or-leave-it basis. This bill had the blessing of Albert Shanker, who participated in negotiations as though he was a legislative leader himself, torpedoing every substantive compromise that gained any traction.[111] The bill finally passed, and Governor Rockefeller signed it as soon as it hit his desk. The new law was a defeat for the Community Control movement, and a disaster for the city's communities of color.

- It mandated the establishment of 30 to 33 local districts that would elect boards with very limited powers. Each would have at least 20,000 students, making them too large to be real "community" school districts, but ripe for picking by political machines and the UFT. The elections would be held during the spring of 1970, and the new boards would take power almost immediately thereafter.
- It authorized the local school boards to hire district superintendents, but they would have no power at all over hiring and firing teachers, who would continue to be assigned by the central Board. Local authorities would not even have the power to transfer teachers between districts.
- It maintained the Board of Examiners' eligibility lists for supervisors, but changed them from "competitive" to "qualifying." This would allow the boards to choose anyone who had passed the exams; they would not be required to hire from among the few top names on the list. However, the eligibility lists then in existence were frozen. There could be no additions until those lists were exhausted or expired. (At the time, there were 106 names on the list for junior high school principal, including

only one Puerto Rican and no blacks. Since this list was not due to expire until 1975, there could be no black principals hired for at least the next six years.)[112]

- It gave the local boards authority to select textbooks, but only from a centrally approved list. The central board would maintain jurisdiction over all high schools, school lunches, school construction, budgeting, most maintenance and collective bargaining.
- It gave the local boards power to contract for repair and maintenance services up to an annual maximum of $250,000 and to administer any federal and state discretionary funds that came into the districts, including the hiring of paraprofessionals and purchasing of supplementary materials.
- It dissolved the existing central Board, and replaced it with one in which a majority of members would be appointed by the borough presidents, all of whom were creatures of the county party machines.
- It eliminated the Ocean Hill–Brownsville, IS 201 and Two Bridges demonstration districts, which would be absorbed into the new, larger districts after the 1969–70 school year.[113]

It was ironic that a decentralization law stamping out the hope for real community control of the schools was passed in New York just as that idea was gaining national traction. By the end of 1969, the dream that came alive at IS 201 in 1966, and sparked the two-year confrontation over Ocean Hill–Brownsville, had spread across the nation. Some form of genuine decentralization or actual community control was being discussed, planned, or implemented in nearly every American city.[114]

Besides dismantling the community control experiments before they ever had a chance to prove anything, the new law cast in stone the privileges and prerogatives of the old bureaucracy, and of the unions. The new local boards would have a limited amount of money to spend, and the power to hire paraprofessionals, but they would have almost no power to improve the education in their schools by bringing in more effective teachers and supervisors. It was a recipe for manipulation by local political machines, and for the corruption that inevitably followed down that path. It also created an opportunity for the UFT to use its political muscle to handpick local board members, trading political patronage and financial profit for the union's continued prerogative to actually run the schools. The teachers would now be in charge of their supervisors, and it would remain, commented Fred Siegel, "virtually impossible to fire even deranged, let alone merely incompetent, teachers."[115]

"What the legislature and unions have done, and whoever else participated in this legislative outrage," exclaimed Milton Galamison, "is to embalm a thoroughly unjust system in legislation."[116] In a letter to the *Times*, he wrote, "The bill masquerades as a compromise, but the only thing compromised is the survival of black children. No wonder they are in open revolt against official neglect of their education and official contempt for their welfare."[117]

Even those who had little enthusiasm for community control blasted this legislation. The *New York Times*, in a May 2 editorial entitled, "The Legislature Gets a D," called the new law "a bad measure, patched together in an outrageous travesty of the legislative process . . . a monstrosity." The editorial continued . . .

> It is hardly surprising that the new law has been cheered by the UFT and (the CSA) . . . Nor is it surprising that it has been denounced by virtually everybody else.
>
> Abolition of the experimental districts can only serve as a reminder that the opponents of any extension of power within the local communities, even on an experimental basis, are the real winners. . . .

The day after the law's passage, the Ocean Hill–Brownsville Governing Board announced that it would close IS 55 and JHS 271 on May 5, "in protest of the Legislative Act that killed community control." It was more a day of mourning than of protest.

I was reminded of W. E. B. DuBois's sardonic commentary on the white Southern elites, as their Civil War defeat led to the brief experiment in racial democracy known as Reconstruction . . .

> It had been insistently and firmly believed by the best minds of the South: (1) that the Negro could not work as a free laborer; (2) that the Negro could not really be educated, being congenitally inferior; (3) that if political power were given to Negroes, it would result in the overthrow of civilization.[118]

A century later, in a sophisticated Northern metropolis, minor variations on these same attitudes had once again prevailed, bringing another brief experiment in racial democracy to an end. It was an even greater tragedy that the force which spearheaded the legislative triumph of those attitudes was the union representing the teachers who were entrusted with the minds of black and Puerto Rican children.

A more specific epitaph was written by the Ford Foundation team that had most closely followed the experimental districts:

> All things considered, it is remarkable that the districts survived at all. So much else of an innovative nature in the New York City public schools had, in the past, failed utterly, far outside the glare of public attention. The demonstration districts were to die not of their own shortcomings but under a legislative edict. They did not collapse administratively or educationally; they did not lose community support; they did not fall captive to racist control.[119]

James Baldwin penned a more concise epitaph. "The experiment was discontinued after three years," he wrote, "not because it failed, but *because it did not fail*."[120]

Albert Shanker had his own view to contribute. "Things," he said, "have worked out fine."[121]

Choosing Sides

The legislative defeat only intensified the brewing internal conflicts at JHS 271. Before long, the unity that characterized the various elements of Ocean Hill–Brownsville's community control forces during the UFT strikes would shatter in a surprising array of pieces.

Many teachers were planning to take our classes to a community celebration of Malcolm X's birthday on May 19 in nearby Malcolm X Park. In preparation, Campbell asked Harris for permission to use ten minutes of each morning, during the week leading up to the event, to play brief excerpts of Malcolm's speeches over the school's PA system. This, he argued, would reinforce the occasion's relevance to the students. Without offering any reasons, the principal delivered a firm written refusal. This came as a surprise, since Harris had never objected to the playing of Malcolm's speeches inside the classrooms, to the distribution of full transcripts of those speeches, or even to the student-made Black Panther bulletin board. Some teachers felt that Harris was provoking a confrontation as a means to take back control of the school.

If that was Harris's objective, Campbell walked right into the trap. In what he freely described as a "clear-cut case of insubordination on my part," he disobeyed the directive and broadcast a Malcolm X speech excerpt the following morning. Harris immediately suspended him and took the matter directly to McCoy. He presented it as a "him or me" issue, and a formal charge of insubordination ensued.

While Campbell was admittedly guilty of the charge, since he had openly disobeyed the principal's directive, the issue was not so clear-cut in the minds of many teachers. His teaching, his leadership, and to no small degree the target for attack that he wore on his back, had made Campbell a citywide symbol of the struggle for black self-determination. He had the support of thousands of high school students and dozens of community groups. If he could be eliminated, who would be next? Furthermore, the legitimacy of "insubordination" itself was under attack. This was, after all, the age of rebellion and revolution. Had not the entire community been insubordinate to the establishment? Had not Harris himself, along with McCoy and the Governing Board, been insubordinate to legally constituted central authority? And what example had been set by the settlement of the illegal UFT strikes, which rewarded serial lawbreakers instead of punishing them?

Factions coalesced on each side. Marvand Holland, who had been quiet since his aborted power play in the fall, now seized the opportunity to organize the principal's supporters. The Campbell forces were led by Al Vann, who dramatized the issue by himself playing a Malcolm X speech over the PA system, this one not very subtly chosen. In it, Malcolm described the distinction between the "house niggers," who benefited by collaborating with racial oppression, and the "field niggers," representing the masses of the oppressed. Harris did not immediately react.

Later that morning, Campbell was ordered to report to the district office. Within an hour after he left the building, the situation had become so tense inside the school, the climate so volatile, the children so anxious, that Harris played it safe by dismissing the students at noon. He announced a one o'clock faculty meeting, and convened what he called a meeting of the acting department chairs in his office.

Harris's meeting included some opponents who actually were department chairs, such as Alberta Brown of the science department and Rudy Clarke, the Dean of Students, but they were outnumbered by supporters of the principal who had no leadership positions. At one point during that meeting, I was told, Holland made the surprising declaration that "Afro-American History doesn't serve any purpose in the curriculum." This incensed Clarke, who quickly denounced him as a "house nigger" and an "Uncle Tom." Milfred Fierce, the assistant principal, had to restrain Clarke from reacting physically.

For anyone who felt a stake in the school's future, neutrality was not an option. One was either with Harris or with Campbell, and some people made unpredictable choices. Lillie Curtis, previously an emotional Campbell supporter whose October outburst in the teachers' lounge resulted in charges filed by the union, now parroted his detractors, accusing him of "teaching racism" and "preaching hate." Sitting with her at a cafeteria table, I asked if she ever witnessed any of this. She replied that she didn't have to, that it was "all in the newspapers." Then she accused *me* of being an instigator. She was very upset. It seemed to me that all the months of conflict were generating more stress than she could handle.

Clarence Eastmond came over to calm her down. I changed tables and sat with Louis DeFreitas, another math teacher, who had worked with Harris in his 600-school for three years. During his many conversations with me during the year, he often praised Harris's administrative abilities, and made excuses for the principal's apparent failings. Now, though, he explained his choice this way: "I look upon Harris as my father, man, but Les is my brother. I'm with him."

In most cases, though, the configuration of forces was generally predictable. Campbell's black supporters, led by the ATA cadre, were comprised primarily of teachers who considered themselves militants, radicals, or nationalists. Many viewed community control of schools as the first step in a broader program to gain black control of the institutions that determined life in their communities. They were joined by a fairly well-organized group of more than twenty white teachers who supported that concept, including Steve Mayer, Steve Bloomfield, Judy Russell, and myself.

Many of Harris's white supporters were not having classroom success, and blaming the other faction for their difficulties. Some had a real fear of black youngsters, and of potential student disorders. They joined forces with Holland and a number of other conservative black teachers. Most of these were older teachers who had long ago made peace with the system. Among them were some excellent teachers, such as Lillie Curtis and Dorothy Hopkins, who had also been temporarily suspended earlier in the year along with Campbell and Vann, while others were finding genuine difficulty in relating to our aroused students. A number of the black conservatives held administrative posts instead of teaching classes, and were dependent on Harris for these prized positions.

Some of these reminded me of a group of teachers that sociologist E. Franklin Frazier profiled in *Black Bourgeoisie*, which I had just finished reading.

> The Negro teachers had accepted their teaching positions because of the social status and economic security which the positions provided . . . They were conservative . . . and had no interest in social questions . . . Their interest was in automobiles, furniture, and household appliances, the same values as the rising white middle class . . . From the standpoint of their values, the Negro teachers could have found . . . congenial association with the prejudiced white middle class. In fact, in their struggle to attain American middle-class ideals, they gave the impression of being Super-Americans.[122]

They had every right to make the decisions they did, but, as a class, their traditional leadership role in the community was being shredded by the Young Turks of the Black Power movement. In the street parlance of the day, these were the people now disparagingly referred to as "Negroes."

This group went far beyond supporting a principal who had disciplined an insubordinate teacher. Developing in miniature was a class conflict within an already beleaguered black caste, pitting the Negro bourgeoisie against the militant advocates of the black masses. It was a conflict that mirrored developments in every nation recently emerged from colonial rule.

On the day of Campbell's ouster and the early dismissal, these two factions assembled in the auditorium for the scheduled one o'clock faculty meeting. Instead, at that hour, the principal figures in the dispute were gathered in Harris's office. McCoy, Harris, Vann, Campbell, and a few members of the Governing Board met behind closed doors to decide what many felt was not only Campbell's fate, but also that of the entire school, if not the district. Campbell, with or even without his supporters, could have easily closed the school down in protest of a negative verdict. McCoy's options, however, were limited. If he supported an admittedly insubordinate teacher over a principal, his relations with the other schools' principals could collapse.

The negotiations dragged on for hours. Two o'clock came and went, as did three and, finally, four o'clock. Most of the teachers went home after three hours of factional arguments, tired and frustrated with no news of an outcome. We were still in the dark over how the issues were being resolved.

The disposition was finally announced the next day. Vann explained to a stunned faculty meeting that Campbell had "voluntarily" transferred to the district office. He argued that the battle for community control was not over, and that internal squabbling had to be contained so "the real enemy" could be confronted. "Les Campbell, who is worth any ten teachers in this or any school," Vann continued, "sacrificed himself because he was looking to the greater picture." He emphasized that closing the school in protest, or taking any other action that drew attention to our internal divisions, would ultimately be self-defeating. Vann's speech was a concession that the militant faction was over a barrel. What the UFT and its allies had been unsuccessful in doing for months was finally accomplished, with the help of the Ocean Hill–Brownsville administration. Les Campbell was out of the classroom.

But what was the "greater picture" to which this sacrifice had been offered? Some Ocean Hill–Brownsville leaders thought the experiment might continue under the new law, as an autonomous unit within a larger school district. Some thought the Governing Board could retain control of the Community Education Center, when and if its funds were released. There were potential rewards for maintaining its distance from "extremists." We would soon find out what other sacrifices would be required.

With Campbell out of the way, it was not long before the innovations that Vann instituted in Harris's absence were reversed. There were no more cultural presentations. The Dean's office and the student hall patrols were disbanded, an incredibly counterproductive step considering the state of discipline in the school. More than symbolic was the canceling of *Lift Ev'ry Voice and Sing*, which by then had become the school's anthem.

Additional per-diem substitutes were put in our classrooms, with instructions only to "keep the kids in the room." An encounter I had with one of these substitutes was typical. After the bell signaled the end of my class's reading period, an unfamiliar person entered the room, substituting for the science teacher. In a matter-of-fact, almost professional tone, she asked, "What should I teach them?" I knew that the regular science teacher would leave lesson plans available in case of an unexpected absence, and asked if she had them.

"Well, yes," whined the substitute, "but I really don't know anything about science. I was thinking of teaching them to sing some songs, but I don't sing too well."

I tried to keep the sarcasm out of my voice. "But you must know something! Don't you have a few stock lessons that you use when you substitute?"

"Nope."

"Well, what the hell do you do for forty minutes?"

Wide-eyed and innocent, she replied, "Usually, I just end up chasing the kids around the room." I walked out the door shaking my head, hoping that she was only putting me on. This was a mistake, though, since the class became unmanageable for the rest of the day.

Later, I taught an eighth-grade class that was also becoming jittery and restless in reaction to the school's deteriorating atmosphere. To change the tone, I decided to break them into small teams, using Madison Project materials to tackle a series of problems. I circulated the room, helping if difficulties arose, but the project was largely teacher-independent. It was designed to guide the students to discover for themselves, and to help each other discover, a new algebraic concept. It seemed to work, but I took no credit for it. With these materials, almost any teacher could have done the same thing. I only wondered why anyone would rather "chase the kids around the room" than use a simple device like this one on a particularly difficult day.

I arrived at my next class a few minutes early, toward the end of a social studies lesson that Ron McFadden was conducting. Even though formal Afro-American History classes had been sacrificed in the latest reorganization, he and others continued working that subject into whatever classes they were teaching. When I came in, he was playing African music as background to help illustrate certain points about connections to "the ancestral homeland." The students seemed to be responding well to it, and that gave me another idea: Why not play music during a math class?

During the last period of the following day, when stress levels were at their peak, I repeated the Madison Project unit with another class. Once the teams were set up and ready to go, I placed a stack of records on the phonograph and adjusted the volume so the music could be heard only inside the room. The sounds of John Coltrane, Miles Davis, and the Edwin Hawkins Singers drifted out of the machine like a cool breeze on a hot, sticky day. Sometimes humming, sometimes "tappin' and groovin'," the students went through their assignment in record time. Many stayed in the room to dance after the dismissal bell rang.

While this experiment yielded one of my better moments in recent weeks, I was annoyed with myself for not having thought of it earlier. In many meetings, I had nodded in agreement when Preston Wilcox urged teachers to "build on what the kids bring to school with them." Still, I hadn't been creative enough in using music, a central part of the children's lives, as a building block to learning. Thinking back, I noted that Vann, Campbell, McFadden, and other black teachers understood the value of this tool from their own experience. They were raised in the same environment as their students, so it was entirely natural for them to harness parts of that culture for the children's education. This was a reminder of how important it was for me, and for my white colleagues, to deepen our understanding of African-American culture if we wanted to be effective teachers in a black school. It was also an example of why it is essential for ghetto schools to have a critical mass of black and Latino teachers and leadership, not only for the children, but for the white teachers as well. It made understandable the demand of a small group of activists for exclusively "Black Teachers for Black Children."

Enter the Republic

One group advocating that demand was the Republic of New Africa (RNA), which had been establishing a beachhead in the community since November, through its "Ocean Hill–Brownsville Independence Project." The RNA, based in Detroit, maintained that black people comprised a separate nation within the borders of the United States, and could declare their independence from it. Its slogan was, "Now We Have a Nation."

One of its first contacts with the Governing Board was later described by Rev. Oliver:

> Representatives from the Republic of New Africa came and requested a meeting with the Governing Board, and we gave them an audience. They wanted us to separate from the United States, declare Ocean Hill–Brownsville an independent state, and apply

> to the United Nations for membership. Our response was that we were not elected to set up a new nation. We were elected only to run the schools. And if we attempted to set up a new nation, the people who elected us would be the first to say, "Get out of here. We didn't elect you for that purpose." So, we didn't. We couldn't go along with that.[123]

By now, the RNA had been out on the streets, organizing and proselytizing, for six months, and it was ready to assert itself. Shortly before a May 20 open meeting of the Governing Board, the RNA issued a leaflet which, for the first time, brought out into the open the incident at JHS 271, when a black male teacher was found having sexual relations with a female student. It alleged that the delegation it formed to investigate the matter had received little cooperation from district officials, and had been given a runaround by Harris and McCoy. As far as they could determine, the teacher had been quietly transferred to another district, and to this they had strong objections.

> We asked if the Governing Board was going to make a public statement relating to this, as we understood the significance of the Governing Board, being the first that has been elected by a community to govern its schools. They were not only obligated to the Black community of Ocean Hill–Brownsville, but to all Black people and communities throughout the United States, to deal with this incident. It was their job to find out the truth and not to sweep the matter under the rug. This is what the Board of Education has been doing and we certainly don't need our elected board of our own people to do the same thing . . . Just to transfer Mr. Young from this black community to another is not enough. If, in fact, this teacher is guilty of this crime, he should not be allowed to teach in any school in the black community.[124]

Soon after the well-attended meeting began, a spokesman for the RNA stood and demanded an explanation of the teacher's status. In response, McCoy stated that the girl now denied anything had happened. Since she would not press charges, formal action could not be taken against the teacher. The group was not satisfied by this explanation, but seemed to accept that nothing could be done within normal legal or bureaucratic channels. Its spokesman then asked McCoy about another concern: "*Why isn't Les Campbell teaching his classes anymore?*"

McCoy alleged "complaints from parents about Campbell's teaching methods." He cited "numerous acts of insubordination," although he noted his own defiance of outside pressure by defending and retaining Campbell for so long. Finally, he closed the matter by explaining that this was really the principal's prerogative, and that he had no power to reverse Harris's decision. Harris had been standing in the rear of the auditorium at the beginning of the meeting, but had by now disappeared. The RNA delegation, and other vocal Campbell supporters, now demanded that the ousted teacher be allowed to speak for himself.

Campbell addressed his speech to the parents and community citizens who had come to the meeting uncommitted to his position, many of whom weren't even aware of his dismissal. These excerpts present the gist of it . . .

> When you people all learn the history of our people, you'll find out that the white man, whenever he was forced to evacuate his African colonies, always tried to put natives in charge who he could depend on. These would be blacks who sold out their own people, time and time again, for the gold that the white man offered. The people were confused at first, but soon they realized that these "Toms" were just as bad as the imperialists, that they were traitors.
>
> Malcolm X was a living symbol of our self-determination . . . When I asked Mr. Harris if I could broadcast one of Malcolm's speeches, he refused for no good reason. So, I dealt with him as I would deal with anyone who stands in the way of my people. I ignored his order, and did what had to be done . . . When I return to JHS 271, it will not be to work for any traitors or lackeys of the power structure . . .
>
> We must beware of those who pretend to lead us with big talk but no action. They are no less the enemy than the man downtown.

Campbell sat down to a standing ovation. The meeting soon broke up. Out in the lobby, he was confronted by one of McCoy's senior staffers, who apparently felt that Campbell had been slandering him when he spoke about the "Uncle Toms." He was angry, and he was loud. "Listen, Les, I can see what you're doing. I'll match my commitment against yours any day of the week, but I'm warning you now about these references you're making to me."

Campbell quietly smiled down at the man. "Sorry the shoe pinches, brother."

After this, the RNA continued to act as self-appointed conscience of the Governing Board, exposing incidents of brutality in the schools and inaction by the district staff. Had this been done months earlier, it might have become a positive force, but it was too late by this time to do very much except attract attention to the RNA itself.

He Said, He Said

After months of adjournments, postponements and delays, my court case, arising out of the October arrest, was finally brought to trial on June 5. My attorney was John E. Silverberg, who had in the past volunteered his services to Thelma Hamilton and the Brownsville parents, and represented the coalition that had fought for the East Brooklyn educational park. He had generously offered to represent me without fee.

Silverberg and I first met a few months earlier, in organizational meetings for the new Council of Jews for Social Justice. The Council was primarily comprised of Jews who were prominent in various fields, though none were leaders of specifically Jewish organizations. Most members supported community control, but all were horrified by the UFT campaign to paint that issue with the brush of anti-Semitism. Among its approximately 75 members were Nat Hentoff, Aryeh Neier, Ira Glasser, Henry Foner, Jason Epstein, Ellen Lurie, David Rogers, Nat Schwerner, Immanuel Wallerstein, Seymour Melman, and Celia Zitron. After endless drafts and negotiations, we issued a statement entitled, "A Call to Reason in the Jewish Community," which accused the UFT of cynical manipulation and said in part, "We Jews will not abide the abuse of our history and identity for the purpose of repressing the just aspirations of the Black and Puerto Rican communities."[125] We also traveled together to Albany, where we lobbied Governor Rockefeller on behalf of the Regents Bill. Both efforts were stunningly ineffective, but I did get to meet some truly interesting people.

I never really took my harassment charge seriously, since I knew I hadn't committed any crime. Further, it was a minor charge (carrying a maximum sentence of fifteen days and a $200 fine), and the arresting officer, Amadeo, had repeatedly assured me that his testimony would stick to the truth. Anyway, it was my first offense. Most cases like this ended with an "adjournment contemplating dismissal," which meant that the charges would be automatically dismissed as long as I stayed out of trouble for a few months.

Silverberg was not so optimistic. He warned that the disposition of the case might have little to do with the actual facts, but his admonitions were in vain. I didn't even ask any witnesses to testify in my defense, since I felt they had more important work to do back at our school.

I still had some illusions about justice in the courtroom. After all, had not Amadeo himself said he would have dropped the charges if it was left up to him? And, if this is what he said, couldn't he be trusted at least to tell the truth on the witness stand about what had happened?

No, he could not. Amadeo in private conversation seemed a decent human being, but on the witness stand, he did what he was told. He had obviously been prepared by a prosecutor who, for some reason, was intent on a conviction. He testified that he told me to move to the opposite side of the barricades and that I "attacked" him rather than comply with the orders. The rules of evidence did not require him to speculate as to what may have motivated this unprovoked attack on one of fifty cops in a small area by a lone, admittedly sober, schoolteacher. For the first time, I realized that I just might be in some trouble, an awakening not dispelled by the look of rapt, almost eager, attention with which the judge was devouring his testimony.

Silverberg, in cross-examination, uncovered a few contradictions in Amadeo's testimony, but the judge, by this time, seemed to have his mind on other matters. He appeared totally disinterested in the lawyer's questioning. Anyway, there could not be many contradictions, since the story had obviously been made up and rehearsed for the occasion. It was not difficult to maintain internal consistency in such an account.

The judge seemed equally uninterested when I took the stand to tell what actually happened that morning, when the only physical contact had been committed by police officers. When my cross-examination began, though, he seemed to wake up again, just in case the prosecutor needed some help.

> *Question:* "Did you shove the officer before or after he told you to move on?"
>
> *Answer:* "Now, wait a minute. I didn't push him—"
>
> *Judge:* "Young man! This is no way to speak to an officer of the court. You were asked a direct question. Did you push the officer before or after you were ordered out of the area? You will answer it directly."
>
> *Answer:* "But I can't answer the question, since I didn't push—"
>
> *Judge:* "Answer the question!"
>
> *Answer:* "All right. Neither. I didn't push him at all."

I felt like asking, "Why don't you ask if I've stopped beating my wife yet?" It seemed as though there were two prosecutors in the room, and no judge. Amadeo and I were the only ones to testify. He told one story, and I told another. The presumption seemed to be, though, that police tell the truth on the witness stand, and defendants do not. This puts the burden of proof not on the prosecution, as I was taught in law school, but on the defense. Finally, it did not matter that my story, since it was true, stuck together. I wondered whether witnesses testifying in my defense would have even made a difference.

It didn't come as a big surprise that, when Silverberg moved for dismissal on grounds of insufficient evidence, the judge replied, "Denied. I find the defendant guilty as charged!"

Before sentencing, Silverberg was allowed to make a plea for leniency. "Your honor," he began, "I wish to emphasize that this is my client's first arrest. He has never been in trouble before and will not be again. While he might have erred in the confusion of the moment in question . . ." I was a little disheartened that I had to depend on such an evaluation for a light sentence. I wanted to interrupt the lawyer when the gist of his argument was uttered in one sentence: "Surely, your Honor, you can agree that my client poses no threat to our orderly society." That day, I sure felt like I wanted to pose exactly such a threat. It appeared that I was the only one telling the truth in court that day.

Standing for sentencing, I was treated to an exposition of His Honor's professional philosophy. "You must realize," he said, "that your position as a teacher is a public trust, requiring more than ordinary adherence to the law. Your actions will influence young people, and your indiscretions will surely lead them in the wrong direction. . . ."

Finally, the harangue ended, and sentence was imposed: "Five days or seventy-five dollars." Justice had struck again. I decided $75 wasn't an outrageously expensive tuition for this advanced course in my legal education.

Silverberg felt worse than I did about the whole proceeding. He was kicking himself for not insisting that I pay more attention to preparation, and for not moving the venue to federal court. He buttonholed the prosecutor out in the hallway, and asked why these charges hadn't simply been dropped, like so many similar ones had been in the recent past. In fact, this was the only Ocean Hill–Brownsville case that had been pursued to a conviction. "I wanted to drop the charges," said the prosecutor, "and so did Officer Amadeo. But the District Attorney sent instructions that we had to proceed." If this was an indication of a more repressive attitude on the horizon, it was much more troubling than the outcome of my little case.

Back at school, I told only those who asked about the trial, being embroiled once again in the battle for survival that was daily taking place in the hallways and classrooms. The eighth grade's graduation had been moved up to the following week, probably to preserve what was left of order in the school. We would soon discover another reason the older students were graduated early.

The eighth-graders welcomed this change. Many had not been attending regularly anyway. One of my more sophisticated students showed up on June 9 after being absent for five consecutive weeks, ever since the last reorganization. When I asked where he'd been for so long, he replied, quite innocently, "Didn't you know?"

"Didn't I know what?"

"Man, school's been over for a month already!" He had cut through all the jabber about new programs, consolidated classes, early dismissals, and extended homeroom periods, to speak the obvious truth. The emperor had no clothes. I could only give him a wink, and a little smile.

The Empire Strikes Back

Still another disaster was looming, this one over the Community Education Center (CEC), which had promised great hope for the community. Budget and personnel approval for the $2.2 million granted by the State had to be funneled through the central Board's bureaucracy, which was doing everything in its power to stunt the program and hold back the funding. By now, the Governing Board had endured eight months of bureaucratic obstruction, preventing the hiring of 500 staff members, including hundreds of community residents, and the opening of educational programs that could fulfill the promise of integrating the schools with the community.[126]

A major roadblock concerned staff credentials. The Governing Board maintained that the CEC positions were outside the civil service system, and that the Board of Examiners had no role in approving appointments. Superintendent Donovan, though, took the position that everyone hired would have to pass exams administered by the Board of Examiners, just like schoolteachers and supervisors. This would mean that no programs could start until a lengthy process of credentialing could be completed, overseen by an entity that was reviled in communities of color for discriminating against black and Puerto Rican professionals. Nothing could have been more contrary to the spirit of the CEC.

On May 13, Galamison put this question on the central Board's agenda. He introduced, campaigned for, and won a resolution directing Donovan to bypass the Board of Examiners and process the pending CEC appointments. Following the vote, the CSA, representing the school system's supervisors, immediately announced that it would file a complaint with the State Education Department, and file a lawsuit to stop all CEC supervisory appointments.[127]

By mid-June, two-thirds of the funds granted to the CEC, for the current school year, had still not made their way into the community. Rent, salaries, and benefits were not being paid and, if the central Board did not release the remaining $1.5 million by the end of the month, that funding would disappear. It would also jeopardize the $4.5-million program scheduled for the following school year.

Something had to happen fast if this logjam was to be broken. And it did.

Implosion

On June 16, whatever peaceful coexistence remained between the warring factions at JHS 271 was shattered. After months of being urged to crack down on incompetent teachers, Harris finally did dismiss four members of the faculty. He shocked everyone, though, by choosing not from among the incompetents, but rather from among the school's best teachers: Les Campbell, Rudy Clarke, Clarence Eastmond, and Floyd Sparrow. They received letters of dismissal effective two weeks hence, at the end of the term. The letters offered no grounds, except that it would be "in the best interests of the students and the school." In addition, Al Vann was demoted from acting assistant principal to guidance counselor. Under Board of Education regulations, June 16 was the last day that Harris could take this action against the four teachers. It was also the first school day after the accelerated June 13 graduation, which explained why Harris really wanted the eighth-graders out of the school early.

The ATA-led faction, of whom the five teachers formed the leadership core, interpreted Harris's actions as a political purge. Those who had devoted the most energy and strength to supporting McCoy and the Governing Board, in their own battle with the educational establishment, were now being sacrificed. The atmosphere was polluted with the stench of "sell-out."

It was believed by some that Harris had only been able to get support for these moves because some kind of a deal was in the works. There were only two weeks left for the central Board to release the $1.5 million of state funds it had withheld from the Community Education Center. The $4.5 million budgeted for 1969–70 was still pending. It cannot be proven that the price of breaking that logjam was a break with the ATA and the sacrifice of its leadership, but it was certainly a plausible interpretation. The Governing Board also had hopes, however slight, of retaining district autonomy under the new decentralization law.

A more benign explanation is also plausible. McCoy and the Governing Board had appointed Harris as the city's first black secondary school principal, and fought to retain him through all the legal challenges mounted by the UFT and the CSA. When he was challenged by a revolt in his own school, triggered by a teacher's act of open insubordination, they may have felt they had no choice but to back him up, whoever the teacher was and whatever the wisdom of Harris's orders. In addition, Harris drew on a long personal and professional relationship with McCoy, having once been his assistant principal. Walter Lynch, an influential board member and a sophisticated political operator, was a close friend and neighbor. In Rev. Oliver's current recollection of the incident, the Governing Board had no role in the dismissals other than to allow the principal's decision to stand.[128]

The tenor of the times also played a role. On the polarized social battlefields of the late 1960s, willingness to compromise was in short supply. It was further discredited by the successful outcome of Shanker's stubborn intransigence all year. From the beginning, he not only refused to compromise in the strike settlement negotiations, but continually escalated his demands. In the end, he got both the settlement and the legislative package that he wanted without giving up anything of consequence. The clash between Harris and Campbell, and between their respective supporters, might under other circumstances have been resolved through discussion, negotiation, mediation. In this charged environment, though, these tools did not seem accessible. This drama would play itself out to the bitter end, a Shakespearean tragedy in the making.

Each of the supporting actors in this unfolding drama was free to make a choice. The school was polarized. One could support Harris, one could support Campbell and the ATA, or one could bury one's head in the sand and hope it all blows over. My own choice was based on my personal experience inside the school. In my view, nearly everything positive that had happened there grew out of initiatives taken by the ATA cadre, while it still had the support of McCoy and the Governing Board. Campbell's presence and teaching had given poor children of color a sense of themselves, a respect for themselves that the school system had squeezed out of so many who came before them. Without Vann's leadership, the school might never have been able to reopen after the November strike settlement, let alone thrive as it did for a brief time. If not for the dedication of their closest supporters, Harris would never have been able to keep the school running at all.

It was also not lost on me that these men had put their careers, perhaps their futures, on the line for what they believed was best for the black community. In my mind, any tactical errors they might have made along the way paled in contrast to this fact. (I felt the same way about McCoy and many of the Governing Board members.) Either Campbell or Vann could have parlayed their intelligence and charisma into any position of power they desired, had they been willing to betray their principles. Whatever the consequences might be, I chose to cast my lot with them. Others made different choices. In the heat of the moment, sad to say, few on either side could find much value in civil discussion with those on the other.

The morning after the dismissals, the ATA teachers' supporters met in a music room to plan a response. The gathering included about forty teachers, fully half of the remaining faculty. It was evenly split between black and white, which came as a pleasant surprise to some. Vann said that, for him, this meeting was "like Malcolm's trip to Mecca," the pilgrimage where Malcolm X said he witnessed for the first time in his life a black-white alliance based on complete racial equality. The ousted assistant principal announced that he had given the district office an ultimatum: If McCoy did not contact this meeting within forty-five minutes, "all bets are off." As we waited for the Unit Administrator, the school lay in a state of suspended animation.

McCoy arrived to an icier reception than he had ever received from this group of his own loyal faculty. He was asked immediately why, with so many inept whites in the classrooms, the strongest of the black teachers were chosen for dismissal. Not surprisingly, there was no answer to these questions, prompting further exclamations of indignation and bitterness. McCoy pleaded ignorance. He said all he knew was that Harris had also sent such letters to seven white teachers. (This was never verified.)

"But I will do something," he continued. "As of now, you may consider those letters rescinded, just as though they had never been sent. At the Governing Board meeting on Thursday, the entire situation will be cleared up." It sounded as though we had won without a fight. But this particular audience, in this place, at this time, was not inclined to fully trust McCoy's promises.

Sensing the flatness of his impact, it seemed, and perhaps surprised by it, McCoy added some sugar. "In addition, I will have to advise the Governing Board that, since such a large segment of the faculty opposes their principal, consideration should be given to replacing Mr. Harris." Now what more could we ask for?

Although he agreed to put these two promises in writing as soon as possible, McCoy was still not able to fully dispel the teachers' suspicions. We decided to support the ATA press conference that had already been scheduled. At noon that day, the group gathered in front of the organization's office in Bedford-Stuyvesant, where it released a scathing statement:

> . . . These teachers are being dismissed as the beginning of a purge of militant Black teachers who have worked hard in behalf of, and sacrificed much to, the concept of "Community Control."
>
> The new interim Board of Education has begun to promise Black District Boards lucrative money packages, if the Community Boards and their present administration will act against the so-called "Community Control Extremist." For the entire year, the UFT, CSA, Board of Education, the Mayor's Office, and other similarly inclined groups, have attempted to secure the dismissals of black teachers, specifically Messrs. Campbell and Vann.
>
> The continued unity and solidarity of the Black community has, so far, protected us from the vultures screaming for our blood. But the power of the dollar is winning. Once again, Black people are betraying Black people for the promise of additional money, programs, and guaranteed positions. The Ocean Hill–Brownsville

Governing Board and Mr. Rhody McCoy have effectively acted as hatchetmen for the power structure and its agents.

We believe in the principle of Community Control. Should the people of Ocean Hill–Brownsville and Bedford-Stuyvesant no longer desire our services, *because of our inability to educate our children*, then we will leave and seek employment elsewhere. However, if we are to be used as pawns in a game to enable a few selfish people to gather crumbs from the master's table, *we will not be party to such an unscrupulous plot.*

As corroborative proof of the above conspiracy—it is significant to note that *not one of the inefficient, inept, immoral, non-teaching, UFT teachers received any notice, whatsoever, of termination . . .*

WE WILL NOT, VOLUNTARILY, SURRENDER THE LIVES AND FUTURES OF BLACK CHILDREN INTO THE HANDS OF THESE SABOTEURS![129]

As scheduled, the Governing Board met on June 19, but no action was taken on this issue. Nor did McCoy introduce any recommendation, either to rescind the letters of dismissal or to consider replacing Harris as principal.

Figure 3.6. Al Vann speaking at ATA press conference. Author is at upper left. (June 17, 1969).

Early in the year, the faculty had been told that "there is more due process in Ocean Hill–Brownsville than in any UFT-run school." The Governing Board had set up an appeal procedure, the heart of which was the opportunity for dismissed teachers to receive a hearing before the full board. This actually was an improvement over the terms of the UFT contract since, in any other district, untenured teachers would have had no right to any appeal. The hearing was scheduled for the very last day of the school year, June 27, at one o'clock, an hour after issuance of the final paychecks, and 59 minutes after most teachers traditionally embarked on their summer vacations.

Dozens of parents and teachers, as well as some students, crowded into the oppressive heat of a conference room, waiting for the acrid finale to weeks of bitterness. One o'clock carne and went, then two o'clock. As room and body temperatures soared, many wondered whether the hearing would ever take place. Three o'clock passed, marking the official close of the 1968–69 school year. Still, there was no sign of the Governing Board. At 3:20, with nearly all board members finally present, Rev. Oliver was ready to open the proceedings. Before they could begin, though, the accused teachers exchanged hostile remarks with a few members of the Governing Board. The Ocean Hill–Brownsville drama moved irresistibly to its *denouement*.

Rev. Oliver began by announcing the unprecedented nature of this appeal process, and his wish to hold it with a minimum of formality. Harris would present his case for dismissal; the teachers would have an opportunity for rebuttal; the Governing Board would then meet in executive session to reach a decision. Campbell, who acted as spokesman for the group, asked when he could call witnesses for the defense. This provoked a fierce debate as to not when, but if, witnesses would be allowed. Rev. Oliver ruled that testimony would be welcomed.

Before any testimony could begin, new arguments broke out among members of the board, the accused teachers, and the spectators, quieting down only when Campbell raised his voice above the din. He pleaded for all parties to "cool it" and to "handle this as *a family affair*, not as a fight between enemies." "Isn't this stupid?" he asked rhetorically. "Brothers and sisters fighting among ourselves, while The Man sits peacefully in his air-conditioned office!" For the time being, his admonition shamed the contestants into a restless calm.

Harris began his presentation by conceding the pedagogical competence of the teachers he had dismissed. Instead, he charged them with a "lackadaisical attitude" and "inattention to assigned duties." He acted as a prosecutor, directing questions at the teachers. "Where were you on May 15 at nine o'clock?" "Why were you late on May 22 for your hall patrol?" "Why did you leave your class during the fifth period on May 16?" The defendants answered as best they could under the circumstances. This was the first time they had been confronted with these accusations, which demanded an impossible degree of on-the-spot recollection.

As the hearing wore on, tempers frequently flared. Angry remarks were exchanged and old wounds torn open. An entire year's worth of frustration was pathetically acted out. "So this," I thought, "is what defeat looks like."

The defendants, assisted by a number of friendly witnesses, attempted to lay bare the essential weakness of the charges. When Sylvia Vaughn and Louis DeFreitas testified as to the excellence of the teachers' performance in the classroom, it was declared irrelevant by a board member, since that was "not the issue in question. Only non-performance of administrative duties is to be debated." Steve Mayer objected. "A double standard is at play here," he charged, "We have many white teachers at 271 who are both professionally *and* administratively incompetent, but were never challenged, and are, in fact, returning in September."

Others insisted on being heard as well, including students fighting to keep their teachers in the school, and parents on both sides of the debate, many speaking at the same time, sometimes shouting to drown one another out. Throughout the proceedings stood Rhody McCoy, silently smoking his omnipresent pipe, watching from the back of the room.

At the point of collective exhaustion, Rev. Oliver called the hearing to a close, informing the teachers that they would be notified of their cases' disposition in the mail. Campbell made it clear that the five wished to be judged collectively, since each wanted to be held responsible for the actions of the others. They would face conviction or vindication as a group.

While this drama was drawing to a conclusion, the UFT leveraged its legislative victory into a new three-year contract with the city. In an election year, the Lindsay administration was not going to risk another war with a union that had demonstrated such political might. In addition to gaining unprecedented increases in salary and pension benefits, the highest in the nation, Shanker finally obtained a provision that had eluded him in each of the previous strikes. The city school system would now be an "agency shop," requiring all non-union teachers to pay the union a "fee" equal to the dues paid by its members. This would strike a major blow to the ATA, whose own members would have to sustain financially both the organization they supported and the one they opposed.[130]

In a television interview during the weekend after the Governing Board meeting, McCoy and Rev. Oliver both expressed their support for the five teachers, and said none of them were being dismissed. In the end, however, none would ever return to JHS 271.

Campbell was correct in characterizing this dispute as a "family affair." All the parties had previously been united in facing the power and the hostility of the educational and political establishments. Once defeated in that battle, we turned on one another with a level of rancor that can be found only in a family dispute, driven as they often are by bitter feelings of disappointment, betrayal, and resentment. About twenty years later, most of the leading figures in this affair attended the first of three Ocean Hill–Brownsville reunions. By then, the passage of time had returned perspective to this old dispute. It was mentioned in passing, but all had been forgiven. The family, for that one night, was happy to be back together again.

Graduation Day
June 13, 1969

Notwithstanding all the infighting and political maneuvering among the adults, the students did enjoy a festive graduation ceremony at Friendship Baptist Church. The valedictory address was given by one of my mathematics wizards, Cherylle Edwards. It was a speech that resonated with Al Vann's message to the students gathered in assembly on the first day of school. It gave voice to the fundamental spirit of Ocean Hill–Brownsville and the Community Control movement. It promised hope for that spirit's endurance, whatever new challenges the future might bring. There is no better way to conclude the 1968–69 narrative of Junior High School 271 than to present these unedited words, written and delivered by this 13-year-old prodigy.

> Our ancestors were brutally forced to an unknown land, to be enslaved and looked down upon as animals by the white man. They were separated from their tribes and unable to speak to their own people because of language barriers. Forced to speak the language of the oppressors, they have since that time been struggling from what was considered the lowest of worldly creatures, slaves in bondage, to achieve a respected place in the world. All blacks weren't Booker T. Washington or W. E. B. DuBois, but they all still wanted, and most tried, to be something.
>
> Today, though no longer in legal slavery, black people are still technically in bondage. Our minds and spirit are enslaved and still in shackles. We must struggle to break the shackles and chains that bind our minds. Though we long to be free, we must learn to be free. We must live and die to be free, and we must not wait for the Man to free us. We must get together and liberate ourselves.
>
> The Man has been limiting our education, keeping us from getting jobs, and keeping us in slums. Though our Black men are the last to be hired and the first fired in times of peace, they are the first to be hired to die in times of war.

We must awaken and be aware of our history, our problems, of who we are. We must be aware and proud of our blackness.

I feel that we must also get out of the "hate whitey" bag that so many of us developing awareness fall into. Do not think that there are no white persons who are going to be a help to you in school and in your studies. A white person may be a great friend and a valuable asset to your career later on, but remember that even God first helps those who try to help themselves.

In high school, we should start so many new things: African-American History clubs; ASA chapters; and other black innovations. When you finish school, try to finish first. Whatever job you get, be the best. You shouldn't be afraid of competition. Try for a job that not many blacks hold, so you can come back to your younger brothers and sisters and help them learn. Give them inspiration, and make them aware. Help them rise!

You have to go out of 271 with pride. Be proud of how you look. Let people who look at you know that you have pride in yourself. Carry yourself proudly. Look proud; think proud; be proud. If you're really Black, you'll do all of this. Have pride in your heritage. Be proud that you are part of a great people. Be proud that you can share in that greatness, and remember that being black and proud means more than just hollering loud. It means self-respect, responsibility, and togetherness.

We, as blacks, have to strive for self-enlightenment and education. Well, seek and you shall find: Plot your own course. Pursue knowledge of your own culture. Develop yourself to the highest point intellectually, educationally and culturally. Go to school, even though it's hard. Don't say you'll never make it because you're black, because you *can* make it. Don't cop out and be a dropout!

We students have a responsibility to our people. We are the might and the strength of our race. We of young blood set the pace. We are the Hopes, the Dreams, the Future that must be fulfilled. Black and Puerto Rican students must go to high school and finish; go to college and finish; and come back to our community and finish the job that has been left unfinished for over 400 years. We must help each other to get ahead. We must seek truth and knowledge about ourselves and others, and spread truth about ourselves and others. Seek knowledge and encourage others to find it with you. Be active in school. Spread your truth. Work and strive. Set a high goal and meet it. Be BLACK, be BEAUTIFUL, be BRILLIANT, and be YOURSELF![131]

IV

Aftermath

> For the first time in three years, the city's schools are opening today free of threat from large-scale disruption. A union contract that gives New York's teachers a salary scale unsurpassed in any major city has removed the usual cliff-hanging suspense . . . The future of the schools . . . and the viability of the city (now) depend on the ability of the United Federation of Teachers to turn itself into an ally of those disadvantaged minorities whose children now constitute a majority of the school population.
>
> —Editorial, *New York Times* (September 8, 1969)

The JHS 271 I returned to in September 1969 was not the school it had been during the previous year. William Harris was still the principal, but the teaching staff had changed. The dismissed black teachers, along with the rest of the ATA cadre and many of the other politically active teachers, were gone. Most of those teachers, and others, transferred to other districts. Several left the school system entirely, moving on to pursue their political and educational ends through different means. The Board of Education had filled nearly all the vacancies, making the faculty both whiter and less political. Even though Rhody McCoy and the Governing Board were still in place, the culture of innovation and the spirit of Afrocentrism were on the wane. There was even a UFT chapter (which no one invited me to join).

The deterioration of the educational program since the strike settlement was a factor in several teachers' decisions to leave. Alan Kellock, our popular European-American teacher of African history, cited the solidarity that existed during the strike among the teachers, the students and the community. "The conditions for teaching during the strike," he said, "were idyllic. I think we accomplished more during the strike than any time since."[1] His new vocation was to work through two universities in a program he devised to teach white teachers black history and culture, which he hoped would lead to an understanding of white racism.

Les Campbell, now Jitu Weusi, left the school system to found The East, an independent pan-African cultural center in Bedford-Stuyvesant. In addition to hosting a full array of popular cultural programs and adult classes, The East sponsored food and clothing cooperatives, a bookstore, a radio program and a catering service. Its newspaper, *Black News*, was distributed in 32 states and five countries.[2] The East's flagship was an accredited private school called the Uhuru Sasa Shule (Kiswahili for "Freedom Now School"), which enrolled several hundred students each year. Weusi served as director of The East and headmaster of Uhuru Sasa for a decade, and would continue building community institutions, among them the International African Arts Festival, for many more.[3] He eventually returned to the school system as assistant principal of JHS 258, the school where it could be said this whole story began back in the early 1950s, and eventually retired from JHS 35, where his own teaching career had begun.[4]

Al Vann entered electoral politics as an insurgent. He formed a political club, also in Bedford-Stuyvesant, and defeated the machine's candidate to win election to the State Assembly in 1974, the same year that Major Owens accomplished the same feat in a Brownsville State Senate race. In 1982, after Owens was elected to Congress, they founded the Coalition for Community Empowerment, which eventually ended white domination of Brooklyn's Democratic Party organization. After leaving the Assembly in 2001, Vann was elected to the New York City Council, where he served three terms. Vann and Owens were in the vanguard of the black community's political awakening that was heir to the Black Power movement.

At JHS 271, the leadership had vanished. The saving grace for me was that there was still no one looking over my shoulder. I could sense hostility from Harris, but he did not retaliate for my support of Campbell, and we left each other alone. No assistant principal ever asked to see my written lesson plans (which didn't exist), or attempted to interfere with what I did in the classroom. They were satisfied that my students stayed in the classroom and seemed to be engaged with whatever I was doing there. Left to my own devices, I took advantage of that, enjoying my classes and teaching what and how I wanted. I also knew I would have access to McCoy if I needed his help, which, as it turned out, I didn't.

The Selective Service System, in an attempt to divide and demobilize the anti-war movement, instituted a lottery system on December 2, 1969. Some of our remaining teachers, lucky enough to draw the high numbers that constituted a free pass out of the Vietnam draft, left teaching to try other lines of work or return to graduate school. (I had no deferment, and drew a low lottery number, which would soon require some fancy footwork to avoid a federal prison term.) The relative ease with which these new vacancies were filled (albeit with more inexperienced teachers) validated our contention that the central Board bureaucracy was deliberately preventing McCoy from filling vacancies during the previous year. As long as decentralization bills were pending in the Legislature, both the bureaucracy and the union did whatever they could to interfere with our educational program. Once the new law was passed, they had no reason not to give JHS 271 the same third-rate treatment as any other ghetto school.

Staff turnover at the district's other schools was not as dramatic as at JHS 271. They didn't have so many vacancies to fill in September, and they were able to retain most of the dedicated teachers who had been hired by the Governing Board. They were still developing exciting, innovative programs. At PS 178, trained paraprofessionals were visiting children's homes, helping them with their reading, and teaching parents how to help them as well. At IS 55, Everhard Barrett and Percy Jenkins, the popular principal, introduced a program called "Words in Color," that extended the concept behind the Cuisenaire Rods to reading. The clock was ticking on Ocean Hill–Brownsville, though. Wishful thinking could go a long way, but no one could see a clear path to continuing this experiment beyond June, 1970.

Brownsville Battles On

Much of the excitement in Ocean Hill–Brownsville, during the 1969–70 school year, centered on the state-funded Community Education Center (CEC). Its $4.5-million budget allocation had been released, and it was able to employ several hundred local residents. Programs were run for both children and adults, including tutoring, counseling, parenting, substance abuse treatment, literacy, English as a Second Language, Latino Studies, African-American Studies, career guidance, preschool, after-school, a photography studio, and a newspaper. It had its own "campus," consisting of leased trailers occupying what had been one of Brownsville's numerous vacant, rubble-strewn lots, remnants of an "urban renewal" program that demolished block after block of houses, then forgot them. Programs were also run in storefronts on the commercial streets. It was operated under the jurisdiction of the Governing Board, which hoped to maintain this arrangement even after the scheduled dissolution of the district.

Here, outside the purview of the Board of Education bureaucracy, the spirit of innovation could truly thrive. A child care center located in Father Powis's church, for example, spawned a unique pre-literacy program. It hired teenagers, gave each of them a few children's books every day, and dispatched them to the streets where Brownsville children of all ages spent their days. Their job was to approach groups of small children and ask if they'd like to hear a story. Every day, stoops and benches all over the community were filled with teenagers reading stories to preschoolers. It was an inexpensive, multipurpose program with multidimensional benefits to the community.[5]

Albert Shanker attacked the CEC as soon as it began operating, charging that it was teaching "near-revolutionary courses."[6] He must have been privy to information unavailable to anyone else.

In December 1969, the new Board of Education finalized its redistricting plan for the new "decentralized" school system. While some Board members were sympathetic to the demonstration districts, they were bound by the new state law's requirement that each district contain at least 20,000 students.[7] In Manhattan, though, the legislature granted a waiver to that rule, with the stipulation that it would not extend to the retention of its two demonstration districts.[8] This double standard attracted little notice at the time.

It is also worth noting that the minimum requirement of 20,000 students had no precedent in New York state law, since few of the state's other school districts could have met it. The City of Poughkeepsie, for example, had 5,200 students. White Plains, the county seat of Westchester, had 8,700.[9] There are upstate districts with total enrollments that could not fill a dozen urban classrooms. The state's average school district size, outside New York City, is just 2,300.[10] The only purpose of the enrollment requirement, as demonstrated by the Manhattan waiver, was to mollify the UFT by foreclosing any possibility that the demonstration districts might survive.

Ocean Hill–Brownsville's eight schools were combined with sixteen other schools in a new Community School District #23. The boundaries of this new school district approximated those of Samuel D. Wright's Assembly District, his political base. He quickly formed a slate of candidates for the coming school board election. Rev. Oliver, seeing the handwriting on the wall, called for a boycott of the election.

It was during this time that Queens College's Institute for Community Studies, in cooperation with the National Opinion Research Center, conducted a scientific survey of parent attitudes toward the Ocean Hill–Brownsville demonstration district.[11] Among their findings:

- 77 percent of the parents expressed a positive evaluation of the teachers.
- Only 14 percent did not think the teachers were interested in the children.
- 83 percent thought the teachers would "try to do something about a problem in the school if contacted."
- 75 percent said the principals were doing an "excellent" or pretty good" job.

- 86 percent had visited their child's school during the current school year.
- 72 percent said the schools were better than they were before the creation of the demonstration district.
- *Two percent* thought the Governing Board had done a poor job.
- The prospect of abolishing the district pleased *six percent* of the parents.

The total indifference of the ruling forces to the will of the people most affected by the district's abolition could be measured by their indifference to these and other results of the ICS/NORC research.

As the March 19 school board election approached, Sam Wright enlisted the help of the Democratic Party machine, which controlled Brooklyn's judiciary, to disqualify the candidacy of all but two opposition candidates. Those disqualified had run afoul of obscure technical petitioning requirements that existed nowhere in the country outside of New York City. The two surviving candidates were elected, but they would be powerless since members of Wright's political club took the other seven seats.

The actual winner, in the most Pyrrhic of victories, was the boycott. Only 883 votes were cast by less than 5 percent of the eligible voters. This was far fewer than the number that voted in the 1967 Governing Board election, in a district one-third the size of the new District 23. It was the lightest vote in the city, where the average district turnout was 14.5 percent.[12]

The new local board was installed on July 1, 1970. Three weeks earlier, the outgoing central Board strongly recommended maintaining the Ocean Hill–Brownsville district as an autonomous "special experimental unit."[13] This was not to be. The Wright-controlled board's first action was to obtain a court order evicting the Governing Board from both the district offices and the Community Education Center. Eleven people were arrested in the physical eviction, including Rev. Oliver, who still refused to recognize the authority of the gerrymandered school district's new board.[14] Now in control of the community's two largest employers, the school district and the CEC, Wright set his sights on its only independent power center, the Brownsville Community Council (BCC).

During that summer, Rhody McCoy, no longer the Unit Administrator, left Brooklyn for the University of Massachusetts, where he would complete his doctorate and teach for a few years before returning to the urban fray, this time in Washington, DC. Wright's board appointed a new District Superintendent, Nellie Duncan, at a tumultuous open meeting attended by over 300 protesters. It quickly replaced the 350 CEC workers who were loyal to the old

Governing Board, and ended their innovative programs. By summer's end, the Community Education Center was walled off from the community by fences twenty feet high, and guarded by police patrols.[15] It now functioned primarily as a patronage mill for Wright's political club.

During the three years of its existence, the Ocean Hill–Brownsville demonstration district was untouched by even a whiff of financial scandal, even though it functioned under a microscope the entire time. Nor did it have any need for twenty-foot-high fences to protect its buildings from the community. The typical ghetto school vandalism and its most obvious sign, broken windows, were never a problem. These conditions would change abruptly under the Wright regime.

I returned to JHS 271 for a third year in September 1970, along with only about two dozen other veterans of 1968–69. The new local board had replaced the Governing Board. Both Harris and McCoy were gone. In actual charge of the school's day-to-day activity was neither Wright's board nor the new principal, though, but the local chapter of the United Federation of Teachers. This reflected the deal that put union muscle behind Wright's pre-ordained election victory. The counter-revolution was complete.

I encountered surprisingly little hostility from either the new supervisors, who seemed to be apolitical bureaucrats, or the newly appointed teachers, many of whom seemed oblivious to the recent history. There were so many new and out-of-license teachers that I was asked, with my lengthy experience of two whole years, to become acting chairman of the Math Department. Even though this position would have reduced my class load, I declined for a couple of reasons. First, because the position required reviewing teachers' formal lesson plans, not one of which I had ever prepared myself; and second, because I would not take responsibility for a department that had no chance of being effective.

Teaching in this relatively calm climate was a breeze. Since I was assigned to eighth-grade classes, I was already a known quantity to most of my students, particularly the former sixth-graders who I had begun teaching two years earlier. They appreciated this bit of stability. My classroom confidence continued to grow, and the class schedule was easy to handle. Before long, though, I started chafing under the bureaucratic demands of the new administration. Creativity became cause for suspicion once the remaining embers of the innovative spirit that flourished under McCoy were stamped out.

During the previous two years, I had never been tempted to leave Ocean Hill–Brownsville, even when colleagues I respected made that decision. Whatever the pressures and challenges may have been, I always felt grounded by accountability to the Governing Board, and by the implicit promise I made to Rev. Oliver when we first met, but things had now changed. I had no intention of holding myself accountable to a corrupt local board, a racist central Board, or supervisors who represented what we fought so hard against. I felt that my days as a "welcome guest" were over. After a couple of months, when I was offered a position at a CUNY community college, I said a sad good-bye to my students and to the school where I had learned so much.

As it turned out, my days there would have been numbered anyway. Not long after I left, parents protesting the new regime organized a lengthy boycott. The Wright-controlled board retaliated by transferring out of the district 32 teachers, including all of those who had been loyal to the old Governing Board.[16] There were no charges filed or hearings held. There were no complaints from the UFT about "due process violations." The press did not appreciate the irony of this event, or find it of any interest at all.

Besides my evening graduate work at the New School, my own education was continuing through a new association with Preston Wilcox, the intellectual godfather of the Community Control movement. Now the head of an Afrocentric consulting firm, he hired me as a part-time community organizer. I traveled out to rural northern Michigan for a few days of field work each month, where I worked with poor white parents. Wilcox was a valued friend and one of my best teachers.

Another was Annie Stein, Rev. Galamison's former aide and a fighter for social justice since the 1920s, who I first met in 1972. Along with Thelma Hamilton and other parent leaders, and about two dozen teachers and paraprofessionals, we founded a citywide organization called People Against Racism in Education (PARE). I was elected chairman, but Annie was the senior partner and our actual leader.

In a very small way, our partnership joined the 1930s Communist-led Old Left with the 1960s anti-authoritarian New Left and Community Control movement. Or what was left of them, for all three had passed their peak of effectiveness. The Old Left was devastated by government repression before the other two movements were born. The New Left was then descending into sectarian factionalism, aided by the FBI's COINTELPRO program of infiltration and dirty tricks. The parent movement, demoralized by the defeat of community control, had been scattered by the structure established in the 1969 decentralization law. Nevertheless, PARE was able to make its voice heard, from time to time, during the five years of its existence.

We focused on issue analysis, advocacy, and anti-racist educational programs for teacher training and curriculum development. When parent groups galvanized around local issues, we were often invited in to provide whatever outside assistance they requested. My favorite project was writing a monthly column in *The City Star*, a alternative newspaper, deconstructing and sometimes parodying Albert Shanker's union-funded column, "Where We Stand," that appeared each week in the Sunday *Times*.

What I learned from working with Preston Wilcox and Annie Stein remains a treasured personal legacy of my time in Ocean Hill–Brownsville.

Figure 4.1. Annie Stein (1975).

As many had predicted, the 1969 Decentralization Law established an order that made educational reform unlikely, but corruption and personal enrichment certain. No community school board was a better showcase for these two outcomes than that of District 23 while it was under the thumb of Samuel D. Wright. PARE maintained a Standing Committee on District 23 throughout its existence.

In March 1971, a split occurred between Wright and his handpicked District Superintendent, Nellie Duncan. "Mr. Wright," she said, "is interested only in the political power base he can establish."[17] Duncan was echoing the charges being made by Joseph François and Thelma Hamilton of the BCC that the CEC had become a cesspool of patronage jobs, and that Wright had even put "goons" on the payroll to act as his personal enforcers. His board illegally transferred Duncan's powers to appointees at the CEC, who had no qualifications to exercise them. At that month's public board meeting, where Wright's "bodyguards" beat up a BCC official who tried to speak, Duncan was fired.[18] This became a regular practice, backed up by enough weaponry to create a climate of intimidation.[19]

Now, seven of District 23's nine board members, and more than fifty of its school officials, were members of Wright's political club.[20] At its August meeting, the board fired ten principals, including Luis Fuentes, Ralph Rogers, and David Lee, leaving in place only one of the principals who had been hired by the Governing Board. Having squandered the CEC's budget, it voted to close it down for "reorganization." The meeting was adjourned prematurely when shouting and fistfights broke out after these decisions were announced.[21]

During that year, Wayne Barrett, who taught in Ocean Hill–Brownsville during the time I did, and lived with his wife, Fran, in one of its tenements, compiled a 133-page bill of particulars that documented the local board's corrupt practices. It charged that Wright and his board . . .

- Awarded bogus and inflated contracts as political payoffs;
- Misappropriated funds;
- Extorted political contributions from 162 school district personnel, including the superintendent, 12 principals, senior district office employees, and CEC workers;
- Extorted contributions from 32 outside vendors;
- Spent $900,000 leasing and renovating a building that had been purchased by the president of Wright's political club for $80,000; and, among many other things,
- Hired a consulting firm that employed the board member who greased the wheels for the award of its contract.

In October 1971, a coalition of 47 Brownsville organizations, led by Thelma Hamilton's Brownsville Parents Association, sent this document to Chancellor Harvey Scribner, with a cover letter demanding the board's removal. Scribner appointed a hearing officer who recommended further action, but the Chancellor only issued a reprimand.[22]

Six months later, Barrett produced a more detailed indictment, this one backed up with several thousand pages of documentation. It, too, was ignored at the central Board. Barrett referred to it as the "longest dead letter in the history of education."[23]

The group then brought the case to the Brooklyn District Attorney. He assigned the case to an assistant who was a former UFT chapter chairman as well as a personal friend of Wright's lawyer, who also represented the political machine that put the DA in office. They never heard from the DA's office after that assignment.

The second school board election under the 1969 law was to be held in May 1973. There would be no boycott this time. Wright's opposition was a coalition of parent leaders, tenant organizers, antipoverty workers and other concerned and outraged citizens. After numerous interviews of prospective candidates, they agreed on a slate headed by Joseph François of the BCC. Maurice Reid, a long-time BCC education activist who was one of the original founders of the Brownsville Parents Association and the director of the local Head Start program, acted as campaign manager. Wayne Barrett was his right-hand man. After a hard-fought campaign, the insurgent slate won four of the nine seats, missing majority control by only 23 questionable votes.

In that election, Wright personally controlled the appointment of all the election inspectors in charge of the polling sites, some of whom were relatives of his candidates. Afterwards, Barrett and Arnold Rothbaum, a Legal Services attorney, wrote a report documenting numerous cases of ballot tampering, uncounted votes, and electioneering by election inspectors. The report was equally ignored by the authorities and by the press.

In another 1973 election, Wright was elected, with UFT support, to the City Council. Since conflict-of-interest laws required his resignation from the school board, he turned control over to his niece and personal secretary. Nothing changed in the District 23 schools.

Also in 1973, Woody Allen made a movie called *Sleeper*, in which his lead character wakes up 200 years in the future, where he is told that the world he knew was destroyed "when a man by the name of Albert Shanker got hold of a nuclear warhead." Three decades later, Shanker's biographer noted on Page 1 that, "It is the peculiar fate of Albert Shanker that he is probably best remembered" for this reference, "for something he never did."[24] The reason the laugh line worked, though, was because of what he did actually do.

A third local election held that year was for the BCC Board of Directors. Wright's slate lost that one, and brought a lawsuit before a hack machine judge who overturned the results. Another election was held, which Wright again lost, and again had the results tossed out. This time, the judge specified new rules for a third election, rules that created conditions for a Wright victory. The new board's first action was to appoint Robert Story, one of his political operatives, as executive director, who was soon arrested for selling 72 ounces of heroin to an undercover federal agent. Nineteen months later, during which Story remained on the payroll, he was convicted and sentenced to a five-year prison term.[25] Shortly afterward, Major Owens, who ran the city's antipoverty program, canceled the agency's $2.5 million contract with the BCC, citing egregious misuse of funds, and charging that the election was "riddled with gross violations and corruption." He called for a federal investigation.[26]

In 1974, the Nixon Administration eliminated the Office of Economic Opportunity, which funded the antipoverty programs. In taking this action, it was supported by Democratic Party mayors and political bosses in every city, whose power monopolies were threatened by the independent voices of the community action programs.[27] The threat to the Brooklyn bosses took a different form that year, when Owens resigned his post as Commissioner, announced his candidacy for the State Senate, and defeated the well-entrenched machine-backed candidate.

In Brownsville, BCC veterans reinvented the organization as the Brownsville Community Development Corporation, focusing on education, including its Head Start program, and on health care. It secured funding to open the Brownsville Multi-Service Family Health Center, providing desperately needed integrated health services to a community with few doctors. Led at first by Joe François, Maurice Reid took it into the twenty-first century on a steady course of expansion. By the time Reid retired in 2007, it was servicing 20,000 patients annually in eight centers, employing 250 professionals and support staff, many drawn from the local community. It has since opened a charter school, preparing students for careers in the health care professions. "BMS," as it is known, has had from its inception a community-based Board of Directors. On its Web site, it proudly traces its origins to the Ocean Hill–Brownsville school wars.[28] Rev. Paul Chandler, Ocean Hill's young firebrand of the 1960s, became a future Chairman of the BMS Board. As an institution, BMS is probably the greatest positive legacy of the Community Control movement to survive in Ocean Hill–Brownsville.

By 1975, when the two sides faced off in the next school board election, People Against Racism in Education geared up to help. We worked in a supportive role with the insurgent slate for months. At a strategic planning retreat during that campaign, Thelma Hamilton introduced me to Carole Stern. Carole was a single mother of three, an antipoverty worker, a longtime fighter for peace and civil rights, and the most beautiful woman I'd ever known. I had admired her from a distance at previous community meetings, but this was my first opportunity to talk to her.

Carole and I were married three years later, in a ceremony presided over by Rev. C. Herbert Oliver. Wayne Barrett was my Best Man. Mrs. Hamilton was the designated Mother of the Bride. Celebrants included Jitu Weusi, Maurice Reid, Annie Stein, and many other veterans of the school wars. The lifelong friendships that developed during those wars, the "instant family" I acquired that day, and the three wonderful grandchildren our sons have given us, are daily reminders of the debt that I can never repay Ocean Hill–Brownsville.

At 5 a.m. on Election Day 1975, PARE's convoy of several dozen volunteers arrived at insurgent headquarters. Campaign manager Reid assigned us as poll-watchers to every voting site. In this capacity, we were able to document and object to instances of election fraud, but we were not authorized to stop them. I did, however, manage to get into a loud argument with Sam Wright

Figure 4.2. Rev. Oliver presiding (April 9, 1978).

himself that day, which the police officer on duty had to break up. When the votes were counted, Wright's slate again won five of the nine seats, with only 75 votes keeping the insurgents from wresting control of the district.

Later that year, I taught a seminar at Staten Island Community College that I curiously titled, "Anthropology of Education." As an introduction to the grittier side of the subject, I took my students on a field trip to a public meeting of the District 23 school board. Some major decisions were to be made that night, and there was talk that one board member was going to switch sides, which would put the insurgents in the majority.

The auditorium was packed when we arrived. I spotted Barrett, Reid, and other insurgent leaders in the audience, all of whom had their physical security protected by other activists. The walls were lined with young men, standing with their arms folded. These were employees of the programs Wright controlled, deployed this night to intimidate the opposition. I was approached by one of these men, who recognized me from the days of the teacher strikes, when he was an active ally on the street in front of JHS 271. "Tell your folks to stay cool," he advised. "Things have changed around here." He was certainly right about that.

Once the meeting began, it became clear that Wright's majority was indeed in jeopardy. Before any votes could be taken, though, fistfights erupted (prearranged, I thought) on each side of the room. When a gunshot rang out, the auditorium cleared. Meeting adjourned, by unanimous consent. My class would have plenty to talk about. The majority faction was, for the time being, safe.

It was not safe, though, from the relentless team of Barrett and Rothbaum, which had gone back to work. (Barrett was then beginning a career in which he would become New York's most prominent investigative journalist.) In addition to gathering the poll-watchers' reports, they spent a month at the city's Board of Elections headquarters, dissecting the results in the most minute detail. Their report documented an irrefutable case of massive election fraud, including:

- More ballots cast in most election districts than there were registered voters;
- Hundreds more votes counted than ballots actually cast;
- Ballot tampering by Wright-appointed election inspectors;
- Open electioneering for the Wright slate inside polling sites; and
- Election inspectors telling voters how to fill out their ballots.

The greatest instances of fraud occurred at the polling site where Wright's wife, Josephine, was the chief election inspector.[29]

The Barrett/Rothbaum 1975 report was sent to the U.S. Department of Justice, which had jurisdiction because Brooklyn was covered by the 1965 Voting Rights Act, along with Barrett's earlier investigative reports. There was no immediate response.

It would be another year until the Brownsville insurgents got someone to listen. David Trager, the newly appointed U.S. Attorney for the Eastern District of New York, reviewed the file in 1976. He decided to focus on a single, easily proven transaction, a $5,000 bribe Wright was paid to secure a $760,000 contract for reading materials. The resulting indictment charged a five-year scheme of corruption.[30]

In the 1977 community school board elections, UFT-slate candidates won 172 of the 288 contested seats. They did not, however, prevail in District 23, where a slate connected to the BCC insurgents and Thomas Boyland, the new assemblyman, won a clear majority.

Wright was finally convicted of extortion and conspiracy in 1978, forced to resign all his elected positions, and sentenced to three months in prison.

Even that prison sentence reflected his political connections, since the maximum was twenty-five years.[31] In any case, the reign of Wright had finally come to an end.

Much damage had been done by this time. The children who started school when Wright took control of the local board were now graduating from junior high school, with a literacy rate estimated at 15 percent.

At his peak of power, in addition to his elected positions, Wright controlled the school boards in both District 23 and District 17; the BCC; the local Manpower Center; three large summer lunch contracts; an adult home; and five child-care centers. One of these centers, located next door to his political clubhouse, was named for him and employed his wife as executive director. He had a voting address in Brownsville, but actually lived in a home with a swimming pool on the ritzy North Shore of Long Island.[32]

In all the elections that Sam Wright stole, and in any that he might have won even without stuffing the ballot boxes, he had two crucial sources of support that made these victories possible. The first was the powerful Brooklyn Democratic Party machine, whose attorneys and judges helped Wright knock opposition candidates off the ballot, and which introduced him to Howard J. Rubenstein, New York's best-connected public relations counsel. With Rubenstein paving the way for three years, Wright was the subject of glowing reports and profiles in even such respected outlets as the *New York Times*. It was only after the indictment that the machine abandoned him. Then, for the first time in his career, he had to hire his own lawyer and do his own public relations.

Wright's other perennial base of support was Albert Shanker's United Federation of Teachers. The UFT supported Wright in every one of his elections after 1965: for Assembly; for the City Council; for control of the BCC board; for Congress in a failed 1976 effort; and, most enthusiastically, for control of the District 23 school board. In the 1975 school board election, which was widely expected to be close, Shanker personally wrote to the district's teachers, asking them to volunteer time to support Wright's slate. The union supplied lawyers, campaign literature, its money, and its phone bank. In certain areas, it even distributed palm cards listing Wright's candidates under the heading, "Vote the UFT Slate."

Why would the teachers' union go to such lengths to support a politician who knew nothing about education and cared even less, who used the district's budget as a piggy bank, and who was widely rumored to be selling appointments to supervisory positions? First, Shanker wanted every vestige of the demonstration district demolished, a goal that Wright shared for his own selfish reasons. Second, as a quid pro quo, Wright's board was quite willing to cede effective control over the district's schools to the UFT, as long as its own patronage and kickback schemes were left untouched.

Jews, Whites, and Others

> Learn to do good! Seek justice, relieve the oppressed, defend orphans, plead for the widow.
>
> —*Isaiah 1:17*

> At dozens of Jewish fund-raisers around the country, I hear whispers on every dais about Negro anti-Semitism. But all I interpret in those whispers is the voice of a man who wants *out* on a commitment.
>
> —Harry Golden (1967)[33]

As it plunged into whiteness during 1969, much of New York City's Jewish community severed itself from the social justice ethos of Judaism's ancient prophetic tradition. This tradition had done more than set the foundation for the historic black-Jewish coalitions that fought for social justice. It had also forced into furtive, whispered conversation whatever personal racist attitudes existed among the Jewish rank-and-file. After the Ocean Hill–Brownsville conflict, such attitudes became acceptable in polite company, often expressed with great conviction. With the exception of a few Manhattan neighborhoods, racial attitudes expressed in the many Jewish enclaves became largely indistinguishable from those long identified with other white ethnic groups. This shift was a lasting legacy of the UFT's demagogic campaign of fear against the bogeyman of "Black Anti-Semitism."

Collective political behavior shifted correspondingly, beginning with the 1969 mayoral election, only a year after the teacher strike. Mayor Lindsay's unapologetic concern for the poor had alienated much of white New York, even costing him the nomination of his own (Republican) party. Running on a third-party line in 1969 against two conservative Italian-Americans, he won reelection with only a 42 percent plurality, thanks to 85 percent of the black vote, 65 percent of the Puerto Rican vote, and a split opposition. Almost 60 percent of Jewish voters joined the more than 80 percent of white Catholics who cast their ballots against him. Spearheading the anti-Lindsay campaign was a series of articles and rants in the *Jewish Press* written by Meir Kahane, the head of the Jewish Defense League. According to Lindsay aide Richard Aurelio, "The biggest problem we had in the campaign was with a certain element of the Jewish population that felt Lindsay had gone overboard in favoring the blacks."[34] This was the first election where anything close to a majority of New York City Jews voted against the more progressive candidate.

Things turned uglier in 1972, when 31 black children from Brownsville's Tilden Houses were rezoned from an East Flatbush school to JHS 211, just across the Canarsie border, "tipping" the school's racial balance by approximately one percent. The children arrived to find white parents, Jews and Italians united, blocking the school steps in an ugly tableau resonant of the infamous 1957 Little Rock High School confrontation. Boycotts and sit-ins followed. The bus from Brownsville was met for days running by over a thousand angry Jewish and Catholic demonstrators. Eggs and rocks were thrown at the children. Gangs of armed white teenagers roamed the blocks around the school. When a similarly armed gang from Brownsville came into the area, war was prevented only when they were talked into turning back by 18-year-old Rev. Al Sharpton.[35]

During the Canarsie school crisis, the established community leadership, including Brooklyn's foremost Democratic Party organization and equally well-organized PTAs, was supplanted by a paramilitary alliance of the Mafia-affiliated Italian-American Civil Rights League, whose membership was 40 percent Jewish at one point, and the Jewish Defense League. It was a racist revolt justified, in a curious twist of logic, as "deferred white vengeance for the New York school crisis of 1968."[36] Both the Canarsie boycott and the 1968 UFT strike were supported, in a 1973 poll, by 60 percent of New York City's Jews.[37]

Press reports generally categorized incidents like the Canarsie crisis as "white backlash," though they rarely identified what whites were "backlashing" against. This term was succinctly defined by Carmichael and Hamilton in *Black Power*. "The so-called white backlash against black people," they wrote, "is . . . the embedded traditions of institutional racism being brought into the open and calling forth overt manifestations of individual racism . . . In the black community, this is called 'white folks showing their color.' "[38]

The authors of a contemporaneous study of voting patterns offered another perspective on this turning point. "1972 was a very bad year for many Jews," they concluded, "because of their discovery of a new and painful truth: Jewish self-interest and liberalism were apparently not one and the same thing."[39] Emblematic of that "discovery" was Norman Podhoretz's editorial in the February 1972 *Commentary* entitled, "Is It Good for the Jews?"[40] His argument was that, after a generation in which American anti-Semitism had been virtually obliterated in business, government, and academia, during which the Jews had embraced universalism, it was now time to turn inward again, to look after only their own parochial interests. Those who were persuaded by this argument had to decide, like the schoolteachers of 1968 did, whether or not the spirit of *Isaiah 1:17* had outlived its usefulness to them. Had *Justice*, in other words, become *Just Us*?

The Jewish Canarsians who justified racist actions as "vengeance" may not have been aware that this is a behavior expressly forbidden by Talmudic law.[41] In any case, it was no short-term phenomenon. Two full decades after Lindsay's reelection, history was made when New York City elected David

Dinkins as its first African-American mayor. Dinkins's Republican opponent, Rudolph Giuliani, held right-wing views on education, housing, capital punishment, homelessness and abortion, all of which had miniscule support among the Jewish electorate. In contrast, Dinkins's campaign had a conventionally liberal platform. The candidate himself made a determined effort to attract the Jewish vote. He announced resolute support for the State of Israel; distanced himself from Jesse Jackson; ran TV commercials denouncing Louis Farrakhan; forced Jitu Weusi out of the campaign (under pressure from the ADL)[42]; and courted Jewish leaders. As Election Day approached, he won wide support among the mainstream Jewish leadership.[43] Polls were predicting a landslide, double-digit, victory.[44]

These predictions proved incorrect. When election results came in, Dinkins's victory margin was a mere 2.4 percent. Still, history was being made. In his victory speech at the late-night celebration, the mayor-elect specifically thanked his Jewish supporters. "Tonight," he proclaimed, "the Jewish community is a light unto the nation."[45]

The exit polls did not become public until a few days later. In a heavy turnout, the Jewish vote had actually gone almost 2 to 1 not *for* Dinkins, but *against* him. In some predominantly Jewish neighborhoods, Giuliani received nearly 80 percent of the vote. The 1989 election statistics told a story much like that of 1969. Dinkins, like Lindsay, won a close vote only because of a one-sided majority among African-Americans (91 percent) in a record turnout, and a substantial majority (65 percent) among Latinos. In another poll, more than a third of Giuliani voters said they cast their votes not because they supported his policies, but in order to "stop the other candidate."[46]

While the Black Power movement had provoked alarm and soul-searching among Jewish leaders in every big city, New York's black-Jewish schism was not part of a national pattern. In other trailblazing elections, African-American candidates won office with heavy Jewish majorities. Ron Dellums of Oakland, California, was the first of these in 1970, when he won the first of his thirteen successful campaigns for Congress. Tom Bradley, the 20-year mayor of Los Angeles was another, winning his first election in 1973 with 80 percent of the Jewish vote. Perhaps most notable was Harold Washington's 1983 mayoral campaign in Chicago, where overwhelming Jewish support helped carry him to victory over a Jewish opponent. In 2008, Barack Obama received almost 80 percent of the Jewish vote. Nationally, Jews and African-Americans remain the most reliably liberal voting blocs on nearly every issue. In New York, though, it has been a rare event since 1968 when the Jewish leadership mobilized its constituency to support any civil rights but their own.

During the late twentieth century, relocation from the cities to the suburbs cut New York City's Jewish population by more than half, from 2.5 million in the 1950s to 2 million in 1973 to less than 1 million 30 years later. A fifth of these were recently arrived immigrants from the former Soviet Union.[47] While a great many actively progressive Jews still resided in the city, its only identifiably Jewish voting bloc in 2012 was made up of over a quarter million members of socially conservative ultra-Orthodox and Hasidic sects. These sects feature prolific birth rates that reversed the declining population trends, increasing the city's Jewish population by 12 percent between 2002 and 2011. They are concentrated in a few Brooklyn neighborhoods where, back in 1980, four out of five votes went to Ronald Reagan.[48] While this bloc aligns itself with the fundamentalist Christian right in support of Israeli expansionism and opposition to marriage equality in every sense of the term, registration is predominantly Democratic. In practice, it has become perhaps the city's largest swing vote in local elections. Its consistent pattern has been to vote for the candidate or party that promises them greater access to social services, and government funding for their religious schools.[49] I don't know whether or not *Isaiah 1:17* is taught in those yeshivas.

Decentralization Reaps What Was Sown

While Shanker had a special animus for the parents and activists of Ocean Hill–Brownsville, and would have supported anyone who protected his teachers from their demands for accountability, the UFT's original District 23 strategy was not substantially different from its citywide approach to community school board elections. In every district, the union cut deals with whatever forces would agree to the type of arrangement it had with Wright. It forged common cause in some districts with slates sponsored by the Catholic Church, in others with such right-wing religious groups as the Christian Coalition, and in still others with well-known political crooks and gangsters.[50]

The rules of these elections were based on a complicated vote-sharing system called Proportional Representation, which even experienced election workers had to be trained to understand. These rules favored well-funded, tightly organized blocs like those that the UFT assembled. The UFT-supported slates were union-financed, backed by legal expertise, and allied with local vote-pullers. For inner-city voters, though, whose experience in ordinary elections was limited, the arcane rules discouraged participation. Whatever the intent might have been in establishing this system, its prime beneficiary was the UFT. In low-turnout elections, union-endorsed slates won control of nearly every community school board.[51]

White teachers, who did not live where they taught, could run for school boards where they lived. Black and Puerto Rican paraprofessionals, who usually did live in the districts where they worked, were ineligible under the law. No barrier to local democracy had been overlooked in the 1969 legislation.[52]

In the 1977 elections, where the UFT-backed candidates won almost two-thirds of the school board seats, turnout dropped to 8 percent of the electorate. Some blamed the low turnout on parent apathy, but David Seeley, director of the Public Education Association, blamed the electoral machinery established by the decentralization law. "It is an insult to the people of this city," he said, "to accuse them of apathy when the election system is almost impossible to relate to. Nobody knows who is running or what they stand for, and the whole thing is a travesty on the democratic process."[53] It worked just fine, though, for the UFT.

Walter Thabit, in his study of East New York, summed up the results. Noting the enormous patronage base gained by the political clubs, he concluded, "The teaching staff and the Community School Board played ball with each other; education of the children was not a major part of the agenda."[54]

The union did not fare as well, however, in protecting its members from budget cuts. In 1975, at the beginning of a lengthy, massive municipal fiscal crisis, the city demanded equally massive sacrifice by all public employee unions. The UFT, which had ridden a tide of victories, refused. It struck the schools again in September. Not a single voice in the city's black and Puerto Rican leadership spoke out in support of this strike. It met with hostility in every community of color. Without that support, and without the white, race-based support the union had manipulated to its own ends in 1968, the union was left to fend for itself. This was the UFT's first unsuccessful strike. It was forced to accept the city's pre-strike offer, including wage freezes, tightened work rules, and layoffs. Fifteen thousand teachers and paraprofessionals were laid off, a fifth of the union membership.[55]

After another round of budget cuts the following year, the teaching force had been reduced by 25 percent. Additional layoffs, in accordance with the seniority provisions of the UFT contract, raised the average age of teachers from 28 to 41 years old. Eliminated as well were the innovative programs some of the laid-off young teachers had developed, as well as most elective courses, bilingual and adult education, sports, after-school centers, guidance counselors, teacher aides, crossing guards, paraprofessionals, and black and Latino teachers hired after the community control conflict. Non-white teachers had only increased from 8 percent to 11 percent of the professional staff between 1969 and 1974; the layoffs dropped their representation to 3 percent.[56]

The community control conflict was recalled at the time, without actually mentioning it, by Stephen Berger, executive director of the State's Emergency Financial Control Board, which had taken control of the city's finances. Berger's critique of the Board of Education echoed David Rogers' pre-decentralization *110 Livingston Street*. "The board," he said, "is the classic example of a system designed to protect its infrastructure, its vested interests, its pedagogues. What it is is a matrix of Balkan protectorates, whose interests are primary. The delivery of educational services is secondary. The end product is third rate."

"What the union had gained," Berger added, "has worked to the detriment of the school system." The solution he espoused was to eliminate the Board, dismantle the central administration, and truly decentralize the system to one "where districts negotiate separately and make individual pleas to the State Education Department." Asked why, he replied, "Because the central Board doesn't know how to run schools."[57] It sounded familiar.

In its next contract, the UFT negotiated salary raises for the remaining teachers rather than use those funds to rehire some of the laid-off staff and to reduce class sizes, which had shot up 25 percent, and in some schools doubled, because of the cuts. As Shanker explained back in 1968, "I don't represent children. I represent the teachers."[58]

The huge short-term gains won by the UFT in its 1968–69 campaigns against community control were outlived and outweighed by its long-term loss of support in the communities of color. A generation later, that relationship was summed up by a District 23 board member. "The bitterness that took place during Ocean Hill," he said, "was never healed."[59] Even in the twenty-first century, a more progressive UFT must struggle to gain the support of African-American and Latino parents. The pain of Ocean Hill–Brownsville, even for those who were born later and know nothing of the history, has become ingrained in institutional memory.

The widespread corruption that characterized District 23 during the Sam Wright years was replicated, to a greater or lesser degree, in nearly every school district. Its was the most widely reported, though, because of Ocean Hill–Brownsville's notoriety and because no other district had an investigative hound dog like Wayne Barrett. Once Wright was gone and the insurgents gained a board majority, many serious problems remained, but financial scandal was not among them.

By 1988, 27 percent of local school board members were school system employees.[60] The UFT had established such a level of control that, according to Nathan Quinones, a former schools chancellor, "A tremendous amount of trading of positions was taking place. For example, a school board member saying, 'I want to become an assistant principal in your district; I'll trade you for a job in my district.'"[61]

During the 1980s and 1990s, the new poster child for chicanery was the Bronx's District 9, which had the city's lowest math and reading scores. Promotions there required service to political clubs and campaigns. Allegations, indictments, and convictions involved extortion of school employees, misuse of funds, kickbacks, calls to pornographic phone lines, even the theft of a grand piano and a bribery charge featuring a white cashmere men's coat. A principal arrested on crack cocaine charges was later charged with sanctioning corporal punishment and routinely cheating on reading tests. By 1992, nine of the district's school board members had been arrested.[62]

This was the legacy of the 1969 decentralization law, which gave the local school boards control over better jobs and larger pots of money than their communities had ever seen, but denied them the tools needed to improve the quality of education. Those attracted to, and able to secure, board positions were far too often those interested in the former at the expense of the latter. Local corruption was made inevitable by the Faustian bargain struck between the teachers' union and the grifters.

There were exceptions, most notably two African-American and Latino districts that accomplished substantial educational progress and avoided corruption. The District 4 board in East Harlem hired Anthony Alvarado, who became the city's most innovative District Superintendent. He created a network of magnet and experimental schools, and allowed parents, for the first time, to choose among the districts' elementary and intermediate schools. In Bedford-Stuyvesant's District 13, Superintendent J. Jerome Harris brought reading scores up to the levels of the white, middle-class districts.[63] He served for fourteen years, before leaving to head the Atlanta school system. These were, however, the exceptions that proved the rule.

In 1995, the *New York Daily News* surveyed the 288 members of the local boards, and interviewed 236 of them. While some members were exceedingly well-informed, the vast majority had no idea of their districts' math and reading scores, their budgets, their enrollments, or which of their schools were overcrowded. The guesses they made were wildly inaccurate.

On the subject of decentralization, the *Daily News* survey elicited surprisingly honest answers. Only 13 percent of the board members thought the 1969 decentralization law was successful; 46 percent deemed it an outright failure. Many of the boards were made up entirely of political aspirants and had no parent members. UFT influence had made the board demographics much whiter than their districts. Only 18 percent of board members even claimed to have taken the job for the children's benefit. There was almost unanimous agreement that the Board of Education had done nothing to train them to meet their responsibilities. In their comments, many board members echoed those who, in 1969, declared that the new system was designed to fail.

> Corruption and mismanagement were not the only reasons the system has failed, the members insisted. Decentralization was doomed from the start, they said, not because local school boards have too much control, but too little. "Local control never happened; it's a figment of people's imagination," said James Meyerson, a member of District

> 2 in Manhattan. "We have virtually no control of our money and how it gets spent," said Margaret Nuzum of Brooklyn's District 15. "People are not getting involved with school boards because they don't think they have any power," she added.[64]

The inability of the local boards to improve educational results, combined with widespread publicity about scandals like those of District 9, eventually discredited the flawed regime of decentralization. There was no chance, though, that it would be replaced by true community control, since the press had falsely conflated the two concepts for 25 years. The pendulum began swinging in the opposite direction.

When Mayor Rudolph Giuliani proposed legislation in 1996 that transferred the few powers of the local boards to the District Superintendents, whose appointments could themselves be vetoed by the Chancellor, there were few defenders of the status quo. Even Assemblyman Al Vann wouldn't oppose the new law. Members of the District 23 board, some of whose parents had been soldiers in the community control struggle, raised no opposition to the effective end of the diluted decentralization regime.[65]

The Bloomberg Era

> (History repeats itself), the first time as tragedy, the second time as farce.
>
> —Karl Marx[66]

Upon taking office as the city's new mayor in 2002, Michael R. Bloomberg began a campaign to finish off the remnants of school decentralization. There was no effort to evaluate it educationally, or to identify any positive aspects that might be worth retaining. After five months of intense negotiation with the State Legislature, during which parent groups were consulted neither formally nor informally by any party to the conversation, he got his wish. A century after the city school system was first centralized in 1898, history would now repeat itself. This time, the entire system was put under the direct control of the mayor, and this mayor had big plans. In the media, mayoral control of the schools was "widely considered the greatest legislative achievement of Bloomberg's first year in office."[67]

The Board of Education was abolished, replaced by a "Panel on Educational Policy." Presided over by the mayor-appointed chancellor, eight of the Panel's thirteen members would also serve at the mayor's pleasure. The Panel's ostensible role was limited to voting on budgets and on certain policy changes, but in practice it simply rubber-stamped decisions made at City Hall. Local school boards were eliminated. District Superintendents and all 135,000 other employees would now be hired and fired by the chancellor, who would report directly to the mayor.

Bloomberg appointed as chancellor Joel I. Klein, a former antitrust lawyer and corporate executive with no background in education and no record of any previous interest in it. Klein hit the ground running with an eight-member cabinet, including an investment banker, a foundation executive, a telecom executive, a former state deputy comptroller, a lawyer, and the son of his former law partner. Later, he added two members who knew something about education.[68]

There was some historical irony in this arrangement. During the UFT's crusade against community control in the late 1960s, one of Albert Shanker's mantras was that lay people on local boards were incapable of making sound educational policy. Now the entire system was being run by non-educators. This in itself was really only an apparent contradiction, since Shanker's reference to "lay people" was actually just a euphemism for "black and Puerto Rican parents." Bloomberg, in enthusiastic agreement with Shanker on that score, took it a step further, extending the exclusion from power to all parents.

It would have been a self-defeating scandal if there were no provision at all for parent involvement. The new system provided for 1,185 paid Parent Coordinators, who were to serve as links between the parents and the principals of their schools. It was the principals themselves, though, who would hire and fire these people. Since their jobs depended on pleasing the principal, there was no possibility of independence. In practice, they became the principals' agents, more likely to dampen parent activism than to encourage it. Under this new regime, parents would be not only powerless, but ignored as well. After all, "consulting with parents," sniffed Klein, "can create gridlock." Parent outreach was redefined as mobilizing them to support Bloomberg's policies and sing his praises, without ever asking their advice. The Panel for Educational Policy, whose five non-mayoral appointees were parents, was characterized by one close observer as "good preparation for knowing how to sit in a chair and keep silent."[69] Bloomberg set a precedent early, removing two of his own appointees who cast votes against his wishes.

The Board's archaic old Brooklyn headquarters at 110 Livingston Street was shut down, which drew no tears, but closed as well were all the local school district offices, which were the parents' last face-to-face contact with the system above the school level. The new Department of Education (DOE) was housed around the corner from City Hall in the old Tweed Courthouse, a relic that for decades had no purpose except as a reminder of Tammany Hall's corrupt nineteenth-century regime. The building was brought up to date, and restored to its former majesty, at the cost of only $100 million.

New, packaged, "cookie cutter" curricula and lesson planning for math and English were made mandatory for elementary and middle schools throughout the system. Standardized tests were developed to measure children's progress in learning the material. These new curricula were implemented citywide before undergoing any real-world evaluation.

In 2007, a new reorganization grafted a full-fledged corporate model onto the school system. Principals became the "CEOs" of their schools, with wide authority over budget allocations and staffing. Test scores became the analog of sales quotas, with principals' jobs, as well as teachers' evaluations and tenure decisions, dependent on reaching specified targets. Cash bonuses were offered to teachers and principals whose students outperformed these targets. Schools were given report cards based on the test scores, and shut down if they received failing grades.[70] With the stakes raised so high, the entire enterprise became data-driven. Testing and test preparation became, in the minds of many, the actual curriculum of the new order.

Pre-school testing now became the gateway for admission into the "Gifted & Talented" programs. Private preschools and test-preparation services sprang up to train the four-year-olds of the upper-middle-class in test-taking. Deborah Meier, a widely respected educational expert, observed that . . .

> Pre-Kindergartens are devoted now to prepping, with test-like skill sheets, and nary a block, a live animal or a plant—not even an easel . . . Anxious parents are plotting how to get their four year-olds in Gifted classes, prepping them for IQ tests that no serious scholars consider reliable, and that overwhelmingly favor white children from wealthy families.[71]

In seven black and Latino districts, Gifted & Talented programs were completely eliminated by 2009 because, based on these test results, not enough children qualified for admission.[72] Forty percent of those admitted to the elite programs came from the four wealthiest and whitest of the city's 32 districts.[73]

Consistent with the market-based ideology of those in charge, privatization became another of the system's new themes. Charter schools, publicly funded but privately controlled, proliferated. These schools are free to sharply increase teacher salaries, cap enrollments and class sizes, extend the school day and/or the school year, and toss students they deem "disruptive" back into the public schools. With admission based on lotteries, they skim many of the most motivated students, and parents, from the public school system. Many have budgets substantially enhanced by corporate and foundation grants.

By 2011, after less than a decade of mayoral control, the city's education budget had more than doubled, from $11.5 to $24 billion, with no increase in student enrollment. Teacher salaries were raised by 43 percent, and untold millions were spent on the design, preparation, implementation, and evaluation of standardized tests. It was not deemed important to reduce class sizes or to alleviate overcrowded schools, both of which increased steadily between 2006 and 2011.

Perhaps the most effective effort to reduce class sizes under mayoral control has been a massive expansion of student suspensions, based on a new code of conduct that tripled the number of suspension-triggering behaviors. During 1968, when high school students were in open rebellion against the school system, suspensions hit a record high of about 13,000.[74] During the law-and-order mayoralty of Rudolph Giuliani, annual suspensions surpassed 28,000. Under the Bloomberg-Klein regime, this figure hit 74,000 during 2008–09, and remained well above 70,000 in each succeeding year. Nine of every ten students suspended each year are black or Latino.

The regime's other innovation in enforcing student discipline has been the outsourcing of this task to the Police Department. According to a 2011 report by the NY Civil Liberties Union,

> The overuse of suspensions combines with heavy-handed street policing tactics . . . to push students from classrooms into the criminal justice system. School safety officers (NYPD personnel assigned to the schools) have become increasingly involved in maintaining school discipline. Students, some as young as five, have been handcuffed, taken to jail, and ordered to appear in court for infractions such as writing on a desk or talking back.[75]

All these fundamental changes in policy were implemented without ever consulting parents (let alone students), or even holding public hearings. Only one man needed to approve them, and he was apparently convinced they were all terrific, game-changing ideas. Bloomberg charged his public relations team with bringing his constituents into agreement. The Department of Education hired a dozen public relations professionals to work full-time promoting its effectiveness. Klein even set up a private foundation that spent millions on an ostensibly independent, self-congratulatory, advertising program.

Miracle or Mirage

There did indeed seem to be much to crow about when the state issued the results of its 2009 standardized math and English tests for grades 3 through 8. In New York City, 82 percent of its students passed the math exam, up from 74 percent in 2008 and just 57 percent in 2006. On the English tests, 69 percent passed, up from 58 percent the year before. Further, the racial achievement gap was finally shrinking. Math proficiency rates for black students, which had trailed those of white students by 31 points in 2006, now trailed by only

17 percent. The DOE's report cards rated 84 percent of the schools with an "A" grade.

For the mayor, the timing could not have been better. Mayoral control was up for renewal in the state legislature, and he was up for reelection to a third term. The public relations apparatus went into overdrive.

At press conferences, "Mr. Bloomberg trumpeted the results as evidence that mayoral control had produced revolutionary improvements." "Groundbreaking" was Klein's favorite adjective. He described the test results an "a milestone in his reform efforts." "This is a big victory for the city," he announced, "and we should really bask in it."[76] Despite the reservations of some scholars about the test results' validity, and those expressed by the Chancellor of the State Board of Regents, who noted that "statistics . . . sometimes obscure the facts,"[77] the Bloomberg-Klein reforms became a nationally hailed success story. School systems across the country rushed to emulate their model.

It took only a few months for the bubble to burst. State education officials gave a hearing to scholars who had been claiming for years that the tests had an inherent defect. Because of the way they were structured, coaching by teachers would make them easier to pass each year. The tests, they argued, were gauging the amount of preparation more than the mastery of subject matter. These arguments finally prevailed. Changes were made in the 2010 tests to correct the defects, and passing grades were recalibrated.[78]

Scores plummeted. The citywide proficiency rate in English dropped from the false 69 percent to 42 percent, in math from 82 percent to 54 percent, and the racial achievement gap was back. The 17-percent gap in math, for example, climbed to 35 percent, four points higher than four years earlier. At one Bronx school, the third-grade math proficiency rate reversed digits, from an apparent 81 percent to an actual 18 percent. Not only were the scores lower than Bloomberg and Klein had been trumpeting for a year, but substantially all the measurable gains of their entire eight-year regime had suddenly vaporized.[79]

The recalibration must have triggered a sense of déjà vu for Bloomberg. Back in 2005, he held a celebratory news conference to announce a similar miracle his policies had supposedly wrought. In a Bronx public school, children's reading proficiency had jumped in one year from 34 percent to 83 percent. Like most things that sound too good to be true, it was. The following year's results had only 42 percent meeting the state standards. The school's 2010 proficiency rate was 37 percent, about the same as it was back in 2004.[80]

This wasn't the first miracle turned mirage in big-city standardized testing. Score inflation had been exposed in Chicago, Dallas, Charleston, Oakland, Houston, Philadelphia, Atlanta, Tacoma, and Washington DC. Cheating scandals had been erupting for years, which can only be expected when the futures of students, teachers, and schools depend on test scores, particularly when the integrity of these high-stakes tests is not protected by high-security measures. After a national study of 46 state education departments the *Atlanta Journal-Constitution* concluded in 2012 that, "Most state-designed security systems have failed to find blatant cheating even when the evidence is right in front of them."[81]

By 2010, a rising number of voices were questioning the validity of such tests, particularly since cheating scandals were becoming routine national news, with some arguing that they were actually a corrupting influence on the entire educational process. Such voices were not heard in the Bloomberg administration. During the 2010–2011 school year, though, hundreds of test-tampering and grade-changing allegations in the city were reported to state officials. Reports to state investigators of test-tampering in the city's high schools multiplied sevenfold during the Bloomberg-Klein era.[82]

Scores in the much-heralded charter schools also took a nosedive in the 2010 recalibration. At one of the highest ranked charter schools, third-grade math proficiency plunged from a celebrated 100 percent to 56 percent. At a charter school operated by the UFT, the eighth-grade proficiency rate plummeted from 79 percent to 13 percent. Overall, the charter schools were shown to be performing only slightly better than the public schools, despite their higher level of funding and freedom to innovate.[83]

This was consistent with the findings of a large national study by the Center for Research on Education Outcomes (CREDO), a research institute affiliated with Stanford University, which compared charter school students' performance with that of public school students with similar background characteristics. In math, it found that 46 percent of the charter schools' outcomes were statistically insignificant from those of the public schools, that 37 percent performed worse than the public schools, and that only 17 percent had superior outcomes. In reading, it found that the average charter school performed slightly worse than the public schools.[84] If Bloomberg and Klein were aware of this study, they chose to ignore it.

The CREDO study was controversial. Other studies (sponsored by the charter school movement itself) reported different results. Certainly, there are excellent charter schools. Certainly, educators could learn from their successes. Some are reminiscent, though, of a spectacularly successful program called "Higher Horizons" that the Board of Education began during the 1950s, when it poured enormous resources into a single junior high school. When the Board tried to duplicate that success elsewhere, within nearly normal budgetary limitations, the total ineffectiveness of the expanded program quickly relegated it to the crowded dustbin of the city's educational history.[85]

There have always been some superlative schools, even school districts, in New York's communities of color, their most common denominator being the skills and vision of their leadership. Some charter schools have joined that number; others have not. In any case, writes John H. Jackson of the Schott Foundation for Public Education,

> We cannot become so affixed on the spotlights that we ignore the larger headlights from the train wreck facing our country, (or) by the 1.2 million (young black males) we are losing each year.[86]

Testing and Its Discontents

Given the explosiveness of other issues in Ocean Hill–Brownsville, to test or not to test was only a peripheral point of contention between Rhody McCoy and the Board of Education. It was the only district, though, whose chief executive refused to mandate administration of the Board's standardized reading tests. McCoy's instruction to principals was that they could use the tests if they wanted to, but only as a tool for internal self-evaluation. No instructional time was to be wasted in test preparation. Results were to be kept confidential. Personally, he believed that such tests were meaningless and potentially harmful. Given the results of the data-driven Bloomberg-Klein regime, it may be time to take another look at this position.

Tests that are used only for diagnostic purposes, which are administered without prior coaching, are now known as "audit tests." The "gold standard" for audit tests is the National Assessment of Educational Progress (NAEP), which contains built-in mechanisms to prevent the corruption associated with tests that have high-stakes consequences. NAEP results have shown no statistically significant improvement, in either reading or math, during the entire Bloomberg-Klein regime. In 2011, for example, three out of four eighth-graders, who were in kindergarten when mayoral control was instituted, scored less than proficient in both subjects, almost exactly the same percentage as in 2003.[87]

Standardized testing seems to have proliferated over the years in step with the technological capacity to administer, grade, and analyze the exams. It wouldn't be unfair to call this a case of "Because we can, we will." It's also a big business, employing untold numbers of statisticians, lobbyists, and sales people. Since the passage of the federal, poorly titled "No Child Left Behind" law in 2002, schools are required to administer tests in English Language Arts and in Math in the third through eighth grades. The Obama administration, in its "Race to the Top" program, raised the stakes on these tests, tying teacher evaluations to their results.

In New York City, these and additional tests have come to determine the fates of students, teachers, principals, and even schools, hundreds of which have been closed due to low scores. Teachers and supervisors now had an incentive to spend an inordinate amount of time "teaching to the test," to sometimes teach the test itself and, in some cases, to cheat. None of this has anything to do with education.

Such exams have always had their critics, though. The Association for Childhood Education International, after studying the issue, reached the same conclusion in 1991 as Rhody McCoy did in 1968. It called for the abolition of standardized testing, after concluding that the testing regime . . .

- Puts undue pressure on children, setting them up for devastating failure and lowered self-esteem;
- Provides no useful information, but becomes the basis for life-changing judgments and decisions;
- Leads to harmful tracking and labeling;
- Compels teachers to spend precious instructional time on test preparation;
- Harms education by distorting curriculum, teaching and learning;
- Lowers teacher expectations; and
- Interferes with cooperative learning and problem-solving.[88]

In the world of the twenty-first century, this last point deserves serious consideration. At a time when business, industrial, and even military challenges are tackled through team efforts, what is the predictive quality of individual, competitive exams? There are other ways to evaluate student performance, methods that allow students to work together in teams with a common purpose. They might even learn to become citizens of a democracy that way.

A better and much less expensive measure of teacher quality was the student questionnaire that my eighth-graders developed at JHS 271. It was only a prototype, of course, which we unfortunately didn't have the opportunity to further develop. Even that crude experiment, though, gave the teachers specific useful feedback, which some used to improve their performance. It also gave the students their first sense of empowerment. Their voices were heard. They were now citizens of their school, taking their first steps toward citizenship of the larger community. When student input is left completely out of the teacher evaluation process, the most important stakeholders are left unheard. No successful business would even think of completely ignoring consumer feedback.

Over-reliance on test data also denies the fact that teaching and learning are *human* activities, involving the engagement of active minds with one another. Here's another radical idea for teacher evaluation, borne of my Ocean Hill–Brownsville experience: Team qualified professionals with parents to conduct classroom observations, and rate teacher performance on the following six criteria:

1. Energy;
2. Enthusiasm;
3. Expectations of the students;
4. Mastery of the subject matter;
5. Ability to communicate in an age-appropriate manner; and
6. Respect for the students, their families, and their cultures.

Any teacher who ranks high on these six criteria will, I firmly believe, be successful. Time and money does not have to be wasted on designing, preparing for, administering, and grading standardized exams. Further, this method lends itself to subjects that are impossible to quantify in any useful way. Teachers of art, music, and even physical education, can be meaningfully evaluated this way (in schools where these subjects haven't been decimated by budget cuts, or squeezed out by the testing regime). Since all of these qualities can be enhanced in workshop settings and internships, and observed in practice, there might be no further need for teacher certification exams or even for schools of education. All the money budgeted for teaching children could actually be used for that purpose.

Point #6 is of particular importance when teachers and students come from different backgrounds. One of the sparks of the Community Control movement was the typically superior, condescending attitude of white teachers toward their black and Puerto Rican students, and toward the students' parents as well. As Paul Becker, a veteran teacher activist, told historian Daniel Perlstein, "Racial insults were part of teacher culture in ghetto schools. Making fun of the children's accents and speech patterns was considered great fun in the teacher lounges."[89]

That "white teacher" culture was an impetus for some to demand only black teachers for black students. More common, though, was the attitude expressed by Margaret Wright of the Los Angeles Community Black Board of Education. "We don't care whether they're black, white or yellow," she told *Newsweek* in 1968, "just as long as they respect the values of the community."[90] Central to the Community Control movement's philosophy, in its early articulation by Preston Wilcox, was the idea that the schools should celebrate the cultures of their students, not reject them. It is a precondition to realizing the organic linkage John Dewey recognized between experience and education.[91] Wherever schools today make an effort to put this concept into practice, the spirit of that movement lives on.

This does not only apply to white teachers in communities of color. Harvard Professor Vito Perrone used to tell a story from his days of teaching high school in a rural area.[92] There were two brothers in his history course who were consistently late to class. He learned that they were tardy because they had to set traps near the local swamps before leaving for school. Since Perrone grew up in the city, he didn't have any idea what trapping even was. When he showed an interest, they offered to show him.

Walking through the forest that day, Perrone was impressed by the brothers' knowledge of flora and fauna. "They seemed to understand everything about the growth of plants and the habitats of various wildlife," he recalled. Then he heard that the brothers were struggling with, of all things, their biology class. Clearly, their science teacher was missing something important.

Perrone said he learned a valuable lesson from these two boys. "To teach students well," he said, "you must know them well, understanding more fully what *they* are all about." In other words, to be a good teacher, one must learn from the students. This was the same lesson I learned in Ocean Hill–Brownsville.

The End Product

> The legislature shall provide for the maintenance and support of a system of free common schools, wherein all the children of this state may be educated.
>
> —*NY State Constitution, Article XI, Section 1 (1854)*

> That Article (XI) requires the State to offer all children the opportunity of a sound basic education. Such an education should consist of the basic literacy, calculating, and verbal skills necessary to enable children to eventually function productively as civic participants. . . .
>
> —*NY State Court of Appeals (1995)*[93]

> Government and its institutions are accountable to power alone. The schools serving the poor will continue to shortchange their students until such time as the poor can obtain a meaningful voice in the public arena.
>
> —Prof. Henry M. Levin, Stanford University[94]

According to the *2011 Mayor's Management Report*, the Department of Education is the worst-performing of the city's 44 agencies. Its own data indicates backsliding in more than half of the rated categories, including class sizes, academic proficiency, overcrowding, and parent contact. It further reports that 61 percent of students who began high school in 2006 successfully graduated four years later, although it offers no information about the 39 percent who did not. The graduation rate among white students was 76 percent; among black students, it was 56 percent.

"No one could have predicted in their wildest dreams," declared the mayor, "that we would be this successful."[95]

How many graduates were ready for college? Following an analysis of previous years' data, state and city community colleges have concluded that high school seniors scoring at least 80 percent on their Regents exams in math, and 75 percent in English, would be capable of achieving "C" grades in those colleges without additional remedial preparation. Based on this rough benchmark, only one-third of the city's 2011 graduates were prepared for college after four years of high school. In 25 high schools where the graduation rate was over 80 percent, less than 20 percent were college-ready. Three schools with over 80 percent graduation rates had less than 2 percent college-ready. Some high schools could not manage to graduate 1 percent of their seniors college-ready, including one that boasted an 86 percent graduation rate.[96]

During the first decade of mayoral control, 135 new, small high schools were created to replace the large comprehensive institutions that were closed. Their 2011 graduation rate was 61 percent, the same as the citywide rate. Their college-ready graduation rate was 12 percent. Less than one of every eight students who started in these high schools in 2007 graduated ready for college work in 2011.[97]

What happens to those failed by our public schools? The dual labor market that characterized the U.S. economy during the century following the Civil War no longer exists. The low-paid dirty industrial jobs for which the public schools supplied uneducated, unskilled black and Latino workers have largely gone overseas, or vanished entirely. Between 1969 and 1999, New York City lost 68 percent of its manufacturing jobs, as apparel manufacturing moved to Asia and the printing industry was transformed by technology.[98] Then, during the Bloomberg mayoralty, almost half of those remaining disappeared.[99] Opportunities in job categories employing unskilled and uneducated workers, in the city and in the nation, cannot begin to absorb those whose options are so limited.

As the nation's need for these workers vaporized, its prison population exploded, from about 320,000 in 1980 to 2.4 million in 2013. Black men, less than 7 percent of the nation's population, comprise more than 40 percent of its prisoners. The United States now has the world's highest incarceration rate, higher than those of Iran, Russia, and China. We have more people in prison than the next 36 countries combined. A higher percentage of blacks are in American prisons now than were in South African prisons at the height of apartheid. This, increasingly, is the fate of those failed by our public school systems, mass incarceration of a disposable population.[100]

During the first decade of the twenty-first century, according to the Pew Center on the States, one of every nine African-American men aged 20 to 34 is behind bars (versus one of every 100 whites).[101] One out of every three is "in the system" (in prison, in jail, on probation, or on parole), tallying more than were enslaved in 1850. In many cities, as many as 80 percent now have criminal records, subjecting them to legalized discrimination, for the rest of their lives, in housing, employment, voting, public benefits, education, and even jury service. "These young men," writes law professor Michelle Alexander, "are part of a growing undercaste, permanently locked up and locked out of mainstream society."[102]

Young black males have become an endangered species. The Schott Foundation's 2010 national study of this problem concluded that, "The rate at which black males are being pushed out of school and into the pipeline to prison far exceeds the rate at which they are graduating and reaching high levels of academic achievement."[103] Its national survey found that only 47 percent were graduating from high school in four years, compared with 78 percent of whites.

The Schott Report also studied the 2008 four-year college-ready graduation rates of black males in the nation's 59 largest school districts. New York City, with the nation's largest black male enrollment, ranked among the country's ten worst large districts. Among males, the rates were 28 percent for blacks and 50 percent for whites. "New York City, lauded for its education reforms," the report concluded," is one of the least successful districts."

Among states, New York had the worst record of all fifty, graduating only 25 percent of its black males college-ready, versus 68 percent of its whites: a 43 percent gap. The substandard education provided to New York City's African-American students, combined with contract-mandated seniority policies and shifting certification requirements that have consistently favored whites, goes a long way toward explaining the school system's persistent failure to adequately diversify its teaching and supervisory staff.

The campaign to abolish the city's Board of Examiners began in 1969, when there were eleven black principals in the one thousand city schools and Luis Fuentes was the only Puerto Rican principal, with the filing of *Chance v. Board of Examiners* by the NAACP Legal Defense and Education Fund. Chancellor Harvey Scribner refused to oppose that suit, finding the existing system indefensible. The UFT, though, filed an *amicus curiae* brief in opposition to the black and Puerto Rican plaintiffs,[104] even though Albert Shanker himself regarded the principals' exam "ridiculous."[105] Notwithstanding the Court's 1972 ruling in that case that the Board's supervisory exams were discriminatory and unconstitutional, it would not be until 1990 that the State Legislature finally put an end to the Board of Examiners. During the two intervening decades, as the walls of discrimination slowly crumbled, African-American representation on the teaching staff climbed from 8 percent to 20 percent, although a substantial proportion of these teachers were uncertified. (The annual failure rate on the national exam, required for certification since 1984, was 20 percent for whites and 60 to 70 percent for blacks and Latinos.)[106]

By 2002, the year Mayor Bloomberg took control of the schools, only slight further progress had been made. African-Americans then comprised 22 percent of the teaching staff. They were, however, 27 percent of the new hires that year. Since then, during each year of the Bloomberg reign, the black new-hire percentage has dropped. By 2008, it was down to 13 percent, and black representation among the staff was back to its 1990 level of 20 percent. A stunning 4 percent of African-American applicants were achieving state certification. While whites declined to 14 percent of the student body, white teachers never comprised less than 60 percent of the staff. The *New York Sun* reported,

> Educators and advocates said they have been troubled by the data for several years—and they said they are especially troubled this year, the 40th anniversary of the Ocean Hill–Brownsville crisis, in which black community leaders challenged the city to make school staff more representative.[107]

Coda

In the mid-twentieth-century, at the time of the *Brown v. Board of Education* decision, New York City's black and Latino children attended inferior, segregated schools. Now, well into the twenty-first century, their grandchildren attend inferior, segregated schools. In 2010–2011, black and Latino children comprised more than 90 percent of the student body in more than 900 of the city's 1,600 schools, while the teaching and supervisory staffs remain overwhelmingly white.[108] According to a 2011 Brown University study, New York is the nation's third most segregated city, behind only Detroit and Milwaukee. Further, the study found that blacks and Latinos with annual incomes higher than $75,000 live in poorer neighborhoods than whites earning less than $40,000.[109]

In 2011, according to the National Assessment of Educational Progress, only one of every six black and Latino eighth-graders, and not even 10 percent of the black boys, scored proficient or better in reading. Less than one of every eight black and Latino eighth-graders demonstrated proficiency in mathematics.[110] By the benchmarks that the Bloomberg-Klein regime itself established, however questionable these benchmarks might be, the city's schools continue to churn out black and Latino students who are unprepared for either college or career. These children are processed through a segregated system that not only institutionalized a refusal to implement *Brown v. Board of Education*, the law of the land since 1954, but does not even meet the "separate but equal" standard the Court set in 1896. Upstate prisons await their arrival.

On the other side of the ledger is the excellent Stuyvesant High School, one of the city's eight elite secondary schools. In 2012, 1.2 percent of Stuyvesant students were African-American, down from 13 percent in 1980. A few more were Latino. Blacks and Latinos comprised over 72 percent of the city's student body.[111] "What the racial gap in admissions represents," wrote Jonathan Kozol, "is the devastating end result of the failure to educate black and Latino children effectively from the age of 2½ up to their 8th grade year." This, he argues, is nothing less than "Apartheid Education."[112] Admission to these elite schools is determined by a single competitive exam, a policy challenged in a 2012 federal civil rights lawsuit by the NAACP Legal Defense and Educational Fund and other organizations.

Shortly after leaving the chancellorship to become a senior advisor to Rupert Murdoch, with a multi-million dollar annual salary, Joel Klein acknowledged the paucity of results during his tenure, claiming that all the creative reforms he attempted were blocked by the UFT.[113] Both of the new UFT contracts during this time were negotiated during mayoral election years, which magnified the union's negotiating leverage. In this sense, "mayoral control" sounds like more than it really is. It was Bloomberg's administration that negotiated and signed these contracts, though, and it was the mayor who made education his signature issue.

What have rank-and-file New Yorkers themselves concluded about mayoral control of the schools? Approval peaked after Bloomberg's self-congratulatory celebration of the phony 2009 test scores. In a subsequent Quinnipiac University poll, 56 percent supported mayoral control; only 24 percent considered it a failure. The results were reversed in 2011, after two years of the recalibrated, lower-scoring tests. Now, 56 percent branded it a failure; only 24 percent still thought it was successful.[114]

These results were echoed in an August 2011 *New York Times* poll, which found only 34 percent of residents approving of how Bloomberg had handled the schools. Answering "not satisfied" were 64 percent of African-Americans, 57 percent of Latinos, and 50 percent of whites. The most often-cited complaint was the school system's obsession with testing and test preparation.[115] In the newspaper's 2013 poll, which yielded generally positive reviews of Bloomberg's 12-year mayoralty, three out of four respondents thought the city's schools had not improved, and one out of three thought they had gotten even worse.[116]

Leonie Haimson, the founder of Class Size Matters, an information and advocacy group, summed up the verdict many had reached in a 2009 essay.

> The enthusiasm for privatization and market mechanisms, the obsession with data, even when much of it was statistically unreliable, was accompanied by a tendency on the part of the Mayor and the Chancellor to continually shift blame onto incompetent administrators, lazy teachers, uninvolved parents, and the "culture of excuses," rather than accept the increased accountability that mayoral control was supposed to bring. Though the mayor and chancellor have been in office for more than six years, with nearly complete authority over our schools, they remain fond of disparaging critics as defenders of the status quo. Bloomberg and Klein insist on holding everyone accountable except themselves.[117]

New York Times columnist Jim Dwyer, in 2011, fired a particularly telling jab at the new school system's relationship with parents, nine years after the demise of decentralization. "For many parents," he wrote, "the school system has become more remote, more obtuse, more bewildering than the reviled community boards that were shut down."[118]

This is not just a New York City story. Mayoral control of urban education systems became fashionable nationwide during the early twenty-first century. These institutions have, by and large, failed to effectively educate their children, particularly children of color. The magnitude of this failure has been documented by a bewildering array of standardized tests that have themselves become fetishized, dominating school calendars and budgets, and substituting for the education they are supposed to measure. Mayoral control of education, like its predecessor fads and fashions, will eventually join them in the dustbin of urban history.

It seems paradoxical that these big-city school systems have been willing to try almost anything *except* the active, meaningful engagement of the schools' primary stakeholders: children and their parents.

It also seems paradoxical, today, that in the public school system of the ever-evolving, ever-changing organism of a city that is New York, so little of substance has changed since 1970, when journalist Robert Campbell penned this eulogy to the Ocean Hill–Brownsville Demonstration School District:

> . . . a sulphurous malaise envelops the city, a stifling stillness, an educational inversion that hangs in there as it always has, an inversion in which no wind blows. Yet suppose that for a time there had indeed been a breath of air, a small wind that breathed some life into a few ghetto schools, before they were blown away? Suppose

> you had seen that? Suppose Rhody McCoy had indeed held the keys to the kingdom. Suppose that the first real revolution in ghetto education had actually occurred. . . .[119]

Perhaps that life-affirming wind will return one day. Perhaps parents, ignored for so long, will once again demand that their voices, and those of their children, be heard. Perhaps community control will one day, finally, be given an opportunity to be fairly judged on its merits. If that day comes, the hope of democracy will be reborn in urban education. And perhaps, if that day comes, and if the level of energy that was unleashed long ago in Ocean Hill–Brownsville can once again emerge, then there can once again be hope for an educational renaissance in our cities. Does anyone have a better idea?

Notes

Part I

1. Harold M. Baron, "The Web of Urban Racism," in *Institutional Racism in America*, ed. Louis L. Knowles and Kenneth Prewitt (Englewood Cliffs, NJ: Prentice Hall, 1969), 146.

2. Fred Siegel, *The Future Once Happened Here: New York, D.C., L.A. and the Fate of America's Big Cities* (New York: The Free Press, 1997), 26.

3. Sidney M. Peck, "The Economic Situation of Negro Labor," in *The Negro and the American Labor Movement*, ed. Julius Jacobson (Garden City, NY: Anchor Doubleday, 1968), 215.

4. Mario Michaelides and Peter Mueser, *Recent Changes in the Characteristics of Unemployed Workers* (U.S. Department of Labor, 2009), 21.

5. A 1963 survey conducted by the NYC Commission on Human Rights found that the Board of Education employed a smaller proportion of black and Puerto Rican professionals (8.8%) than any city agency except the Department of Finance.

6. George R. LaNoue and Bruce L. R. Smith, *The Politics of School Decentralization* (Lexington, MA: D.C. Heath & Co., 1973), 164.

7. Annie Stein, "Strategies for Failure," *Harvard Educational Review*, 41:2 (May, 1971), 159–60.

8. Sol Stern, "'Scab' Teachers," *Ramparts* (November 17, 1968), 20.

9. David Rogers, *110 Livingston Street: Politics and Bureaucracy in the New York City School System* (New York: Random House, 1968), 196n.

10. Joshua B. Freeman, *Working-Class New York: Life and Labor Since World War II* (New York: The New Press, 2000), 12.

11. Siegel, *The Future Once Happened Here*, 28.

12. Herbert Hill, "The Racial Practices of Organized Labor: The Contemporary Record," in *The Negro and the American Labor Movement*, ed. Julius Jacobson (Garden City, NY: Doubleday Anchor, 1968), 292.

13. Freeman, *Working-Class New York*, 48, 180.

14. Philip Foner, *Organized Labor and the Black Worker: 1619–1973* (New York: International Publishers, 1976), 341.

15. Freeman, *Working-Class New York*, 182.

16. *Brown v. Board of Education of Topeka* 347 US 483 (1954).

17. *Brown v. Board of Education of Topeka* 349 US 294 (1955).

18. Clarence Taylor, *Knocking On Our Own Door: Milton A. Galamison and the Struggle to Integrate New York City Schools*, (New York: Columbia University Press, 1997), 52–4.

19. Board of Education of the City of New York, "Resolution for Action," December 23, 1954.

20. Peck, "The Economic Situation of Negro Labor," 212.

21. Freeman, *Working-Class New York*, 106.

22. August Meier and Elliot M. Redwick, *From Plantation to Ghetto: an Interpretive History of American Negroes* (New York: Hill & Wang, 1966, 1968), 189.

23. Craig Steven Wilder, *A Covenant With Color: Race and Social Power in Brooklyn* (New York: Columbia University Press, 2000), 182.

24. Martha Biondi, *To Stand and Fight: The Struggle for Civil Rights in Postwar New York City* (Cambridge, MA: Harvard University Press, 2003), 121, 230.

25. Freeman, *Working-Class New York*, 184; Siegel, *The Future Once Happened Here*, 47.

26. Earl Lewis, "The Need to Remember: Three Phases in Black and Jewish Educational Relations," in *Struggles in the Promised Land: Toward a History of Black-Jewish Relations in the United States*, ed. Jack Salzman and Cornel West (New York: Oxford University Press, 1997), 246.

27. Freeman, *Working-Class New York*, 184.

28. Brian Purnell, "Taxation Without Sanitation is Tyranny," in *Civil Rights in New York City: From World War II to the Giuliani Era*, ed. Clarence Taylor (New York: Fordham University Press, 2011), 54.

29. David K. Shipler, "The Brownsville Way of Life: Grinding Poverty and Squalor," *New York Times* (May 6, 1971).

30. Harold X. Connolly, *A Ghetto Grows in Brooklyn* (New York: New York University Press, 1977), 140.

31. *Ibid.*, 212–13.

32. Wilder, *A Covenant With Color*, 182–94.

33. Biondi, *To Stand and Fight*, 223–24.

34. Stein, "Strategies for Failure," 162.

35. Rogers, *110 Livingston Street*, 71–2.

36. Stein, "Strategies for Failure," 162.

37. Leon F. Litwack, *North of Slavery: The Negro in the Free States, 1790–1860* (Chicago: University of Chicago Press, 1961), 132.

38. Adina Back, "Blacks, Jews and the Struggle to Integrate Brooklyn's Junior High School 258: A Cold War Story," *Journal of American Ethnic History* 20:2 (Winter, 2001), 44.

39. Taylor, *Knocking On Our Own Door*, 72.

40. "A Tribute to Thelma Hamilton," *City Star* (April, 1975).

41. Daniel H. Perlstein, *Justice, Justice: School Politics and the Eclipse of Liberalism* (New York: Peter Lang, 2004), 99; Clarence Taylor, ""Conservative and Liberal Opposition to the New York City School-Integration Campaign," in *Civil Rights in New York City*, 104.

42. Taylor, *Knocking On Our Own Door*, 92ff.

43. Carl Bernstein, *Loyalties: A Son's Memoir* (New York: Simon & Schuster, 1989), 95–7.

44. Perlstein, *Justice, Justice*, 100.

45. Taylor, *Knocking On Our Own Door*, 103.

46. Rogers, *110 Livingston Street*, 267; Barbara Carter, *Pickets, Parents and Power: The Story Behind the 1968 Teachers' Strike* (New York: Citation Press, 1971), 50.

47. Rogers, *110 Livingston Street*, 244.

48. Carter, *Pickets, Parents and Power*, 27.

49. Rogers, *110 Livingston Street*, 305ff.

50. Stein, "Strategies for Failure," 164.

51. Siegel, *The Future Once Happened Here*, 31.

52. Foner, *Organized Labor and the Black Worker*, 339.

53. Carter, *Pickets, Parents and Power*, 50.

54. Real Estate Board of New York, *Rebuilding Manhattan: A Study of New Office Construction* (1972), 28.

55. Freeman, *Working-Class New York*, 190.

56. Herbert Hill, "The Racial Practices of Organized Labor," 304, 315; Perlstein, *Justice, Justice*, 103–4, 136; Foner, *Organized Labor and the Black Worker*, 337.

57. Leaflet, "50-50 or Fight!" (Author's Collection).

58. Jonathan Rieder, *Canarsie: The Jews and Italians of Brooklyn Against Liberalism* (Cambridge, MA: Harvard University Press, 1985), 15.

59. Connolly, *A Ghetto Grows in Brooklyn*, 216; Stein, "Strategies for Failure," 165.

60. Taylor, *Knocking On Our Own Door*, 133ff.

61. Taylor, "Opposition to the New York City School-Integration Campaign," 112.

62. Marjorie Murphy, *Blackboard Unions: The NEA and the AFT, 1900–1980* (Ithaca, NY: Cornell University Press, 1990), 238.

63. Perlstein, *Justice, Justice: School Politics and the Eclipse of Liberalism*, 87.

64. Miriam Wasserman, *The School Fix: NYC, USA* (New York: Outerbridge & Dienstfrey, 1970), 315.

65. Herbert Hill, "The Racial Practices of Organized Labor," 286–7; Murphy, *Blackboard Unions*, 207–8.

66. Perlstein, *Justice, Justice*, 25; Rogers, *110 Livingston Street*, 196.

67. Clarence Taylor, *Reds at the Blackboard: Communism, Civil Rights and the New York City Teachers Union* (New York: Columbia University Press, 2011), 271; Back, "Blacks, Jews and the Struggle to Integrate Brooklyn's Junior High School 258," 51–6.

68. Freeman, *Working-Class New York*, 48, 70, 75.

69. Taylor, *Reds at the Blackboard*, 312.

70. Robert J. Braun, *Teachers and Power: The Story of the American Federation of Teachers* (New York: Simon & Schuster, 1972), 61.

71. Taylor, *Reds at the Blackboard*, 303.

72. Wasserman, *The School Fix*, 316.

73. Interview, Jitu Weusi (January 7, 2012).

74. Taylor, *Knocking On Our Own Door*, 141–5.

75. Taylor, *Knocking On Our Own Door*, 148–4.

76. Fred Powledge, "More than 10,000 March in Protest on School Pairing," *New York Times* (March 13, 1964), 1, 20.

77. Taylor, *Knocking On Our Own Door*, 161–2.

78. George Corley Wallace, "Inaugural Address," (January 14, 1963).

79. New York State Education Commissioner's Advisory Committee on Human Relations and Community Tensions, "Desegregating the Public Schools of New York City" (May 12, 1964).

80. Transcript of interview with Reverend John Powis, conducted by Blackside, Inc. on November 4, 1988, for *Eyes on the Prize II: America at the Racial Crossroads 1965 to 1985*. Washington University Libraries, Film and Media Archive, Henry Hampton Collection.

81. Interview with Msgr. John Powis, conducted by Prof. Stephen Brier on April 26, 2011.

82. Wendell Pritchett, *Brownsville, Brooklyn: Blacks, Jews and the Changing Face of the Ghetto* (Chicago: University of Chicago Press, 2002), 224.

83. Monifa Edwards, Excerpt from "Naïve Child," (1996), reprinted by permission.

84. Pritchett, *Brownsville, Brooklyn*, 226.

85. Charles G. Bennett, "City Seeks Delay in Industry Park," *New York Times* (January 13, 1966), 42.

86. Douglas Robinson, "Mayor Walks Alone Into Angry Crowd and Draws Cheers," *New York Times* (July 20, 1966), 1, 26.

87. Joseph Featherstone, "Community Control of Our Schools," *The New Republic* (January 13, 1968), 18.

88. Ossie Davis, Foreword to *Schools Against Children: The Case for Community Control*, ed. Annette T. Rubinstein (New York: Monthly Review Press, 1970), 19.

89. Taylor, *Knocking On Our Own Door*, 159.

90. Malcolm X and James Farmer, "Separation or Integration: A Debate," originally in *Dialogue Magazine* 2:3 (May, 1962), reprinted in *Negro Protest Thought in the Twentieth Century*, ed. Francis L. Broderick and August Meier (New York: Bobbs Merrill, 1965), 361.

91. Clayborne Carson, *Malcolm X; The FBI File* (New York, Carroll & Graf, 1991), 24–5.

92. Preston Wilcox, "Releasing Human Potential: A Study of the East Harlem–Yorkville Bus Transfers," East Harlem Project for New York City Commission on Human Rights (1961), 12ff. (Author's Collection).

93. Kenneth B. Clark, *Dark Ghetto: Dilemmas of Social Power* (New York, Harper & Row, 1965), 129–33.

94. Eleanor B. Leacock, *Teaching and Learning in City Schools* (New York: Basic Books, 1969), 205; Robert Rosenthal and Lenore Jacobson, "Teacher Expectations for the Disadvantaged," *Scientific American* 218 (April, 1968), 19–23. Rosenthal and Jacobson's classic study in the "self-fulfilling prophecy" was published in book form as *Pygmalion in the Classroom* (New York: Holt Rinehart & Winston, 1968).

95. Carter, *Pickets, Parents and Power*, 7–9.

96. Henry Hampton and Steve Fayer, *Voices of Freedom: An Oral History of the Civil Rights Movement From the 1950s Through the 1980s* (New York: Bantam Books, 1990), 291.

97. Jerald E. Podair, *The Strike That Changed New York: Blacks, Whites and the Ocean Hill–Brownsville Crisis* (New Haven, CT: Yale University Press, 2002), 60.

98. Fred M. Hechinger, "Negroes' Priority Demand," *New York Times*, (October 13, 1968). 1. 80; "The Use and Misuse of Power," *Time* (October 25, 1968), 52.

99. Stein, "Strategies for Failure," 171–2.

100. Lewis, "The Need to Remember," in *Struggles in the Promised Land*, ed. Salzman and West, 243.

101. Stokely Carmichael and Charles V. Hamilton, *Black Power: The Politics of Liberation in America* (New York: Random House, 1967), 54.

102. Featherstone, "Community Control of Our Schools," 18.

103. Wilder, *A Covenant with Color*, 239.

104. Milton A. Galamison, "Educational Values and Community Power," *Freedomways* 8:4 (Fall, 1968), 312–13.

105. Leonard J. Fein, *The Ecology of the Public Schools: An Inquiry into Community Control*, (New York: Pegasus, 1971), 2.

106. Thelma J. Hamilton, Unpublished autobiographical fragment, Author's Collection; Interview, Paul Chandler (June 11, 2012).

107. Pritchett, *Brownsville, Brooklyn, 197*.

108. Pritchett, *Brownsville, Brooklyn, 198*.

109. Siegel, *The Future Once Happened Here*, 34.

110. Fred C. Shapiro, "The Talk of the Town," *The New Yorker* (September 21, 1968), 39.

111. Diane Ravitch, *The Great School Wars: New York City, 1805–1973* (New York: Basic Books, 1974), 308.

112. Ravitch, *The Great School Wars*, 316.

113. Fein, *The Ecology of the Public Schools*, 24.

114. Preston Wilcox, "Control of Schools Within the Black Community," Third Annual Black Power Conference, September 1, 1968 (Author's Collection).

115. Charles V. Hamilton, "Education in the Black Community: An Examination of the Realities," *Freedomways* (Fall, 1968), 323.

116. Leaflet issued by SCOPE (undated), Author's Collection.

117. Charles E. Wilson, "Lessons of the 201 Complex in Harlem," *Freedomways* (Fall, 1968), 406.

118. Marilyn Gittell et al., *Local Control in Education: Three Demonstration School Districts in New York City* (New York: Praeger, 1972), 59; William L. Van Deburg, *New Day in Babylon: The Black Power Movement and American Culture, 1965–1975* (Chicago: University of Chicago Press, 1993), 121; Murphy, *Blackboard Unions*, 243.

119. Rhody A. McCoy, "Year of the Dragon," in *Confrontation at Ocean Hill-Brownsville*, ed. Maurice Berube and Marilyn Gittell, (New York: Frederick Praeger, 1969), 167–8.

120. Stein, *Strategies for Failure*, 195.

121. *Chance v. Board of Examiners*, 458 F.2d 1167 (2d Cir. 1972).

122. Jonathan Kaufman, *Broken Alliance* (New York: Simon & Schuster, 1988, 1995), 134.

123. Transcript of interview with Reverend John Powis, conducted by Blackside, Inc. on November 4, 1988, for *Eyes on the Prize II: America at the Racial Crossroads 1965*

to 1985. Washington University Libraries, Film and Media Archive, Henry Hampton Collection.

124. Interview, "Rhody A. McCoy," in *Why Teachers Strike: Teachers' Rights and Community Control*, 115.

125. Rhody McCoy, "Why Have an Ocean Hill–Brownsville?" in *What Black Educators are Saying*, ed. Nathan Wright Jr. (New York: Hawthorn Books, 1970), 253.

126. Bernard Mackler, "The Punitive Use of Suspensions and Transfers in the New York City Schools," in *Schools Against Children: The Case for Community Control*, ed. Annette T. Rubinstein (New York: Monthly Review Press, 1970), 152.

127. Interview, Jitu Weusi (June 7, 2012).

128. Thomas A. Johnson, "Negro Teachers Give School Plan," *New York Times* (September 20, 1967), 37; C. Gerald Fraser, "Negro Teachers Define Their Stand," *New York Times* (September 21, 1967), 52.

129. Albert Vann, "Goals of ATA," *African-American Teachers Forum* (November, 1968), 1.

130. Preston Wilcox, "Africanization: The New Input to Black Education," *Freedomways* (Fall, 1968), 397.

131. LaNoue and Smith, *The Politics of School Decentralization*, 178.

132. Wasserman, *The School Fix*, 332–3.

133. "It's the Most Effective of Four Teacher Strikes," *New York Times* (September 10, 1968), 36.

134. Stein, *Strategies for Failure*, 173.

135. Murphy, *Blackboard Unions*, 237.

136. Richard D. Kahlenberg, *Tough Liberal: Albert Shanker and the Battle Over Schools, Unions, Race and Democracy* (New York: Columbia University Press, 2007), 81.

137. Ravitch, *The Great School Wars*, 332–3.

138. Kahlenberg, *Tough Liberal*, 87.

139. Ravitch, *The Great School Wars*, 335.

140. Lenora E. Berson, *The Negroes and the Jews* (New York: Random House, 1971), 316.

141. Carter, *Pickets, Parents and Power*, 47–9.

142. Interview, C. Herbert Oliver in *Why Teachers Strike: Teachers' Rights and Community Control*, ed. Melvin Urofsky (Garden City, NY: Anchor Doubleday, 1970), 216.

143. Carter, *Pickets, Parents and Power*, 60.

144. Transcript of interview with Les Campbell, conducted by Blackside, Inc. on November 3, 1988, for *Eyes on the Prize II: America at the Racial Crossroads 1965 to 1985*. Washington University Libraries, Film and Media Archive, Henry Hampton Collection.

145. Leonard Buder, "8 Brooklyn Schools Boycotted by 6,000: Control Demanded," *New York Times* (April 11, 1968).

146. William M. Birenbaum, *Something for Everybody Is Not Enough* (New York: Random House, 1971), 229.

147. Ravitch, *The Great School Wars*, 354.

148. Braun, *Teachers and Power*, 215.

149. Rogers, *110 Livingston Street*, 337.

150. Ellen Lurie, *How to Change the Schools: A Parents' Action Handbook on How to Fight the System* (New York: Random House, 1970), 135.

151. Interview, C. Herbert Oliver, *Why Teachers Strike: Teachers' Rights and Community Control*, 216.

152. Interview, Paul Chandler (June 12, 2012).

153. Leonard Buder, "Shanker Backs Ousted Teachers," *New York Times* (May 14, 1968), 1, 44; Carter, *Pickets, Parents and Power*, 66.

154. Leonard Buder, "Parents Occupy Brooklyn School as Dispute Grows," *New York Times* (May 14, 1968), 1, 44; Carter, *Pickets, Parents and Power*, 66.

155. C. Gerald Fraser, "Members of Troubled School Board Tell of Agony," *New York Times* (May 17, 1968), 37.

156. Leonard Buder, "Three Schools Closed to Ease Tensions," *New York Times* (May 16, 1968), 1, 41.

157. Ocean Hill–Brownsville Governing Board, "Fact Sheet" (May 15, 1968), Author's Collection.

158. Stern, "'Scab Teachers," 24.

159. "School Boycott Ends in Brooklyn," *New York Times* (May 21, 1968) 1, 30.

160. Leonard Buder, "Ousted Teachers Back in Classes," *New York Times* (May 22, 1968) 1, 33.

161. Stern, "'Scab Teachers," 20.

162. Sydney H. Schanberg, "Teachers Union Reportedly Blocking Mild School Decentralization Plan in Albany," *New York Times* (May 24, 1968), 35.

163. Editorial, "Decentralization Shambles," *New York Times* (May 28, 1968).

164. Gene Currivan, "Ocean Hill Unit Dismisses 350," *New York Times* (June 21, 1968), 24.

165. Carter, *Pickets, Parents and Power*, 87, 91.

166. The Rivers Report is reprinted in *Confrontation at Ocean Hill–Brownsville*, 83–101.

167. Carter, *Pickets, Parents and Power*, 100.

168. Declaration of Ocean Hill–Brownsville Governing Board (September 8, 1968), Author's Collection.

169. M.A. Farber, "Lindsay Insists Schools in City Will Open Today; Union Insists Strike Is On," *New York Times* (September 9, 1968) 1.

170. "5 Union Teacher Demands," *New York Times* (September 10, 1968).

171. Siegel, *The Future Once Happened Here*, 32.

Part II

1. Maurice Goldbloom, "The New York School Crisis," *Commentary* (January, 1969), 44.

2. The full poem could not be reprinted here because of copyright issues. It first appeared in *Opportunity* (December, 1940), 364. It is also included in *The Collected Poems of Langston Hughes*, ed. Arnold Rampersad (New York: Alfred A. Knopf, 1994), 402. It is readily available through a simple Internet search.

3. Jonathan Kozol, *Death at an Early Age: The Destruction of the Hearts and Minds of Children in the Boston Public Schools* (Boston: Houghton Mifflin, 1967), 225.

4. Rogers, *110 Livingston Street*, 292.

5. Martin Mayer, "Close to Midnight for the New York Schools," *New York Times Magazine* (May 2, 1965), 35.

6. Leonard Buder, "Two Negro Groups Accuse Schools of Discrimination in Promotion," *New York Times* (November 4, 1966), 29.

7. *Chance v. Bd. of Examiners*, 458 F.2d 1167 (2d Cir. 1972).

8. Rogers, *110 Livingston Street*, 288.

9. Rogers, *110 Livingston Street*, 288.

10. Kaufman, *Broken Alliance*, 147; Carter, *Pickets, Parents and Power*, 38–9.

11. "It's the Most Effective of Four Teacher Strikes," *New York Times* (September 10, 1968), 36.

12. Gene Currivan, "School Supervisors Join the Strike," *New York Times* (September 10, 1968).

13. Editorial: "Destructive Strike," *New York Times* (September 10, 1968).

14. Leonard Buder, "School Strike is Settled; Shanker Claims Victory," *New York Times* (September 11, 1968), 1.

15. Leonard Buder, "New Teachers Strike is Called for Tomorrow," *New York Times* (September 12, 1968), 1, 52.

16. *Ibid.*, 52.

17. cf. Podair, *The Strike That Changed New York*, 117; Ravitch, *The Great School Wars*, 367–8; Martin Mayer, *The Teachers Strike: New York, 1968* (New York: Harper & Row, 1969), 71.

18. "Teacher Power vs. Black Power," *Time* (September 20, 1968), 60.

19. Carter, *Pickets, Parents and Power*, 93.

20. Kahlenberg, *Tough Liberal*, 99.

21. Interview, C. Herbert Oliver in *Why Teachers Strike*, 229.

22. Interview, Rev. C. Herbert Oliver (June 22, 2013).

23. Interview, Paul Chandler and Brother Sun (June 12, 2012).

24. Interview, Rhody A. McCoy, in *Why Teachers Strike: Teachers' Rights and Community Control*, 148.

25. Transcript of interview with Dolores Torres, conducted by Blackside, Inc. on October 31, 1988, for *Eyes on the Prize II: America at the Racial Crossroads 1965 to 1985*. Washington University Libraries, Film and Media Archive, Henry Hampton Collection.

26. Sidney E. Zion, "Five Black Panthers Held in Brooklyn," *New York Times* (September 13, 1968), 93.

27. Podair, *The Strike That Changed New York*, 117.

28. Kathleen Teltsch, "Foreigners Told of a Beating Here," *New York Times* (September 12, 1968), 53.

29. Thelma J. Hamilton, Unpublished autobiographical fragment, Author's Collection.

30. Leonard Buder, "New Teachers' Strike is Called for Tomorrow," *New York Times* (September 12, 1968), 1.

31. Fred Ferretti, "New York's black anti-Semitism scare," *Columbia Journalism Review*, 8:3 (Fall, 1969), 19.

32. Podair, *The Strike That Changed New York*, 113.

33. Author's Collection.

34. Author's Collection.

35. Maurice Carroll, "Giant City Hall Rally Backs Teachers," *New York Times* (September 17, 1968), 1, 41.

36. "The Meaning of Rosh Hashanah—The Jewish New Year" (Author's Collection); "Ocean Hill Students Get Holiday With a Lesson," *New York Times* (September 21, 1968).

37. Stein, "Strategies for Failure," 195.

38. Ravitch, *The Great School Wars*, 370.

39. Fred Ferretti, "New York's black anti-semitism scare," 20.

40. Interview, Bernard E. Donovan in *Why Teachers Strike*, 210.

41. Leonard Buder, "Schools Reopening Today," *New York Times* (September 30, 1968), 1.

42. Resolution, Ocean Hill–Brownsville Governing Board (September 30, 1968), Author's Collection.

43. Murray Kempton, "The Busting of Rhody McCoy," *New York Post* (October 1, 1968).

44. Nancy Hicks, "Ocean Hill Parents and Teachers Voice Their Unity," *New York Times* (October 1, 1968), 36.

45. "With Love," *Newsweek* (October 7, 1968), 76.

46. Leonard Buder, "School Clashes Draw Warning of a New Strike," *New York Times* (October 2, 1968), 1.

47. Earl Caldwell, "Presence of Police at Schools Stirs Resentment," *New York Times* (October 2, 1968), 31.

48. Stern, "'Scab' Teachers," 18.

49. Podair, *The Strike That Changed New York*," 122.

50. Ravitch, *The Great School Wars*, 372.

51. Leonard Buder, "School Clashes Draw Warning of a New Strike," *New York Times* (October 2, 1968), 1.

52. Mayer, *The Teachers Strike*, 80.

53. Leonard Buder, "McCoy and 7 Aides Ousted for Barring 83 Teachers," *New York Times* (October 9, 1968), 1, 36.

54. Carter, *Pickets, Parents and Power*, 103.

55. Transcript of interview with Karima Jordon, conducted by Blackside, Inc. on April 18, 1989, for *Eyes on the Prize II: America at the Racial Crossroads 1965 to 1985*. Washington University Libraries, Film and Media Archive, Henry Hampton Collection.

56. Annie Stein, "Containment and Control: A Look at the Record," in Rubenstein ed., *Schools Against Children*, 39.

57. Carter, *Pickets, Parents and Power*, 105.

58. Carter, *Pickets, Parents and Power*, 107.

59. Mayer, *The Teachers Strike*, 1.

60. Kahlenberg, *Tough Liberal*, 125.

61. Sylvan Fox, "Death Threat Cited at Brooklyn School," *New York Times* (October 15, 1968), 1, 38.

62. Peter Kihss, "Charges Handed to Four Teachers," *New York Times* (October 22, 1968).

63. "The Use and Misuse of Power," *Time* (October 25, 1968), 52.

64. Transcript of interview with Reverend John Powis, conducted by Blackside, Inc. on November 4, 1988, for *Eyes on the Prize II: America at the Racial Crossroads 1965 to 1985*. Washington University Libraries, Film and Media Archive, Henry Hampton Collection.

65. "Mayor Jeered at Jewish Center As He Speaks on School Crisis," *New York Times* (October 16, 1968), 1, 32.

66. Robert I. Friedman, *The False Prophet* (Brooklyn, NY: Lawrence Hill Books, 1990), 102.

67. Friedman, *The False Prophet*, 121–26.

68. "Defense League Scored by Rabbi," *New York Times*, May 18, 1969.

69. Milton A. Galamison, "The Ocean Hill-Brownsville Dispute," *Christianity and Crisis* 28:12 (October 14, 1968), 239, 241.

70. "Why Weren't Your Schools Open Today?" Leaflet issued by "Supervisors and Teachers of District 18, CSA, UFT," Author's Collection.

71. James Haughton, "The Role of the Board of Education in Perpetuating Racism in the Building Trades and Vice Versa," in *Schools Against Children*, 167.

72. Bayard Rustin, "From Protest to Politics: The Future of the Civil Rights Movement," *Commentary* 39:2 (February, 1965), 26.

73. Sylvan Fox, "40,000 Marchers Support Teachers," *New York Times* (October 18, 1968), 50.

74. Agee Ward, "Ocean Hill: Education, Community, Power and the Media," *The Center Forum* (November 13, 1968), 7. This author, who I knew personally, chose to write the article under a *nom de plume*. I could never fathom that decision, but I respect it here.

75. Paul Buhle and Robin D. G. Kelley, "Allies of a Different Sort," in *Struggles in the Promised Land*, ed. Salzman and West, 201.

76. Karl Marx, *Capital, Volume I* (Moscow: Progress Publishers, 1887 English edition, 1954), 284.

77. *Ibid.*, 206–7.

78. "Regents Approve School Decentralization Plan," *New York Times* (October 18, 1968), 51.

79. Carter, *Pickets, Parents and Power*, 123.

80. New York Civil Liberties Union, "*The Burden of Blame: A Report on the Ocean Hill–Brownsville School Controversy* (October 9, 1968).

81. David Bird, "Shanker, in Speech in Houston, Says Cities Face Schools Crisis" *New York Times* (October 21, 1968), 44.

82. William Ryan, *Blaming the Victim* (New York: Random House, 1971, 1976), 248.

83. John Dewey, *Experience and Education* (New York: Collier Books, 1938), 55.

84. Transcript of interview with Les Campbell, conducted by Blackside, Inc. on November 3, 1988, for *Eyes on the Prize II: America at the Racial Crossroads 1965 to 1985*. Washington University Libraries, Film and Media Archive, Henry Hampton Collection.

85. Author's Collection.

86. Transcript of interview with Rhody McCoy, conducted by Blackside, Inc. on October 12, 1988, for *Eyes on the Prize II: America at the Racial Crossroads 1965 to 1985*. Washington University Libraries, Film and Media Archive, Henry Hampton Collection.

87. Hampton and Fayer, *Voices of Freedom*, 500–01.

88. Fred C. Shapiro, "The Talk of the Town," *The New Yorker* (December 14, 1968), 53.

89. Melissa F. Wiener, *Power, Protest and the Public Schools: Jewish and African-American Struggles in New York City* (New Brunswick, NJ: Rutgers University Press, 2010), 112–13.

90. Horace M. Kallen, "Democracy Versus the Melting-Pot (Part II)," *The Nation* (February 25, 1915), 217–20.

91. According to the 1960 Census, the area's median annual income was between $3,000 and $5,100. Marilyn Gittell et al., *Local Control in Education: Three Demonstration Districts in New York City* (New York: Praeger, 1972), 44. The Board of Education's 1968 statistics had more than half the households living on less than $5,000. Bill Kovach, "School Crisis Helps Ocean Hill's Search for a Community" *New York Times* (October 31, 1968), 49–51.

92. Bill Kovach, "Teachers Working on JHS 271 Staff Feel a 'Vibrance.'" *New York Times* (October 21, 1968).

93. *I. F. Stone's Weekly* (November 4, 1968), 2.

94. Rogers, *110 Livingston Street*, 336.

95. Richard Armstrong, "McGeorge Bundy Confronts the Teachers," *New York Times Magazine* (April 20, 1969) 25, 122.

96. Stern, "'Scab' Teachers," 19.

97. Author's Collection.

98. Kaufman, *Broken Alliance*, 155.

99. Author's collection. The full text is reprinted in *Confrontation at Ocean Hill-Brownsville*, 167–68.

100. Perlstein, *Justice, Justice*, 35.

101. Jason Epstein, "The Issue at Ocean Hill," *New York Review of Books* (November 21, 1968).

102. Friedman, *The False Prophet*, 94.

103. Fred Ferretti, "New York's black anti-semitism scare," 22.

104. Fred M. Hechinger, "Racism and Anti-Semitism in the School Crisis," *New York Times*, September 16, 1968.

105. "How Do You Stop an Anti-Semitic Leaflet?" *Jewish Currents*, 22:11 (December, 1968), 13.

106. Fred Ferretti, "New York's black anti-Semitism scare," 23.

107. "Anti-Semitism? A Statement by the Teachers of Ocean Hill–Brownsville to the People of New York," *New York Times* (November 11, 1968); reprinted in *Confrontation at Ocean Hill-Brownsville*, ed. Berube and Gittell, 170.

108. Ferretti, "New York's black anti-semitism scare," 21, 24.

109. "Anti-Semitism Held an Artificial Issue," *New York Times* (October 22, 1968).

110. Jimmy Breslin, "Albert Shanker's Game," *New York Post* (October 23, 1968).

111. "A Statement of Jewish Teachers for Community Control," issued November 1, 1968 (Author's Collection); Excerpts reprinted in *Jewish Currents* (December, 1968), 9.

112. Edith Evans Asbury,"Jewish Teachers Back Ocean Hill," *New York Times*, November 2, 1968, 24.

113. Interview, Paul Chandler and Brother Sun (June 12, 2012).

114. Fred Ferretti, "Who's to Blame in the School Strike?" *New York Magazine* (November 18, 1968), 22–35.

115. Carter, *Pickets, Parents and Power*, 122.

116. Transcript of interview with Sandra Feldman, conducted by Blackside, Inc. on October 31, 1988, for *Eyes on the Prize II: America at the Racial Crossroads 1965 to 1985*. Washington University Libraries, Film and Media Archive, Henry Hampton Collection.

117. Kaufman, *Broken Alliance*, 154.

118. John Kifner, ""Echoes of a New York Waterloo," *New York Times* (December 22, 1996), D5.

119. Kahlenberg, *Tough Liberal*, 107.

120. Kahlenberg, *Tough Liberal*, 95.

121. Carter, *Pickets, Parents and Power*, 68.

122. Philip Taft, *United They Teach: The Story of the United Federation of Teachers* (Los Angeles: Nash Publishing, 1974), 179.

123. Copies of drafts and related materials are in NYU's Robert F. Wagner Labor Archives, UFT Collection (WAG.022), Sub-Series II-B, Box 92, Folders 28–30.

124. Leonard Buder, "Admit Teachers, McCoy is Ordered," *New York Times* (May 24, 1968), 1, 35.

125. Morris Kaplan, "Board of I.S. 148 Yields in Protest," *New York Times* (April 24, 1968), 31.

126. Podair, *The Strike That Changed New York*, 116.

127. "Negro Unionists Back Ocean Hill," *New York Times* (October 26, 1968).

128. Podair, *The Strike That Changed New York*, 134.

129. "The Use and Misuse of Power," *Time* (October 25, 1968), 52.

130. Editorial, "Killing Hope for School Peace," *New York Times* (November 13, 1968).

131. Major R. Owens, *The Peacock Elite* (New York: Grant House Publishers, 2010), 14.

132. Ward, "Ocean Hill: Education, Community, Power and the Media," 3.

133. Charles S. Isaacs, "A JHS 271 Teacher Tells It Like He Sees It," *New York Times Magazine* (November 24, 1968), 53–79. Reprinted in *Confrontation at Ocean Hill–Brownsville*, 192–205.

134. Leonard Buder, "Donovan Orders JHS 271 Closed After Disorders." *New York Times* (October 10, 1968) 1, 41.

135. Kenneth G. Gross, "Bad Show for Reporters," *The Nation* (November 18, 1968), 522–25.

136. Letter, *New York Times Magazine* (December 8, 1968).

137. Author's Collection.

138. Michael Lerner and Cornel West, *Jews and Blacks: Let the Healing Begin* (New York: G.P. Putnam's Sons, 1995), 83.

139. Alexander S. Kohanski, "An Open Letter to Charles S. Isaacs," *Reconstructionist* 35:1 (February 28, 1969), 13–19.

140. Fred C. Shapiro, "The Talk of the Town," *The New Yorker* (November 23, 1968), 53.

141. Jason Epstein, "The Issue at Ocean Hill," *New York Review of Books* (November 21, 1968).

142. Dwight MacDonald, "An Open Letter to Michael Harrington," *New York Review of Books* (December 5, 1968).

143. Ward, "Ocean Hill," 7, 9.

144. Carter, *Pickets, Parents and Power*, 108–9.

145. Statement of Commissioner of Education James E. Allen, Jr. (November 17, 1968), Author's Collection.

146. Murray Schumach, "Teacher Shifted Over Harassing," *New York Times* (November 17, 1968) 1, 83.

147. Carter, *Pickets, Parents and Power*, 128.

148. Arnold H. Lubasch, "Discord at Teachers' Rally Puts Off Vote Until Today" *New York Times* (November 18, 1968), 1, 51.

149. Robert Campbell, *The Chasm: The Life and Death of a Great Experiment in Ghetto Education* (Boston: Houghton Mifflin, 1974), 173–4.

Part III

1. "Rhody McCoy Blames Sabotage on Shanker," *The Harvard Crimson* (December 6, 1968), 1.

2. Homer Bigart, "Boy and Teacher Differ on Hurt-Thumb Incident," *New York Times* (November 27, 1968), 30.

3. Sylvan Fox, "Eight Union Teachers Barred 3½ Hours From JHS 271," *New York Times* (November 22, 1968), 1, 31.

4. Author's Collection.

5. Statement of Ocean Hill–Brownsville Governing Board (November 25, 1968), Author's Collection.

6. Leonard Buder, "Oliver, Defiant, Re-Enters School," *New York Times* (November 27, 1968), 1.

7. Leonard Buder, "35% of Students Boycott Schools," *New York Times* (November 30, 1968), 1, 34.

8. Peter Khiss, "Student Bands Disrupt at Least 12 City Schools," *New York Times* (December 3, 1968), 1, 41.

9. Homer Bigart, "4 Seized as Lindsay Order Protection for Houses of Worship," *New York Times* (November 28, 1968), 1.

10. Martin Tolchin, "Racial Exchanges Mar Talks of Leaders Here," *New York Times* (February 22, 1969), 59.

11. Michael Stern, "Blaze Destroys Old Synagogue in Far Rockaway," *New York Times* (January 4, 1969), 19.

12. "Two Youths Arrested in Synagogue Fire," *New York Times* (January 27, 1969).

13. "Brooklyn Rabbi's Son Accused in Synagogue Fires," *New York Times* (March 31, 1969).

14. Perlstein, *Justice, Justice*, 53.

15. Leonard Buder, "State Closes JHS 271; Dr. Johnson Is Out," *New York Times* (December 3, 1970), 1, 40.

16. Leonard Buder, "New State Aide Hopes to Reopen JHS 271 Monday," *New York Times* (December 4, 1968), 1.

17. Fred C. Shapiro, "The Talk of the Town," *The New Yorker* (December 14, 1968), 53.

18. Buder, "State Closes JHS 271," *New York Times* (December 3, 1968), 1, 49.

19. Ibid.

20. Nancy Hicks, "Clark Blames Firman in McCoy Arrest," *New York Times* (November 12, 1968), 59.

21. Leonard Buder, "State's Trustee Orders McCoy Out of Brownsville," *New York Times* (November 12, 1968), 1, 58.

22. Ravitch, *The Great School Wars*, 377.

23. M.A. Farber, "Nordos Prefers Patience to Force," *New York Times* (December 18, 1968), 36.

24. Interview, Wilbur R. Nordos, in *Why Teachers Strike*, 278.

25. Interview, C. Herbert Oliver, in *Why Teachers Strike*, 226.

26. Interview, Wilbur R. Nordos, in *Why Teachers Strike*, 282.

27. Paul Robeson, Foreword to *Lift Every Voice*, ed. Irwin Silber (New York: People's Artists Press, 1954).

28. Nancy Hicks, "Nine Are Indicted For Obstruction in School Dispute," *New York Times* (December 20, 1968), 1, 51.

29. "Vann is Acquitted in Ocean Hill Case," *New York Times* (May 13, 1970), 18.

30. Baldwin, foreword to *The Chasm*, xx.

31. "Excerpts from Regents' Plan for Schools' Decentralization," *New York Times* (March 4, 1969), 28.

32. Robert G. Weisbord and Arthur Stein, *Bittersweet Encounter: The Afro-American and the American Jew* (Westport, CT: Negro Universities Press, 1970), 205.

33. Gary T. Marx, *Protest and Prejudice: A Study of Belief in the Black Community* (New York: Harper & Row, 1967), 201.

34. Henry Raymont, "Jews Debating Black Anti-Semitism," *New York Times* (January 26, 1969), 1, 59.

35. Editorial, "Appeasement in Ocean Hill," *New York Times* (January 4, 1969).

36. James P. Sterba, "Shanker Scores Reinstatement of Disputed JHS 271 Teacher," *New York Times* (January 3, 1969), 25.

37. Gene Currivan, "Negro Teacher Group's Editorial Assails Jews," *New York Times* (January 5, 1969), 43.

38. Editorial, *African-American Teachers Forum* (November, 1968), 2.

39. Julius Lester, *All is Well* (New York: William Morrow & Co., 1976), 152.

40. Kaufman, *Broken Alliance*, 159.

41. Kaufman, *Broken Alliance*, 160.

42. Henry Raymont, "Teachers Protest Poem to FCC," *New York Times* (January 16, 1969), 1.

43. Lester, *All Is Well*, 154.

44. Julius Lester, *Lovesong: Becoming a Jew* (New York: Henry Holt & Co., 1988), 56.

45. Interview, Jitu Weusi (June 7, 2012).

46. Transcript of interview with Les Campbell, conducted by Blackside, Inc. on November 3, 1988, for *Eyes on the Prize II: America at the Racial Crossroads 1965 to 1985*. Washington University Libraries, Film and Media Archive, Henry Hampton Collection.

47. Hampton and Fayer, *Voices of Freedom*, 502.

48. M. A. Farber, ""Mayor Assailed on Disputed Poem," *New York Times* (January 20, 1969), 22.

49. "Jacob Cohen," in *Negro and Jew: An Encounter in America*, ed. Shlomo Katz (New York: Macmillan, 1967), 13.

50. John Kifner, "Mayor Assails Two at Ocean Hill," *New York Times* (January 22, 1969), 1.

51. Leonard Buder, "Two Teachers' Cases Sent to Donovan," *New York Times* (January 23, 1969), 1, 51.

52. Julius Lester, Transcript of remarks on WBAI-FM (January 30, 1969), *All is Well*, 155.

53. Ferretti, "New York's black anti-semitism scare," *Columbia Journalism Review* (Fall, 1969), 18–28.

54. Lester, *Lovesong*, 57.

55. Nat Hentoff, "Blacks and Jews: An Interview with Julius Lester," *Evergreen Review* (April, 1969), 22.

56. cf. "The Anti-Semitism of Black Demagogues and Extremists," (Anti-Defamation League Research Report: 1992), 25; Marcia Kramer, "Activist Taking Heat; Old Remarks Mar Prep for Mandela," *New York Daily News* (June 19, 1990), 3.

57. "Dishonor in the Senate: Brooklyn's Velmanette Montgomery Lauds Anti-Semite Jitu Weusi," *New York Daily News* (January 7, 2013).

58. Will Lissner, "McCoy Won't Act on Anti-Semitism," (sic) *New York Times* (February 2, 1969), 38.

59. Office of the Superintendent of Schools, General Circular #7, 1968–69 (January 29, 1969).

60. Perlstein, *Justice, Justice*, 44.

61. Stern, "'Scab' Teachers," 21.

62. Bill Kovach, "Court Reinstates Three Principals Here," *New York Times* (January 16, 1969), 1, 48.

63. JHS 271 "Weekly Bulletin" (February 7, 1969), Author's Collection.

64. J. Milton Yinger, *Anti-Semitism: A Case Study in Prejudice and Discrimination* (New York: Anti-Defamation League of B'nai B'rith, 1964), 38–49.

65. Thomas A. Johnson, "Anti-Semitic Role of Negro is Noted," *New York Times* (May 21, 1967), 114.

66. Irving Spiegel, "Jews Are Advised Not to Exaggerate Animosity of Negro," *New York Times* (September 10, 1968), 73.

67. John F. Hatchett, "The Phenomenon of the Anti-Black Jews and the Black Anglo-Saxon," *African-American Teachers Forum* (November-December, 1967), 1–4.

68. Isaacs, "A JHS 271 Tells It Like He Sees It," 73.

69. Author's Collection.

70. "For the Defense," *New York Post* (January 28, 1969).

71. Author's collection.

72. Author's collection.

73. Kahlenberg, *Tough Liberal*, 97.

74. Ferretti, "New York's black anti-semitism scare," 26–7; They received brief mention a year later in Weisbord and Stein, *Bittersweet Encounter*, 196–97.

75. George Dugan, "Back Civil Rights, Jews Are Urged," *New York Times* (February 8, 1969), 21.

76. Ferretti, "New York's black anti-semitism scare," 28.

77. Lerner and West, *Jews and Blacks*, 12.

78. "Arthur Hertzberg," in Katz ed., *Negro and Jew*, 72.

79. Ronald Searle, *Too Many Songs by Tom Lehrer* (New York: Pantheon Books, 1981), 90.

80. Hampton and Fayer, *Voices of Freedom*, 505.

81. *I. F. Stone's Weekly* (November 4, 1968), 4.

82. John Kifner, "Blacks vs. Jews," *New York Times* (January 26, 1969), E7.

83. Julius Lester, Transcript of remarks on WBAI-FM (January 30, 1969), *All is Well*, 156.

84. "C. Eric Lincoln," in *Negro and Jew*, 90.

85. "Arthur Hertzberg," in *Negro and Jew*, 72.

86. Nell Irvin Painter, *The History of White People* (New York: W.W. Norton, 2010), 143.

87. Jerald A. Podair, "The Ocean Hill–Brownsville Crisis: New York's *Antigone*," (Paper presented at the Gotham History Festival, CUNY Graduate Center, New York, NY, October 6, 2001).

88. Weiner, *Power, Protest and the Public Schools*, 174.

89. Martin Mayer, *The Teachers Strike: New York, 1968*.

90. Aryeh Neier, Letter to the Editor, *New York Times Magazine* (February 23, 1969), 14.

91. John O'Neill, Letter to the Editor, *New York Times* (March 16, 1969), 22, 133.

92. Martin Mayer, "Frustration is the Word for Ocean Hill," *New York Times Magazine* (May 19, 1968). 77.

93. Jason Epstein, "The Real McCoy," review of *The Teachers Strike: New York, 1968* by Martin Mayer, *New York Review of Books* (March 13, 1969).

94. Damien Scarf et al., "Pigeons on Par with Primates in Numerical Competence," *Science* 334 (December 23, 2011); 1664.

95. Martin Mayer, "Close to Midnight for the New York Schools," *New York Times Magazine* (May 2, 1965), 34, 104.

96. Rogers, *110 Livingston Street*, 412–13.

97. Fred M. Hechinger, "Ocean Hill Revisited," *New York Times* (March 16, 1969), E11.

98. "C. Eric Lincoln," in Katz, ed. *Negro and Jew*, 92.

99. Interview, Monifa Edwards (December 12, 2011).

100. "Ocean Hill Teacher Loses Fight for Reinstatement," *New York Times* (March 21, 1969).

101. Thomas P. Ronan, "300 Quit Civil Liberties Group to Protest School Stand," *New York Times* (January 15, 1969), 31.

102. M. A. Farber, "Calm Prevailing at City Schools," *New York Times* (June 27, 1969), 44.

103. Lurie, *How to Change the Schools*, 195.

104. cf. William M. Birenbaum, *Overlive: Power, Poverty and the University* (New York: Delacorte Press, 1969), 165–85; and Letter, "Admissions Standards at City Colleges," *New York Times* (February 10, 1965), 40.

105. Martha Biondi, "Brooklyn College Belongs to Us: Black Students and the Transformation of Public Higher education in New York City," in *Civil Rights in New York City*, 163.

106. Ibid., 181.

107. "Attachment No. 1 to Special Circular No. 77 1968–69, (March 22, 1969), Author's Collection.

108. Interview with Jitu Weusi (October 11, 2011).

109. Carter, *Pickets, Parents and Power*, 8.

110. Carter, *Pickets, Parents and Power*, 146. This quote is from a lengthy April, 1969 speech at the University of Chicago that went ignored by the press and future historians, and is recorded only in Carter's narrative.

111. Bill Kovach, "Intense Negotiations Resulted in the Decentralization Law," *New York Times* (May 4, 1969), 84.

112. M. S. Handler, "Donovan Urges the Cancellation of Test for Principal as Futile," *New York Times* (May 16, 1969), 39.

113. Fred M. Hechinger, "Decentralization Bill May Mean More Strife," *New York Times* (May 4, 1969) E8; Ravitch, *The Great School Wars*, 387.

114. Carter, *Pickets, Parents and Power*, 166; William K. Stevens, "Efforts to Decentralize School Gain Over U.S.," *New York Times* (March 18, 1970), 50.

115. Siegel, *The Future Once Happened Here*, 44.

116. Taylor, *Knocking On Our Own Door*, 206.

117. Milton A. Galamison, Letter: "School Bill Failure," *New York Times* (May 6, 1969) 46.

118. W. E. B. DuBois, *Black Reconstruction in America, 1860–1880* (New York: Atheneum, 1935, 1973), 587.

119. Mario Fantini, Marilyn Gittell, and Paul Magat, *Community Control and the Urban School* (New York: Praeger, 1970), 153–54.

120. James Baldwin, Foreword to *The Chasm: The Life and Death of a Great Experiment in Ghetto Education*, by Robert Campbell (Boston: Houghton Mifflin, 1974), xvii.

121. Braun, *Teachers and Power*, 222.

122. E. Franklin Frazier, *Black Bourgeoisie: The Rise of a New Middle Class* (New York: The Free Press, 1957), 83.

123. Transcript of interview with C. Herbert Oliver, conducted by Blackside, Inc. on March 13, 1989, for *Eyes on the Prize II: America at the Racial Crossroads 1965 to 1985*. Washington University Libraries, Film and Media Archive, Henry Hampton Collection.

124. Leaflet, Republic of New Africa (May 20, 1969), Author's Collection.

125. Author's Collection.

126. Jason Epstein, Reply to Letter, "Mayer Culpa," *New York Review of Books* (May 8, 1969).

127. M. S. Handler, "School Board Orders Donovan to Bypass Examiners on 14 Ocean Hill Posts," *New York Times* (May 14, 1969), 26.

128. Interview, Rev. C. Herbert Oliver (June 22, 2013).

129. African-American Teachers Association, Press Release (June 17, 1969), Author's Collection.

130. "Highlights of the 3-Year School Contract Agreement," *New York Times* (June 25, 1969).

131. Author's Collection.

Part IV

1. Philip Sterling, *The Real Teachers* (New York: Random House, 1972), 368.

2. Kwasi Konadu, *A View from the East: Black Cultural Nationalism and Education in New York City* (Syracuse, NY: Syracuse University Press, 2009), 72.

3. Merle English, "Black Community Hails Activist Weusi," *Newsday* (January 17, 1990), 21.

4. Interview, Jitu Weusi (June 7, 2012).

5. Interview, Fran Barrett (December 30, 2011).

6. "Shanker Accuses Board of Ocean Hill Extravagance," *New York Times* (September 29, 1969).

7. M. A. Farber, "Board Details Final Plan on School Reorganization," *New York Times* (December 29, 1969), 1, 17.

8. LaNoue and Smith, *The Politics of School Decentralization*, 185.

9. Carter, *Pickets, Parents and Power*, 54.

10. In 2013, according to the NY State Education Dept., there are 697 school districts outside NYC, enrolling 1.6 million students.

11. Marilyn Gittell et al., *Local Control in Education: Three Demonstration Districts in New York City* (New York: Praeger Publishers, 1972), 44–64.

12. Leonard Buder, "Voter Turnout is 14.5% For City School Election," *New York Times* (March 23, 1970), 1, 81.

13. Leonard Buder, "Ocean Hill and 201 May Keep Identities," *New York Times* (June 9, 1970), 1, 35.

14. Leonard Buder, "Ocean Hill School District Is Losing Its Special Status," *New York Times* (July 10, 1970), 36.

15. M.A. Farber, "Ocean Hill Chief Firm on Opening," *New York Times* (August 9, 1970), 1, 51.

16. John Darnton, "Ocean Hill Schools: Conflict Goes On," *New York Times* (March 24, 1971), 1, 47.

17. John Darnton, "Brooklyn Board Orders Leave for Superintendent," *New York Times* (March 13, 1971) 14.

18. John Darnton, "Ocean Hill Schools: Conflict Goes On," *New York Times* (March 24, 1971), 1, 47.

19. Jack Newfield and Paul DuBrul, *The Abuse of Power: The Permanent Government and the Fall of New York* (New York: Viking Press, 1977), 227.

20. Pritchett, *Brownsville, Brooklyn*, 254.

21. John Darnton, "5 Ocean Hill Principals Reported Ousted," *New York Times* (August 9, 1971), 1, 14.

22. Ronald Smothers, "Charge of Politics Again Raised in Brownsville School Elections," *New York Times* (April 29, 1973), 54.

23. Wayne Barrett, "Stalking Sam Wright: Five Years in Brownsville," *Village Voice* (April 6, 1977).

24. Kahlenberg, *Tough Liberal*, 1.

25. Newfield and DuBrul, *The Abuse of Power*, 226.

26. Pritchett, *Brownsville, Brooklyn*, 253; Peter Khiss, "Community Aide Charges Corruption in Brownsville," *New York Times* (November 29, 1973), 48.

27. Owens, *The Peacock Elite*, 110; Nicholas Lemann, "The Unfinished War," *The Atlantic Monthly* (December, 1988).

28. <http://bmsfhc.org/bms_history.html>; Pritchett, *Brownsville, Brooklyn*, 263.

29. "Report on the New York City Community School Board Election for District 23 Held on May 6, 1975," (Author's Collection).

30. Barrett, "Stalking Sam Wright."

31. Wolfgang Saxon, "Wright Is Convicted On Extortion Charge," *New York Times* (April 16, 1978), 1, 41.

32. Newfield and DuBrul, *The Abuse of Power*, 129, 226.

33. "Harry Golden," in Katz ed., *Negro and Jew*, 60.

34. Friedman, *The False Prophet*, 104.

35. Leonard Buder, "Eggs and Rocks Thrown as Boycott at Canarsie School Continues," *New York Times* (November 1, 1972), 1, 90.

36. Rieder, *Canarsie*, 216–20.

37. William Schneider, Michael D. Berman, and Mark Schultz, "Bloc Voting Reconsidered: Is There a Jewish Vote?," *Ethnicity* 1:4 (December, 1974), 364.

38. Carmichael and Hamilton, *Black Power*, 56.

39. Schneider, Berman and Schultz, "Bloc Voting Reconsidered," 345.

40. Norman Podhoretz, "Is It Good for the Jews?" *Commentary* 53:2 (February, 1972), 7–14.

41. cf. *Leviticus* 19:18.

42. Celestine Bohlen, "Teacher Accused of Past Anti-Semitism Quits Dinkins Camp," *New York Times* (October 12, 1989).

43. Charles Isaacs, "A Light Unto the Nations?" *The City Sun* (November 8–14, 1989).

44. Andrew Rosenthal, "The 1989 Elections: Predicting the Outcome," *New York Times* (November 9, 1989), 1.

45. "Excerpts From Speech by Dinkins," *New York Times* (November 8, 1969).

46. Charles Isaacs, "The Hands That Didn't Reach Back: Dinkins and the White Vote," *The City Sun* (November 15–21, 1989).

47. Murray Friedman, "The Changing Jewish Profile," *American Jewish History* (September, 2003), 433.

48. Schneider, Berman and Schultz, "Bloc Voting Reconsidered," 427; UJA-Federation, *Jewish Community Study of New York: 2011* (June, 2012), Chapter 1.

49. Liz Robbins, "The Orthodox Influence," *New York Times* (May 6, 2012), NJ6.

50. Newfield and DuBrul, *The Abuse of Power*, 235.

51. Ravitch, *The Great School Wars*, 389.

52. Fantini, Gittell, and Magat, *Community Control and the Urban School*, 170.

53. "Teacher Federation Says it Won Smashing Victory in School Vote," *New York Times* (May 18, 1977).

54. Walter Thabit, *How East New York Became a Ghetto*, (New York: New York University Press, 2003), 194.

55. Podair, *The Strike That Changed New York*, 194.

56. Freeman, *Working-Class New York*, 271.

57. Fred Ferretti, "Financial Crisis Crippling New York's Public Schools," *New York Times* (December 12, 1976).

58. Kahlenberg, *Tough Liberal*, 214.

59. Joseph Berger, "Seeking Change Where It All Began," *New York Times* (December 20, 1996).

60. Philip S. Gutis, "School Board Bill Gaining in Albany," *New York Times* (December 1, 1988).

61. Sarah Lyall, "School Board 9 in Bronx Has History of Accusations," *New York Times* (November 28, 1988).

62. Adam Nossiter, "School District's Excesses Mirror the Faults of the System," *New York Times* (February 20, 1996).

63. Heather Lewis, "Protest, Place and Pedagogy: New York City's Community Control Movement and its Aftermath, 1966–1996" (PhD diss., New York University, 2006).

64. Raphael Sugarman, "Fear and Greed As Easy as ABC," *New York Daily News* (June 1, 1995).

65. Joseph Berger, "Seeking Change Where It All Began."

66. Karl Marx, *The Eighteenth Brumaire of Louis Bonaparte* (1852), 1; V. Adoratsky, ed. *Karl Marx: Selected Works, Volume II* (New York: International Publishers, 1933), 315.

67. James Traub, "A Lesson in Unintended Consequences," *New York Times Magazine* (October 6, 2002).

68. Wayne Barrett, "The Underside of Bloomberg's School Reforms," *Village Voice* (October 21, 2003).

69. Gail Robinson, "A New Chief for Parent Involvement," *Gotham Gazette* (July 26, 2011).

70. Sarah Garland, "Bloomberg Moves Schools Toward Corporate Model," *New York Sun* (January 19, 2007).

71. Deborah Meier, "NYC Schools, Then and Now," in *New York City Schools Under Bloomberg and Klein: What Parents, Teachers and Policymakers Need to Know*, ed. Diane Ravitch et al. (New York: Lulu, 2009), 160.

72. Hazel Dukes, "Has the Bloomberg/Klein Agenda Served the Cause of Equity?" in *New York City Schools Under Bloomberg and Klein*, 96.

73. Diane Ravitch, "Introduction," in *New York City Schools Under Bloomberg and Klein*, 4.

74. Stein, "Strategies for Failure," 201.

75. New York Civil Liberties Union, *Education Interrupted: The Growing Use of Suspensions in New York City's Public Schools* (January, 2011).

76. Javier C. Hernandez, "New York City Shows Gains in Math," *New York Times* (June 2, 2009).

77. Jennifer Medina, "More New York Students Meet State Standards in English," *New York Times* (May 8, 2009).

78. Jennifer Medina, "On New York School Tests, Warning Signs Ignored," *New York Times* (October 10, 2010).

79. Sharon Otterman and Robert Gebeloff, "When 81% Suddenly Becomes 18%," *New York Times* (August 1, 2010).

80. Diane Ravitch, op-ed, "Waiting for a School Miracle," *New York Times* (May 31, 2011).

81. M. B. Pell, "More Cheating Scandals Inevitable, as States Can't Ensure Test Integrity," *Atlanta Journal-Constitution* (September 30, 2012).

82. Sharon Otterman, "Under Bloomberg, a Sharp rise in Accusations of Cheating by Educators," *New York Times* (August 22, 2011).

83. Sharon Otterman and Robert Gebeloff, "When 81% Suddenly Becomes 18%," *New York Times* (August 1, 2010).

84. Center for Research on Education Outcomes, *Multiple Choice: Charter School Performance in 16 States* (June, 2009).

85. Rogers, *110 Livingston Street*, 403–04; Ravitch, *The Great School Wars*, 60, 298.

86. John H. Jackson, "Preface," *Yes We Can, The Schott 50 State Report on Public Education and Black Males* (Schott Foundation for Public Education, 2010), 1.

87. "The Nation's Report Card: The Official Site for Results from the National Assessment of Educaitonal Progress," National Assessment of Educational Progress (NAEP), 2011, <http://nationsreportcard.gov/>.

88. Association for Childhood Education International, *Position Paper on Standardized Testing* (1991).

89. Perlstein, *Justice, Justice*, 53–4.

90. "Who Should Run the Schools?," *Newsweek* (October 28, 1968), 82.

91. Dewey, *Experience and Education*, 73ff.

92. Nicole Jacovino, "Vito Perrone: Teaching the Teachers," *Harvard University Gazette* (September 25, 1997).

93. *Campaign for Fiscal Equity v. State of New York*, 86 NY2d 307, 316 (1995).

94. Sterling, *The Real Teachers*, 315.

95. Sharon Otterman, "37 Percent of New York Graduates are College-Ready, Data Show," *New York Times* (June 15, 2011).

96. Anna M. Phillips, "At Most High Schools, Fewer Than Half of Graduates Are Ready for College," *New York Times* (October 25, 2011).

97. Rachel Monahan, "Mayor's Schools Set Students Up for Failure When it Comes to College Preparation, But More Graduate," *New York Daily News* (October 27, 2011).

98. Jason Braun and Michael Anderson, "Declining Manufacturing Employment in the Mew York-New Jersey Region, 1969–99," *Current Issues in Economics and Finance* 7:1 (2001).

99. Sarah Crean, "Did City's Industrial Policy Manufacture Defeat?" *City Limits* (January 3, 2011).

100. Michael Tonry, *Punishing Race: A Continuing American Dilemma* (New York: Oxford University Press, 2011), 28ff.

101. *One in 100: Behind Bars in America 2008* (Pew Center on the States, February 2008).

102. Michelle Alexander, *The New Jim Crow: Mass Incarceration in the Age of Color Blindness* (New York: The New Press, 2010), 3.

103. *Yes We Can, The Schott 50 State Report on Public Education and Black Males* (Schott Foundation for Public Education, 2010).

104. Herbert Hill, "The AFL-CIO and the Black Worker: Twenty-Five Years After the Merger," *The Journal of Intergroup Relations* 10:1 (Spring, 1982), 42.

105. Kahlenberg, *Tough Liberal*, 71.

106. Sam Howe Verhovek, "Accord to End License Board for New York City Teachers," *New York Times* (June 20, 1990).

107. Elizabeth Green, "Fewer Blacks, More Whites Hired as City Teachers," *New York Sun* (September 25, 2008).

108. N. R. Kleinfeld, "Why Don't We Have Any White Kids," *New York Times* (May 13 2012), NJ1.

109. John R. Logan, Separate and Unequal: The Neighborhood Gap for Blacks, Hispanics and Asians in Metropolitan America (Brown University US 2010 Project: July, 2011).

110. <www.ed.gov/nces/naep>. Accessed May 11, 2012.

111. Fernanda Santos, "Black at Stuy," *New York Times* (February 26, 2012), NJ1.

112. Jonathan Kozol, "Segregated Schools: Shame of the City," *Gotham Gazette* (January 16, 2006).

113. Joel Klein, "The Failure of American Schools," *The Atlantic* (June, 2011).

114. David W. Chen, "Bloomberg Given Poor Marks in New Poll," *New York Times* (May 11, 2001).

115. Sharon Otterman and Allison Kopicki, "New Yorkers Say Mayor Has Not Improved Schools," *New York Times* (September 6, 2011).

116. Michael Barbaro and Megan Thee-Brenan, "The Constituents Speak," *New York Times* (August 18, 2013), NJ9–10.

117. Leonie Haimson, "Children First: A Short History," in Ravitch ed., *NYC Schools Under Bloomberg and Klein*, 15–16.

118. Jim Dwyer, "How Not to Rid New York City Schools of Bad Apples," *New York Times* (March 1, 2011).

119. Campbell, *The Chasm*, 19.

Illustration Credits

Abbreviations

DWN: Daily World & Daily Worker Negative Collection (Photos 223.1), Robert F. Wagner Labor Archive, Tamiment Library, New York University
DWP: Daily World & Daily Worker Photo Collection (Photos 223), Robert F. Wagner Labor Archive, Tamiment Library, New York University
UFT: UFT Photo Collection (NP19), Robert F. Wagner Labor Archive, Tamiment Library, New York University

Cover Photo: DWP, Box 13D, #680279

Fig. i.1 Author's Collection

Fig. 1.1 UFT, Box 3, Folder 49

Fig. 1.2 UFT, Box 4, Folder 57

Fig. 1.3 UFT, Box 4, Folder 59

Fig. 1.4 Author's Collection

Fig. 1.5 Author's Collection

Fig. 1.6 UFT, Box 2, Folder 25

Fig. 1.7 SR: Photo by Sam Reiss. Sam Reiss Negative Collection (Photos .021), Robert F. Wagner Labor Archive, Tamiment Library, New York University

Fig. 1.8 UFT, Box 1, Folder 10

Fig. 1.9 UFT, Box 3, Folder 42

Fig. 2.1 UFT, Box 2, Folder 25

Fig. 2.2 UFT, Box 4, Folder 59

Fig. 2.3 DWP, Box 13D, #680279

Fig. 2.4 DWP, Box 13D, #680279

Fig. 2.5 DWP, Box 100, #19286

Fig. 2.6 UFT, Box 2, Folder 38

Fig. 2.7 DWP, Box 100, #19286

Fig. 2.8 Photo by David Fenton. Courtesy, Rev. C. Herbert Oliver

Fig. 2.9 Author's Collection

Fig. 2.10 UFT, Box 4, Folder 57

Fig. 2.11 DWN, Box 31, #680288

Fig. 2.12 DWN, Box 31, #680288

Fig. 3.1 UFT, Box 4, Folder 58

Fig. 3.2 UFT, Box 5, Folder 71

Fig. 3.3 Courtesy, Rev. C. Herbert Oliver

Fig. 3.4 Author's Collection

Fig. 3.5 UFT Photo Collection (WAG.022), Robert F. Wagner Labor Archive, Tamiment Library, New York University, Box 53, Folder 1

Fig. 3.6 Author's Collection

Fig. 4.1 Author's Collection

Fig. 4.2 Author's Collection

Sources

In addition to the author's collection of contemporaneous notes and documents, the following sources were consulted.

Books

Abubadika, Mwlina (Sonny Carson). *The Education of Sonny Carson*. New York: W.W. Norton, 1972.

Alexander, Michelle. *The New Jim Crow: Mass Incarceration in the Age of Color Blindness*. New York: The New Press, 2010.

Bernstein, Carl. *Loyalties: A Son's Memoir*. New York: Simon & Schuster, 1989.

Berson, Lenora E. *The Negroes and the Jews*. New York: Random House, 1971.

Berube, Maurice, and Marilyn Gittell, ed. *Confrontation at Ocean Hill-Brownsville*. New York: Frederick Praeger, 1969.

Biondi, Martha. *To Stand and Fight: The Struggle for Civil Rights in Postwar New York City*. Cambridge, MA: Harvard University Press, 2003.

Birenbaum, William M. *Overlive: Power, Poverty and the University*. New York: Delacorte Press, 1969.

Birenbaum, William M. *Something for Everybody Is Not Enough*. New York: Random House, 1971.

Broderick, Francis L,. and August Meier, ed. *Negro Protest Thought in the Twentieth Century*. New York: Bobbs Merrill, 1965.

Braun, Robert J. *Teachers and Power: The Story of the American Federation of Teachers*. New York: Simon & Schuster, 1972.

Campbell, Robert. *The Chasm: The Life and Death of a Great Experiment in Ghetto Education*. Boston: Houghton Mifflin, 1974.

Carmichael, Stokely, and Charles V. Hamilton. *Black Power: The Politics of Liberation in America*. New York: Random House, 1967.

Carson, Clayborne. *Malcolm X: The FBI File*. New York: Carroll & Graf, 1991.

Carter, Barbara. *Pickets, Parents and Power: The Story Behind the New York City Teachers' Strike*. New York: Citation Press, 1971.

Clark, Kenneth B. *Dark Ghetto: Dilemmas of Social Power*. New York: Harper & Row, 1965.

Deburg, William L. Van. *New Day in Babylon: The Black Power Movement and American Culture, 1965–1975*. Chicago: University of Chicago Press, 1993.

Dewey, John. *Experience and Education*. New York: Collier Books, 1938.

Connolly, Harold X. *A Ghetto Grows in Brooklyn*. New York: New York University Press, 1977.

DuBois, W. E. B. *Black Reconstruction in America, 1860–1880*. New York: Atheneum, 1935, 1973.

Fantini, Mario, Marilyn Gittell, and Richard Magat. *Community Control and the Urban School*. New York: Praeger, 1970.

Fein, Leonard J. *The Ecology of the Public Schools: An Inquiry into Community Control*. New York: Pegasus, 1971.

Foner, Philip S. *Organized Labor & the Black Worker, 1619–1973*. New York: International Publishers, 1976.

Frazier, E. Franklin. *Black Bourgeoisie: The Rise of a New Middle Class*. New York: The Free Press, 1957.

Freeman, Joshua B. *Working-Class New York: Life and Labor Since World War II*. New York: The New Press, 2000.

Friedman, Robert I. *The False Prophet: Rabbi Meir Kahane*. Brooklyn, NY: Lawrence Hill Books, 1990.

Fuchs, Estelle. *Pickets at the Gates*. New York: The Free Press, 1966.

Geltman, Max. *The Confrontation: Black Power, Anti-Semitism and the Myth of Integration*. Englewood Cliffs, NJ: Prentice-Hall, 1970.

Gittell, Marilyn, et al. *Local Control in Education: Three Demonstration School Districts in New York City*. New York: Praeger, 1972.

Gordon, Jane Anna. *Why They Couldn't Wait: A Critique of the Black-Jewish Conflict Over Community Control in Ocean Hill-Brownsville*. New York: RoutledgeFalmer, 2001.

Greer, Colin. *The Great School Legend: A Revisionist Interpretation of American Public Education*. New York: Basic Books, 1972.

Halpern, Ben. *Jews and Blacks: The Classic American Minorities*. New York: Herder & Herder, 1971.

Hampton, Henry, and Steve Fayer. *Voices of Freedom: An Oral History of the Civil Rights Movement From the 1950s Through the 1980s*. New York: Bantam Books, 1990.

Jacobson, Julius, ed. *The Negro and the American Labor Movement*. Garden City, NY: Doubleday Anchor, 1968.

Kahlenberg, Richard D. *Tough Liberal: Albert Shanker and the Battles over Schools, Unions, Race and Democracy*. New York: Columbia University Press, 2007.

Katz, Shlomo, ed. *Negro and Jew: An Encounter in America*. New York: Macmillan, 1967.

Kaufman, Jonathan. *Broken Alliance: The Turbulent Times Between Blacks and Jews in America*. New York: Simon & Schuster, 1988, 1995.

Knowles, Louis L., and Kenneth Prewitt, ed. *Institutional Racism in America*. Englewood Cliffs, NJ: Prentice Hall, 1969.

Konadu, Kwasi. *A View from the East: Black Cultural Nationalism and Education in New York City*. Syracuse, NY: Syracuse University Press, 2009.

Kozol, Jonathan. *Death at an Early Age: The Destruction of the Hearts and Minds of Children in the Boston Public Schools*. Boston: Houghton Mifflin, 1967.

La Noue, George R., and Bruce L. R. Smith. *The Politics of School Decentralization*. Lexington, MA: D.C. Heath & Co., 1973.

Landesman, Alter F. *Brownsville: The Birth, Development and Passing of a Jewish Community in New York*. New York: Block Publishing Co., 1969.

Leacock, Eleanor B. *Teaching and Learning in City Schools*. New York: Basic Books, 1969.

Lerner, Michael, and Cornel West. *Jews and Blacks: Let the Healing Begin*. New York: Grosset/Putnam, 1995.

Lester, Julius. *All is Well*. New York: William Morrow & Co., 1976.

Lester, Julius. *Lovesong: Becoming a Jew*. New York: Henry Holt & Co., 1988.

Lewis, Heather. "Protest, Place and Pedagogy: New York City's Community Control Movement and its Aftermath, 1966–1996." PhD diss., New York University, 2006.

Litwack, Leon F. *North of Slavery: The Negro in the Free States, 1790–1860*. Chicago: University of Chicago Press, 1961.

Lurie, Ellen. *How to Change the Schools: A Parents' Action Handbook on How to Fight the System*. New York: Random House, 1970.

Marx, Gary T. *Protest and Prejudice: A Study of Belief in the Black Community*. New York: Harper & Row, 1967.

Marx, Karl. *Capital, Volume I*. Moscow: Progress Publishers, 1887 English Edition, 1954.

Marx, Karl. "*The Eighteenth Brumaire of Louis Bonaparte* (1852)," in *Karl Marx: Selected Works, Volume II*, edited by V. Adoratsky, 315–426. New York: International Publishers, 1933.

Mayer, Martin. *The Teachers Strike: New York, 1968*. New York: Harper & Row, 1969.

Meier, August, and Elliot M. Redwick. *From Plantation to Ghetto: an Interpretive History of American Negroes*. New York: Hill & Wang, 1966, 1968.

Murphy, Marjorie. *Blackboard Unions: The AFT and the NEA, 1900–1980*. Ithaca, NY: Cornell University Press, 1990.

Newfield, Jack, and Paul DuBrul. *The Abuse of Power: The Permanent Government and the Fall of New York*. New York: Viking Press, 1977.

Owens, Major R. *The Peacock Elite: A Case Study of the Congressional Black Caucus*. New York: Grant House Publishers, 2010.

Painter, Nell Irvin. *The History of White People*. New York: W.W. Norton, 2010.

Perlstein, Daniel H. *Justice, Justice: School Politics and the Eclipse of Liberalism*. New York: Peter Lang Publishing, 2004.

Podair, Jerald E. *The Strike That Changed New York: Blacks, Whites and the Ocean Hill–Brownsville Crisis*. New Haven, CT: Yale University Press, 2002.

Purnell, Brian. *Fighting Jim Crow in the County of Kings*. Lexington, KY: University Press of Kentucky, 2013.

Pritchett, Wendell. *Brownsville, Brooklyn: Blacks, Jews and the Changing Face of the Ghetto*. Chicago: University of Chicago Press, 2002.

Rampersad, Arnold, ed. *The Collected Poems of Langston Hughes*. New York: Alfred A. Knopf, 1994.

Raskin, Jonah. *Out of the Whale: Growing Up in the American Left*. New York: Links Boos, 1974.

Ravitch, Diane. *The Great School Wars: New York City, 1805–1973*. New York: Basic Books, 1974.

Ravitch, Diane, et al., ed. *New York City Schools Under Bloomberg and Klein: What Parents, Teachers and Policymakers Need to Know*. New York: Lulu, 2009.

Rieder, Jonathan. *Canarsie: The Jews and Italians of Brooklyn Against Liberalism*. Cambridge, MA: Harvard University Press, 1985.

Robeson, Paul, foreword to *Lift Every Voice*, ed. Irwin Silber. New York: People's Artists Press, 1954.

Rogers, David. *110 Livingston Street: Politics and Bureaucracy in the New York City School System*. New York: Random House, 1968.

Rosenthal, Robert, and Lenore Jacobson. *Pygmalion in the Classroom*. New York: Holt Rinehart & Winston, 1968.

Rubinstein, Annette T., ed. *Schools Against Children: The Case for Community Control*. New York: Monthly Review Press, 1970.

Ryan, William. *Blaming the Victim*. New York: Random House, 1971, 1976.

Salzman, Jack, and West, Cornel, ed. *Struggles in the Promised Land: Toward a History of Black-Jewish Relations in the United States*. New York: Oxford University Press, 1977.

Searle, Ronald. *Too Many Songs by Tom Lehrer*. New York: Pantheon Books, 1981.

Siegel, Fred. *The Future Once Happened Here: New York, D.C., L.A., and the Fate of America's Big Cities*. New York: The Free Press, 1997.

Sleeper, Jim. *The Closest of Strangers: Liberalism and the Politics of Race in New York*. New York: W.W. Norton, 1990.

Sterling, Philip. *The Real Teachers*. New York: Random House, 1972.

Taft, Philip. *United They Teach: The Story of the United Federation of Teachers*. Los Angeles: Nash Publishing, 1974.

Taylor, Clarence, ed. *Civil Rights in New York City: From World War II to the Giuliani Era*. New York: Fordham University Press, 2011.

Taylor, Clarence. *Knocking On Our Own Door: Milton A. Galamison and the Struggle to Integrate New York City Schools*. New York: Columbia University Press, 1997.

Taylor, Clarence. *Reds at the Blackboard: Communism, Civil Rights and the New York City Teachers Union*. New York: Columbia University Press, 2011.

Thabit, Michael. *How East New York Became a Ghetto*. New York: New York University Press, 2003.

Tonry, Michael. *Punishing Race: A Continuing American Dilemma*. New York: Oxford University Press, 2011.

Urofsky, Melvin, ed. *Why Teachers Strike: Teachers' Rights and Community Control*. Garden City, NY: Anchor Doubleday, 1970.

Wasserman, Miriam. *The School Fix: NYC, USA*. New York: Outerbridge & Dienstfrey, 1970.

Weiner, Melissa F. *Power, Protest and the Public Schools: Jewish and African American Struggles in New York City*. New Brunswick, NJ: Rutgers University Press, 2010.

Weisbord, Robert G. and Arthur Stein. *Bittersweet Encounter: The Afro-American and the American Jew*. Westport, CT: Negro Universities Press, 1970.

Wilder, Craig Steve. *A Covenant With Color: Race and Social Power in Brooklyn*. New York: Columbia University Press, 2000.

Wright, Nathan Jr., ed. *What Black Educators are Saying*. New York: Hawthorn Books, 1970.

Zitron, Celia Lewis. *The New York City Teachers Union, 1916–1964: A Story of Educational and Social Commitment*. New York: Humanities Press, 1968.

Journal Articles and Papers

Aronowitz, Stanley. "The Dialectics of Community Control." *Social Policy* 1:1 (May/June, 1970): 47–51.

Back, Adina. "Blacks, Jews and the Struggle to Integrate Brooklyn's Junior High School 258: A Cold War Story." *Journal of American Ethnic History* 20:2 (Winter, 2001): 38–69.

Berube, Maurice. "Social Change and the White Working Class." *Social Policy* 1:3 (September/October, 1970): 38–39.

Braun, Jason, and Michael Anderson. "Declining Manufacturing Employment in the Mew York–New Jersey Region, 1969–99." *Current Issues in Economics and Finance* 7:1 (2001).

Brooks, Thomas R. "Tragedy at Ocean Hill." *Dissent* (January/February, 1969): 28–40.

Carmichael, Stokely. "What We Want." *New York Review of Books* (September 21, 1966).

Carmichael, Stokely. "Toward Black Liberation." *The Massachusetts Review* 7:4 (Autumn, 1966): 639–651.

Epstein, Jason. "The Issue at Ocean Hill." *New York Review of Books* (November 21, 1968).

Epstein, Jason. "The Real McCoy." Review of *The Teachers Strike: New York, 1968*, by Martin Mayer. *New York Review of Books* (March 13, 1969).

Epstein, Jason. Reply to Letter, "Mayer Culpa." *New York Review of Books* (May 8, 1969).

Fantini, Mario, and Marilyn Gittell. "The Ocean Hill-Brownsville Experiment." *The Phi Delta Kappan* 50:8 (April, 1969): 442–445.

Ferretti, Fred. "New York's black anti-semitism scare." *Columbia Journalism Review* 8:3 (Fall, 1969): 18–28.

Friedman, Murray. "Is White Racism the Problem?" *Commentary* 47:1 (January, 1969): 61–65.

Friedman, Murray. "The Changing Jewish Political Profile." *American Jewish History* (September-December, 2003): 423–438.

Galamison, Milton A. "Educational Values and Community Power." *Freedomways* 8:4 (Fall, 1968): 311–318.

Galamison, Milton A. "The Ocean Hill-Brownsville Dispute." *Christianity and Crisis* 28:17 (October 14, 1968): 239–41.

Goldbloom, Maurice. "The New York School Crisis." *Commentary* 47:1 (January, 1969): 43–58.

Hamilton, Charles V. "Education in the Black Community: An Examination of the Realities." *Freedomways* 8:4 (Fall, 1968): 319–324.

Hentoff, Nat. "Blacks and Jews: An Interview with Julius Lester." *Evergreen Review* (April, 1969).

Hill, Herbert. "The AFL-CIO and the Black Worker: Twenty-Five Years After the Merger." *The Journal of Intergroup Relations* 10:1 (Spring, 1982): 5–79.

Jacoby, Tamar. "Sonny Carson's Politics of Protest." *NY: The City Journal* 1:4 (Summer, 1991): 29–40.

Jacovino, Nicole. "Vito Perrone: Teaching the Teachers." *Harvard University Gazette* (September 25, 1997).

Kohanski, Alexander S. "An Open Letter to Charles S. Isaacs." *Reconstructionist* 35:1 (February 28, 1969) 13–19.

Lemann, Nicholas. "The Unfinished War (Part I)." *The Atlantic Monthly* (December, 1988): 37–56.

Levy, Peter. "The New Left and Labor: The Early Years (1960–1963)." *Labor History* 31:3 (Summer, 1990): 294–321.

MacDonald, Dwight. "An Open Letter to Michael Harrington." *New York Review of Books* (December 5, 1968).

McCoy, Rhody A. "A Black Educator Assails the White System." *Phi Delta Kappan* 49:8 (April, 1968): 448–49.

Podair, Jerald A. "The Ocean Hill–Brownsville Crisis: New York's *Antigone*." Paper presented at the Gotham History Festival, CUNY Graduate Center, New York, NY, October 6, 2001.

Podhoretz, Norman. "Is It Good for the Jews?" *Commentary* 53:2 (February, 1972): 7–14.

Raab, Earl. "The Black Revolution and the Jewish Question." *Commentary* 47:1 (January, 1969): 23–33.

Ravitch, Diane. "Community Control Revisited." *Commentary* 53:2 (February, 1972): 69–74.

Rosenthal, Robert and Lenore Jacobson. "Teacher Expectations for the Disadvantaged." *Scientific American* 218 (April, 1968): 19–23.

Rustin, Bayard. "From Protest to Politics: The Future of the Civil Rights Movement." *Commentary* 39:2 (February, 1965): 25–31.

Scarf, Damien, et al. "Pigeons on Par with Primates in Numerical Competence," *Science* 334 (December, 2011): 1664.

Schneider, William, Michael D. Berman, and Mark Schultz. "Bloc Voting Reconsidered: Is There a Jewish Vote." *Ethnicity* 1:4 (December, 1974): 345–92.

Stein, Annie. "Strategies for Failure." *Harvard Educational Review* 41:2 (May, 1971): 158–204.

Taylor, Clarence. "Robert Wagner, Milton Galamison and the Challenge to New York Liberalism." *Afro-Americans in New York Life and History* 31:2 (July, 2007): 121–137.

Ward, Agee. "Ocean Hill: Education, Community, Power and the Media." *The Center Forum* 3:3 (November 13, 1968): 1–10.

Wilcox, Preston. "Africanization: The New Input to Black Education." *Freedomways* 8:4 (Fall, 1968): 395–398.

Wilcox, Preston. "Social Policy and White Racism." *Social Policy* 1:1 (May/June, 1970): 41–46.

Wilson, Charles E. "Lessons of the 201 Complex in Harlem." *Freedomways* 8:4 (Fall, 1968): 399–406.

Reports and Position Papers

Anti-Defamation League, "Anti-Semitism in the New York City School Controversy" (January 23, 1969).

Anti-Defamation League, "The Anti-Semitism of Black Demagogues and Extremists," (1992).

Association for Childhood Education International, *Position Paper on Standardized Testing* (1991).

Barrett, Wayne, and Arnold Rothbaum: "Report on the New York City Community School Board Election for District 23 held on May 6, 1975."

Center for Research on Education Outcomes, *Multiple Choice: Charter School Performance in 16 States* (June, 2009).

City of New York, "Fiscal 2011 Mayor's Management Report."

Council of Jews for Racial Justice, "A Call to Reason in the Jewish Community" (May, 1969).

Logan, John R., *Separate and Unequal: The Neighborhood Gap for Blacks, Hispanics and Asians in Metropolitan America* (Brown University US 2010 Project: July, 2011).

Michaelides, Mario, and Peter Mueser, *Recent Changes in the Characteristics of Unemployed Workers* (U.S. Department of Labor, 2009).

National Assessment of Educational Progress, "The Nation's Report Card: The Official Site for Results from the National Assessment of Educational Progress" (2011), <nationsreportcard.gov>.

New York Civil Liberties Union, *The Burden of Blame: A Report on the Ocean Hill–Brownsville School Controversy* (October 9, 1968).

New York Civil Liberties Union, *Education Interrupted: The Growing Use o Suspensions in New York City's Public Schools* (January, 2011).

New York State Education Commissioner's Advisory Committee on Human Relations and Community Tensions, "Desegregating the Public Schools of New York City" (May 12, 1964).

Pew Center on the States, *One in 100: Behind Bars in America 2008* (February, 2008).

Real Estate Board of New York, *Rebuilding Manhattan: A Study of New Office Construction* (1972).

Report of the National Advisory Commission on Civil Disorders (1968).

Schott Foundation for Public Education, *Yes We Can, The Schott 50 State Report on Public Education and Black Males* (2010).

UJA-Federation, *Jewish Community Study of New York: 2011* (June, 2012).

Wilcox, Preston. "Control of Schools Within the Black Community." (Third Annual Black Power Conference, September 1, 1968).

Wilcox, Preston. "Releasing Human Potential: A Study of the East Harlem–Yorkville Bus Transfers." (East Harlem Project for New York City Commission on Human Rights, 1961).

Court Decisions

Brown v. Board of Education of Topeka, 347 US 483 (1954).
Brown v. Board of Education of Topeka, 349 US 294 (1955).
Campaign for Fiscal Equity v. State of New York, 86 NY2d 307, 316 (1995).
Chance v. Bd. of Examiners, 458 F.2d 1167 (2d Cir. 1972).

Newspapers, Newsletters, and Magazines

African-American Teachers Forum
Amsterdam News
ASA *Speaks* (African-American Students Association)
Atlantic Monthly
City Limits
City Star
City Sun
Gotham Gazette
I. F. Stone's Weekly
Jewish Currents
Jewish Press
Jewish Teachers Association Newsletter
Long Island Press
New York Daily News
New York Magazine
New York Post
New York Sun
New York Times
New York Times Magazine
Newsday
Newsweek
Ramparts
The Nation
The New Republic
The New Yorker
The Public Life
Time
Village Voice

Interviews

Fran Barrett
Wayne Barrett
Paul Chandler
Monifa (Cherylle) Edwards

Rev. C. Herbert Oliver
Msgr. John Powis
Maurice Reid
Brother Sun
Albert Vann
Jitu Weusi (Les Campbell)

Interviews conducted by Blackside, Inc. for Eyes on the Prize II: America at the Racial Crossroads, 1965 to 1985. Washington University Libraries, Film and Media Archive, Henry Hampton Collection.

Les Campbell
Sandra Feldman
Karima Jordan
Rhody McCoy
Reverend John Powis
Dolores Torres

Index